D1534867

STUDIES IN ENGLISH LITERATURE

Volume XXXIX

MIMESIS
AND METAPHOR

AN INQUIRY INTO THE
GENESIS AND SCOPE
OF CONRAD'S SYMBOLIC IMAGERY

by

DONALD C. YELTON

1967
MOUTON
THE HAGUE · PARIS

LIBRARY OF CONGRESS CATALOG CARD NUMBER: 67-27213

Printed in The Netherlands by Mouton & Co., Printers, The Hague

75-9004

To Sarah Elisabeth

A work of art should speak for itself. Yet much could be said on the other side; for it is also clear that a work of art is not a logical demonstration carrying its intention on the face of it.

Joseph Conrad to Frank N. Doubleday,
June 2, 1924.

ACKNOWLEDGMENTS

For suggestions and criticism I am indebted chiefly to those members of the graduate faculties of Columbia University who read an earlier version of this study, accepted as a doctoral dissertation under the title *Symbol and Metaphor in Conrad's Fiction* (c1963). First among these are Professors William Y. Tindall, my graduate advisor, John Unterecker, and Daniel Dodson, who read the manuscript as it was produced and who advised on its organization, as well as upon matters of detail. I am also obligated to Professors Robert Gorham Davis, Leon S. Roudiez, and Ludwig Krzyżanowski (distinguished as a student of Conrad's Polish background and reputation), who read the completed draft and from whose suggestions and corrections the book has profited.

Of my fellow graduate students at Columbia during the years when the idea of the book was taking shape I am most indebted for the fruitful exchange of views on Conradian questions to Adam Gillon, then already deep in the Conrad studies which eventuated in his *The Eternal Solitary*, published in 1960.

Since acknowledgements to all the Conrad scholars and critics to whose published writings I am indebted is impracticable in these preliminary pages, it would be comforting to be able to assure the reader that such acknowledgments could be found evenhandedly dispersed through the text and footnotes of the book. But footnotes are fashioned *ad hoc*, arising out of emergent occasions, sometimes in what the lawyers speak of as adversary situations. A book which proposes no modifications of current views can have no legitimate claim to publication; and where modifications are proposed there is an advantage to critical discourse in identifying the views one proposes to modify. In the present context, such a procedure has had the inconvenience, quite unintended, that a number of writers to whom I am in fact obligated for fundamental insights into Conrad's art, and a number of works that have deservedly entered into the common stock of Conrad criticism (and that have enriched my own private stock) appear in the pages that follow solely or primarily as the source of judgments with which issue is taken.

My obligation to Albert J. Guerard, whom I have freely cited, and particularly to his invaluable *Conrad the Novelist* (1958), is great indeed; but so also is my obligation to the late Morton D. Zabel, whose seminal writings on Conrad I have found little occasion to cite – chiefly because of the intimacy with which, by the time I undertook my study, his insights had been assimilated to my own apprehensions of Conrad's craft and Conrad's characters. My somewhat contentious dealings in the text with Thomas Moser, also, are far from indicating my indebtedness to his *Joseph Conrad: Greatness and Decline* (1957), a work, recently reprinted in paperback, that has deservedly become one of the standard items in the Conrad bibliography.

The pioneer biographical work of Conrad's friend and literary executor, the late G. Jean-Aubry, and the more definitive work of Jocelyn Baines (published in 1960) are amply cited in the text, but the indebtedness of Conrad scholars to their work is incalculable and must be acknowledged here. For the sources and the biographical background of Conrad's early works, John Dozier Gordan's *Joseph Conrad: The Making of a Novelist* has been of special value. And like all Conradians in the past decade I am under special obligation to the thorough bibliographical work of Kenneth A. Lohf and Eugene P. Sheehy, published in 1957.

Finally, my enduring thanks to Mrs. Lorraine Przywara, who typed the final copy of the original version, and to my wife who typed the copy for the present version and who gave me the benefit of her criticism and encouragement throughout the time the book was in preparation.

CONTENTS

I

INTRODUCTION

"Where to?"
Mikulin to Razumov

Joseph Conrad's formal writings are not often explicit about his artistic intentions. The "author's notes" and "familiar prefaces" to the published works are, with the notable exception of the preface to *The Nigger of the "Narcissus"*, concerned mainly with the autobiographic sources of character and episode and with anecdotal reminiscence about the circumstances surrounding their production. Though not barren of significant hints for the critic or practitioner, they are far from constituting – as the collected prefaces to the New York edition of Henry James's novels have been taken to constitute – an "art of the novel". Indeed, in the final paragraph of the "Author's Note" to *Youth*, written in 1917 for his collected edition, Conrad, apparently on the verge of some significant commentary regarding the compositional aspects of "The End of the Tether", abruptly turns his back on the question he raises, with the declaration: "But here we are approaching the veiled region of artistic values which it would be improper and indeed dangerous for me to enter." [1]

---

[1] *Youth*, p. xii. In this connection, as in other aesthetic connections, Marlow, the articulate master-mariner who served Conrad as narrator of "Youth", "Heart of Darkness", *Lord Jim*, and *Chance*, supplies a suggestive commentary. I have in mind his remark on the "torpid demeanour" of the French lieutenant in *Lord Jim*: "It had that mysterious, almost miraculous, power of producing striking effects by means impossible of detection which is the last word of the highest art" (*op. cit.*, pp. 141 f.). Except as otherwise noted quotations from Conrad are from the Canter-

That sentence, in its refusal to reveal, is revelatory of an exceptionally secretive temperament. Alongside such near-contemporaries as James, Gide, Proust, Joyce, and Thomas Mann, Conrad appears to be wanting in artistic self-consciousness and in articulateness about the aesthetics of his craft. It is significant that he only once undertook – and then abortively, in the abandoned fragment published posthumously as *The Sisters* – to dramatize the artist's consciousness, that all-but-obligatory subject of the early twentieth-century practitioner of serious fiction. He left no "notebooks", nor, except for the laconic penciled jottings of the Congo diary of 1890, did he keep any journals. His sole venture into formal autobiography, *A Personal Record*, is a work of exceptional elegance (it is the most precise term one can find for its compositional qualities), but only rarely and obliquely does it illuminate – except by example – the problems of literary composition or the springs of artistic creation. The triple-distilled self-consciousness revealed in Thomas Mann's *Making of a Novel* or in Gide's *Journal des Faux-Monnayeurs* – that Chinese-box account of a man writing a novel about a man writing a novel – has no counterpart in Conrad.

The contemporaries named, however, are among the most self-conscious practitioners of a literary epoch of almost unparalleled self-consciousness and confessional candor; and the contrast should not deceive us into thinking of Conrad's own attitude toward his art as fundamentally incurious or naive. The preface to *The Nigger of the "Narcissus"*, written within two years of the publication of his first novel, would of itself discredit such a view; and his correspondence, though it contains repeated testimony to a wide penumbra of unexamined impulse, contains also much deliberate, if unsystematized, comment on his artistic aims, and even occasional hints at his artistic stratagems. "My work", wrote Conrad in the most revealing of the letters to Blackwood, the publisher of *Youth* and *Lord Jim*, "shall not be an utter failure

---

bury edition (Garden City, Doubleday, Page, 1924). The Concord, Kent, Malay, and Personal editions, also issued by Doubleday, have corresponding pagination.

because it has the solid basis of a definite intention." [2] The insistence upon intention, and upon "a strict conception of my method", is recurrent throughout the letter (to say nothing of other letters in the series), as for example in the assertion that "there is in it as much intelligent action guided by a deliberate view of the effect to be attained as in any business enterprise".[3] We do not find – either in this letter or in any other, or for that matter in the preface to *The Nigger of the "Narcissus"* – any all-sufficing formula that serves to make explicit the definite intention or the strict conception of method so confidently alluded to. Indeed we may assume that these were not in fact amenable to any simple and unitary formula, surmising of all his works (as he declared of "The Shorter Tales" published in 1924) that "in each there lurks more than one intention".[4] Partial and tentative formulae can be derived from many sources. However, though there is much that bears obliquely on the question, and much indeed that corresponds strikingly to the writings of avowed "symbolists", there is relatively little in the way of explicit dealings with the role of image and symbol in literary art.[5] It was, in fact, not until the final years of his life – and in a private letter rather than in a formal essay – that Conrad, with his strongest work behind him, expressed unequivocally his view of art as symbolic. Though its terms are general and have nothing to say of the

[2] Joseph Conrad, *Letters to William Blackwood and David S. Meldrum*, ed. William Blackburn (Durham, Duke University Press, 1958), pp. 155 f. (letter of 31 May 1902). The letter, a sort of *apologia pro arte sua*, followed an interview in which Blackwood had kindly but plainly suggested that Conrad was "a loss to the Firm" (*ibid.*, p. 150). The statement quoted purports to be the first article of what Conrad speaks of in the letter as "my creed". The second article, much more particularized, is cited *infra*, p. 72. In my next chapter I take the liberty of identifying the *Preface to The Nigger of the "Narcissus"* as Conrad's artistic "credo", asking the reader to accept the distinction between the Latin and English terms as symbol of the distinction in character between the two statements – the one formal and public, the other private and casual.

[3] *Ibid.*, pp. 154, 155.

[4] *Last Essays*, p. 145.

[5] The preface just cited affords a rare example of Conrad's application of the term "symbolic" in a specific critical context – when he speaks of the typhoon, in the story of the same name, taking on "almost a symbolic figure" (*ibid.*).

function of the symbol as a specific entity within the literary work, the passage in question is the logical point of departure for such an inquiry as I have undertaken.

Replying to a query of Barrett H. Clark regarding the proper interpretation of *Victory,* Conrad, in a letter of May 4, 1918, put before his correspondent the following "general proposition":

that a work of art is very seldom limited to one exclusive meaning and not necessarily tending to a definite conclusion. And this for the reason that the nearer it approaches art, the more it acquires a symbolic character. This statement may surprise you, who may imagine that I am alluding to the Symbolist School of poets or prose writers. Theirs, however, is only a literary proceeding against which I have nothing to say. I am concerned here with something much larger. But no doubt you have meditated on this and kindred questions yourself.

So I will only call your attention to the fact that the symbolic conception of a work of art has this advantage, that it makes a triple appeal covering the whole field of life. All the great creations of literature have been symbolic, and in that way have gained in complexity, in power, in depth and in beauty.

I don't think you will quarrel with me on the ground of lack of precision; for as to precision of images and analysis my artistic conscience is at rest. I have given there all the truth that is in me; and all that the critics may say can make my honesty neither more nor less. But as to "final effect" my conscience has nothing to do with that. It is the critic's affair to bring to its contemplation his own honesty, his sensibility and intelligence.[6]

The literature of symbolism and the symbolic is extensive, a forest in which the literary critic or scholar can wander indefinitely without issue. Perhaps only the terms romantic and romanticism have been so diversely defined or have so stubbornly resisted the efforts of criticism to reduce them to final and categorical formulae. The problem for literary criticism is complicated – as in its dealings with those other terms – by the provenience of the terms symbol and symbolic in extraliterary contexts, so that the

---

[6] G. Jean-Aubry, *Joseph Conrad, Life and Letters* (Garden City, Doubleday, Page & Co., 1927), II, p. 204 f. (hereafter referred to as *Life and Letters*). The passage may also be found in the valuable compilation of Conrad's critical writings recently edited for the Regents Critics series by the distinguished Conrad scholar Walter F. Wright (*Joseph Conrad on Fiction*, Lincoln, University of Nebraska Press, 1964, pp. 36 f.).

terms may be construed on various levels of generality. It is further complicated by the fact that the relation subsisting between the original terms (symbol, the symbolic) and the derived term (symbolism) is – in consequence of an element of the arbitrary in the denomination of the literary movement of *Symbolisme* – itself more questionable than that subsisting between the terms romantic and romanticism.

In what follows I pass over a large body of philosophic literature (e.g., Whitehead, Ernst Cassirer and his American disciple Susanne K. Langer, Wilbur M. Urban) dealing with the symbolic at the highest level of generality. The Cassirer-Langer view of man as the symbolizing animal (*animal symbolicum*), a creature defined, and distinguished from other species, by the need to symbolize, though not necessarily irrelevant to critical discourse, involves predicates outside the scope of any literary context and difficult to relate to specific literary problems. It is rather from the standpoint (still highly generalized, yet firmly situated in a context of critical discourse) of such writers as Goethe, Coleridge, and Croce, in all of whom philosophical and critical impulses were combined in a close nexus, that I shall approach the question here.

The problem for literary criticism of a view of the symbolic which equates it with art itself, or with the individual arts, was made explicit by Croce in the *Aesthetic*:

Now, if the symbol be conceived as inseparable from the artistic intuition, it is a synonym for the intuition itself, which always has an ideal character. There is no double bottom to art, but one only; in art all is symbolical, because all is ideal.

Any other view of the symbol reduced it, in Croce's view, to the (artistically inauthentic) mode of allegory. Immediately following the sentences just quoted Croce declared:

But if the symbol be conceived as separable – if the symbol can be on one side, and on the other the thing symbolized, we fall back again into the intellectualist error: the so-called symbol is the exposition of an abstract concept, an *allegory*; it is science, or art aping science.[7]

---

[7] Benedetto Croce, *Aesthetic as Science of Expression and General Linguistic*, 2nd ed. (London, Macmillan, 1929), p. 34. Dante scholars will

For Croce the meanings that cluster about the terms "symbol" and "symbolic" are polarized at the two terminals: art proper, and allegory or pseudo-art ("art aping science" – or, as he put it elsewhere, "a sort of cryptography"). Tautological at the one pole, deleterious or misleading at the other, the terms were in Croce's view a critical nuisance; borrowing Occam's razor, he excised them from his critical vocabulary.

Near the end of this chapter I quote the only explicit statement on allegory that I have found in Conrad. Meanwhile the Crocean distinction may be inferred from the letter to Barrett Clark in which the writer, identifying the symbolic with art itself (or with art at its apogee, art as ideally conceived and imperfectly realized) defines it in terms of opposition to the willed definiteness, the intellectually imposed exclusiveness of meaning proper to allegory. Conrad's implied identification of the symbolic with art itself, in its ideal character, leaves us with the Crocean question whether the terms symbol and symbolic are tautologies, and thus whether – without falling into the allegorical trap – any valid discrimination of specifically "symbolic" elements of a novelist's art can be made. Can a study of a novelist's symbols or symbolisms be legitimately differentiated from a study of the novelist as artist *tout court*? A strict adherence to Crocean terminology would lead one to assert that it cannot.

There is, however, an earlier vein of philosophical criticism, most conspicuously identified with Goethe and Coleridge, which, anticipating the Crocean distinction between symbol and allegory and the exclusion from the category of the symbolic of the "fixities and definites" of allegory, nevertheless did not, like Croce, infer from these positions the superfluity of the concept of symbol as a tautology for art itself. For Coleridge and Goethe the concept of symbol, akin to the grammatical concept of metonymy,

----

recall Croce's scornful rejection of allegorical interpretations of *The Divine Comedy*, in the opening pages of *The Poetry of Dante*: "Allegory ... is nothing but a sort of cryptography, and therefore a practical product, an act of the will, which decrees that this is to mean one thing and that something else" (*op. cit.*, New York, Holt, 1922, p. 6).

defined the specifically *representative* function of the characters and actions of the highest literary art – their quality, that is, of representing humanity, or the human situation, at large. Thus Coleridge, in one of the most familiar of his statements on the symbolic, defined it as a

> translucence of the special in the individual, or of the general in the special, or of the universal in the general; above all ... the translucence of the eternal through and in the temporal.[8]

And Goethe, in a much-quoted maxim, asserted:

> Das ist die wahre Symbolik, wo das Besondere das Allgemeinere repräsentiert, nicht als Traum und Schatten, sondern als lebendig augenblickliche Offenbarung des Unerforschlichen.[9]

As deduced by Fritz Strich at the conclusion of his able examination of the Goethean *Symbollehre* this body of theory yields a concept of the symbol as "the mythos of an individualized humanity". At this level of generality we may agree with Strich to see in such archetypal characters as Don Quixote, Hamlet, Gargantua, and Emma Bovary the highest evidences of the symbolic imagination. In this perspective one would want to approach Conrad as symbolist (or symbolic novelist) directly through his characters and the actions in which their qualities are revealed and their potentialities realized, relating these to our general intuitions of the human species or the human situation. Measured by the mythopoeic power that gives rise to the great heroes of literature and to the symbolic actions in which they have their being, the sleights and stratagems of a consciously "symbolist" literary art may seem to be quite different things, calling for a quite different characterizing term.

But the Coleridgean passage just quoted presents a hierarchy

---

[8] Samuel Taylor Coleridge, *Complete Works*, ed. W. G. T. Shedd (New York, Harper's, 1853), I, p. 437. The passage is from *The Statesman's Manual*.

[9] Goethe, *Maximen und Reflexionen; Sämtliche Werke,* Jubiläums-Ausgabe (Stuttgart und Berlin, Cotta, 1940), XXXVIII, p. 266. The passage is a *locus classicus*. I have recently encountered it in Hermann Pongs' study of the contemporary novel (*Im Umbruch der Zeit*) and in Erich Heller's essay on Kafka, in *The Disinherited Mind*.

of relations, in which we may find warrant for a more special and particularized view of the symbolic function in literature, and one which cannot be said to be incompatible with the larger and more generalized view. If the characters and actions of a novel stand in a symbolic relation to an intuited "actual" world and generalized humanity, as images or epitomes of these implied universals, so within the microcosm of the novel itself, many compositional elements – images, episodes, landscapes, local details of every description – may serve to focus or to epitomize the intuited meanings, or motifs, of the work in which they figure. In this sense the individual art-work, concrete epitome (or symbol) of an implied universal, is itself a universe, a coherent system of implied symbolic relations, more or less deliberately planned, with more or less of expressive power in the local details and in their inter-relationships.

We may agree with Fritz Strich to see in Don Quixote (in the character and in the book) a unitary symbolic conception, the product of a total act of the imagination, scarcely distinguishable from that which at an earlier stage of culture produces myth. The symbol in this perspective acquires the stature of myth, so that we may, indeed, with no sense of impropriety, substitute the term "mythic" for "symbolic" in characterizing Cervantes' hero and his adventures. We may further agree that Don Quixote as symbolic creation contains an element of the irreducible, or at any rate of the unanalyzable into terms of deliberate art. But we should immediately have to acknowledge that his symbolic potency is, to an appreciable degree, conveyed through a succession of distinct episodes or images – for most readers, in fact, through no more than a handful of such images (the episode of the windmills before all; perhaps also the attack on the sheep, the liberation of the convicts, the *retablo* of Maese Pedro) in which the character of quixotism is distilled and epitomized. As vehicles of the total symbolic import which we posit of the character and of the novel, these images clearly command the attention of criticism as symbolic elements of the whole. For indeed criticism has no way of coming to grips with artistic wholes except through a prior attention to their component parts. If we cannot fully account for our sense of the symbolic character Don Quixote through reference to the local images through which the character is actualized, it is more certain that we cannot even partially account for it without such reference.

The concept of a specific and local symbolism entails (upon the critic as upon the artist himself) two obvious risks, both widely canvassed in contemporary critical discourse. I shall have occasion to return to them in specific contexts farther on; here I need only identify them. One is the risk of compromising, of reducing to self-conscious fussiness and triviality, the larger and more universal conception of the symbolic, as expressed by Goethe, Coleridge, and Conrad himself – the concept which sees in the symbolic nothing less than the ideal goal of the artistic enterprise, the representative condition to which art aspires. The other is the risk of confusion with the allegoric – that is to say, of converting the local symbol into cryptogram, depriving it of its autonomy and of its actuality as part of the living fabric of the whole, in the misconceived effort (as Erich Heller has put it) to translate it "into what it really means". In the face of these risks there is a temptation to avoid the term as irreparably compromised, or at any rate drained of specific meaning. But the word, however compromised, and the conceptual nexus it represents, however difficult of definition, are indispensable.

To adopt the term metaphor as a generic term embracing Conrad's symbolic imagery in all its range and formal diversity entails other difficulties – among them the embarrassment of having to reject the Coleridgean opposition between the categories of the metaphoric and the symbolic. In this instance the weight of contemporary terminological usage is preponderant, and one is obliged to conclude that the Coleridgean distinction originated in a too restrictive conception of metaphor.

It is true that contemporary discourse, in positing a relationship of mutuality between symbol and metaphor, falls short of full agreement as to the precise character of that relationship. On the one hand metaphor has been defined as "perhaps the most vital principle of all symbolism" (Susanne Langer); on the other hand the symbol has been seen as a special, and "transcendent", case of metaphor (Wilbur M. Urban). For our purposes metaphor, in the sense attributed to it in the title, expresses in conjunction with the Aristotelian concept of mimesis the symbolic operancy of images originating out of the novelist's engagement with the sense data and the moral entanglements of a lived reality. This "symbolic operancy" is in brief the reciprocal relation among the parts that bind them into the coherent and intelligible whole which is the work of art – a unitary "symbol" as the term is employed at a higher level of generality.

Moreover, I have found it heuristically valuable – in the face of Conrad's disclaimer of any allusion to "the Symbolist School of poets or prose writers" – to compare his own artistic dicta, his scattered hints as to his compositional methods and objectives, with the more systematic pronouncements of the French *Symbolistes* and their congeners (particularly Mallarmé) and of their acknowledged precursor, Baudelaire. Theirs may have been, as Conrad asserted in the letter to Clark, "only a literary proceeding", but the proceeding had more in view than Conrad's letter suggests: it may safely be said, in fact, that it aimed at a gain in all of those qualities attributed by him to the symbolic conception of art – a gain, that is, "in complexity, in power, in depth and in beauty".

Much of the chapter to follow will be devoted to a comparative inquiry into Conrad's aesthetic doctrine and that of *Symbolisme,* with a view to elaborating the concepts which underlie my subsequent synoptic examination of his metaphoric and symbolic usage (chapters V to IX) and my detailed scrutiny of two of his representative works (chapters X and XI).

Since the doctrines of *Symbolisme* were developed largely by poets and with special (though not exclusive) reference to poetic composition, a *rapprochement* between Conrad's artistic views and procedures and those of the *Symbolistes* is exposed to objections based upon the distinction of genres. Complex and interesting questions are involved here, having to do with the proper function of both novelist and critic of the novel. I shall touch briefly upon these questions as occasion arises. For the present I shall say only that the inquiry to which my second chapter is devoted is empirically conceived and will be empirically conducted. It is true that I start from a persuasion that Conrad, in the exercise of his craft, exploited the evocative resources of verbal and objective image beyond (so to speak) the call of a novelist's duty as conceived by most of the major figures who established the tradition of the novel in the eighteenth and nineteenth centuries. He was, in short, the exponent of a fictional art that might aptly be identified by Otto Ludwig's term "poetic realism". It is an art that, by a sort of atmospheric saturation and by a constant system of linguistic and metaphoric cross-reference, produced novels of which the parts (as Edward Crankshaw put it) are "bathed suggestively in the light of the whole".[10] But I have no doubt that Conrad's practice owed more to the practice of precursors in his own craft than to the practice – or the doctrine – of poets. My third and fourth chapters are devoted to examination of this question. There remains, however, the inescapable fact that the movement of *Symbolisme* left a body of artistic precept which entered into the life-stream of European literature, affecting all literary genres, and which no critic concerned with the symbolic in any of its subsequent literary manifestations can afford to neglect. Since I am interested in placing Conrad's work within a current of ideas and aesthetic principles as a preliminary to my detailed examination of metaphoric texture and symbolic structure in his fiction, some consideration of *Symboliste* doctrine becomes obligatory.

Complaining that he had not generally been well understood, Conrad defined his artistic goal as an effort to realize "the 'ideal' value of things, events and people".[11] But if there can be no doubt that the *terminus ad quem* of his art lay in the realm of ideal – or

---

[10] In his pioneering study of 1936, recently reissued in paperback. Edward Crankshaw, *Joseph Conrad: Some Aspects of the Art of the Novel* (London, John Lane, 1936), p. 173.
[11] "I have been called a writer of the sea, of the tropics, a descriptive writer, a romantic writer – and also a realist. But as a matter of fact all my concern has been with the 'ideal' value of things, events and people. That and nothing else. The humorous, the pathetic, the passionate, the sentimental *aspects* came in of themselves – *mais en vérité c'est les valeurs idéales des faits et gestes humains qui se sont imposés à mon activité artistique*" (Letter to Colvin, 18 March 1917; *Life and Letters*, II, p. 185).

symbolic – values, he was clear from the first as to the primacy of the image (of the "human acts and gestures") in the creative process. "You must remember", he wrote to his friend Cunninghame Graham in 1899, apropos of "Heart of Darkness", "that I don't start with an abstract notion. I start with definite images and as their rendering is true some little effect is produced." [12] The juxtaposition of these two statements of Conrad's offers a convenient occasion to make the distinction, fundamental to my view of Conrad's art, between the symbolic and the allegoric. The asserted priority of the image points to an imaginative operation precisely the opposite of that identified by Coleridge as the method of allegory (in a passage immediately following the definition of symbol quoted above). Deploring "the blindness of self-complacency" which led his contemporaries to confound symbols with allegories, Coleridge, having defined the symbolic, declared of the opposed term: "Now an allegory is but a translation of abstract notions into a picture-language, which is itself nothing but an abstraction from objects of sense." [13] The relation between this sentence and Conrad's declaration to Cunninghame Graham could scarcely be more striking if Conrad had written with the Coleridgean definition in mind. The word allegory does not appear in the Conradian context; but in denying the primacy of the "abstract notion" (the identical term is used by both writers), Conrad affirms the solidarity of his artistic method with the symbolic method as contradistinguished by Coleridge to the allegoric.

The Coleridgean distinction is reaffirmed in substance, though with differences of detail, by the late C. S. Lewis:

On the one hand you can start with an immaterial fact, such as the passions which you actually experience, and can then invent *visibilia*

---

[12]   *Life and Letters*, I, p. 268. Cf. Conrad's assertion to H. G. Wells, in a letter of 1905: "But since, O Brother!, I am but a novelist I must speak in images" (*ibid*, II, p. 16).
[13]   Coleridge, *Complete Works*, I, p. 437. In other contexts also – e.g., in *Aids to Reflection* and in the lecture on Cervantes – Coleridge insisted upon the distinction ("*toto genere*") between symbol and allegory (*ibid.*, I, 270*n*.; IV, 264 f.).

to express them. If you are hesitating between an angry retort and a soft answer, you can express your state of mind by inventing a person called *Ira* with a torch and letting her contend with another invented person called *Patientia*. This is allegory. . . . But there is another way of using the equivalence, which is almost the opposite of allegory, and which I would call sacramentalism or symbolism. . . . The difference between the two can hardly be exaggerated.[14]

I do not quote Lewis's definition of symbolism. Avowedly hermetic and Platonic, it involves (as the synonymy with "sacramentalism" indicates) an extra-literary element not relevant to the present discourse. I am concerned here only to invoke his considerable critical authority – as an outstanding contemporary scholar in the literature of allegory and a practicing allegorist – for the distinction between the two categories of allegory and symbol and for a view of allegory substantially congruent with Coleridge's and equally opposed to Conrad's account of his own artistic method. Lewis, like T. S. Eliot, held allegory in far higher esteem than did Coleridge; but he is at one with Coleridge in insisting upon a radical distinction between the allegoric and the symbolic. In the face of these testimonies, and of many others (including that of Yeats, who saw his own poetic development as a progression from allegory to symbol [15]), the widespread contemporary neglect of the distinction must be seen as a critical regression. Specifically, the tendency of a number of critics to see Conrad's fiction as allegorical seems to me a mistaken one. Without preferring Coleridge's charge against such criticism, I shall merely say that I see in it either a radical confusion of categories or a radical misreading of Conrad.

[14] C. S. Lewis, *The Allegory of Love: A Study in Medieval Tradition* (London, Oxford University Press, 1938), pp. 44 f.
[15] Cf. Yeats's distinction, in his essay on "William Blake and His Illustrations to The Divine Comedy", between "symbolic imagination", which he sees as revelatory in its operations, and allegory, in which he sees only "one of many possible representations of an embodied thing". In this essay Yeats testified to having torn up "hundreds of pages in my endeavor to escape from allegory". (Quoted in William York Tindall, *The Literary Symbol*, New York, Columbia University Press, 1955, p. 33.) Tindall's entire second chapter (pp. 28-67), devoted to the concepts of symbol, allegory, and metaphor, and containing many valuable insights, canvasses a wide spectrum of critical formulae from Dante to Wallace Stevens.

That Conrad thought of his art as symbolic was established on the fourth page of this study in a quoted passage that has become a *locus classicus*. That he distinguished between the symbolic and the allegoric, and that he emphatically did *not* identify his own artistic method or vision with the latter mode, is irrefragably conveyed in a much earlier and largely unnoticed letter. I quote it here in the fond hope that it also may enter into the bloodstream of Conrad scholarship and exert a restraining influence upon critics tempted to convert into allegory one of the great bodies of symbolic fiction in our language:

And so [wrote Conrad to Cunninghame Graham] poor Watts is coming to the end of his august career. What a full and rounded life. And yet it seems poor in stress and passion, which are the true elixirs against the majestic over-powering tediousness of an existence full of allegoric visions. *Dieu nous préserve de cette grandeur!* Better be born a lord, – a king, – better die archpriest of an incredible religion.[16]

The god who amply endowed him with stress and passion preserved Conrad alive from that unwished-for grandeur. It will not be inflicted upon him in the present study, in which his fiction (though arguably skirting the fringes of allegory at one or two points on his artistic journey) will be considered as a product of the symbolic imagination, realizing its intrinsically novelistic vision through the medium of presented images, both objective and verbal.

In the graphic, sometimes violent, intensity of his visualization, in the frequent effect as of cinematic montage conveyed by what he called (in a letter to Richard Curle) his "unconventional grouping and perspective", Conrad's fiction sometimes suggests the cinematic art of the great Russian director Eisenstein. And indeed Conrad, in his later years, was not unaware of the cinema, or of a relation between his own fictional art and the art of cinema. On the eve of his departure for his visit to the United States he sketched the outline of the lecture he was later to present to a private gathering at the Long Island house of Mrs. Ellen Curtiss James. As he described it in a letter to his agent Eric Pinker it was developed

[16]   Letter of 2 July 1904; *Life and Letters*, I, p. 331.

on the (apparently) extravagant lines of the imaginative literary art being based fundamentally on scenic motion, like a cinema; with this addition that for certain purposes the artist is a much more subtle and complicated machine than a camera, and with a wider range, if in the visual effects less precise . . .[17]

The image, then, is both genetically and functionally important in Conrad's fiction – which is to say, tautologically speaking, that his imagination operated "imaginally"; and we may expect that much of the burden of his meaning will be carried by his images. The statement that "I start with definite images" suggests the aesthetic doctrines of T. E. Hulme and the Imagist poets of 1908 – a group which has been found to have owed something to the example of Conrad's prose.[18] But behind the Imagists was (in addition to the putative example of Conrad himself and to the metaphysical speculations of Bergson) a more formidable school of doctrinaires and a more imposing poetic movement, that of *Symbolisme*, for which music rather than the plastic arts served as ideal model. At this point I want to embark on my inquiry into the relation of *Symboliste* aesthetic to Conrad's precept and practice. The inquiry will serve, among other things, to develop the concept of musical structure as ideal model for the system of thematic relations among images in which Conrad's symbolic method largely inheres.

---

[17] Letter of 9 April 1923; *Life and Letters*, II, p. 302. Edward Crankshaw developed the "cinematic" aspects of Conrad's art in the study cited above. Cf. also Edwin Muir on Conrad's fictional method: "Mr. Conrad writes in pictures, for the pictures come, and what he shows us is not action, but a progression of dissolving scenes, continuous and living, which in the end reflect action and give us a true apprehension of it" (Edwin Muir, "A Note on Mr. Conrad", *Latitudes*, New York, Huebsch, 1924, p. 50).
[18] Cf. Hugh Kenner, *The Poetry of Ezra Pound* (Norfolk, Conn., New Directions, 1951), p. 267.

II

POETICS OF THE NOVEL

> Dans la musique, comme dans la peinture et même dans
> la parole écrite, qui est cependant le plus positif des arts,
> il y a toujours une lacune complétée par l'imagination de
> l'auditeur.
>
> Baudelaire, *L'Art romantique*

The tenure of *Symbolisme* as a distinct literary movement was precarious and short. Jean Moréas, a moderately gifted poet and a *blagueur* of genius, who baptized the movement in a manifesto of 1885, pronounced its obituary six years later, in the course of his manifesto of "l'école romane", declaring that the movement had had "only the interest of a phenomenon of transition". Moréas accomplished, not a liquidation of *Symbolisme* (if dead it declined vociferously to lie down), but only a schism in its ranks – if we may speak of ranks in connection with an action in which most of the troops operated independently as guerrillas and pioneers. For *Symbolisme* as poetic school or aesthetic movement enjoyed from the first only a tenuous existence – in the view of Paul Valéry, in fact, a largely illusory existence.[1] But although

---

[1] In his essay on "The Existence of Symbolism" (1936) Valéry defined the movement in terms rather of a common "ascesis" than of a common aesthetic – viz., a common rejection of "the appeal to a majority" and an insistence upon "freedom of research, absolute adventure in the realm of artistic creation" (Paul Valéry, "The Existence of Symbolism", tr. by Malcolm Cowley, *Kenyon Review*, XIX, Summer, 1957, pp. 425-447). In an earlier essay, however, Valéry had discovered the "secret" of the movement in "the intention common to several families of poets to 'reclaim from music their heritage' ". Here Valéry was quoting from Mallarmé. Such an intention, one would say, must be construed as an aesthetic rather than as an ethical aim (Cf. *Variété*, Paris, Gallimard, 1924, p. 97).

Mallarmé, the one incontestably great poet whose work is generally assimilated to the movement – as distinguished from the poets generally thought of as precursors – did not proclaim himself a *Symboliste*, the term was contemporaneously employed, during the years 1885-1900, having been adopted in preference to the journalist's term "Décadent" by a number of poets who stood in a close relation to Mallarmé. If, as Valéry declared, there was no aesthetic of *Symbolisme*, there is a Mallarméan aesthetic, or the *disjecta membra* of one, dispersed through a score of short-winded but pregnant utterances on his art.

Moreover, the term *Symbolisme* was not entirely an adventitious one. Granted that the group was held together rather by a shared passion for independent technical experimentation than by shared dogmas, one may still say that both Mallarmé, independent of schools, and his lesser contemporaries who were avowedly *Symbolistes* were aware of an aesthetic problem of the Symbol and found occasion in their writings (though less systematically than we might have expected) to broach the problem. Whatever the tenure or contemporary "existence" of *Symbolisme* as movement or school, its influence has persisted in twentieth-century letters to our own day, and it is not unrelated to the problem of the symbolic in literature.[2]

Granting it a trajectory through the decade of the nineties the movement – if we are to call it that – coincides with the gestation of Conrad's first novel, with his literary début, with the formulation of his artistic credo in the Preface to *The Nigger of the "Narcissus"*, written in August 1897, and with the full maturation of his art in *Youth* and *Lord Jim*. These events took place in an exceptional isolation from literary contacts of any sort; moreover,

[2] On the identity and tenure of *Symbolisme* as a self-conscious and more or less coherent movement, see especially Kenneth Cornell, *The Symbolist Movement* (New Haven, Yale University Press, 1951). On the propriety of the term "Symbolisme" – i.e., on the identity and function of the symbol in *Symboliste* art – with specific reference to Mallarmé, see Albert Thibaudet, *La Poésie du Stéphane Mallarmé: Étude littéraire*, 11ième éd. (Paris, Gallimard, 1926), p. 114. Or cf. the definition in Moréas' manifesto, as quoted, e.g., in Pierre Martino, *Parnasse et Symbolisme (1850-1900)*, 3ième éd. (Paris, A. Colin, 1930), p. 151.

except for his correspondence with the Belgian novelist Marguerite Poradowska, the scant literary acquaintance Conrad did enjoy during the years intervening between the publication of *Almayer* and the writing of the Preface – it was confined largely to Galsworthy, Edward Garnett and Cunninghame Graham – entailed no contacts with contemporary French letters and little contact with the aesthetic movement in general. It is true that Conrad's early literary culture was rather French than English; and the comparative dearth of testimony with regard to his reading during his seafaring years leaves room for conjecture in any direction. Yet George Moore, acquainted with Mallarmé and Verlaine and Villiers de l'Isle-Adam, had immeasurably greater opportunity to absorb, in his formative years, direct influences from the *Symbolistes*.

But George Moore, the most plastic of minds, was exposed to diverse and contradictory influences, and his fiction at this period, reflecting rather the influence of Zola than of Villiers, was dismissed by Conrad in his single recorded comment on his confrère as "très vieux jeu"; while Conrad, on the other hand, all but isolated from any first-hand literary influences, betrays the most striking congruence with the *Symbolistes* in his aesthetic theory and his professed artistic goals. The phenomenon is curious and deserves some examination. We shall find that the evidence of direct and formative influence is largely negative. There is certainly nothing that permits us even remotely to compare it with the evidence of his life-time devotion to Flaubert and Maupassant; and we may finally conclude that the *example* of Flaubert, as intuitively apprehended by Conrad and articulated in his own quasi-*Symboliste* terms, is much more implicated in the formation of his aesthetic than any conjectured influence of *Symboliste* doctrine. I shall touch on the evidence for such a view in my fourth chapter; for the present, since the actual vocabulary of his artistic credo corresponds more closely to *Symboliste* doctrine than to anything in Flaubert, I want to review the evidence, tenuous as it is, of his acquaintance with the movement.

With the writers (chiefly poets) who frequented Stéphane Mallarmé's "*mardis rue de Rome*" in the eighties and nineties

Conrad's acquaintance, whether personal or literary, was limited; and it was subsequent both to the dissolution of *Symbolisme* as a more or less coherent movement and (as indicated above) to the formation of his own literary character. Of the most extended of these relations (that with André Gide) I shall speak briefly in another connection; here it is sufficient to say that their initial acquaintance was subsequent by two decades to the period in which *Symboliste* influences were uppermost in Gide's own work – the period of *Le voyage d'Urien* (1892), which was precisely the time at which Conrad was forging his style and his artistic outlook with the writing of *Almayer's Folly*. With only three other habitués of the rue de Rome did Conrad at any period enter into personal relations: Henri de Régnier, Paul Valéry, and Arthur Symons.

The personal relations with Régnier (an exchange of courtesies in 1922) and with Valéry were too late and too casual to be in any way implicated in our inquiry. The conjecture of a prior literary acquaintance is not inadmissible, particularly since Régnier was one of the French writers with whose work Conrad displayed (on Jean-Aubry's testimony [3]) an "astonishing acquaintance"; but I find no critical comment on either writer in his correspondence or his published writings.

Only Conrad's association with Arthur Symons, among initiates of Mallarmé's "chapel", offers ground for conjecture of a direct and fertilizing influence upon Conrad of Mallarméan views through personal contact. But since their infrequent correspondence commenced only in 1908, when Conrad had half his work behind him, and their first-hand acquaintance dated only from 1911, we can obviously not look for any formative influence via personal contact. The interest of the relationship lies rather in the evidence we find of sympathy and a certain congruence of outlook, and in the way Symons assimilates Conrad, in his critical remarks, into the *Symboliste* orbit.

Conrad's response to Symons's appreciation of his work, though not without emphatic reservations (having to do with the critic's

---

[3] In the preface, written in 1929, to his edition of Conrad's *Lettres françaises*.

attribution to his subject of deliberate cruelty), betrays a special quality of gratitude. Indeed Symons's admiration for Conrad's talent was great and fervent. His judgments, though warped toward the bias of his predilection for the decadent, betray a fellow-feeling which, in part illusory, is in the main significant. In his maddeningly digressive *Notes on Joseph Conrad* Symons finds in his subject resemblances to Laforgue and Villiers de l'Isle-Adam, and he repeatedly applies to his friend's art (together with formulae which might better have been applied to the Marquis de Sade) all the tags which had been *mots d'ordre*, and almost the personal property, of the *Symboliste* movement: mystery and suggestion, magic and sorcery, and "the wonderful power of evocation".[4] They are terms which we shall find applied to Conrad by others among the epigonoi of *Symbolisme*; and they are, moreover, among the key terms of the Preface of 1897.

More moderately, Conrad reciprocated his friend's esteem, approving his verse (if we are to trust Jessie Conrad's testimony), at any rate borrowing a scrap of it as epigraph to *'Twixt Land and Sea*, encouraging him two years earlier by commending a translation of Verlaine. But appreciation of Symons's verse (which strikes one rather as post-Preraphaelite than as post-*Symboliste*) can scarcely have been significant for Conrad's imaginative development, even if it antedated his acquaintance with the poet; and what he might have derived from those versions of Mallarmé and Verlaine which Yeats justly praised must remain conjectural in the want of any testimony that he read any other than the *Crimen Amoris*. At all events Conrad, praising his friend's version, offered no remarks on Verlaine himself; and I find no other evidence of his acquaintance with the poet's work, nor any evidence whatever of an acquaintance with Mallarmé.

There is testimony – and early testimony – to an acquaintance with Rimbaud, but it is testimony of incomprehension. Of the most formidable of Verlaine's "poètes maudits" Conrad remarked

---

[4]   Arthur Symons, *Notes on Joseph Conrad with Some Unpublished Letters* (London, Myers & Co., 1925), pp. 11 f., pp. 28-30, and *passim*. Cf. also the essay on *Lord Jim*, in *Dramatis Personae* (Indianapolis, Bobbs-Merrill, 1923).

in a letter of August 1898 to Cunninghame Graham: "Can't understand Rimbaud at all. You overrate my intelligence. Je ne suis bon qu'à lire Cyrano and such like coglionerie." [5] This is emphatic enough, and there seems to be no evidence to indicate that Conrad modified his position with regard to Rimbaud – or, indeed, that he ever again accosted the poet's work. Nor (in the face of Symons's rapprochement between the two writers) does one find any evidence to implicate Jules Laforgue in the shaping of Conrad's outlook, or any evidence of his acquaintance with Laforgue's verse. Concerning Maeterlinck, with whose "outlook on life" another critic (Edwin Björkman) found "much in common" with Conrad's, the subject of this odd comparison expressed himself, on more than one occasion, with a disdain approaching savagery, speaking of the dramatist in a letter of 1907 as a "farceur, who has been hiding an appalling poverty of ideas and hollowness of sentiment in wistful baby-talk".[6] There can be little ground for conjecture of an influence from this direction, other than to heighten Conrad's blood-pressure – and the evidence for this effect comes ten years after the composition of the Preface to *The Nigger of the "Narcissus"*.

There is, on the other hand, convincing evidence – external in the one case, internal in the other – that Conrad read, and imaginatively responded to, primary texts of two major writers who stood as it were in a parental relation to *Symbolisme*; but in neither case does the ascertained chronology support the inference of a formative impact upon his art.

There is, first, in the epigraph to *The Shadow-Line*, testimony to

[5] *Life and Letters*, I, p. 246. That Conrad's appetite for poetry extended beyond *coglionerie* has already been suggested. Clearly it was less voracious than his appetite for prose, nor did his poetic taste approach the catholicity or sophistication of his taste in prose, which ranged comfortably from the simplicities of Marryat to the sophistications of Proust and the later James. However, it would not be difficult to demonstrate (if detailed demonstration were required) that his poetic culture, if not profound, was extensive and far from contemptible.

[6] *Life and Letters*, II, p. 62; and cf. such expressions as "the pretty-pretty of Maeterlinck", in a letter to Garnett written four years later. *Letters from Joseph Conrad, 1895-1924*, ed. with Introduction and Notes by Edward Garnett (Indianapolis, Bobbs-Merrill, 1928), p. 227.

a genuine imaginative encounter with the poetry of Baudelaire, the universally acknowledged ancestor of the *Symboliste* movement. The evidence itself (viz., the epigraph) is, of course, in the public domain, and within the purview of the most casual reader. What has to be emphasized is its evidential value, which does not emerge from a casual reading of Conrad's novel. Since I devote a chapter to *The Shadow-Line* (ch. XI), I shall postpone consideration of the symbolic nexus which I see as existing between the novel and the poem ("La Musique") from which the epigraph is taken. For the present I shall only say that the relation of the organizing symbols of the novel to those of the poem suggests a more intimate penetration into the symbolic mode of Baudelaire's imagination than one gathers from the mere fact of quotation.[7] In his 1898 essay, "Tales of the Sea", Conrad credited Fenimore Cooper with treating nature not as the "framework" but as "an essential part of existence", and said that "in his sea tales the sea interpenetrates with life".[8] Without presuming to challenge the inference that Cooper served as a model for Conrad in this respect, we may well suspect that his example was strongly seconded by the greater expressive resources which Baudelaire deployed on the same theme, in the poem in question and others (e.g., "l'Homme et la Mer"), and which elsewhere (in "Correspondances" and many other poems) he brought to bear on the more general theme of man's reciprocity with all created nature.

The only other explicit Baudelaire reference I find in Conrad – his application to himself of the Baudelairean phrase "stérilités des écrivains nerveux" [9] – is significant in two respects: first that its source is in Baudelaire's prose rather than in his verse; second that it bespeaks, as early as 1905, and even more explicitly than the epigraph, a sense of intimate identification with the poet, suggesting the identification Conrad felt with "the shade of old

---

[7] Though the fact of quotation on a Conrad title-page was itself, according to Jessie Conrad, of considerable significance. For her testimony to the care with which Conrad selected his epigraphs see her *Joseph Conrad as I Knew Him*, p. 49.

[8] *Notes on Life and Letters*, p. 55.

[9] Letter to Edmund Gosse, 28 March 1905 (*Life and Letters*, II, p. 14).

Flaubert". One would like to have more positive testimony to the imaginative relationship of Conrad to Baudelaire, and particularly to the date of his first acquaintance with him, which I suspect to go back to his Marseilles days. But the scraps of evidence available are suggestive out of all proportion to their size.

Finally, there is Villiers de l'Isle-Adam to be considered – another precursor of *Symbolisme*, perhaps the one first-rate *prosateur* claimed by the movement, and a writer whose prestige among his contemporaries rivalled that of Mallarmé himself and has (I should judge) been at least partially restored after some subsequent diminution. I have found no mention of Villiers in Conrad's correspondence or his published writings: the evidence of his acquaintance with him is all internal, but that evidence would seem to be inexpugnable. Miss Katherine H. Gatch's comparative study of Conrad's *Victory* and the *Axël* of Villiers de l'Isle-Adam leaves no margin for doubt that Conrad had read, and intimately responded to, Villiers's drama.[10]

I shall not recapitulate at length the clues Miss Gatch adduces in support of her thesis. However great the disparities in the conception of the two works, and in the details of plot and catastrophe, certain radical similarities in the situation and destiny of the two Axels will be apparent to all who are acquainted with both works. The physical isolation of each (the one in his castle in the Black Forest, the other on his island); the temperamental detachment of each from the world – a detachment in each instance philosophically based (the one in Rosicrucian, the other in Schopenhauerian, principles); the invasion of the hero's solitude by a woman, in each instance suggestive of a feminine archetype, and subsequently by a dangerous enemy, in each instance embodying The World, in its devilish aspect – these are some of the striking resemblances in the conduct of the two works. Add to these the common motif of the fabulous concealed treasure (in *Victory*, fabulous in a strict sense; in *Axël* an actual treasure, fabulous only in its magnitude and splendor), the common evocation of a storm for the heightening of dramatic tension, and the

[10] Katherine H. Gatch, "Conrad's Axel", *Studies in Philology*, XLVIII (January, 1951), pp. 98-106.

resemblances of compositional detail noted by Miss Gatch
– resemblances of phrase, of attitude and gesture, of costume –
and the evidence is conclusive that Conrad knew Villiers's drama,
and that, whatever his critical judgment of the work may have
been, he responded to it imaginatively. This is not to say that he
"adapted", or even voluntarily imitated Villiers; but we can
scarcely doubt that we have to deal here with a case of first-hand
literary influence.

For our purposes, however, the case is only significant as an
indicator of imaginative affinity, since whatever influence we may
detect on the Conrad of 1915 can do nothing to account for the
original formation of his artistic objectives. Conrad may, of
course, have read *Axël* at any time during the quarter-century
between its publication in 1890 and the composition of *Victory*:
but there is no warrant for assuming an earlier influence that
cannot be traced.

Before proceeding to the comparative view of principles and
terminology shared by Conrad and the *Symbolistes*, I want to
devote several pages to a succinct account of Conrad's contemporary reputation in France – suggestive for the purposes of this
inquiry in view of the persistence in that country (if only as a
rumor in the air, in the face of strong counter-currents) of
Symboliste influences. Almost from the first, an impressive seg-
ment of the French literary world acclaimed Conrad as "one of us",
as though unwilling to acknowledge his abandonment of the
country and the language which during three of his formative
years he had made his own.[11]

The Mercure de France, in which the *Symboliste* tradition
remained most alive, was consistently appreciative; in 1910 or
thereabouts Gustave Kahn, theoretician of *Symbolisme*, acclaimed
Conrad (in the *Gil-Blas*, as Conrad remembered it) as "un

---

[11] "Qui est des nôtres", as H. D. Davray put it in the review of *Tales of
Unrest*, in the July, 1899, issue of the *Mercure de France*. Cf. *Lettres
françaises*, p. 38. Davray, who favorably reviewed a number of Conrad's
books and who later (1928) published a translation of *The Secret Agent*,
had as early as 1897 been a reviewer of *Symboliste* verse in the columns
of *l'Ermitage*. Cf. Cornell, *The Symbolist Movement*, pp. 179, 183.

puissant rêveur"; [12] and there is evidence of a friendly relation (casual, it is true, and late in Conrad's career) with that other veteran of "la mêlée symboliste", Henri Ghéon. St.-John Perse visited Conrad at Capel House in 1913 or thereabouts. The *Symboliste* playwright H.-R. Lenormand, who encountered Conrad in Corsica in 1921 and left enthusiastic testimony of his regard, rendered him the sincerest flattery in his play *Le Simoun*, which shares with *Almayer's Folly* its central situation (complicated by the theme of incest which Lenormand, a good Freudian, found latent in Conrad's treatment of the relations between Almayer and Nina) and some of the detail of its plot. Paul Claudel, an early discoverer of Conrad, introduced Gide to his work in 1905, instructing his friend, in response to the question what titles he should read, to read them all.

Exceeding Claudel's instructions, Gide subsequently assumed the direction, in collaboration with Jean-Aubry, of the translation and publication of Conrad's *Oeuvres complètes* – a task discharged over a period of two decades or so – under the auspices (and the imprimatur) of the *Nouvelle Revue française*. Gide himself translated *Typhoon* for this edition; one of the co-translators of *Victory* was Isabelle Rivière, wife of the *NRF*'s founder and joint editor. By far the largest and most appreciable memorial issue of a periodical published at the time of Conrad's death was the December 1924 issue of the *NRF*, to which (among French writers) Gide, Valéry, Lenormand, Jean-Aubry, Estaunié, André Maurois, Edmond Jaloux, Joseph Kessel, and Ramón Fernández contributed their "hommages".

Gide's own long attachment to Conrad, both as artist and as friend, is well known and need not be detailed here. Like most of the data of Gide's life and consciousness it has found its way into the public domain through the medium of the Journals and the published correspondence, in both of which one may find frequent judgments of Conrad's work. He was undoubtedly Conrad's most effective champion and publicist in France; and though there was no question of any reciprocity of literary services by the older writer, there is evidence of a reciprocity of esteem, with Conrad

[12] *A Personal Record*, p. 111.

bestowing upon Gide in his letters the salutation "Cher Maître" (sometimes "Très cher maître et ami") otherwise reserved for Henry James, and even speaking on one expansive occasion of Gide's affectionate friendship as a gift of the gods, as "certainement le 'Grand Prix' de ma vie littéraire".[13] Gide, for his part, wrote in his contribution to the *NRF* memorial issue (republished in *Feuilles d'automne*): "De mes aînés, je n'aimais, ne connaissais que lui." Years before he had attached a sentence from *Lord Jim* as epigraph to one of the chapters of *Les Caves du Vatican*; years later he was to dedicate to Conrad's memory his *Voyage du Congo*.

This summary review might be amplified by the names of other acquaintances and admirers among Conrad's French contemporaries – including such nonliterary figures as Debussy (an admirer of *The Secret Agent*) and Ravel, with whom Conrad in 1922 struck up a late and lively acquaintance ("vive amitié"). But the foregoing roster, taken together with the antecedent evidence (restricted as it is) of Conrad's acquaintance with the literature of *Symbolisme*, will suffice for my purposes. These are, in the first instance, to evoke an image of Conrad from about mid-career, or somewhat earlier, involved – if at a distance – in an ambience of French literary thought distinct from that which he encountered in his relations with Garnett and Graham and Galsworthy, with Wells and Bennett; distinct also, in certain respects, from the Flaubertian ambience which hung over his collaboration with Ford and his occasional relations with James and Crane. In the second instance it is intended to enforce the inference that certain qualities of Conrad's imagination and artistic method (specifically those qualities examined in this study) met with their liveliest response in the literary climate of post-*Symboliste* France. Indeed the French reception of Conrad in the first quarter of the present century can be compared with Faulkner's reception by the succeeding generation. The comparison suggests the reserve with which my inference should be received. It would not be difficult to show that the French response to the two novelists was in large

---

[13]   *Lettres françaises*, p. 140; pp. 132-146 *passim*.

degree based upon qualities that by no critical license can be related to the ideals or procedures of *Symbolisme*. Indeed André Gide, who spanned the two generations, responding to the appeal and contributing to the French reputation of each novelist in turn, left little doubt in his writings on Conrad that his response was all to specifically "novelistic" qualities (the conduct of narrative and dramatic peripety, the wealth of moral and psychological insights) which attracted him also to Dostoevsky – with the fluid psychology of whose characters he found a resemblance to that of Conrad's and a liberating departure from the constricting tradition of French classicism.

Conrad's French success was not, then, a simple phenomenon, and does not admit of a simple or tendentious explanation. It *was* a "phenomenon", however; and its relevance will emerge in the following pages when some of the other grounds of French appreciation are canvassed. I can suggest these qualities and direct our inquiry to that comparative view of artistic aims which is the principal task of this chapter by quoting from a review by one of Conrad's earliest French admirers, the Franco-Polish poet and journalist Teodor de Wyzewa. Another veteran of the *Symboliste* eighties and nineties, who had acclaimed Conrad as early as 1903, Wyzewa eleven years later contributed to the *Revue des deux Mondes* an extended commentary on "An Outpost of Progress" – that brief but impressive dress rehearsal for "Heart of Darkness". Having praised the enveloping "atmosphere" of the tale, he proceeded to characterize Conrad's art in a paragraph which contains in series a number of the key terms of *Symboliste* and Mallarméan aesthetic. Unlike Kipling and Stevenson (Wyzewa wrote),

M. Conrad ne nous donne pas cette impression [de la justesse pittoresque du "détail"], en "peintre", mais bien plutôt en "poète", avec un étrange talent d'*évocation* quasi "*musicale*", qui lui permet de substituer aux longues et complètes peintures habituelles de ses confrères l'emploi, savamment gradué, d'un petit nombre de traits "*suggestifs*".

Pressing his contrast Wyzewa declared that, instead of presenting his figures full face and in full relief, "toujours M. Conrad nous force plus ou moins à les *deviner*"; and he concluded by acclaiming "la séduction qu'exercent sur nous les hommes et les choses qui nous semblent porter en soi une part de *mystère*".[14]

Now if we turn from this appreciation of Conrad to Mallarmé's interview with Jules Huret – a *locus classicus* of *Symboliste* theory published almost a quarter-century earlier – we shall find in a brief and famous passage that all but one of the key terms indicated in Wyzewa's paragraph are used by Mallarmé (two of them repeatedly), and that Wyzewa's analysis corresponds strikingly in other respects to Mallarmé's prescription (out of respect for the italics in the original text I refrain in the quotation that follows from supplying my own):

> La contemplation des objets, l'image s'envolant des rêveries suscitées par eux, sont le chant: Les Parnassiens, eux, prennent la chose entièrement et la montrent: par là ils manquent de mystère; ils retirent aux esprits cette joie délicieuse de croire qu'ils créent. *Nommer* un objet, c'est supprimer les trois-quarts de la jouissance du poème qui est faite de deviner peu à peu: le *suggérer*, voilà le rêve. C'est le parfait usage de ce mystère qui constitue le symbole; évoquer petit à petit un objet pour montrer un état d'âme, par une série de déchiffrements. ... Il doit y avoir toujours énigme en poésie, et c'est le but de la littérature – il n'y en a pas d'autres – d'*évoquer* les objets.[15]

"Suggestion", "evocation", "divination", "mystery" – here, together with their congeners "enigma" and "decipherment", are the same four sacred words of *Symbolisme* that Wyzewa, in the course of another dozen or so lines written more than two decades later, was to apply in a context of strikingly similar phrases to a minor production of Conrad's. And these words, it will be noted, define in their discursive context the Mallarméan concept of the poetic symbol.

Is the correspondence significant, or have we to do in Wyzewa's review only with the *snobisme* of an aging reviewer, epigone of a

[14] Teodor de Wyzewa, "Un conteur anglais: M. Joseph Conrad", *Revue des deux Mondes*, 6ième période, XX (Apr. 15, 1914), p. 939 f. My italics.

[15] Mallarmé, *Œuvres complètes*; texte établi et annoté par Henri Mondor et G. Jean-Aubry (Bibliothèque de la Pléiade) (Paris, Nouvelle Revue française, 1945), p. 869. The text of the interview can also be found in Jules Huret, *Enquête sur l'Evolution littéraire* (Paris, Charpentier, 1901), pp. 55-65. The Mallarmé interview was one of sixty-four originally published in *l'Echo de Paris* from 3 March to 5 July 1891.

moribund movement, parading the remembered jargon of his literary novitiate? The question, which can of course be confidently answered only by reference to Conrad's story, may be left open to the reader's own curiosity. For purposes of this chapter I need only say that, however applicable to "An Outpost of Progress", Wyzewa's *Symboliste* predications express with some precision certain of Conrad's professed artistic objectives. What we have to examine now is the relation to *Symboliste* doctrine of these objectives or principles as expressed by Conrad himself. The crucial text is, of course, the Preface to *The Nigger of the "Narcissus"*, his self-proclaimed artistic credo, a sort of condensed Poetics of the novel, which I take to be Conrad's one formal effort in the realm of criticism to which one may confidently assign the status of a classic. It is a production of a quite special character, being rather an apologia or *confessio fidei* than a work of conventional criticism; and in it we shall find, in significant contexts, all the Mallarméan key-words identified above.

Before turning to this celebrated document, however, I want to consider the implications of certain more casual pronouncements which, in their specific contexts, and in some instances by their very informality and by their remoteness in time from the aesthetic climate of the nineties, have a special evidential value. Here, for example – in a burst of spleen directed against Richard Curle, almost half a life-time later than the Preface – we find Conrad no less explicit than Mallarmé about the artistic disadvantages of explicitness and the corresponding advantage of suggestion:

It is a strange fate that everything that I have, of set artistic purpose, laboured to leave indefinite, suggestive, in the penumbra of initial inspiration, should have that light turned on to it and its insignificance (as compared with, I might say without megalomania, the ampleness of my conceptions) exposed for any fool to comment upon or even for average minds to be disappointed with. Didn't it ever occur to you, my dear Curle, that I knew what I was doing in leaving the facts of my life and even of my tales in the background? Explicitness, my dear fellow, is fatal to the glamour of all artistic work, robbing it of all suggestiveness, destroying all illusion. You seem to believe in literalness and explicitness, in facts and also in expression. Yet nothing is more clear than the utter insignificance of explicit statement and also its power to call attention away from things that matter in the region of art.[16]

Conrad's asperity was prompted by his friend's identifying, in the manuscript of a critical article, the Eastern port of "Youth" with the port – "a damned hole without any beach and without any glamour" – of the actual voyage of which "Youth" was "the record of 'poeticised' sensations". If we feel that the *ad hoc* character of this outburst may limit its validity as generalization, we shall find no want of other and more equable testimonies, from all periods of Conrad's career, to the central importance of suggestiveness in his artistic scheme – as for example in his profession to Galsworthy, a decade earlier, of his "ineradicable mistrust of the theatre as the destroyer of all suggestiveness".[17]

Suggested to me by one Mallarméan text, Conrad's remonstrance to Curle recalls another, more succinct and even more celebrated than that cited above – the famous sentence from the poet's "Crise de Vers" (which he thought important enough to repeat verbatim in a later essay, the "Avant-dire" to René Ghil's *Traité du Verbe*):

Je dis: une fleur! et, hors de l'oubli où ma voix relègue aucun contour, en tant que quelque chose d'autre que les calices sus, musicalement se lève, idée même et suave, l'absente de tous bouquets.[18]

As Mallarmé aspired musically to conjure the idea of a flower, the flower absent from all bouquets, so Conrad strove in "Youth" to evoke a port of the mind, absent from all earthly shores. Or we might say that the effort of the one artist was to evoke the flower, and of the other the port, that never was on sea or land – a paraphrase which incidentally serves to remind us of the parent stock from which both poet and novelist derived the seed of this ideal aspiration.

---

[16] *Conrad to a Friend: 150 Selected Letters from Joseph Conrad to Richard Curle* (Garden City, Doubleday, Doran & Co., 1928), pp. 112 f. The letter bears the date-line April 24, 1922.
[17] Apropos of his speculation upon the success in performance of one of Galsworthy's plays. Letter of 28 March 1911 (*Life and Letters*, II, p. 128).
[18] Mallarmé, *Œuvres complètes*, p. 368; p. 857.

Again, if we compare our earlier Mallarméan text with Conrad's letter to Barrett Clark, quoted in the introductory chapter, we shall find in Conrad's discrimination between the tasks of artist and critic and in his assertion "that a work of art is very seldom limited to one exclusive meaning and not necessarily tending to a definite conclusion", an analogue to Mallarmé's notion of the reader's complicity in the creative process ("cette joie délicieuse de croire qu'ils créent").

Here a reservation must be made, although its implications need not be developed at length. Mallarmé speaks of the delicious joy of readers in believing that they create. A more extended view of Mallarméan doctrine – e.g., his assertion to Edmond de Goncourt that "a poem is a mystery to which the reader must search for the key"; his announced goal, derived from Poe's account of the genesis of "The Raven", of abolishing "le hasard" from poetry – supports the inference that Mallarmé saw in the creative pretentions of his readers a salutary illusion. An "algebraist" of poetry (as Valéry remarked), he claimed more than other poets except Poe himself, and certainly more than Conrad, for deliberate strategy and conscious intent, having apparently no doubt (at least in his doctrinaire moods – one finds hints *en passant* of an opposing strain of thought) that the keys to poetic mysteries could be fashioned by poets as well as the locks, so that the collaborative role of readers is reduced in fact to the discovery of meanings implanted by the poet in full consciousness. This suggests on the face of it the sort of cryptographic activity identified in my introductory chapter as proper to allegory rather than to the symbolic. On this question – since an examination of Mallarmé's verse in its relations to his critical dogma falls quite obviously outside the scope of a study of Conrad – I shall say only that in my view Mallarmé's verse, and *Symboliste* verse in general, did not entirely avoid the allegoric, but that Mallarmé's poetic instinct, far more frequently than Poe's, outwitted the more constricting rigors of his poetic dogma.

In terms of precept, however, as distinguished from practice, it is clear that on the point in question it is the novelist, with his explicit allowance for "plurisignation", who is more nearly in accord than the *Symboliste* poet with the general theory of the symbolic.[19] He is at the same time, in his implicit recognition of the role in art of unconscious activity, closer than Mallarmé to romantic doctrine as represented, for example, by Coleridge's dictum: "There is in genius an unconscious activity; nay, that is the genius in the man of genius"; [20] closer also to the position of his contemporary Valéry when he wrote apropos of *Cimetière marin*:

On n'y insistera jamais assez: *il n'y a pas de vrai sens d'un texte*. Pas d'autorité de l'auteur. Quoi qu'il ait *voulu dire*, il a écrit ce qu'il a écrit. Une fois publié, un texte est comme un appareil dont chacun se peut servir à sa guise et selon ses moyens; il n'est pas sûr que le constructeur en use mieux qu'un autre.[21]

It is true that Conrad, to whom it was important to establish a continuity between his two vocations, found more than one occasion to protest his "full responsibility", the conscious deliberation of his artistic *procédés*, as when he declared to Davray (apropos of his intention in writing "The Duel"): "Savoir ce que l'on veut faire est le fait d'un artiste",[22] or when, in the "Familiar Preface" to *A Personal Record*, he told his readers: "The fact is that I have a positive horror of losing even for one moving moment that full possession of myself which is the first condition of good service."

Now I should say here that nothing in this study is intended to deny or to minimize the role of deliberate intention and conscious artistic strategy in his work. Indeed, to deny this would be to deny the relevance (to his own work at least) of the inquiry here under-

[19]   On "plurisignation" as a quality of the symbol, cf. Philip Wheelwright, *The Burning Fountain: A Study in the Language of Symbolism* (Bloomington, Indiana University Press, 1954), pp. 61 f. Wheelwright's book is an important contribution to its subject.
[20]   Coleridge, *Complete Works*, IV, p. 332. Cf. also the distinction between symbol and allegory in the Lecture on Cervantes *(ibid.,* IV, 264 f.).
[21]   Valéry, *Variété III*, p. 68. The marks of emphasis are Valéry's. W. Y. Tindall quoted from this passage at the end of his *Literary Symbol*, a work in which full justice is done to the symbolic plurisignation here insisted upon (Tindall, *The Literary Symbol*, p. 267).
[22]   *Lettres françaises*, p. 87.

taken into his aesthetic principles. If there are events in his biography (some of them faithfully reflected in his fiction) which suggest that the state of "possession" with him was not always one of self-possession, the evidence of responsible intention in his art is nevertheless ubiquitous and undeniable. Equally ubiquitous, however, is the evidence that he recognized, in his own practice, the limits of conscious volition, of the *vouloir faire*; and the public assertion of full responsibility was sometimes categorically denied in private, as when, in an early letter to Garnett, he wrote in response to his friend's urgings that he rewrite the last chapter of *An Outcast of the Islands*:

I shall try without faith, because all my work is produced unconsciously (so to speak) and I cannot meddle to any purpose with what is within myself. ... It isn't in me to improve what has got itself written.[23]

Inclined as he was to the adoption of desperate positions in private colloquy and correspondence, he expressed himself hyperbolically. He did revise the chapter in question; and most of his published works underwent repeated and sometimes drastic revision.

Yet his conscious intentions were often baffled or checkmated, as in the long and exhausting struggle with *The Rescue* or the aborted effort of *The Sisters*. Only by exception did he commence a work with a clear consciousness of its dimensions or trajectory: we know, for example, that two of his longest novels were conceived as short stories. Indeed it would be difficult to name a novelist in whom so rigorous an artistic conscience and so deliberate an ideal of his craft consorted with so incalculable a creative impulse. Clearly the truth of the matter lay for Conrad – as it does for all major artists, but in his case with a peculiarly aggravated sense of tension – somewhere between the two extremes of full self-possession and full possession by the daimon, at the *Brennpunkt* where the cunning of the artificer converges with the obscure impulse of the seer.

[23] *Letters from Joseph Conrad*, p. 42. Cf. Conrad's advice to Garnett, in a letter written twenty-five years later: "But before everything switch off the critical current of your mind and work in darkness – the creative darkness which no ghost of responsibility will haunt" (*ibid.*, p. 273).

But however this may be, Conrad and Mallarmé are at one – and they are at one with Valéry and Arthur Symons and all the heirs of *Symbolisme* – in their assertion of the aesthetic value of the suggestive or evocative as against the merely explicit and demonstrative, and in their insistence upon the active (collaborative or co-creative) role of the reader in the realization of the text and the potentiation of the symbol. And Conrad was, I would hold, justified in his faith; for granting to the concept of the symbolic a dimension finally inaccessible to any stratagems of method or mere technique, any deliberate *Suggestionskunst*, we must still define it, at any level of generality, by its inexhaustibility (*Unendlichkeit*), which is precisely its quality of suggesting or evoking more than it fully reveals or more than we can finally apprehend.

We may grant that Conrad in pursuit of the suggestive sometimes exceeded his visible resources of meaning, achieving rather what John Bayley characterized as the "queerly portentous" or the "shadowy and pseudo-meaningful"; but the method of suggestion, grounded in instinct or become by habit a second instinct, is none the less essential to his talent and deeply implicated in the symbolic value we derive from his fiction. And though we may sometimes be tempted to see a sort of verbal conjuring-trick in his repeated invocation of those *Symboliste* key-terms identified above – as of those resounding Marlovian modifiers, "inscrutable", "inconceivable" and the like, to which F. R. Leavis, without reflecting upon their appropriateness to Marlow, took exception – they in fact respond precisely, for Conrad as for Mallarmé, to his vision of reality and to his ideal of an art which should reflect such a reality.

The terms "mystery" and "enigma", two of the dark particular stars of his rhetorical firmament, had unquestionably a symbolic value for Conrad, as for Mallarmé and for Baudelaire (to whom "le mystère" was an indispensable ingredient of "le Beau"). His effort, epitomized by recurrent imagery of veil and cloud, to suggest a realm of arcana behind the veil of surface appearances was deeply grounded in temperament, even obsessive. It prompted more than one French critic to characterize him, incautiously, as a mystic.[24] He was not a mystic, in any proper sense; but he lost no opportunity to proclaim a mystery.

In the Preface to *The Nigger of the "Narcissus"*, in which he characterizes the world as an "enigmatical spectacle", he proclaims of the artist that "he speaks to our capacity for delight and wonder, to the sense of mystery surrounding our lives". "Mystery" is the climactic word in that rhetorical paragraph in *A Personal Record* (p. 92), in which Conrad proposes his doctrine of the "spectacular" universe, of which the final sentence invokes "our conscience, gifted with a voice in order to bear true testimony to the visible wonder, the haunting terror, the infinite passion and the illimitable serenity; to the supreme law and the abiding mystery of the sublime spectacle". It is invoked in *Lord Jim*, in that central scene between Marlow and Stein in which Marlow, in a moment of revelation which Joyce would have termed an epiphany, is granted a vivid insight into Jim's case,

as though [he tells us] in our progress through the lofty silent rooms amongst fleeting gleams of light and the sudden revelations of human figures stealing with flickering flames within unfathomable and pellucid depths, we had approached nearer to absolute Truth, which, like Beauty itself, floats elusive, obscure, half submerged, in the silent still waters of mystery. (p. 216)

In "Youth", it is the word "enigma" that is the focal term in Marlow's account (the climax of the tale) of his first impression of "the mysterious East":

[24] "Sous le masque du disciple de Flaubert et des réalistes français, vivait un mystique qui s'inquiétait d'écouter battre le cœur du monde" (Daniel-Rops, *Carte d'Europe*, Paris, Perrin & cie., 1928, p. 75). And cf. the opening statement of André Chevrillon's tribute in the memorial issue of the *NRF*: "C'est un réaliste romantique et mystique" (*Nouvelle Revue française*, XXIII, Décembre 1924, p. 704). More frequently French criticism contented itself with signalizing the sense of mystery in the work. Thus Louis Gillet, in an early review of *The Arrow of Gold*: "Le caractère originel de l'auteur des *Histoires inquiètes*, celui qui fait le fond permanent de sa poétique, et auquel on est toujours obligé d'en revenir, toutes les fois qu'on parle de lui, c'est le sens du mystère" (*Revue des deux Mondes*, 6ième période, LIII, 1 Octobre 1919, p. 677). Cf. Wyzewa, quoted *supra*, pp. 33 f.; also the able paragraph in Ujejski's study of Conrad in which the attribution of mysticism is rejected (Joseph Ujejski, *Joseph Conrad*; tr. du polonais par Pierre Duméril, Paris, Société française d'éditions littéraires et techniques, 1939, pp. 113 f.).

And I sat weary beyond expression, exulting like a conquerror, sleepless and entranced as if before a profound, a fateful enigma.[25]

In the first of many letters to Arnold Bennett, written in March 1902, Conrad, after praise of *The Man from the North*, nevertheless impugned the realism of the novel: "You stop just short of being absolutely real because you are faithful to your dogmas of realism. Now realism in art will never approach reality." [26] Of explicit criticism there is nothing adverse but the remark that "what it wants is a more emphatic modelling; more relief", so that we can only guess at the identity of the "larger and freer faith" which he urged upon his correspondent. Certainly Conrad's strictures upon Bennett's realism implied no quarrel with his subject-matter. His own *Nigger of the "Narcissus"* is a "tale of the forecastle", a narrative of workaday existence which, had his experience been different, might have found its setting in shop or mine. Unquestionably the fact that his experience was what it was is consequentially related to the original and ineffaceable strain of the "incorrigible Don Quixote"; but the suggestion of the exotic in the Malay novels (in part illusory, since their world was after all a world of his familiar observation) was largely sublimated in his rigorous devotion to his two crafts. The objection to "realism", then, must be seen as an objection to the systematic impoverishment of imagination and suppression of temperament its dogmas implied: not to a sober concern with the data of everyday life and common appearances, but to an incapacity or unwillingness to penetrate their surfaces – or, as he put it elsewhere, defining his own effort in *The Nigger of the "Narcissus"*, to "get through the veil of details at the essence of life".

No doubt his strictures on realism, like Mallarmé's on the Parnassians, originate in a temperamental revolt, the intrinsic nineteenth-century revolt, with which even Zola came in the end to identify himself, against a prevailing positivism and materialism, with their attendant erosion of individuality and vulgarization

---

[25] *Youth*, p. 38 (cf. also the use of the word in two contexts in "Heart of Darkness": *ibid.*, pp. 60, 105).
[26] *Life and Letters*, I, p. 303.

of art – as expressed, for example, in his outburst to Cunninghame Graham in a letter of 1905:

Vous – vous êtes né trop tard. The stodgy sun of the future – our early Victorian future – lingers on the horizon, but all the same it will rise – it will indeed – to throw its sanitary light upon a dull world of perfected municipalities and W.C.s sans peur et sans reproche. The grave of individual temperaments is being dug by G.B.S. and H.G.W. with hopeful industry. Finita la commedia! [27]

Characteristically, Conrad added: "Well, they may do much, but for the saving of the universe I put my faith in the power of folly." His corrosive insight into the workings of that power counts for much in the universe of his fiction. As deliberate artist, however, as "maker", he put his faith – or so much of it as was not invested in the rendering of sensory impression, "to make you *see*" – in mystery and enigma, in inquietude, in "the magic suggestiveness of music", as he conceived that "art of arts".[28]

Indeed, as with the proponents in painting of the so-called "magic realism", though with technical means more nearly suggesting those of impressionism, the plastic and pictorial impulse was deeply implicated with the suggestive and "musical" impulse. *The Nigger of the "Narcissus"*, from the Preface of which I have just quoted, was sometimes proclaimed – together with the slightly earlier *Red Badge of Courage* – as one of the earliest triumphs of literary impressionism in the English language. But the much-cited predicate, "to make you *see*", like that other no less familiar formula in the second sentence of the Preface ("to render the highest kind of justice to the visible world"), must be construed within its context, and particularly in relation to the allusions to "magic" and to "music".

A recent student of Ezra Pound has credited Conrad, in an elegant metaphor, with introducing into the English tradition the element of "phanopoeia" – the word by which Pound defined the

---

[27] *Life and Letters*, II, p. 12. For the anti-positivist bias of the *Symbolistes*, cf. Martino, *op. cit.*, p. 138: "Le positivisme croyait pouvoir bien expliquer le monde, le peindre et le régenter; eux, insatisfaits de ces explications, ils trouvaient partout l'énigme, le mystère, l'inquiétude."
[28] *The Nigger of the "Narcissus"*, p. xiii.

quality of immediate visual presentment.[29] But if Conrad was pre-eminently a man for whom (as for Gautier) the visible world existed, in all its concreteness, if as artist he betrays a Flaubertian passion for the rendering of external appearance, it is no less true that for him "seeing" was more than an optic function, that it implied seeing into and beyond the external appearances, seeing "through the veil of details" to an intimated essence. "Justice to the visible world", if it respected the surfaces of things, was nevertheless achieved, as that opening paragraph tells us, "by bringing to light the truth, manifold and one, underlying its every aspect". The artist's obligation toward his material (as the seventh paragraph of the Preface declares) is "to show its vibration, its colour, its form; and through its movement, its form, and its colour, reveal the substance of its truth – disclose its inspiring secret: the stress and passion within the core of each convincing moment". If the task is achieved, i.e., "by the power of the written word, . . . to make you *see*", then everything is achieved, including also "that glimpse of truth for which you have forgotten to ask".

In such passages may be found the clue to his exasperated struggle with words, attested by the manuscripts, and by Ford in his account of their collaboration. Conrad had the sort of imperial sense of the prepotency of the word that Mallarmé (and following him Valéry) expressed by the majuscule in their invocations of "le Verbe". "Give me the right word and the right accent and I will move the world", he proclaimed in the "Familiar Preface" to *A Personal Record*. The famous sentence on the power of words in paragraph five of the Preface to *The Nigger of the "Narcissus"* expresses the sense of that power in the *Symboliste* formula of "magic suggestiveness" – a striking equivalent of the Baudelairean definition of poetry as "magisme, sorcellerie évocatrice" [30]:

[29] "It was by way of the Impressionist novel in the French manner that phanopoeia finally got a toehold in the English tradition, notably at the hands of Conrad, whose aim was 'above all, to make you see' " (Kenner, *The Poetry of Ezra Pound*, p. 268).

[30] It may be noted also that the terms magic and sorcery ("ensorcellement") were among the common counters of critical appreciation of Conrad in both France and England – as employed, for example, by Louis Gillet in a review of *The Rover*, by Desmond MacCarthy in a passage to

It is only through an unremitting never-discouraged care for the shape and ring of sentences that an approach can be made to plasticity, to colour; and the light of magic suggestiveness may be brought to play for an evanescent instant over the commonplace surface of words: of the old, old words, worn thin, defaced by ages of careless usage.

In terms of his own affirmation of the power of the word it is tempting to speculate on the reflexive influence of his repeated invocation of "magic suggestiveness" (the phrase occurs also in the sentence immediately preceding the one quoted) in producing that incantatory strain that marks many tracts of his early prose. Undoubtedly the pages of *An Outcast* and of such a story as "The Lagoon" are marred by a sort of inflated verbal currency (in which we may discover some words worn thin by Conrad himself), yielding a prose style whose musical qualities one might characterize by Verlaine's term "cymbaliste". But by the summer of 1897 he had taken stock of this danger and pruned his excesses. He did not drop the term "magic" from his critical vocabulary – it appears as the characterizing term for all creative art in his 1905 essay on Henry James; and Anatole France, in an essay of 1908, is spoken of as a "magician". But that Conrad employed the term "magic suggestiveness" as a metaphor for the symbolic function of language, conceived as a latent energy to be kept under scrupulous control, is strongly inferrable from another passage on the power of words, written some two years later than the Preface in a letter to Hugh Clifford:

Words, groups of words, words standing alone, are symbols of life, have the power in their sound or their aspect to present the very thing you wish to hold up before the mental vision of your readers. The things "as they are" exist in words; therefore words should be handled with care lest the picture, the image of truth abiding in facts, should become distorted – or blurred.[31]

---

be cited shortly, and by Edwin Muir, who attributed to Conrad "that last gift called 'magic' whereby the object is made to leap before our eyes by a power beyond mere description" (Edwin Muir, *Latitudes*, New York, Huebsch, 1924, p. 51).

[31] *Life and Letters*, I, p. 280. A Conrad concordance would show a considerable number of entries under the word "symbol" and its cognates.

Reduced to the concision of epigram, this would come to much the same thing as Axël's dictum in the "Traité des Causes secondes": "Tout verbe, dans le cercle de son action, crée ce qu'il exprime. Mesure donc ce que tu accordes de volonté aux fictions de ton esprit."

It is not part of my purpose to supplement this inquiry into the key-words of Conrad's aesthetic with an attempt to discriminate specific "symbolic" words in his fiction. There is room here for an inquiry of some interest; but my concern is rather with the symbolic image, and though a word in isolation may of course evoke an image and may, as Conrad himself declared, be construed as a unitary symbol, it is through the ensemble of words in a phrase or image, of phrases and images in a paragraph or episode, that the symbolic as here construed is communicated.

The term "magic suggestiveness" may be seen as a sort of elegant pleonasm, since in the aesthetic of Conrad's Preface (as in that of Baudelaire and the *Symbolistes*) the modifier, if we take it as a substantive, is virtually interchangeable with the noun.[32] But when, earlier in the fifth paragraph, Conrad further modified the noun by the addition of his musical reference, as a sort of *tertium comparationis*, he introduced an element of more than rhetorical value. Asserting the primary importance of an appeal to and

---

Marlow sees Jim as "symbolic" (*Lord Jim*, p. 265); he applies the term to the voyage of the *Judea* in "Youth" (*Youth*, pp. 3 f.). The word is used to characterize Hervey's wife in "The Return" (*Tales of Unrest*, p. 139); it is applied to Edith Travers' lost sandal (*The Rescue*, p. 396); to Peter Ivanovitch's escape from Siberia (*Under Western Eyes*, p. 121); and repeatedly to Rita de Lastaola (*The Arrow of Gold*, pp. 85, 142, 312). These are only random samples: an exhaustive list would have only symptomatic interest, since the symbolic, whatever it may be, is obviously not attained in art by a mere act of designation. I have supplied instances in my introductory chapter of Conrad's rare employment of the terms in critical contexts (*supra*, pp. 15 f.).

[32] It is in terms of the linked, and indeed identified, concepts of "suggestion" and "magic" that the German critic Fritz Strich, in an essay on "The Symbol in Poetry", characterized the *Symboliste* movement. Proposing the term *Suggestionkunst* as a more precise term for the movement than *Symbolismus*, he added the remark: "Es ist eine Kunst der Beschwörung, der Magie. Denn die moderne Magie heisst eben: Suggestion" (Fritz Strich, *Der Dichter und die Zeit*, Bern, A. Francke, 1947, p. 17).

through the senses if fiction is "to reach the secret spring of responsive emotions", he invokes the sister arts:

It must strenuously aspire to the plasticity of sculpture, to the colour of painting, and to the magic suggestiveness of music – which is the art of arts.

The synthesis of the plastic (or more generally the visual) and the "musical" here put forth as the ideal goal is of the essence of the view of Conrad's art which underlies my subsequent examination of his metaphoric and symbolic usage, in which the image vividly visualized and plastically rendered exists in musical, as it were motival, relation to other images and to the intuitively apprehended themes of the work. I shall have more to say about the analogy of music in my chapter on the Conrad-Flaubert relation. However, it is a topic that imposes itself unavoidably in the present context and must be dealt with, if only summarily.

If Conrad's reference to the visual arts suggests Flaubert and the Parnassians, the primacy accorded to the example of music brings the passage in touch with the Mallarméan aesthetic, in which the "souci musical" was not simply a dominant theme, but the *Leitmotiv*, the theme of themes. The evoked flower of the "Crise de Vers" – "l'absente de tous bouquets" – emerged, it will be recalled, "musically" from the poet's phrase; and elsewhere in that seminal text Mallarmé defined the task of poets as one of achieving the transposition of the symphony into the Book, of reclaiming from music their heritage ("de reprendre notre bien") – an intention in which Valéry, in one of his prefaces, professed to see the entire secret of the *Symboliste* movement. For Conrad, as for the *Symbolistes*, music was the vehicle par excellence, and thus the paradigm for the other arts, of the "evocative" and the "suggestive" in art.

Or so the Preface of 1897 would have us believe, and such, I think, one may take to be the case, however ideal and abstract his notion of music may have been. Conrad had none of the musical sophistication of a Proust or a Thomas Mann; he had, unlike Gide, no musical avocation; and the art of music, on the few occasions of musical performance in his fiction, is travestied (e.g., Zangiacomo's all-girl orchestra in *Victory*; Babalatchi's music-box concert for Lakamba in *Almayer's Folly* – an opéra-bouffe parody of David and Saul). Of musical knowledge he probably had less even than Baudelaire or Mallarmé, both professed Wagnerians, though perhaps more on aesthetic principle than by conviction. Such musical preference as he evinced was for the more accessible reaches of the operatic repertory. We have Galsworthy's testimony that " 'Carmen' was a vice with both of us", but that "the blare of Wagner" left his friend cold; and Conrad himself in a letter of 1910 remarked ironically to Galsworthy: "I suppose that I am now the only human being in these Isles who thinks Myerbeer [sic] a great composer."

Yet the Preface speaks of music as "the art of arts"; and whether the passage consciously echoes Pater's familiar dictum [33] or some remembered fragment of *Symboliste* prose, or whether it expresses an original intuition, Conrad's musical reference is, in its context, of great suggestive value for an approach to his fiction. Here I shall only illustrate briefly a single mode of "musical" suggestion discoverable in his prose.

The *Symboliste* concept of music did not preclude a concern with the structural aspect of the art (as witness Mallarmé's conjecture, in the Preface to *Un coup de dés*, that the genre which he hoped that work would establish, might become, little by little, "like the symphony compared to the monody"); but its primary significance for poetry lay in the realm of semantic suggestion and cross-reference, after the example of *Leitmotiv*, and of rhythmic and phonetic relations – of Aristotle's melopoeia. To illustrate here the consequences of Conrad's musical ideal as it expressed itself in the phonetic texture of his prose (particularly in his employment of assonance and alliteration) would be interesting, but of doubtful relevance. More relevant is his occasional recourse to expressive, or symbolic, rhythmic patterns. This again – like

[33] Omit the references to sculpture and painting and it will be apparent that Conrad's sentence is a somewhat elaborated paraphrase of Pater's "All art constantly aspires towards the condition of music" (in the essay on "The School of Giorgione"). The verb is the same. Scarcely less striking is the phonetic resemblance between Conrad's "strenuously aspire" and Pater's "*Anders-streben*" (in the same essay).

the matter of the Conradian vocabulary – is a special topic, outside the current of my principal concern, so that a single example must suffice to indicate Conrad's awareness of the expressive possibilities of rhythm. The passage in question has the advantage, for exemplary purposes, of incorporating one of the rather scarce Conradian similes having a musical referent, and the further advantage of having an approximate prototype in *L'Education sentimentale*, thus enabling me to anticipate the material to be dealt with in chapter IV and to indicate its relatedness to the material of the present chapter.

I have in mind an extended (eight-line) sentence in "The End of the Tether", in which the movement of the *Sofala* upriver into the Malay forest is described. The opening lines, with divisions supplied to mark the rhythmic periods expressive of the engines' pulsation, are as follows:

The thump of the engines / reverberated regularly / like the strokes of a metronome / beating the measure / of the vast silence. . . .

The rest of the sentence, moving out of the orbit of the metronomic image, falls into a quite different periodic structure, the more leisurely and extended movement of which serves to evoke the interminable forward movement of the steamer against the current:

the shadow of the western wall had fallen across the river, and the smoke pouring backwards from the funnel eddied down behind the ship, spread a thin dusky veil over the sombre water, which, checked by the flood-tide, seemed to lie stagnant in the whole straight length of the reaches.[34]

The image of the metronome is Conrad's own; but the opening rhythm of the sentence may well have originated in an unconscious memory of the more extended sequence in the first chapter of *L'Education sentimentale* in which the harpist competes with the engines of the steamer as it moves upriver toward Nogent-sur-Seine:

les battements de la machine / coupaient la mélodie / à fausse mesure; / il pinçait plus fort: / les cordes vibraient, / et leurs sons métalliques /

[34]   *Youth*, p. 257.

semblaient exhaler des sanglots, / et comme la plainte d'un amour / orgueilleux et vaincu.[35]

A rhythmic pattern, then, can itself constitute a symbol – or, speaking more generally, the rhythms of a passage, together with the sonorous quality of the vocables themselves, are implicated in the symbolic operancy of the image. The passages quoted suggest a literal sense in the common metaphor whereby images are said to set up "resonances" in a work. I shall try to show in chapter IV how a number of the Flaubertian images which appear to have haunted Conrad's imagination were appropriated, or adapted, as rhythmic units, retaining their rhythmic identity substantially unimpaired in their transit from French to English, in spite of semantic alterations.

But it is by definition the category of the visual rather than of the auditory that primarily concerns us in our dealings with the image; and it is Conrad as *"Voyant"*, pursuing his avowed purpose "to make you *see*", that I want here to consider, in a summary way, before proceeding to more detailed considerations. The purpose here is to suggest the interfusion of optic vision and evocative power which ideally, for Conrad, constituted the faculty, or the act, of "seeing" – in which is implied a penetration into "the stress and passion within the core of each convincing moment".

We can find no better comment on that ideal faculty of vision proclaimed in the Preface of 1897 than Marlow's speculation on the genesis of Anthony's love for Flora de Barral, when he speaks of the lover as

called out in all his potentialities often by the most insignificant little things – as long as they come at the psychological moment: the glimpse of a face at an unusual angle, an evanescent attitude, the curve of a cheek often looked at before, perhaps, but then, at the moment, charged with astonishing significance. These are great mysteries, of course. Magic signs.[36]

[35]   Flaubert, *L'Education sentimentale*, p. 7. All citations from Flaubert, except as otherwise noted, are from the Conard edition of 1921: *viz.*, Gustave Flaubert, *Œuvres complètes* (Paris, Louis Conard, 1921).
[36]   *Chance*, p. 217. Cf. in this connection the paragraph in Desmond MacCarthy's essay on Conrad, written shortly after his death, in which his "master faculty as an imaginative writer" is defined as a power of evocation, of creating "magic moments" conveyed by "those descriptions of

To this we might add that it is such things also that challenge the artist, like the lover a creature impassioned and obsessed; or the further corollary that it is by such "magic signs", perceived in a state of preternatural awareness (Baudelaire would have said "surnaturel"), that the artist communicates his meanings to the reader, provoking in him a corresponding awareness and calling forth from him his own creative potentialities. We may, in short, without extravagance read this passage as a Marlovian venture – appropriately disguised – into post-*Symboliste* aesthetics. Regarded in this light it harks back over a half-century to one of the most famous of pre-*Symboliste* texts – Baudelaire's pronouncement on the genesis of the symbol in the *Journaux intimes* (*Fusées*, XVII):

Dans certains états de l'âme presque surnaturels, la profondeur de la vie se révèle tout entière dans le spectacle, si ordinaire qu'il soit, qu'on a sous les yeux. Il en devient le Symbole.

Typically, a Conrad scene recurs to mind associated with some visual detail or ensemble of details which, if it does not determine it, is at any rate intimately identified, as by a fusion of metals under pressure, with the emotional tonality of the scene or with some apprehended theme or moral crux of the narrative. I have already quoted a passage in which such an intention is made explicit, in which the symbolic identification is (uncharacteristically) presented as a datum of consciousness of one of the characters involved. The passage in question is that from *Lord Jim*, already cited above. In a "moment of vision", prepared for by an antecedent paragraph of more vivid particularization, Marlow sees his candle-lighted progress with Stein through the moving shadows of Stein's rooms as an approach, through obscurities and ambiguities, to Truth. The image stands at the center of the book, and spreads, like the concentric waves that expand around a stone dropped into a pool, over the entire field of Marlow's inquiry into Jim's case.

I recall Mallarmé's precept, cited above: "to choose an object

---

scene and place which create in us such a strange expectancy" (*Portraits*, New York, Oxford University Press, 1954, p. 77).

and disengage from it a psychic state (*état d'âme*), by a series of decipherments". To such a procedure Conrad's temperament repeatedly led him: a number of his characteristic fictions are precisely a series of moral decipherments, the final import of which, never free from ambiguity, the reader must, by a contributory effort of the imagination, "divine little by little". Frequently, since Conrad like Henry James is obsessed with the drama of consciousness, the effort of divination is itself embodied in the novel or tale, as in *Lord Jim*: the reader follows in the footsteps of a narrator or commentator equipped, as it were, with an inner divining-rod, fallible but incessantly responsive. This characteristic procedure is parabolically defined by the narrator of *Chance* when he remarks to Marlow (in a metaphor that attests the imaginative appeal to Conrad of Fenimore Cooper's novels, and suggests an unexpected symmetry in their procedures):

"You are the expert in the psychological wilderness. This is like one of those Redskin stories where the noble savages carry off a girl and the honest back-woodsman with his incomparable knowledge follows the track and reads the signs of her fate in a footprint here, a broken twig there, a trinket dropped by the way. I have always liked such stories. Go on.[37]

Taking the metaphor simply, as it is offered, we have a vivid figure of the novelist's psychological involvements and the excitements of unraveling them, availing ourselves of "aids to detection" (gestures, attitudes, visibilia of all sorts) cunningly disposed along the narrative trail.

But we may fetch the metaphor farther, seeing in the back-woodsman's visible traces a whole great class of visibilia – Marlow's passage with Stein, let us say, through the dimly-lit chamber; the moon rebounding between the prongs of the cleft mountain of Patusan; the black silk hat inverted upon the white marble balustrade in the corridor of the Château Borel; or Verloc's black bowler by the sofa on which his body lies; or the cracked marble urn ornamented with masks and garlands which engages

[37] *Chance*, p. 311. Reading this passage one thinks of Almayer's obliteration of Nina's footprints, after her elopement with Dain (*Almayer's Folly*, p. 195); of Jim letting fall Stein's talisman ring in the moment before his death (*Lord Jim*, p. 415).

the absent attention of Charles Gould in the bare hall of an Italian villa – which we cannot see as "aids to detection", or direct betrayals of psychological states, and which only to the impoverishment of the text and of our own imaginative response can we see as mere denotative counters whose significance is exhausted when we have assigned them meanings, in the sense of explicit designata. And yet though we may assent to John Bayley's pronouncement that Conrad's scenes and images, like his characters, "are only revelatory because they are what they are" – and are, we might add, intensely and vividly what they are – we cannot as readers accept that their existence excludes them from a world of meaning. Like Marlow's "magic signs", such images seem to us charged with significance: they are often, whether we approve or disapprove, *portentously* what they are. Though we cannot "decipher" them or treat them as signs in the strict semeiotic sense without "denaturing Conrad's reality", we shall find, I believe, that in allowing them to penetrate our consciousness, responding to them in their context of moral and physical event, they may illuminate and focus the drama of consciousness enacted by the novelist's characters. They may or may not evoke psychic states (*états d'âme*); but their *modus operandi* is legitimately symbolic: as local symbols they serve to communicate and enforce the total symbolic import of the works in which they figure.[38]

However deliberate Conrad may have been in his pursuit of the "suggestive" as a quality of art, such images, and many others among his most effective, seem rather to have invaded the con-

---

[38] Cf. John Bayley, *The Characters of Love* (New York, Basic Books, 1960), p. 267, source of the several quotations in the foregoing paragraph. Bayley's paragraph, directed at the misconception of Conrad's achievement implied in E. M. Forster's complaint of a "central mist" at the heart of his thought, assimilates Conrad to his general view of narrative and dramatic art, which, asserting "the supremacy of personality in the greatest literature" (*ibid.*, p. 266), protests against a "discernment that [loses itself] far below the surface of ... actuality" (p. 268). Apart from the qualifications indicated above, involving my belief that his restriction of the concept of the symbol is inadmissible, I see in Bayley's brief remarks on Conrad valuable details in a valuable book. For further consideration of what Bayley speaks of as "the dangers of 'deep' criticism of Conrad" see my discussion of an essay by Philip Rahv at the commencement of the chapter following.

sciousness of the author himself by the way of suggestion – the unsought reward of that effort of total vision, of total saturation in the elements of his fictional world, of which we have moving evidence in the correspondence. Given such a mood of receptivity – variously defined by Baudelaire and Yeats – we may well conceive that the images to which we attribute a symbolic import may (as Goethe postulated) be achieved by an author unaware, or only tardily aware, of their revelatory character ("ohne es gewahr zu sein, oder erst spät"). Ramón Fernández' hypothesis is convincing for much of Conrad's revelatory imagery. Adapting a punning word of Paul Claudel's, he spoke of a sort of "conaissance" of event and image, the image seeming to grow out of the same ground as the event: the product of a single impulse, image and event coexist in an indissoluble imaginative unity.[39]

In the want of direct testimony, however, questions of the relation of unconscious impulse to conscious intent, though endlessly challenging, are both unanswerable and inessential. What we have to consider, in any case, is a body of fiction incorporating a system of felt correspondences between the experiencing agents and the objects or images that constitute their material environment or that, evoked in metaphor, constitute as it were their ideal ambience.

Sir Kenneth Clark, devoting his Romanes lecture of 1954 to the symbolic effect of "occasions of intensified physical perception", drew his illustrations from both painting and poetry, citing as "eminent instances" such diverse items as Leonardo's whirlpools, Wordsworth's daffodils, Dürer's hands, Giorgione's seated woman, and a familiar image from one of the closing stanzas of "The Eve of St. Agnes" ("And the long carpets rose along the gusty floor"). Of the first four items in the series we may say that the image, when not the exclusive occasion, is a major element, of the whole in which it figures. The final example, on the other hand, is a minute detail in an extensive whole, a single line in a poem that approaches four hundred lines – and, one might add, a single image in a poem exceptionally prolific of sensory images.

[39] Ramón Fernández, "L'Art de Conrad", *Nouvelle Revue française*, XXIII (Décembre 1924), p. 733.

If we grant Sir Kenneth the somewhat disconcerting disparity of his series, we may readily grant the "eminence", in its own kind, of the instance from Keats, even seeing in that eminence a particularly compelling testimony to the imaginative phenomenon in question – the phenomenon described by Conrad as an "appeal through the senses" to "the secret spring of responsive emotions". Keats's image has, of course, certain contextual advantages over other images in the poem: it comprises a single terminal line of its stanza, and it marks the crest of the wave of physical excitement incident to the narrative and dramatic climax of the poem – from which it clearly derives an increment of power. There is, then, a reciprocity, an exchange of potency between image and context; but the significant aspect is the contribution of the image to our imaginative apprehension of the context – of the dramatic crux, and of the enveloping mood of the whole.

I linger over the instance, not only by reason of its eminence, but because the image recalls a like image – the disturbance of a sheet of paper by a gust of wind at a moment of narrative tension – by which Conrad in two separate contexts (in *Nostromo*, and later in *Victory*) enforced, and even to a degree evoked, by aid of the image the response called for by the event.[40] The Conradian images are not "eminent instances", being minute details of much vaster wholes than "The Eve of St. Agnes" and wanting the specific advantages of the Keats image – notably its identity as a metrical integer. They serve, however, to illustrate the primary symbolic function performed by Conrad's images – the evocation of feelings or psychic states by physical means, by that "appeal through the senses" proclaimed in the Preface of 1897.

No suggestion is intended that in appropriating to prose fiction the conscious and even systematic awareness – common to poets

[40] "A piece of paper scurried out from somewhere, rustling along the landing" (*Nostromo*, p. 423: the moment after Nostromo catches sight of the shadow of Hirsch's hanged body in a room of the abandoned Custom House); "From the dark slope of a tall stand-up writing-desk a forgotten, solitary sheet of paper flew up and settled gracefully on the floor" (*Victory*, p. 275: at the moment of Wang's forced entry of the disused bungalow which Heyst has offered for the accommodation of Mr. Jones and his satellites).

in all ages – of the psychological nexus between man and his material environment, and thus of the symbolic potential of material objects and physical phenomena, Conrad's originality was absolute and his achievement unexampled. Nor have I intended, in relating his aesthetic position to the doctrines of French *Symbolisme*, to seduce the reader into absurd conclusions by suggesting a closer approximation than can possibly be demonstrated between the end-product of Conrad's artistic effort and the characteristic productions of that movement.

On the first point it is demonstrable that the method of Flaubert is based upon a like insight and pursued a like goal, and it may be strongly inferred that Flaubert's example, abetted to a degree by that of some other novelists (notably Turgenev, Dickens, the early Henry James, in whom objective image and metaphor can be shown to operate in like ways) counted for more in the formation even of this aspect of Conrad's art than either the example or the precept of avowed *Symbolistes*. (My next two chapters are devoted to this question.) On the second point it may be said that in introducing into the novel "poetic" modes of apprehending reality – in the interests largely of that gain in intensity and immediacy which prompted him also, under obscurer and less articulate impulsions, to such devices as multiple narration and interrupted time-scheme – he obeyed no impulse to overturn the fictional genre. If, following the bias of his native temperament and inflamed by French influences, he reconnoitred the terrain, and indeed occupied large tracts, of a "poetic" novel – of a novel more intensely visualized, more densely imaged, more thematically organized, and more musically evocative than the novel of tradition – the reconnaissance was conducted with the impedimenta of a novelist, from a base firmly anchored in novelist's country. An artistic pioneer, and even an innovator, Conrad was not a revolutionary. Nor was he (as allegorical interpretations would imply) an artistic reactionary in his conception of the fictional genre. Though the Preface of 1897 suggests as much the sketch of a general aesthetic as the working creed of a novelist, Conrad was, nevertheless, a professional novelist who acquiesced in the fundamental convention of his art – the convention that required the novelist (as he put it in a letter addressed to Blackwood five years after the composition of the Preface) to deal with the "action of human beings that will bleed to a prick, and are moving in a visible world". The art of fiction was for Conrad an art of mimesis.

Indeed it is too little to say, in this connection, that Conrad acquiesced in a convention: he embraced with passion, as the novelist's birthright, the requirements of action and of surface observation, as one would expect of a mariner turned novelist who was steeped in Cervantes and Dickens, who had much of Balzac and Flaubert by heart, who was one of the first of his generation to relish Proust, and who yet devoured with no less appetite works of history, personal memoirs, and the literature of voyages and exploration. To his account of the life of ships and the sea in particular he brought the devoted attention to detail of a professional; and he would have made no shadow of sense of the complaint of Vernon Young that, in a work like *The Nigger of the "Narcissus"*, he had "overloaded his mundane treatment of the crew", at the expense of the "subaqueous world" which was his real subject.[41] As it happens, Conrad knew better than his critic what he was about. Like other major artists he had, I believe, insights into a realm that may be metaphorically defined as "subaqueous", as also into metaphorically "translunar" realms. In certain major and diffusive images (the sea repeatedly; the forest, in the Malay novels and in "Heart of Darkness"; the river in "Heart of Darkness"; the fog-drenched city in *The Secret Agent*; the system of cosmic and meteorological metaphor in *Lord Jim*), and even in certain minor but obsessive images (the mirror for example, or the veil, whether objectively presented or metaphorically evoked) we may detect an intent and an operancy that transcend the account of the function of sensuous imagery offered in the Preface to *The Nigger of the "Narcissus"*, as commented on

---

[41] "Fearful of overstressing the subaqueous world of the underconsciousness, the symbol-producing level of the psyche which, in fact, was the most dependable source of his inspiration, Conrad overloaded his mundane treatment of the crew" (Vernon Young, "Trial by Water: Joseph Conrad's *The Nigger of the 'Narcissus'* "; Robert W. Stallman, ed., *The Art of Joseph Conrad: A Critical Symposium*, East Lansing, Michigan State University Press, 1960, p. 119).

above. There is in a valid sense of the word a metaphysical, as well as a physical, dimension to Conrad's system of imagery. But his more penetrating or aspiring insights into subaqueous or translunar realms could, in his artistic scheme, only be refracted through a surface that was firm, authentically realized, and materially dense.

Conrad was, in short, a novelist, and not a poet *manqué*. We may call him a poet-novelist if we do not take the first term of the compound as a derogation from the second; it is likely, in any case, that he introduced into the practice of his art more of the available resources of poetry than any novelist before him. But we would do better to think of him simply as a novelist with something of a poet's intensity of vision who created fictional structures which, like all works of primary literature, are symbolical. Certainly the man who created Marlow was, whatever else he was, a born narrator. So thoroughly did he transform himself into a man of letters that one has to remind oneself that he was not a born "homme-plume" like Flaubert – he was rather (in a more exclusive sense than Flaubert) an *homme-gueuloir*, a compulsive raconteur whom obscure impulses of heredity and temperament propelled into literature at an age when almost every other writer one can name has either firmly established himself or decisively failed.

As practitioner of a narrative art Conrad required an audience, and he meant to be accessible to it. He was not notably successful in this, having a low opinion of the public ("Car enfin", as he once wrote to Davray, "le public est si bête qu'il faut lui montrer le soleil du doigt pour qu'il puisse comprendre que cela luit"), and having no more instinct for compromise than Flaubert – or for that matter than Mallarmé. In another letter to Davray he spoke once of the writer's giving his soul to "the devil of domestic economy",[42] but the Blackwood correspondence reveals how little capable that devil was of hurrying his rate of production when he had under hand any work with which he was intimately involved.

---

[42]   "Parole d'honneur quand on se met à écrire on donne son âme [*sic*] au diable – le diable de l'économie domestique" (*Lettres françaises*, p. 69). For the parenthetical quotation above cf. *ibid.*, p. 51.

Until the publication of *Chance* (1913), almost two decades after his literary début, his sales were pitiably meagre and his living precarious. Obsessed as he was with the "mysterious" and the "enigmatic" in human character and destiny, and concerned to communicate these in his art, he warded off innumerable readers whom he might have attracted by his sheer narrative *élan*, had that been uncomplicated by his obsessions and by the artistic ideals set forth in the Preface to *The Nigger of the "Narcissus"*. But his artistic goals did not at all require of him (any more than his domestic circumstances would have permitted him) Mallarmé's calculated effort to make of his productions arcana unveiled "au seul prédestiné", or "hieratic formulas" deliberately contrived "to ward off the importunate". Conrad had no notion of reading as "a desperate practice".

When this has been said, it has to be added that the Mallarmé-an phrase defines with some strictness Conrad's experience of *writing* – as all readers of his correspondence are aware. I know of no English writer who has left such insistent and painful testimony to the pangs of literary parturition: to match it one must go to the correspondence of Flaubert. All students of Conrad will recall, in this connection, Henry James's characterization of his colleague (apropos of *Chance*) as "absolutely alone as a votary of the way to do a thing that shall make it undergo most doing"; [43] and it is manifestly impossible that this way of doing a thing should not make exactions upon the reader. The exactions are not (or not all) of the same sort as those made by Mallarmé and by post-*Symboliste* poetry in general, since – in the tradition of his own art and after the example of Flaubert – much of his compositional effort was expended on the achievement of a perspicuous surface: on clarity of syntax, on precision of diction and imagery (a different thing from "explicitness", which is a matter of reference). [44] In this effort his professional conscience and the instinct

---

[43] Henry James, *Notes on Novelists, with some other Notes* (New York, Scribner's, 1914), p. 345.

[44] "As to precision of images and analysis my artistic conscience is at rest" (*Life and Letters*, II, p. 205; from the letter to Barrett Clark cited *supra*). With this cf. the following from a letter of 1910 to Mrs. E. L. Sanderson: "In letters suggestiveness itself – a great quality – must be

of workmanship were implicated; but he had anguish left over from that effort to expend on those evocations – whether from some metaphoric realm of the "subaqueous world", or from the luminous realm of "valeurs idéales" – to which he was obsessively driven and which he saw as essential to his task.

The problem for a writer driven by two such distinct ideals may be suggested by Marlow's outburst in "Heart of Darkness":

"When you have to attend to things of that sort, to the mere incidents of the surface, the reality – the reality, I tell you – fades. The inner truth is hidden – luckily, luckily." (*Youth*, p. 39)

I am aware that this can be taken as testimony to the incompatibility of the two artistic impulses – toward a clear rendering of surfaces and toward an evocation of "depths" – which (as in Philip Wheelwright's definition of the symbolic) I here attribute to Conrad. Specifically it can be taken to support the Vernon Young thesis that Conrad went astray, misconceived his talent in his attention to the surface. I take it, on the contrary, as testimony to the heroic difficulty of the task he set himself (or which his genius set him) and to the high accomplishment of a performance which demonstrates that his two impulses, though distinct, are not incompatible. By scrupulous attention to the surface he fashioned a medium – translucent rather than transparent – through which the "inner truths", the subsurface intimations, are refracted. The symbolic in Conrad is inextricably involved with the actual, the metaphoric with the mimetic, in the Aristotelian sense.

Whatever we make of the suggestive but strained thesis of Gustav Morf [45] that Conrad's work embodies an attempt at expiation of guilt for his "desertion" of his native country, there can be no question that the consciousness of exile and isolation reverberates in his fiction and that certain archetypal themes

---

obtained by precise expression. ... To awaken a responsive feeling, something exact must be said. ... In writing and especially in descriptive writing one must guard oneself against the '*à peu près*', – the horrid danger of the 'near enough' " (*Life and Letters*, II, p. 118). The admonition against the "à peu près" may perhaps derive from Maupassant's preface to *Pierre et Jean*, one of Conrad's sources of Flaubertian doctrine.

[45] Gustav Morf, *The Polish Heritage of Joseph Conrad* (London, Sampson Low, Marston, 1930), especially Chapter V, on *Lord Jim*.

– notably the theme of initiation (*rites de passage*) and that of the Fall or the Lost Paradise, as sounded in the epigraph to his first novel – are recurrent, even obsessive, in his work. But these patterns, where discernible, are not imposed as allegories but are symbolically implicit in the human actions; and the concept of the human in Conrad at all times implies the predicate of existential actuality. Fictional "existence" in Conrad is the precondition and determinant of symbolic "essence".

III

THE NURSERY OF THE CRAFT

> Rendre fidèlement le monde visible, tel que l'on le voit,
> et exprimer son sentiment vrai dans la vie intérieure (qui
> est l'âme de l'activité humaine) dans une œuvre d'imagi-
> nation, – c'est bien difficile.
>
> Conrad, Letter to K. Waliszewski

It should require no demonstration that Conrad – however close
to Mallarmé in the terms of critical discourse he found to justify
his art to the public – was, in the fundamentals of his craft, the
inheritor in natural succession of the European tradition of prose
fiction. An exhaustive inventory of the elements of that tradition
is not required here: the following brief affirmation by Conrad
himself (the Conrad of the most productive period) will suffice:

> In its essence it is action (strange as this affirmation may sound at the
> present time) nothing but action – action observed, felt and interpreted
> with an absolute truth to my sensations (which are the basis of art
> in literature) – action of human beings that will bleed to a prick, and
> are moving in a visible world.[1]

This, succinctly expressed (and susceptible, of course, of any
amount of refinement or elaboration), defines the genre of prose
fiction. If the "absolute truth to my sensations" derives from
Flaubert, the rest goes back to Defoe, or for that matter to
Cervantes – who for Conrad as for Flaubert was the master of
those who know the world and man and who cast their knowledge
into the forms of prose narrative.

---

[1] *Letters to William Blackwood*, p. 156. The passage constitutes the second article of that "creed" of which the first article (the claim of a
"definite intention") was cited on p. 14 f., *supra*. For a more succinct expression of the same formula ("action in its essence") see Conrad's 1905 essay,
"Henry James, An Appreciation", *Notes on Life and Letters*, p. 13.

Conrad had, then, a clear sense of the fictional medium and of the novelist's métier; and this sense was never compromised by his experiments with the medium or by his commitment to expressive goals which he shared with a poetic movement. Thus it is clearly to his predecessors in fiction rather than to the poets that one would have to direct one's attention for the terms of comparison required to deal with the more generic aspects of his art.

But the possibility must be considered that Conrad was also influenced by his predecessors in those aspects of his art with which we are specifically concerned. There is evidence for the supposition that he was so influenced, and notably by Flaubert. The theory of the symbolic in literature as it had developed through the nineteenth century was largely the creation of poets and propagandists for poetry (especially Coleridge, Baudelaire, Mallarmé), influenced to a degree by German idealist philosophers. The novelists stood largely outside this theoretical current. So imposing is the historical evidence in the case that Philip Rahv, writing several years ago in the *Kenyon Review*, felt warranted in basing an arraignment of contemporary criticism of fiction on the thesis that its approaches and preconceptions, involving "an identification that confuses the intensive speech proper to poetry with the more openly communicative, functional and extensive language proper to prose", had been smuggled in from the criticism of poetry in a futile effort "to deduce a prosaics from a poetics".[2] Rahv's challenge was delivered not to symbolistic criticism alone, but to a critical complex yielding an approach to fiction in terms of mythic, symbolic, and allegoric patterns (patterns which, incidentally, Rahv found to be inadequately discriminated in current critical discourse[3]); of close stylistic analysis; and of what the writer called "technicism". On the lookout for "differentia distinguishing the prose-narrative from

[2] Philip Rahv, "Fiction and the Criticism of Fiction", *Kenyon Review*, XVIII (Spring, 1956), pp. 276-299. The quoted passages occur on p. 280.
[3] "The younger critics have taken to using all three terms almost interchangeably and always with an air of offering an irrefutable proof of sensibility, with the result that they have been nearly emptied of specific meaning and turned into little more than pretentious counters of approbation" (*ibid.*, p. 281).

the other verbal arts", for "generic critical terms and criteria of value [for the novel] that are unmistakably its own", he proposed a definition which, so far as it goes, seems to me to apply with precision to most of the works in the main stream of the European tradition, Flaubert's and Conrad's included:

The novel . . . is the most empirical of all literary genres; existence is its original and inalienable datum; its ontology, if we may employ such a term in relation to it, is "naive", commonsensical, positing no split between appearance and reality.[4]

Rahv was able, as one would expect, to adduce "absurdities" and "fantastications" illustrative of the risks implicit in the sort of criticism he opposed. Generalizing from the positions adopted in his essay (or from those that immediately concern us), we may fairly say that in Rahv's view symbolic detail, where actually discoverable in an extended fiction, is of little consequence in the total pattern, since it is the whole rather than the parts that is the vehicle of the significantly symbolic;[5] and that the concern of some contemporary novelists for the symbolic (as for myth and allegory) is misconceived. Generally speaking, he finds the alleged symbols of fiction to be vain things fondly invented by critics of poetry strayed from their proper field, in whose excessive emphasis on symbolism he sees an example of the "fallacy of misplaced concreteness" which, "in making for a split between spirit and sense, . . . goes so far in conceptualizing the literary object as to drain it of its existential qualities".[6]

There is much salutary good sense in Rahv's essay, and much that should be cautionary to a writer on Conrad, particularly since recent Conrad criticism supplies Rahv with an interesting example of "fantastication", or of what elsewhere in his essay he characterizes as "Kabbalistic" criticism. As Conrad scholars are aware, Rahv is by no means alone in finding that Conrad criticism

---

[4]   *Ibid.*, p. 286.
[5]   Cf. his assertion – following a hostile glance at critical efforts to "trans-mogrify" *The Red Badge of Courage* into a religious allegory – that "if it is symbolic, it is in the patent sense in which all good art, in so far as it opens out to the world at large by transcending its immediate occasions and fixed, exclusive meanings, can be said to be symbolic" (*ibid.*, pp. 282 f.).
[6]   *Ibid.*, p. 282.

has been productive of "fantastication". The example he adduces (culled from an essay on "The Secret Sharer" by R. W. Stallman) had already been belabored by Marvin Mudrick in the *Hudson Review*; [7] and critics more equable than Mudrick, and with a clearer view of Conrad's stature and the complexity of his method, have added their strictures. John Bayley was cited in this connection in the foregoing chapter. Ian Watt, in an essay on "Conrad Criticism and *The Nigger of the 'Narcissus'* ", has spoken of a tendency toward a "reductio ad symbolum", of the usurpation by the critic of the poet's traditional function of "romantic seer", committed to the enterprise of seeing "what isn't there, or at least has never been seen before".[8] Jocelyn Baines, whose critical biography of Conrad, published in 1959, placed him in the front rank of Conrad scholarship, has complained of the same tendency, in which he finds an extra-literary preoccupation comparable to that of the alchemists.[9]

[7] Marvin Mudrick, "Conrad and the Terms of Modern Criticism", *Hudson Review*, VII (Autumn, 1954), pp. 419-426. Cf. also the same writer's "Communication: Mr. Stallman's Remarks", *Kenyon Review*, XIX (Summer, 1957), p. 483, in which Mudrick, responding to a reference by Stallman to his essay of 1954, remarks, *inter alia*, that "an obtrusive and calculated exploitation of the symbol, as practiced in some of Conrad's fiction and ingenuously reflected in some contemporary criticism (Mr. Stallman's, for example), does not produce valuable fiction or valuable criticism". As indicated in this passage, Mudrick tended to distribute demerits impartially between Conrad and his critics – though he has subsequently (apropos of "Heart of Darkness") attempted to define "the originality of Conrad".

[8] Ian Watt, "Conrad Criticism and *The Nigger of the 'Narcissus'* ", *Nineteenth-Century Fiction*, XII (March 1958), p. 271. Watt's essay followed an essay of Mudrick: "The Artist's Conscience and *The Nigger of the 'Narcissus'* ", *Nineteenth-Century Fiction*, XI (March 1957), pp. 288-297. Rejecting Mudrick's "denigration of *The Nigger*" (Watt, *loc. cit.*, p. 266), he attempts to mediate between Mudrick and the critics he abhors by proposing that Conrad's symbols are characteristically *exoteric* rather than *esoteric*. He supports his distinction by an invented vocabulary which, though interesting, we need not concern ourselves with here *(ibid.*, pp. 273 f.).

[9] Cf., e.g., Baines's characterization of a commentator on "Il Conde" as "one of a number of critics who appear to have assumed the mantle of the alchemists or dabblers in the occult; to them literary texts are arcana offering knowledge to those who can find the key" (Jocelyn Baines, *Joseph Conrad*, New York, McGraw-Hill, 1960, p. 341*n*.). Cf. also his subsequent identification of Stallman as "one of the alchemical critics"

There is, then, a "question of Conrad criticism", itself an aspect of a more general question of the criticism of fiction as currently practiced. I shall have to revert (briefly) to aspects of this controversy in connection with my detailed examination of "The Secret Sharer" and *The Shadow-Line* (chapters X and XI), in which the relation between the symbolic and the allegoric is at issue. In the meantime, since my juxtaposition of Conradian and Mallarméan doctrine exposes me to the distrust of critics of Rahv's persuasion, this is a convenient occasion to assure the reader that I am aware of the controversy, that I am not insensitive to its implications or its seriousness, and that I shall attempt to do justice to the quality of Conrad's symbolic imagination (in which much of apparently unconscious impulse conspired with much of deliberate, but often secretive, intention) without assuming the mantle of the romantic seer or adopting the posture of the Kabbalist, the alchemist, or the mere cryptographer.[10] (I may say here parenthetically that I believe the quest of the alchemist to be a valid symbol of the creative enterprise but a bad one for criticism. The cryptographer, who deals with ciphers involving one-for-one substitutions and equivalences of the order $x = y$, may have something to teach the allegorist; but he can only confuse issues where the symbolic, in the proper sense, is concerned.) But I want to proceed to the question of literary history posed by Rahv's dealings with the novelistic tradition.

Rahv's essay, whatever its merits, suffers from a failure to deal adequately with the "intensive speech" and the symbolically suggestive detail to be found in the work of several major nineteenth-century novelists – notably Dickens and Flaubert, the two novelists with whose works Conrad was most deeply saturated. Not only is there evidence of local symbolism, deliberately employed, in the work of both novelists; there is also a history of critical dealings with the symbolic imagery of the two writers (comprehen-

---

(*ibid.*, p. 365*n*.). One recalls Mallarmé's formula for the poem: "Un mystère dont le lecteur doit chercher la clef."

[10] Cf. Professor Stallman: "A cryptographic novel ... asks for and rewards a cryptographic reader" (Robert Wooster Stallman, ed., *The Art of Joseph Conrad: A Critical Symposium* (East Lansing, Michigan State University Press, 1960, p. xxvii).

sive with regard to Flaubert, restricted in scope with regard to Dickens) that clearly antedates the contemporary critical movement Rahv deplores. As early as 1907 G. K. Chesterton centered his treatment of *Bleak House* upon the continuous diffused symbolism he found in the book. In 1922 Albert Thibaudet, in a critical study of Flaubert by no means tendentious or "Kabbalistic", devoted a number of perceptive pages to the symbolic employment of character, episode, and motif, and particularly of metaphor. Obviously these were not critics under the influence of Messrs. Ransom and Leavis (the critics mentioned by Rahv as "coming to prose with habits of mind acquired in the study of poetry" [11]): their sensibilities, though susceptible to poetry, were formed in other schools than that of the New Criticism, and their assertion of the value of the symbolic texture of the two novelists in question may be taken as innocent of any taint of mere fashionableness, or obsequiousness to the shibboleths of poetic criticism. I press the point here since – though Flaubert and Dickens clearly demand some attention in any inquiry into the antecedents of Conradian symbolism – I cannot, in a study of Conrad, devote to their fiction the sort of detailed scrutiny that would be required to establish clearly the ubiquitousness and the artistic significance of the local symbolisms discoverable in their work.

Since my consideration of these two predecessors, and particularly of Flaubert, affords a convenient passage into the subject of my fifth and following chapters (on Conrad's verbal imagery, and on his symbolic use of atmosphere and objective image), I shall, before examining his relations to them, consider more summarily his relation to several other predecessors whose traces are discernible in his work. By way of a brief abstract of Conrad's recorded views of his other major nineteenth-century predecessors, one may say that he felt affectionate admiration for Turgenev; respected Stendhal but had singularly little to say about him; felt an apprehensive regard for Balzac – against whose "Monstrous Shade" he pronounced a sort of *absit omen* on the occasion of his first encounter with Stephen Crane, brusquely dismissing his style as "just black on white"; was familiarly acquainted with the novels

[11] Rahv, *loc. cit.*, pp. 289-291.

of Thackeray but had little regard for him as artist; could not read
Melville; felt profound distaste for Tolstoy as thinker, though on
one or two occasions granting him as artist a grudging tribute,
hedged about with reservations; and abominated Dostoevsky –
whom he nevertheless did read and was unmistakably impressed
by.[12] Of Conrad's complex relation to Dostoevsky I shall speak
briefly farther on. As for Tolstoy it need only be pointed out that
the later works filled him with disgust ("Ivan Ilyitch" was a
"gratuitous atrocity", "The Kreutzer Sonata" a "monstrous
stupidity"), while of *Anna Karenina* he thought (as he told
Garnett) "but little", and of *War and Peace* itself he found nothing better to say than that "the subtle presentation of Rostov's
squadron under fire for the first time is a mere episode lost in a
mass of other matter, like a handful of pebbles in a heap of
sand".[13] Except for his older contemporary Henry James, I find
no significant comment in Conrad's writings on other nineteenth-
century novelists who might be classed as "major" – unless one
include Daudet, Maupassant, and Anatole France, another older

[12]　Balzac's "monstrous world", whose truth and vitality is nevertheless
acknowledged in a sentence of the 1905 essay on "Books", undoubtedly
formed part of Conrad's imaginative baggage, though he found little occasion to declare it publicly; Jean-Aubry included Balzac's novels among
those of which Conrad revealed an "étonnante connaissance" (*Notes on
Life and Letters*, p. 6; *Lettres françaises*, p. 12. For the quotations in text
cf. *Last Essays*, pp. 105 f.). Stendhal (whose "mind was of the first order")
was briefly and cordially appreciated in the essay just cited (*Notes on
Life and Letters*, p. 8). – For Conrad on Melville see the letter of 15
January 1907 to H. Milford, published in Frank MacShane, "Conrad on
Melville", *American Literature*, XXIX (January, 1958), p. 463 f. Declining
to contribute a preface to the Oxford Press *Moby-Dick*, and recommending
Hudson for the job, Conrad gave the following dismal account of his
dealings with his great predecessor: "Years ago I looked into *Typee* and
Omoo, but as I didn't find there what I am looking for when I open a
book I did go no further. Lately I had in my hand *Moby Dick*. It struck
me as a rather strained rhapsody with whaling for a subject, and not a
single sincere line in the 3 vols of it" (*ibid.*, p. 464).
[13]　In the Preface he wrote to *The Red Badge of Courage* (*Last Essays*,
p. 123). For the quotations in parentheses, cf. *Life and Letters*, II, p. 77.
Jocelyn Baines found in the typescript of *Under Western Eyes* derisory
allusions to two of Tolstoy's later works – in a passage suppressed in the
published versions, in which Peter Ivanovitch is cited as the author of
"The Resurrection of Yegor" and of "the thrice famous Pfennig Cantata"
(Baines, *op. cit.*, p. 372).

contemporary, to all of whom (as also to James) he paid tribute in brief periodical essays or reviews as well as in private letters.

Conrad's relation to James has not been thoroughly explored, and it would doubtless reward the effort. His admiration for the older writer is well attested: by the salutation "très cher maître" in the few letters he addressed to him and in the dedicatory inscription to the copy of the French version of *The Mirror of the Sea* which he sent him; by the tone of homage and the handful of approbative phrases ("the fountain of intellectual youth", "the historian of fine consciences") in the rather diffuse "appreciation" which he contributed in 1905 to the *North American Review*; by occasional expressions struck off in letters to friends, as when he exclaimed to Garnett upon receipt of a letter from the Master: "Such enthusiasm! Wonderful old man, with his record of wonderful work!" [14] A devotion so marked could scarcely have failed to leave some imprint on the imagination of the devotee; but it is doubtful to me (though the question is open to further inquiry) whether any clear influence of James's symbolic ordering of image and episode can be traced in Conrad that could not more probably be subsumed under the influence of their common master Flaubert.

With somewhat more assurance I would say the same of Daudet, and with somewhat less assurance, of Maupassant. Conrad's essay on Daudet (published in 1898) reveals a genuine affection but does not claim greatness for its subject.[15] The quali-

[14] *Life and Letters*, II, pp. 55, 91; *Lettres françaises*, p. 77; *Notes on Life and Letters*, pp. 12, 17; *Letters from Joseph Conrad*, pp. 172 f.

[15] "... a prodigality approaching magnificence. ... Neither his qualities nor his faults were great, though they were by no means imperceptible. It is only his generosity that is out of the common" (*Notes on Life and Letters*, p. 20). The cordial, but critically qualified, appreciation contained in this essay is a more reliable guide to Conrad's mature judgment of Daudet than the more enthusiastic expressions to be found in a letter of 1895 addressed to Marguerite Poradowska. In that letter, in which he asks his kinswoman whether he should send a copy of *Almayer* to Daudet, he speaks of his "worship" for the older writer (*Letters of Joseph Conrad to Marguerite Poradowska: 1890-1920*; trans. from the French and ed. with an Introduction, Notes, and Appendices by John A. Gee and Paul J. Sturm, New Haven, Yale University Press, 1940, p. 91). There is warmth, but no idolatry, in the essay of 1898 – the final paragraph of which expresses frank doubt whether Daudet was an artist at all.

ties he admired were qualities rather of temperament than of art, and Daudet's meridional temperament, infused as it was with Dickensian sentiment, appealed to Conrad. Moreover he was intimately attracted to the subjects and the milieux of Daudet's novels. There are passages in *Le Nabab* (particularly chapter 12, devoted to the Corsican election) which recall episodes in the political life of Costaguana; others that recall the social milieu of *The Arrow of Gold*, whose heroine may claim some kinship with Daudet's Félicia Ruys. But though he responded no doubt to the impressionist vividness and the metaphoric abundance of Daudet's style, it seems doubtful that Daudet as artist had any appreciable influence on him.

Conrad's relation to Maupassant was one of "saturation": it is his own word, and his own repeated testimony is supported by Ford and Jean-Aubry.[16] Moreover he himself acknowledged Maupassant as an "influence" – a rare acknowledgement, in fact all but unexampled. This was in a letter to his Belgian "aunt" written in the year prior to the publication of *Almayer*, in which he wrote:

> You are too late with your advice, my dear Aunt. I am afraid I am too much under the influence of Maupassant. I have studied *Pierre et Jean* – thought, method, and everything – with the deepest discouragement. It seems to be nothing at all, but the mechanics are so complex that they make me tear out my hair. You want to weep with rage in reading it. That's a fact! [17]

Nor can there be much doubt that Maupassant was the unidentified referent of the sentence in the "Author's Note" to *Tales of Unrest* in which Conrad dismissed, with an effect almost of rejection, the story "The Idiots".[18] The story is, in fact, a compe-

---

[16] "Moi qui suis, sans me vanter, saturé de Maupassant" (*Lettres françaises*, pp. 51 f.). The claim is made in a letter of 1903 to Davray, requesting his critical support of a volume of selected stories of Maupassant published by Duckworth in that year, "comme hommage [as Conrad put it] au grand talent, à l'art impeccable (presque) de Maupassant" (*ibid.*). Cf. also Jean-Aubry in his Introduction to *Letters françaises* (p. 12); Ford, *Joseph Conrad*, p. 31.

[17] *Letters to Marguerite Poradowska*, p. 84. Cf. also p. 76.

[18] *Tales of Unrest*, p. ix (" 'The Idiots' is such an obviously derivative piece of work that it is impossible for me to say anything about it here").

tent and well-conducted piece of writing largely free of the typical early Conradian excesses that mar "The Lagoon", for example; but it is so markedly under the seal of Maupassant that one scarcely thinks of it as Conradian at all.

In his essay on Maupassant (1904) Conrad praised the "consummate" artist and singled out his gift of "[concreting] his fearless conclusions in illuminative instances".[19] The importance of concretion, of discovering or inventing what a later criticism has termed the objective correlative of feelings and psychological states, was developed in the well-known preface to *Pierre et Jean*, which Conrad knew and which stands in a determinate relation to the Preface to *The Nigger of the "Narcissus"*.[20] But there is nothing in Maupassant's preface, in which the term "extrême lucidité" may be taken as the *mot d'ordre*, that corresponds to Conrad's invocation of "magic suggestiveness"; and the unquestioned interest of the relationship must yield, for our purposes, to the greater and more relevant interest of the Conrad-Flaubert relationship.

Conrad's two brief appreciations of Anatole France (devoted to *Crainquebille* and *L'Ile des Pingouins*) render due justice to the irony and pity poetically celebrated by Bill Gorton in *The Sun also Rises*, as well as to other imputed qualities of which contemporary criticism is perhaps insufficiently appreciative. In general, however (though Conrad speaks of Anatole France as "a great magician"), these are analyzed as qualities of temperament rather than of art, and there would seem to be little in the two reviews that is directly relevant to our inquiry.[21]

In an earlier essay, contributed to the *Outlook*, Conrad paid homage to the shaping influence of Marryat and Cooper.[22] Ford Madox Ford made much of the influence of Marryat upon Conrad

---

[19] *Notes on Life and Letters*, pp. 26, 31.
[20] The relation has been analyzed in an unpublished dissertation by Edgar Wright, cited in Baines, *Joseph Conrad*, p. 148.
[21] "Anatole France", in *Notes on Life and Letters*, pp. 32-44.
[22] "Tales of the Sea", *Notes on Life and Letters*, pp. 53-57. On Cooper cf. also Conrad's declaration to Arthur Symons, in a letter of August 1908: "F. Cooper is a rare artist. He has been one of my masters. He is my constant companion" (*Life and Letters*, II, p. 73).

"as philosopher *tel quel*, and as English gentleman". But Ford also expressed a doubt that Marryat had exercised "any influence at all on Conrad as a writer" – and in this instance I think we may accept Ford's judgment without question, in the strictly professional sense in which he presumably intended it.[23] With Cooper, Conrad had affinities of outlook and temperament (reflected both in choice of subject and in treatment) more significant, I should say, than the affinities with Marryat, Daudet, or Anatole France.[24] The figure of Lingard that haunted him from the beginning almost to the end of his writing life, developed in his fiction in reverse chronological order and with an increment of quasi-mythical significance in each successive treatment, recalls in more than one respect the Natty Bumppo who occupied so curiously similar a role in Cooper's imaginative life. Though Conrad's heroic present-ment is tempered by irony, Lingard is conceived, like Deerslayer, as the mediating link between two impinging cultures, in a sort of dispersed epic that celebrates a dying order characterized by simplicity of manners and motives, chivalrous instincts, a com-munity of interests governed by the ideals of fidelity and honor. Both radically aristocratic in their outlook, both haunted by dreams of a life of heroic simplicity, the two novelists had much in common in terms of fundamental artistic impulse and of the "poetical feeling" Conrad detected in Cooper. But – though one might detect Conradian anticipations in some of the landscapes of *The Prairie*, for example, as well as in Cooper's seascapes – Conrad as artist, as deliberate craftsman of the novel, is at a wide remove from Cooper and can, one feels, have had little to learn from him. There is no need to doubt, however, that the inter-penetration of the sea and of life which Conrad praised in Cooper's sea tales encouraged in him his own instinctive efforts toward a similar interpenetration in his own fiction.[25]

Except for Chekhov (whom he admired, but on whose works he left no detailed comment) Turgenev was the sole Russian

---

[23]   Ford, *Joseph Conrad*, pp. 61 f.
[24]   Marius Bewley touches on the Cooper-Conrad relation in his chapter on Cooper in *The Eccentric Design* (New York, Columbia University Press, 1959), pp. 85-93.
[25]   Cf. *Notes on Life and Letters*, p. 55.

writer who commanded Conrad's allegiance as artist. Acknowledging that Turgenev was "whole-souledly national", he nevertheless saw his created world as "universal", declaring that "Turgenev's Russia is but a canvas on which the incomparable artist of humanity lays his colours and his forms in the great light and the free air of the world".[26] Ford testified that Turgenev was one of their common subjects of conversation during the period of his collaboration with Conrad, implying that Turgenev's example served to confirm them both in their "poetic" conception of the novel.[27] Conrad's fullest statement on Turgenev is contained in the preface he contributed to Edward Garnett's study of the novelist and republished in the *Notes on Life and Letters*. The preface was elaborated (with some omissions, however) from a letter of 1917 in which he recalls his purely instinctive boyhood response, acknowledges his indebtedness to the Constance Garnett versions for a more mature appreciation, and briefly summarizes the qualities of Turgenev's art as he apprehends them.[28]

What Conrad's practice might specifically have owed to Turgenev it is impossible to say with any precision. The art of *The Nigger of the "Narcissus"* elicited from Constance Garnett, translator-general of the Russians in Conrad's time, a comparison with Turgenev; and Richard Curle found more than one resemblance in his friend's work to episodes in Turgenev.[29] It is not

---

[26] *Ibid.*, p. 46. On the following page Conrad writes, apropos of Turgenev's "essential humanity", that "all his creations, fortunate and unfortunate, oppressed and oppressors are human beings, not strange beasts in a menagerie or damned souls knocking themselves to pieces in the stuffy darkness of mystical contradictions". The reference to Dostoevsky is unmistakable.

[27] Ford, *Joseph Conrad*, p. 30. There is some ambiguity in Ford's account: in identifying Turgenev as "the greatest of all poets", and "Byelshin Prairie" (an episode in *A Sportsman's Sketches*) as "the greatest of all pieces of writing", he is not clear as to the source of the judgments expressed. But whether or not Conrad would have subscribed to the letter of these judgments, there is every reason ot believe that he shared, in general, his friend's admiration: indeed he himself described *A Sportsman's Sketches*, in the preface referred to above, as "those marvellous landscapes peopled by unforgettable figures" (*Notes on Life and Letters*, p. 46).

[28] *Life and Letters*, II, p. 192 f.

[29] John Dozier Gordan, *Joseph Conrad: The Making of a Novelist* (Cambridge, Harvard University Press, 1940), p. 234; Curle, *Joseph Conrad*,

difficult to collect apparent echoes of Turgenev in Conrad, particularly in his treatment of Haldin and the Russian émigrés in *Under Western Eyes*, whose "luridly smoky lucubrations" (p. 35) undoubtedly owe something to Turgenev as well as to Dostoevsky; but it would be little to the purpose to record them here. What is more to the point is Turgenev's device of symbolic foreshadowing – as for example in *Smoke,* in the story of a case of witchcraft recounted in a letter from his father, which, working upon Litvinov's unconscious mind, leads him to associate with Irina the anonymously presented bouquet of heliotrope and strikes the tonic note of their relationship as developed in the chapters that follow.[30] Or the sort of synchronistic image that one sometimes finds in Turgenev – the apparently casual event in the natural world that punctuates an episode, and symbolizes a predicament or fore- shadows a destiny – as for example, from the same novel, the briefly recorded struggles of a butterfly between the curtain and the window of the room in which Litvinov is in the act of de- claring his hopeless love for Irina.[31] It is a procedure employed on a number of occasions by Conrad, sometimes with a clear intent of foreshadowing. A single example will suffice to suggest the rela- tionship – e.g., the image of the rey-zamuro which, after circling Nostromo as he lies in the ruins of the old fort, spent from his swim in the Golfo, alights "on a hillock of rubbish within three yards of that man, lying as still as a corpse".[32] Again Turgenev's symbolic and atmospheric presentment of landscape is strongly suggestive of Conrad's method. An example of this is the present- ment of the dried-up Avduhin pond, with its two pine trees within whose gaunt tops "the wind was for ever droning and sullenly

pp. 127, 168. Cf. the pronouncement on *Under Western Eyes* by an essayist of the English Association in 1920: "a work that might have been written by Turgenev" (F. Melian Stawell, "Conrad", *Essays and Studies by Mem- bers of the English Association*, VI, 1920, p. 96). It is not a judgment that a competent critic would be likely to make today, in the light of the Con- rad criticism of the intervening generation.

[30]   Ivan Turgenev, *Smoke: A Novel*, trans. Constance Garnett (New York, Macmillan, 1896), pp. 60-63 (ch. vi).

[31]   *Ibid.*, p. 190 (ch. xvi).

[32]   *Nostromo*, p. 413. The omen is doubled five pages farther on by the owl with its cry of "ya-acabo!" (*ibid.*, p. 418).

murmuring", with its associations of half-legendary crimes and fatal accidents: a suitably haunted spot for the ill-omened tryst between Rudin and Natalya.[33]

It is in such occasional notations as I have illustrated, and more generally in the skill with which he conveyed mental states through physical impressions, in the scrupulous rendering of the "colours" and "forms" of his world, and in the felt reciprocity between the figures and the landscape, that Turgenev's art may well have exercised a fertilizing influence on Conrad's artistic imagination.

More unmistakable, but (as I see it) less relevant to our subject, is the impact of Dostoevsky – the "grimacing, haunted creature" of Conrad's aversion, whose very name, Gide tells us, made him shudder.[34] From Gide, Curle, Louis Gillet, and Thomas Mann to Zabel and Guerard, Conrad's critics have detected resemblances between the two novelists; and so far as I know only Jean-Aubry (out of deference, one suspects, to his friend's nerves) has categorically denied any affinity.[35]

That Jean-Aubry was mistaken requires, I think, no demonstration here, since the undoubted affinities (discernible chiefly in *Under Western Eyes*, only less markedly in *The Secret Agent*, and sporadically throughout Conrad's mature work) are largely in the realm of theme and situation and what Pierre-Quint, linking

---

[33] Ivan Turgenev, *Rudin: A Novel*, trans. Constance Garnett (London, Heinemann, 1894), pp. 163 f. (ch. ix).

[34] Gide, *Nouvelle Revue française*, XXIII (December 1924), p. 661. Conrad's physical response to the dreadful name was enforced, Gide tells us, by "vague imprecations". His characterization of Dostoevsky as a "grimacing, haunted creature" is from the letter to Garnett cited *supra*, p. 73. For the published preface the phrase was edited to "the convulsed terror-haunted Dostoevski" (*Notes on Life and Letters*, p. 48). A somewhat more qualified reaction to Dostoevsky is expressed in a letter of May, 1912, to the same correspondent, acknowledging the gift of Constance Garnett's version of *The Brothers Karamazov*: "Of course I was extremely interested. But it's an impossible lump of valuable matter. It's terrifically bad and impressive and exasperating. Moreover, I don't know what D[ostoevsky] stands for or reveals, but I do know that he is too Russian for me. It sounds to me like some fierce mouthings from prehistoric ages" (*Life and Letters*, II, p. 140).

[35] G. Jean-Aubry, "Joseph Conrad's Confessions", *Fortnightly Review*, CXV (May, 1921), p. 788. Neither in the *Life and Letters* nor in *The Sea Dreamer* did Jean-Aubry mention Dostoevsky.

the names of the two novelists under this rubric, called "psychological chiaroscuro".[36] There seems to be little doubt that *The Possessed* and *Crime and Punishment* were both laid under contribution in the writing of *Under Western Eyes*, but the evidences are not germane to this study.[37] We may detect in Dostoevsky rather than in Turgenev a contributory source of those "prophetic reflections about the Russian soul" which Gide admired in *Under Western Eyes*; [38] but his head-long style, almost bare of metaphor, is poles apart from the deliberate, and deliberately evocative, style of Conrad. Certainly Dostoevsky is in a large and unimpeachable sense a symbolic writer; but he seems to me to be preëminently the sort of writer in whom Philip Rahv saw the ideal type of the novelist – a writer, that is, in whose works one cannot usefully discriminate a specifically symbolic element other than that which one attributes to the total import of his characters and actions. This at any rate seems to me to be generally true – though one might find evidences of a diffused light-dark symbolism, enforcing the "psychological chiaroscuro" in his novels, and though his brilliant interweaving of fable into the dialectic of his novels (the Legend of the Grand Inquisitor, for example, or Stepan Trofimovitch's reflections upon the episode of the Gadarene swine, from which *The Possessed* derives its title) may be said to have a specifically symbolic character. But there is not, in Dostoevsky's intricate web of emotional and dialectical relations, in the kaleidoscopic rush of his narrative with its multiplication of dramatic and moral crises, anything answerable to that nexus of verbal and objective imagery that constitutes so characteristic an aspect of Conrad's fiction.

Of all Conrad's predecessors it was Dickens who, after Flaubert,

[36]   In his critical biography of André Gide, in which he saw the examples of Dostoevsky, Conrad, and Hardy as instrumental in determining Gide's reaction from "the purely musical lyricism of Symbolism" (Léon Pierre-Quint, *André Gide: His Life and Work*, trans. Dorothy M. Richardson, New York, Knopf, 1934, p. 50).

[37]   Some of the parallels between *Under Western Eyes* and *Crime and Punishment* have been canvassed by Jocelyn Baines (Baines, *Joseph Conrad*, pp. 369 f.).

[38]   André Gide, *The Journals of André Gide*, trans. Justin O'Brien (New York, Knopf, 1947-51), II, p. 219.

may be said to have occupied the highest position in his esteem. His regard for Dickens, and his early and intimate acquaintance with his work, are enthusiastically attested in *A Personal Record*. He clearly found Dickens's peculiar angle of vision sympathetic; Dickens was, in any case, the one English novelist for whom Conrad felt something approximating his devotion to Flaubert. H. G. Wells, in his autobiography, denied to Conrad any comprehension, and indeed any conception, of English humor; yet there are strokes of humor in Conrad, often involving personifications, that one might have thought would infallibly have recalled Dickens to an English reader – as for example this glimpse of the Secretary of State in *The Secret Agent* (p. 138): "Sir Ethelred opened a wide mouth, like a cavern, into which the hooked nose seemed anxious to peer"; or the thumbnail sketch of the boiler-maker in "Heart of Darkness" (*Youth*, p. 85):

His aspect was worried, and his head was as bald as the palm of my hand; but his hair in falling seemed to have stuck to his chin, and had prospered in the new locality, for his beard hung down to his waist.

These are legitimate Conradian coinage, but they would certainly pass in Dickens territory. Again (to approach the matter the other way round), the portrait of Mr. Wemmick in *Great Expectations*, though it is authentic Dickens, strikes me as an anticipation of Conradian impressionism at its most characteristic. Wemmick is presented to us, in chapter twenty-one of the novel, "with a square wooden face, whose expression seemed to have been imperfectly chipped out with a dull-edged chisel". The image, developed through two succeeding sentences, would fit with perfect propriety into the series of Conradian sculptural images to be cited in my next chapter in connection with a similar example from Flaubert.[39] Even more striking is the predilection that Conrad shares with the later Dickens for imagery of sinister import, evocative of violence and death. The way in which the impedimenta surrounding the figure of Jaggers, in *Great Expectations*, are made to be evocative

[39] Cf. especially the image of Winnie Verloc "like a figure half chiselled out of a block of black stone" (*The Secret Agent*, p. 280).

of the potential fate of his clients,[40] and the presentment of the furniture and the occupants of the Clennam household, in *Little Dorrit*, are strongly reminiscent of Conrad's employment of mortuary imagery. I shall speak in my fifth chapter of the Flaubertian vein of "le grotesque triste". The corresponding Dickensian vein – what Conrad called the "freakishly sombre phantasy the Great Master knew so well how to bring out by the magic of his understanding love" [41] – clearly constituted one of Dickens's chief attractions for Conrad. On our first introduction to Flintwinch (in *Little Dorrit*) we are told that, with his twisted neck and sideways cravat, he "had a weird appearance of having hanged himself at one time or other, and of having gone about ever since, halter and all, exactly as some timely hand had cut him down".[42] And here is a sentence from the paragraph that first presents the terrorist Karl Yundt to our scrutiny (in *The Secret Agent*): "When he rose painfully the thrusting forward of a skinny groping hand deformed by gouty swellings suggested the effort of a moribund murderer summoning all his remaining strength for a last stab." [43] The confrontation of these two images suggests, I think, a significant aspect of Dickens's appeal to Conrad's imagination.

Of Dickens's novels it was *Bleak House* that had the strongest claim on Conrad's devotion and to which his imaginative response was most intense.[44] *Bleak House* occupies a special position in the

---

[40]　"Mr. Jaggers's own high-backed chair was of deadly black horsehair, with rows of brass nails round it, like a coffin" (Dickens, *Great Expectations*, ch. xx). Or cf. the following: "The pair of coarse fat office candles that dimly lighted Mr. Jaggers as he wrote in a corner, were decorated with dirty winding-sheets, as if in remembrance of a host of hanged clients" (*ibid.*, ch. xlviii).

[41]　*Notes on Life and Letters*, p. 152.

[42]　Dickens, *Little Dorrit*, Bk. I, ch. iii.

[43]　*The Secret Agent*, p. 42.

[44]　Likening Madame Delestang, his patroness during his Marseilles days, to Lady Dedlock, Conrad spoke of this novel as "a work of the master for which I have such an admiration, or rather such an intense and unreasoning affection, dating from the days of my childhood, that its very weaknesses are more precious to me than the strength of other men's work". He added that he had read it "innumerable times, both in Polish and in English" (*A Personal Record*, p. 124).

Dickens canon. Edgar Johnson, together with many other critics writing in the mid-twentieth century, has found symbolic implications throughout Dickens's work; but it was G. K. Chesterton, writing almost a half-century earlier, who first saw *Bleak House* as a radically symbolic work, singling it out from all the other productions of its author. "The whole tale is symbolic and crowded with symbols", he wrote in his introduction to the Everyman's edition of the novel, which he pronounced to be, not Dickens's "best book", but perhaps his "best novel". He found in the Chancery fog of the opening pages the "alpha and omega" of the book – a detail "not merely good in itself, like the description of the wind in the opening of 'Martin Chuzzlewit' ", but "also good in the sense that Maeterlinck is good". It was, finally, to this density of symbolic texture that Chesterton attributed the "satisfying, almost suffocating" artistic unity of the novel compared to Dickens's earlier novels. There are counterparts throughout Conrad's work of the sort of atmospheric symbolism that is so pervasive an element in the Dickens universe and that, as Chesterton saw in 1907, is most densely palpable in *Bleak House.*

Among Conrad's works it is *Chance* and even more strikingly *The Secret Agent* – in setting and atmosphere as well as in the famous cab-ride at the center of the novel – that most remind us of Dickens. Conrad's London – especially the chaotic, insulating, fogbound City of *The Secret Agent* – is an indigenous product of his own moral vision and his own impressionable senses, the residue of "the memories of my solitary and nocturnal walks over London in my early days", of which he spoke in the "Author's Note" to the novel. Believing this, however, one may still believe that his impressions (like James's as recorded in *The Princess Casamassima,* and like those, perhaps, of all other post-Dickensian noctambulists of London) were, in some indefinable degree, refracted through the recollected medium of Dickens's pages. His sense of a Dickensian atmosphere is, indeed, unmistakably attested in his recollection of his first visit to London in September, 1878, to secure a seaman's berth following his arrival at Lowestoft. In a succession of references he characterizes as "Dickensian" the quarter, the office, and the eating-house which he visited.[45] He incorporated some of these impressions in his account of "Young Powell and his Chance", and the novel to which that episode serves as overture contains suggestions of Dickens throughout.[46]

Conrad's affection did not preclude a critical awareness of Dickens's formal limitations. A review of 1904 (entitled "A Glance at Two Books") implicates Dickens, together with Thackeray, in the charge preferred against "the national English novelist" that he is wanting in a "clear conception of his craft". Apropos of the characters of Mr. Osborne and Pecksniff he saw the two authors as "neglecting the one indispensable thing, neglecting to use their powers of selection and observation". The opening paragraph of the review will suggest the distinction Conrad drew between the Dickensian and the Flaubertian traditions:

The national English novelist seldom regards his work – the exercise of his Art – as an achievement of active life by which he will produce certain definite effects upon the emotions of his readers, but simply as an instinctive, often unreasoned, outpouring of his own emotions. He does not go about building up his book with a precise intention and a steady mind. It never occurs to him that a book is a deed, that the writing of it is an enterprise as much as the conquest of a colony. He has no such clear conception of his craft. Writing from a full heart, he liberates his soul for the satisfaction of his own sentiment; and when he has finished the scene he is at liberty to strike his forehead and exclaim: "This is genius!" [47]

But Conrad had no doubt of Dickens's genius, and he gave himself up to his enchantment in entire surrender, with incalculable effect upon his imaginative development. There can be no doubt that he found in Dickens – whether as the products of conscious art or of unmediated intuition – examples of many of the effects for which he himself deliberately, and with "precise intention", strove.

I conclude, in short, that the examples of Dickens and of Turgenev (and perhaps also of Dostoevsky, though to me less

[45] *Notes on Life and Letters*, pp. 152 f. (essay entitled "Poland Revisited").
[46] *Chance* (1913). Cf. especially Marlow's acknowledgment of the Dickensian element in the novel, at the end of one of the early chapters: "Figures from Dickens – pregnant with pathos" (*Chance*, p. 162).
[47] *Last Essays*, p. 132.

perceptibly) are implicated in those elements of Conrad's fiction
with which we are here concerned. In their figurative language, in
their "atmospheric" evocations, in the sympathetic relation of
figures to landscape or milieu, their art touches upon Conrad's at
many points. The degree to which we see them as "influences"
– in the face of Conrad's own disavowals, seconded by Galsworthy, who could "trace no definite influence on him by any
writer" – must depend upon our own evaluation of the sort of
evidence yielded by local resemblances and apparent echoes.
Affinities of this sort are, in any case, "elective affinities" – even,
one must believe, the affinity with Dostoevsky, though clearly at
a level below the level of consciousness. In matters of literary
influence Coleridge's paradox holds good: the artist receives but
what he gives. If Conrad had not had the root of the matter in
him, if his native instincts had not led him in the direction of
evocative metaphor and atmospheric density, he would scarcely
have been accessible to the influences here postulated.

IV

THE MANTLE OF FLAUBERT

Exactitude et mystère!
Flaubert, Postcript to a
letter to the Goncourts

In turning to Flaubert, the relation of whose artistic procedures to those of Conrad is of a quite special interest and calls for examination in some detail, I want to return momentarily to the essay by Philip Rahv cited near the outset of the previous chapter. I noted there that Rahv had not dealt with the evidences of symbolic intent in nineteenth-century fiction; I should add that his essay entirely omitted Dickens from consideration and that it introduced the name of Flaubert only to dismiss him in a footnote, with a paragraph borrowed from Ernst Robert Curtius, as an "ornamentalist", a writer of "art-prose" whose method, degenerating into a formula in the work of the Goncourts, leads to a blind alley.[1] Such a view of Flaubert was convenient for Rahv's thesis (which is not to suggest that it was not seriously advanced); but if we insist that criticism also must partake of the "empirical" character ascribed by Rahv to the novel – if, that is to say, we insist that criticism, whatever its doctrinal preconceptions, must deal with actual works, and must take account of the demonstrable relations subsisting among them – we are bound to reject the Rahv view of Flaubert (even though backed by the commanding authority of Ernst Robert Curtius) as affording a totally inadequate account of that writer's actual position and influence. The fact, after all, is simple and evident: historically speaking, and regardless of the

[1] Rahv, *Kenyon Review*, XVIII (Spring, 1956), p. 293.

absolute value one assigns to his *oeuvre*, Flaubert's position is unassailable and his influence, manifold and ramifying, cannot for a moment be confined, as Curtius and Rahv would confine it, to the "écriture artiste" of the Goncourts.

When Henry James wrote of *Madame Bovary* that it "covers us with its mantle", that "we flaunt it as the flag of the guild",[2] he spoke not for his generation alone, but for serious practitioners of the novel throughout the second half of the nineteenth century and into the twentieth – generations whose contribution to the novel may be resumed under the names of Zola and Maupassant, of James himself, of Conrad and Ford, of Proust and Joyce. If Flaubert's direct influence is less apparent today, it is still there in the background, mediated through the writers I have named, among others; he remains in the face of all derogations the exemplary figure in the history of the novel, far more available as a model than Joyce or Proust and still, as James called him, "the novelist of the novelist" – though not, perhaps, of the "anti-novelist".

In short, Flaubert's influence did not terminate in the "dead end" of the Goncourts: among other channels it flowed into and through the work of Conrad, with whom he had profound moral and temperamental affinities which need not be catalogued here, but which may in part be suggested by inviting the reader to reflect upon the relations subsisting between the conception and treatment of Emma Bovary and of such early Conradian characters as Almayer, Willems, and Jim.[3] The force of his artistic

---

[2] Henry James, *Notes on Novelists, with some Other Notes* (New York, Scribner's, 1914), pp. 89 f. The passage, familiar to students of James, speaks also of a "loyalty" to Flaubert "unlike ... even the best feeling inspired by any other member of the craft", and goes on to say that Flaubert "may stand for our operative conscience or our vicarious sacrifice".

[3] Conrad's affinity to another aspect of Flaubertian temperament and outlook is unexpectedly betrayed in an extended paragraph in "An Outpost of Progress" (*Tales of Unrest*, pp. 93-95), in which Carlier and Kayerts, reduced to the unfamiliar pastime of reading (Dumas, Cooper, Balzac, the rhetoric of a home journalist), suddenly evoke, by their responses to this unaccustomed stimulus, the archetypes of Bouvard and Pécuchet – as though Flaubert's bonshommes had been suddenly transported to the heart of darkness.

example is discernible in many ways, most of them subsumed under the concept of deliberate craftsmanship and artistic scruple: – in attentive concern for the requirements of formal organization, in awareness of the resources of the verbal medium, in the same deliberate calculation in disposing of those resources as that with which the painter disposes of his pigments and the composer of his tones. Moreover there is evidence for the supposition that among the Flaubertian hallmarks detectable in the post-Flaubertian novel, and specifically in Conrad, are the evocative or symbolic use of metaphor and the symbolic ordonnance of theme and episode which patterns itself, with more or less of deliberateness, upon musical structure.

Admittedly, this aspect of Flaubert's art was not well canvassed until a generation or so after his death. To the dominant criticism of his day such matters were "affaires de cuisine", not precisely contemptible, but largely invisible to an attention directed elsewhere – to questions of morals and social milieu, to questions of genre, to many other questions, but only rarely (as Flaubert himself repeatedly complained) to questions of art. But a novelist like Conrad, saturated with Flaubert's works and alert to their exemplary value for his own practice, cannot be assumed to have required a critical crutch to enable him to make his way into Flaubert's kitchen.

Amid so much that was new in Flaubert's approach to the novel – the instinct for documentation, for example, which he bequeathed to Zola and the *Médanistes*; the effort towards perfection of style and precision of diction which was to arouse the emulation of James and Conrad and Ford – the symbolic organization of his fiction largely eluded the attention of an official criticism preoccupied with other fictional values. Certainly one finds little enough to support the claim of a recent writer in *The Times Literary Supplement* that it was Flaubert, rather than Baudelaire, who was the "decisive influence" in the movement towards symbolism, in verse as well as in prose.[4] On the other hand there is no want of testimony that Flaubert's poetic

[4] "Madame Bovary", *The Times Literary Supplement*, LVI (April 12, 1957), pp. 217-219.

contemporaries found in him a suggestive quality, not clearly defined, but felt as "poetic" and recognized as placing his work on quite another plane from that occupied by the doctrinaire realism of Champfleury. Acknowledging Baudelaire's review of *Madame Bovary* in *L'Artiste*, Flaubert wrote that "vous êtes entré dans les arcanes de l'oeuvre, comme si ma cervelle était la vôtre. Cela est compris et senti *à fond.*" [5] Among the few contemporaries who praised *L'Education sentimentale* the most unreserved was the poet Banville who, upon its publication, acclaimed the novel as bearing "the indestructible seal of perfection", and a decade later declared that "the entire contemporary novel comes from it". Banville was no less admiring of the *Trois Contes*, in which he discerned "la puissance d'un poète sûr de son art".[6] Later Mallarmé, in the course of his interview with Jules Huret, was to speak of "les grandes oeuvres de Flaubert, des Goncourt, et de Zola, qui sont des sortes de poèmes". It is true that in the same sentence he defined the method of these works as consisting "à prendre à la peinture ses moyens pour montrer la forme extérieure des choses", which is rather a different thing from the method of *Symbolisme.*[7] Nevertheless the *Symbolistes* and their allies did find in Flaubert something − a quality of "l'au-delà" tempering that of "l'ici-bas", to apply one of their own distinctions − that was not referable to the doctrine of the naturalism they deplored. Rémy de Gourmont, responding to Jules Huret, characterized the idolized Villiers de l'Isle-Adam as "notre Flaubert, pour nous ce que fut Flaubert pour la génération naturaliste, *qui l'a, d'ailleurs, si mal compris*"; [8] and Huysmans, speaking of Flaubert as one of those who were "morts sans postérité", implicitly denied his apparentation to the Goncourts and Zola. Responding to the

---

[5] Flaubert, *Correspondance*, IV, p. 229. For Baudelaire's review, in which *Madame Bovary* is declared to be "essentiellement suggestif", see "L'Art romantique", in Baudelaire, *Œuvres complètes*, III, pp. 393-408.
[6] René Dumesnil, *Gustave Flaubert: l'homme et l'œuvre; avec des documents inédits* (Paris, Desclée de Brouwer & cie., 1932), pp. 261, 281.
[7] Huret, *Enquête sur l'évolution littéraire*, p. 64 (or cf. Mallarmé, *Œuvres complètes*, p. 871).
[8] Huret, *op. cit.*, pp. 135 f. (my italics). In this connection it is worth noting that Villiers chose his epigraph to one of the *Contes cruels* ("Maryelle") from *La Tentation de Saint Antoine.*

same indefatigable inquisitor, Gustave Kahn (who two decades later was to acclaim Conrad as "a powerful dreamer") singled out *La Tentation de Saint Antoine* as one of the first of symbolic works in the modern sense.[9] Much later Albert Thibaudet, remarking on the "prestige symbolique sur l'imagination" exercised by *Salammbô*, was to declare categorically that "c'est d'elle qu'est née l'*Hérodiade* de Mallarmé"; and though there is no reason to doubt that – as Thibaudet himself was later to suggest – *Hérodiade* derived from other sources as well, one sees, nevertheless, that a filiation exists between Flaubert's conception and Mallarmé's.[10]

In any case, the "suggestive" quality (Baudelaire's term) and the symbolic organization of image and episode were there, in the novels and stories from the respective dates of their first publication, commencing with 1857 – even though it was not until the publication of Thibaudet's study in 1922 that this aspect of Flaubert's work was examined in significant detail.

Thibaudet was followed in 1931 by a scholarly study of prodigious dimensions, the work of D. L. Demorest, in which the "figurative and symbolic expression" of Flaubert's entire production, the juvenilia and the correspondence included, was scrutinized, enumerated and classified with a thoroughness and comprehensiveness which can perhaps be matched only in the literature of sacred commentary.[11] The findings of this invaluable and rather daunting work were summarized in part by René Dumesnil, *doyen* of Flaubertian scholars, as follows:

M. Demorest montre que les images sensorielles prédominent; il montre que Flaubert, devançant les symbolistes, a recherché la nuance autant que la couleur et qu'il a su prolonger sous la surface des choses, des sensations et des émotions et suivre les ramifications obscures et complexes qui les unissent les uns aux autres.[12]

[9]   *Ibid.*, p. 181; p. 394.
[10]   Albert Thibaudet, *Gustave Flaubert, 1821-1880: sa vie, ses romans, son style* (Paris, Plon, 1922), p. 155. Cf. Thibaudet, *La Poésie de Stéphane Mallarmé: Etude littéraire*, pp. 389 f.
[11]   D. L. Demorest, *L'Expression figurée et symbolique dans l'œuvre de Gustave Flaubert* (Paris, L. Conard, 1931). The work, 24 centimeters in height, contains over 700 pages. Demorest discovered some 10,000 metaphors and similes in Flaubert's published works, many hundreds more in his "brouillons".
[12]   Dumesnil, *Gustave Flaubert: l'homme et l'œuvre*, p. 445.

The English critic Martin Turnell, in his *Novel in France*, has domesticated the view of the Flaubertian novel as *au fond* symbolic in conception, a precursor of the symbolic novel of the present century.[13] This view of Flaubert has not gone unchallenged; but even if one feels that it has been pressed in some quarters with an incautious zeal the internal evidence of symbolic intent – and, more importantly, of symbolic realization – is too strong and too ubiquitous to be dismissed. Moreover, the internal evidence of the novels is supported by occasional explicit indications in the worksheets (which have been subjected to much scholarly scrutiny) and by certain critical passages in Flaubert's extensive correspondence.

This is not the place to dig deeply into that mine, but a sampling of the ore will be helpful – and has the special justification that Conrad is known to have delved into the correspondence early in his writing career.[14] Thus the central *Symboliste* doctrine of the suggestive (or evocative) in art is implicit in Flaubert's remark to Feydeau that "le style est autant *sous* les mots que *dans* les mots. C'est autant l'âme que la chair d'une oeuvre." [15] Again the concept of a "poésie pure" – that Siren's rock upon which Mallarmé's art eventually shipwrecked in *Un Coup de dés* – finds its strict counterpart in Flaubert's dream of a "book about nothing", exempt from external attachment or contingency, maintaining

---

[13] Martin Turnell, *The Novel in France: Mme de La Fayette, Laclos, Constant, Stendhal, Balzac, Flaubert, Proust* (Norfolk, Conn., New Directions, 1951). Cf. especially on p. 302: "Even a cursory reading of Flaubert is sufficient to show that each of his books is a 'forest of symbols'. His use of them was a habit of mind – a habit in which he was inclined to indulge to excess. For there is scarcely a sentence which does not refer to something which has happened earlier in the book or which is about to happen or which does not contain some carefully calculated allusion."

[14] Ford reported that he and Conrad "read [the memoirs of Maxime Du Camp and the Correspondence of Flaubert] daily together over a space of years" (Ford, *Joseph Conrad*, p. 57). This would have been during the years of their collaboration, at the turn of the century. Ford certainly exaggerated the frequency, and probably the duration, of these joint readings; but there is no reason to doubt that the works in question were read. The correspondence published at that time was less than half of that now published, but it comprised much of the most valuable material – including the all-important letters to Louise Colet.

[15] Flaubert, *Correspondance*, IV, p. 315.

itself by the internal force of its style, like the earth suspended in air.[16] One may see in this an ideal not of the novel but of the anti-novel – a work of "alittérature", to borrow a word from M. Claude Mauriac – exempt from all the conditions proper to the fictional genre. Flaubert, who remained a novelist, scarcely approximated his ideal in practice, since he did not, even in *Bouvard et Pécuchet* abolish the "subject", or render it invisible; but he did achieve, in part through his system of metaphoric and symbolic reference, fictional structures unexampled in their self-containedness and internal coherence.

It is clear that the type-art here is music, which alone (prior to the advent of abstractionism in painting) could present itself as a pure system of internal relations, independent of subject or material attachment. Flaubert's statement, anticipating the *Symbolistes*, might figure as evidence for that doctrine of the *Anders-streben* of the other arts toward the condition of music which Pater proposed in "The School of Giorgione". But the correspondence yields a number of explicit references to musical art. Flaubert's musical sophistication would appear to have exceeded that of Conrad: at 25 he proclaimed Mozart's *Don Giovanni* to be one of the three finest things in creation (the others being *Hamlet* and the sea); [17] and much later he was overwhelmed by Pauline Viardot-Garcia singing Gluck's *Orpheus*, which he heard twice in 1860.[18] But this was a rare indulgence – two years earlier he had assured a correspondent that he had not set foot in the Opera for four

---

[16] "Ce qui me semble beau, ce que je voudrais faire, c'est un livre sur rien, un livre sans attache extérieure, qui se tiendrait de lui-même par la force interne de son style, comme la terre sans être soutenue se tient en l'air, un livre qui n'aurait presque pas de sujet ou du moins où le sujet serait presque invisible, si cela se peut. Les œuvres les plus belles sont celles où il y a le moins de matière. ... Je crois que l'avenir de l'Art est dans ces voies" (Flaubert, *Correspondance*, II, p. 345). The foregoing is from a letter of 1852. The relation of the Flaubert passage to *Symboliste* aesthetic is attested by Marcel Raymond who cites it in his summarizing paragraph on Mallarmé's poetic ideal. (Cf. Marcel Raymond, *De Baudelaire au Surréalisme*, Paris, Corrêa, 1933, p. 35.)

[17] Flaubert, *Correspondance*, I, p. 352.

[18] "C'est une des plus grandes choses que je connaisse", Flaubert wrote. "Depuis longtemps je n'avais eu pareil enthousiasme" (*Correspondance*, IV, p. 371).

years.[19] For Flaubert, as for Conrad, music figured rather as an ideal concept than as a source of sensuous gratification. Monkishly addicted to the practice of his own art Flaubert found little time to cultivate an acquaintance with the sister arts, and he rarely expatiated on them; but he had antennae for the aesthetic currents of his day. Like his poetic contemporaries he found in the procedures and objectives of the other arts terms of reference for his own; and we may say without hyperbole of the body of Flaubert's work that it resumes, for the prose medium, the pictorial aspirations of the Parnassian movement, which coincided with his period of greatest productivity, and anticipates the musical aspirations of *Symbolisme*.

On the simplest level music for Flaubert was *melopoeia*, epitomizing the auditory quality to be attained in prose by attention to rhythm and phonetic relations:

Tout le talent d'écrire [he wrote to Louise Colet] ne consiste après tout que dans le choix de mots. C'est la précision qui fait la force. Il est en style comme en musique: ce qu'il y a de plus beau et de plus rare c'est la pureté du son.

But a passage from an earlier letter of the same period, starting in a similar vein, ends differently: "De la musique! De la musique plutôt! Tournons au rhythme, balançons-nous dans les périodes, descendons plus avant dans les caves du coeur." In the final clause we detect a more metaphysical concept of music, akin to that of German idealist philosophy and of the *Symbolistes*: here music has become model for the evocative quality of prose style. Later, during the composition of the great set-piece of *les Comices agricoles* in *Madame Bovary*, he proposed a more precise analogy with music:

C'est un dur endroit. J'y ai *tous* mes personnages de mon livre en action et en dialogue, les uns mêlés aux autres, et par là-dessus un grand paysage qui les enveloppe. Mais, si je réussis, ce sera bien symphonique.

A month later he returned to the theme, declaring:

Ce dont je suis sûr, c'est qu'elle sera neuve et que l'intention en est bonne. Si jamais les effets d'une symphonie ont été reportés dans un

[19] *Ibid.*, IV, p. 247.

livre, ce sera là. *Il faut que ça hurle par l'ensemble,* qu'on entende à la fois des beuglements de taureaux, des soupirs d'amour et des phrases d'administrateurs.[20]

We have, then, various indications that music occupied in Flaubert's mind an exemplary position as the "art of arts" – as it did for Mallarmé, as it did for Pater (who made Flaubert the hero of his "Essay on Style"), and as it did for the Conrad of the Preface to *The Nigger,* an essay presumably written, as Jocelyn Baines has shown, under the impression of a recent reading of Pater's *Marius the Epicurean.*[21] I shall consider shortly the bearings of this musical ideal upon the Flaubertian-Conradian concept of fictional structure and thematic organization. The analogy with the symphony, expressly invoked to account for the contrapuntal effect aimed at in the *Comices,* is, in fact, of much wider application. It is latent in all the major novels, as discerned by Demorest in the concluding paragraph of the study mentioned above, where he remarks that Flaubert

est parvenu, en procédant comme les compositeurs avec l'exactitude du savant, mais avec l'intuition et l'imagination du poète, à composer de grandes symphonies qui ne sont jamais parfaites, et qui ne sont pas toujours en équilibre exact, qui laissent parfois l'impression d'un immense effort, que l'on aimera ou non la première fois, ainsi que cela arrive souvent en écoutant les grandes symphonies modernes, mais qui enchantera la troisième fois, et encore plus la dixième.[22]

Our business is with Conrad, and the reader must be referred to Demorest and to the other less compendious critics cited above for the defense and illustration of their thesis. The examples I

[20] Flaubert, *Correspondance,* II, p. 471; II, p. 414; III, p. 335; III, p. 365 (Flaubert's italics).
[21] Garnett sent Conrad a copy of *Marius* in May, 1897. In a letter of 28 August Conrad discussed with Garnett the text of his Preface, already completed and in the hands of his correspondent. Cf. Baines, *Joseph Conrad,* p. 188; Jean-Aubry, *Life and Letters,* I, p. 210. There are unmistakable suggestions of Pater in Conrad's Preface, which have not escaped earlier critical attention. Cf. e.g., Albert Wüscher, *Schau und Veranschaulichung der Aussenwelt bei Joseph Conrad* (Thayngen, K. Augustin, 1934), p. 17.
[22] Demorest, *op. cit.,* pp. 649 f. The passage is cited with approval by René Dumesnil (Dumesnil, *op. cit.,* pp. 445 f.).

shall cite of quasi-musical structure in Flaubert will be such as may be suggested by comparable strategies in Conrad. At this point, however – since it is time to bring this excursus on Flaubert into closer contact with our subject – I want to reverse the procedure and follow the clue furnished by Flaubert's comment on his *Comices* into the labyrinth of *Nostromo*, near the center of which we shall find a scene which, in its execution, equally invites a musical analogy.

There is no need for our purpose to reconstruct Flaubert's *Comices* in detail. It comprises in its entirety chapter eight of Part II of *Madame Bovary* (pages 183-214 in the collected edition of Conard). The scene is set, the "paysage" rendered, in the early pages which constitute a landscape with figures, among them most –if not quite all, as Flaubert claimed – of the "personnages" of the book presented "in action and dialogue". The countrymen flow into the village with their livestock, and the bourgeois, or *villageois*, of Yonville-l'Abbaye perfect their arrangements for the advent of the *Conseiller*. But the portion that is really new and that clearly vindicates Flaubert's musical analogy, is the antiphonal section or movement (comprising pages 196-210) in which Rodolphe's verbal assault upon Emma's conjugal fidelity, conducted behind a window on the second floor of the *mairie* overlooking the square, alternates with fragments of official rhetoric wafted from the platform below and with the announcements of awards. The section closes with the tableau of the receipt of a silver medal by Catherine Leroux, after which Rodolphe abandons his post of vantage, taking Emma with him.

Conrad's "symphonic" movement is similarly set within the frame of an assembly held in the sala of the Casa Gould (comprising chapter five of Part II, pages 173-206 of *Nostromo*). The movement or section begins on page 178 when Antonia Avellanos, followed by her lover Decoud, retires into the balconied embrasure of a window overlooking the Calle de la Constitucion; it ends with the end of their tête-à-tête and their reabsorption into the discursive "tide" that washes about in the sala.

Conrad attempted nothing like an imitation of the *Comices* – a thing which could only have yielded pastiche. The handling of the scene is so far from resembling in its details Flaubert's handling of the *Comices* that no one, so far as I find, has suggested a relation between them. Nevertheless, when one confronts the idea of the *Comices*, abstracted from its particulars as Flaubert presents it in his letter, one sees that Conrad, under a like impulsion toward a "musical" structure, has attempted something at once perfectly distinct in execution and markedly similar in conception.

As in the *Comices* the central grouping is that of a man and a woman in confidential relation in the embrasure of a window – with which any resemblance of detail ends. In the Conradian scene the competing (or counterpointed) discourse is not in a square below, but in the room behind – the great sala at reception time swarming with the representatives of the political Right (Blancos) from whose midst Antonia and Decoud have taken temporary refuge and from whom they are half screened by the window-curtains. The contribution of the street to the symphonic texture of the scene is a succession of images with their appropriate sounds: the people, anonymous, returning from the harbor, the grandees and their families, several of these identified by name, in their swaying carriages; later, as darkness gathers, the glow of brazeros in the plaza and the passage of Nostromo on his silver-gray; still later Padre Corbelàn, who leaves the cathedral to enter under the gate of the Casa Gould and join the assembly of Sulacan notables in the sala. The couple in the window observe and, at intervals, remark on the passersby in the street; at one point (pages 178-9) they are the object of observation by the passersby.

During much of the scene (the first dozen pages) the counterpoint is limited to alternations between balcony and street: the assembly is no more than a felt presence in the background, and a point of reference for the Decoud-Antonia dialogue. During the final pages (from page 189) the counterpoint is between the couple in the window and the conversational tumult in the sala. Decoud's skeptical discourse and Antonia's brief, fatigued responses contrast in their tonality with the note of excitement and expectancy in the sala. At one point the alternating currents of conversation converge – when Decoud, catching from the "boastful tumult" behind him the name of Montero, turns round and shouts into the uproar his Dantesque epithet for the insurgent leader: "Gran' bestia!" (page 191). The scene ends – or rather the contrapuntal movement ends – when the two central figures, who from their post of observation in the window had served to link the stream of life in the Calle and the tide of political speculation in the sala, rejoin the other guests – Antonia to withdraw with Emilia to an inner room, Decoud to engage Father Corbelàn in another dialogue. Apart from the specific content of the discourse, the reader is left with a composite image of Sulaco at a critical juncture, in which many of the principal personages of the novel figure within a single frame.

It is a memorable scene, conducted with novelistic tact and in complete independence of the *Comices* in virtually all matters of detail. There is, I think, no suggestion in the Conradian episode of a tour de force, as in Flaubert's scene, just as there is no such brutally "deflationary" tendency as Flaubert achieved by juxtaposing the diverse rhetorics of love and agriculture, so that the latter (as in the celebrated instance of the Conseiller's "Fumiers!") seems to comment on the former. In particular there is nothing like the frequency of alternation from voice to voice (or from plane to plane, since both scenes invite pictorial as well as musical analogy), which in the *Comices* culminates in an antiphony so rapid as to suggest a badminton set – an exhilarating effect in Flaubert's context, but one that would not at all have consorted with the ironic gravity Conrad clearly aimed at, and achieved.

Whatever the direct relation to the *Comices*, and whether or not Conrad recalled Flaubert's gloss on that scene (a gloss that he may be presumed to have encountered in the Correspondence during the gestation-period of *Nostromo*), the "symphonic" conception of Conrad's scene appears to me palpable. And we may observe here – by way of anticipating the material we shall be considering in the following chapters – that the suggestion of a musical analogy is enforced by the employment of a recurrent verbal image which links thematically the Decoud-Antonia dialogue and the tumult of the sala, and carries over into the final pages of the scene.

Decoud, in support of his skepticism, throws out to Antonia

the bitter metaphor of the Liberator Bolivar, who declared that those who worked for the independence of America "have ploughed the sea". Interrupting Antonia's protest he repeats the figure; and Conrad takes it up from his character, with ironic intent, transmuting it into the figure of "the political tide that once in every twenty-four hours sets with a strong flood through the Gould drawing-room". Three times in the course of the chapter he returns to the figure: – the tide beats high, "as if driven beyond the marks by a great gust of hope"; ebbing, it leaves Gould stranded on the carpet, "as it were a multicoloured shoal of flowers and arabesques under his brown boots", with only a handful of guests still scattered about in the room; ebbing out at length "to the last insignificant drop", it leaves him "standing motionless like a tall beacon amongst the deserted shoals of furniture".[23]

There is not much in the way of external evidence to add to the mention in the Preface to *The Nigger of the "Narcissus"* in attestation of Conrad's sense of music as a model of the structural effects he sought. I find little more, in fact, than a Wagner reference summarizing for Marguerite Poradowska the final chapter of *Almayer's Folly*, which (as he put it) "begins with a *trio* – Nina, Dain, Almayer – and ends with a long *solo* for Almayer which is almost as long as Tristan's in Wagner".[24] It is not much, but it is interesting enough in view of Wagner's relation to the literature of the period; and what significance we see in it is augmented when we consider its early date. Like Flaubert, though from a different standpoint as regards such auditory effects as assonance and alliteration, which he seems more often to have sought than to have avoided, Conrad consciously aspired to "musical" sonorities (*melopoeia*) in his prose: so much is self-evident and has long been a critical commonplace. It is equally evident that the ideal example of music was in some degree mediated, notoriously so in the earlier works, through the practical example of Flaubert. Murry saw Conrad as too consciously disposed to musical effects,

---

[23] The image of the sea is evoked in this scene also to describe the Campo as it appears to the inward eye of the hide-merchant Hirsch (*Nostromo*, p. 203).

[24] *Letters to Marguerite Poradowska*, p. 68.

to the detriment of his style;[25] and some French criticism has seen the specifically Flaubertian influence as not entirely felicitous – though that influence has not yet, to my mind, been thoroughly explored. Ramón Fernández, for example, wrote in the memorial issue of the *NRF* that

Flaubert n'a pas toujours eu sur lui la meilleure influence. Ses phrases sont souvent trop écrites, et l'inévitable *et* qui précède la dernière proposition les rend quelque peu monotones.[26]

The last sentence exaggerates the incidence in Conrad's prose of a Flaubertian stylistic device which he never rejected, but which ceases to be very conspicuous in the works written after about 1900.

There is a similar comparison between the two styles in Huneker's essay on Conrad in *Ivory Apes and Peacocks*. Referring to the same sort of linking of elements in periodic series, terminating in an "and" clause, to which Fernández referred, Huneker – following a parade of musical terms: "fugal", "contrapuntal", "polyphonic" – declared that "a typical paragraph of his shows what might be called the sonata form: an allegro, andante, and presto".[27] Commenting upon a paragraph from "Karain" (*Tales of Unrest*) chosen to illustrate his formula, Huneker saw in its "*coda*" a suggestion of Flaubert; but he did not tell his readers that twenty-five years earlier Émile Hennequin had discovered precisely the same musical pattern in the typical Flaubert paragraph.[28] It seems more than likely that Huneker appropriated the formula, without acknowledgment, from Hennequin; but if so it

[25] "When the musical suggestion is allowed to predominate, decadence of style has begun. I think you will find a great many examples of this sacrifice of the true creativeness of language in Swinburne, and not a few in that much, and within limits rightly, admired modern master, Mr. Conrad" (John Middleton Murry, *The Problem of Style*, London, Oxford University Press, 1922, p. 86).
[26] Ramón Fernández, "L'Art de Conrad", *Nouvelle Revue française*, XXIII (Décembre 1924), p. 737.
[27] James Gibbons Huneker, *Ivory Apes and Peacocks* (New York, Scribner's, 1915), p. 6.
[28] In his *Etudes de critique scientifique*; quoted in Dumesnil, *Gustave Flaubert, l'homme et l'œuvre*, p. 430. The three movements of the "paragraphe type" are illustrated on p. 431, *op. cit.*

would still be significant that he should think that a musical analogy cut to Flaubert's measurements should fit Conrad with no alterations.

Enough has been said to suggest that a stylistic relation, recognizable and critically recognized (not to say exaggerated), obtains between Flaubert and Conrad. The definition of that relation, however tempting a task, does not belong in this study except as it involves the symbolics of style, and specifically the frequency, the form, the range of reference, and the thematic employment of metaphor. With regard to the last-named (thematic employment of metaphor) the analogy of music imposes itself, as illustrated in the example cited from *Nostromo*, in which images of the sea continue, as it were, a theme announced by Decoud in his phrase from Bolivar. I shall have occasion to return to this analogy; for the moment I want to add only one further item to the foregoing considerations regarding the role of that analogy in Conrad's imaginative economy.

As one would expect in the work of any writer not tone-deaf Conrad's metaphoric repertory includes a class of figures with musical referent. It is not large: it is, in fact, trivial in comparison with a number of other classes to be mentioned further on. It bears no comparison with the class of musical images in Proust. Nor can it be claimed that many of the examples are very revealing, being largely of the order of references to the particularities of instruments: to the beating or rolling of drums, the vibration or snapping of strings, pounding of gongs, tolling of bells, grinding of music-boxes. Occasionally they are picturesque, as when a seaman's snoring is likened to the sound of "a water-logged trombone", or Peter Ivanovitch's drone to "the deep muttering of wind in the pipes of an organ"; [29] but none that I find refers to the compositional or structural properties of music.

However, there is in *Nostromo* – perhaps of all the novels the most suggestive of musical analogies – one extended image with musical reference which has, I think, a special relevance both for its emotive quality and because it is among the few unmistakably synaesthetic images in Conrad, involving a transmutation of

[29]   *Typhoon*, p. 156; *Under Western Eyes*, p. 129.

visual perception into musical terms. In the image in question music is invoked to express, at its highest intensity, an affective response to the glow of sunset on the flank of Higuerota – the sort of recurrent natural spectacle to which Conrad's sensibilities remained receptive throughout his life and which he habitually invoked to create that atmospheric envelope within which his figures have their being. I quote it in its entirety:

> In the transparent air of the high altitudes everything seemed very near, steeped in a clear stillness as in an imponderable liquid; and with his ear ready to catch the first sound of the expected diligencia the engineer-in-chief, at the door of a hut of rough stones, had contemplated the changing hues on the enormous side of the mountain, thinking that in this sight, as in a piece of inspired music, there could be found together the utmost delicacy of shaded expression and a stupendous magnificence of effect.
>
> Sir John arrived too late to hear the magnificent and inaudible strain sung by the sunset amongst the high peaks of the Sierra. It had sung itself out into the breathless pause of deep dusk before, climbing down the fore wheel of the diligencia with stiff limbs, he shook hands with the engineer.[30]

It is an effective, if not particularly original, example of synaesthetic imagery, recalling to mind the well-known profession of his poetic goal which Mallarmé made to his friend Cazalis during the composition of *Hérodiade*: "Peindre non la chose, mais l'effet qu'elle produit."

There is, so to speak, a "mirror-image" of the figure quoted above, occurring some twenty pages farther on in *Nostromo*, when Conrad, reversing the order of reference, assimilates the auditory impression of a vesper bell to the visual impression of a sunset.[31] I am far from suggesting that these images, minute details in a vast whole, are to be read as cryptographic allusions to the role

[30] *Nostromo*, p. 40.
[31] "... in mid-air the sound of a bell, thin and alert, was like the throbbing pulse of the sunset glow" (*Nostromo*, p. 62). The auditor here is Emily, living with her guardian in Italy. It is worth adding to these references from *Nostromo* a similar image from Conrad's first novel: "He followed their figures moving in the cruel blaze of the vertical sun, in that light violent and vibrating, like a triumphant flourish of brazen trumpets" (*Almayer's Folly*, p. 194).

of musical or quasi-musical structure that I have suggested is particularly prominent in *Nostromo*. I take them to be strokes of pure impressionism, as I think they are intended. But I take them also as clues – significant in the general dearth of testimony on the question, and especially in the light of the generally trivial or derisory role of music in Conrad's fiction, as noted above – that the reference to the "art of arts" in the Preface to *The Nigger of the "Narcissus"* was not mere *flatus vocis*, but expressed a genuine, if unsophisticated, response to music. To what degree the artistic impulse toward the "magic suggestiveness" of music involved a deliberate awareness of motival or contrapuntal structure as a model for his own art of fiction must remain doubtful; but deliberately or otherwise Conrad did tend toward a quasi-musical organization of his material.

Before undertaking the comparative survey of Conrad's and Flaubert's employment of verbal imagery with which I lead into the material of my fifth chapter, I want to summarize here the external evidence for a view of Conrad as being saturated with Flaubert. This is to be found primarily in Conrad's own correspondence, and the testimony there found is reënforced by the writings of various memorialists, notably Jean-Aubry and Ford Madox Ford. A letter of 1903 to a Polish correspondent, Kazimierz Waliszewski, summarized the devotion of a lifetime in a parenthesis: "Un vrai saint, celui-là"; and the context revealed an acquaintance with one of the least known works in the Flaubert canon, the "féerie", *Le Château des coeurs*.[32] Six years later, in replying to a remark of James Gibbons Huneker, Conrad revealed something of the subjective basis of his attachment to Flaubert and the degree to which Flaubert figured in his mind as a heroic exemplar:

When you overwhelm me with the mantle of Flaubert, it is an ominous garment to put on a man's shoulders. Yet, there is one point in which I resemble that great man; it is in the desperate heartbreaking toil and effort of the writing; the days of wrestling as with a dumb devil for every line of my creation.[33]

[32] *Lettres françaises*, p. 54.
[33] James G. Huneker, *Steeplejack*, 2 vols. in one (New York, Scribner's, 1922), p. 234.

To these passages from the correspondence we may add the evocation of "the shade of old Flaubert" in the opening paragraph of *A Personal Record*,[34] and the succeeding references to the Rouen episodes of *Madame Bovary*.

Ford's testimony is emphatic. "That which really brought us together", he declared, "was a devotion to Flaubert and Maupassant"; and he added that both men had much of *Trois Contes* and "immense passages" of *Bovary* "by heart".[35] Jean-Aubry, in the "Souvenirs" which he contributed to the Conrad memorial issue of the *NRF*, wrote, apropos of the "stupefying" precision of Conrad's literary recollections:

que de fois, par exemple, ne l'ai-je pas entendu, au cours d'une conversation, me rappeler les personnages de troisième plan, les endroits les moins généralement connus de tel conte de Maupassant, de tel roman d'Anatole France, ou de tel livre de Flaubert, celui surtout qu'il chérissait particulièrement et qu'il savait véritablement par coeur: l'*Education sentimentale?* [36]

In the face of these testimonies it is impossible to accept unreservedly Conrad's own judgment, expressed in a well-known letter to Hugh Walpole, that "I don't think I learned anything from Flaubert". The assertion is, in any case, immediately followed by the statement that "what he did for me was to open my eyes and arouse my emulation"; and it is a nice semantic question whether the effects described do not imply a form of "learning", if only of learning to see, and to care, as Flaubert cared, about the rendering of the things seen. It must be added that Conrad's disclaimer is weakened by the context, containing as it does a demonstrable lapse of memory. Here is the entire paragraph:

You say that I have been under the formative influence of *Madame Bovary*. In fact, I read it only after finishing *A.F.*, as I did all the other works of Flaubert, and anyhow, my Flaubert is the Flaubert of *St. Antoine* and *Ed: Sent:* and that only from the point of view of the rendering of concrete things and visual impressions. I thought

---

[34] *A Personal Record*, p. 3. Cf. the closing sentence of the paragraph: "Was he not, in his unworldly, almost ascetic, devotion to his art, a sort of literary, saint-like hermit?"

[35] Ford, *Joseph Conrad*, p. 31.

[36] G. Jean-Aubry, "Souvenirs (Fragments)", *Nouvelle Revue française*, XXIII (Décembre 1924), p. 675.

him marvellous in that respect. I don't think I learned anything from him. What he did for me was to open my eyes and arouse my emulation. One can learn something from Balzac, but what could one learn from Flaubert? He compels admiration, – about the greatest service one artist can render to another.[37]

We can never know with exactitude what one writer has learned from another; but we do know that whatever Flaubertian influence we postulate can be postulated from the beginning of Conrad's writing career, since his correspondence with Marguerite Poradowska, published in 1940, has put it beyond question that his acquaintance with *Madame Bovary* antedated much, if not all, of the writing of his first novel.[38]

What was the nature of the influence, or what in any case were the aspects and qualities of Flaubert's art that aroused Conrad's emulation? First, we may guess that in opening Conrad's eyes, Flaubert's example sharpened in Conrad his own native keenness of vision, balancing the lyrical and introspective tendency that the two writers shared by a concern for visibilia and, more generally, for the sensory aspects of the world. "Voir, et voir comme voient les myopes, jusque dans les pores des choses": this is what it was to see like Flaubert, "qui voudrait vous faire sentir presque *matériellement* les choses qu'il reproduit".[39] It is interest-

---

[37] *Life and Letters*, II, p. 206. The letter is dated June 7, 1918. The *A.F.* of the quoted paragraph is *Almayer's Folly*.

[38] The evidence is contained in the following sentence: "In the [hiatus] and striking simplicity of your descriptions you remind me a little of Flaubert, whose *Mme. Bovary* I have just reread with respectful admiration –" (*Letters to Marguerite Poradowska*, p. 44). The letter is dated 6 April 1892. *Almayer's Folly*, the first proofs of which Conrad received from Fisher Unwin on Christmas Eve, 1894 (*ibid.*, p. 89), was begun in 1889. I find no clue to the date of Conrad's prior reading, or readings, of *Madame Bovary*. Nor do I find any clue to the provenience of that copy of the novel, the existence of which was alleged by Ford Madox Ford, in the end-papers and margins of which were pencilled the first words of *Almayer's Folly* (Ford, *Joseph Conrad*, pp. 7, 31, 97 f.).

[39] In this passage from a letter of 1852 to Louise Colet, Flaubert (who, like Conrad, felt himself to be *homo duplex*) defined one of the "deux bonshommes distincts" coexisting within him. The other he describes as "épris de gueulades, de lyrisme, de grands vols d'aigle, de toutes les sonorités de la phrase et des sommets de l'idée" (quoted in Dumesnil, *Gustave Flaubert*, p. 345). The entire letter (no. 303, in vol. II of the Conard edition) constitutes an artistic testament of the first importance.

ing that French criticism has repeatedly employed the word "hallucinatory" to characterize the visual intensity achieved upon occasion by both writers. Faguet, for example, wrote of the Flaubertian landscape:

Les paysages de Flaubert sont des hallucinations précises. Ils sont d'une réalité absolue et ils ont ce relief, cette saillie forte des angles et des contours, que les objets prennent brusquement, quelquefois, sur le rideau noir du sommeil.[40]

And Ramón Fernández, in a densely-packed study of the psychological implications of Conradian "impressionism" – a study abounding in such optic terms as "projection graphique", "impressions-éclairs", and "relief stéréoscopique" – at one point defined the Conradian novel as "une suite de perceptions qui composent un état dramatique actuel, un présent hallucinant et oppressif".[41]

Flaubert, who had experience of actual (i.e., morbid) hallucinatory states, was careful to distinguish between these and the artist's "interior vision". The former, he declared, in response to an inquiry of Taine's, were always accompanied by terror, the latter by joy. But he acknowledged in the same letter a relation between "artistic intuition" and the hallucinations of dreams ("hallucinations hypnagogiques").[42] Conrad's extensive medical history includes nothing like Flaubert's famous seizure of 1843, no record of morbid hallucinatory states, with images bursting within the head like fireworks, escaping like streams of blood.[43] It seems likely, however, that he was accessible to states of imaginative (or imaginal) vision resembling those which Flaubert likened

[40] Emile Faguet, *Flaubert (Les grands écrivains français)* (Paris, Hachette, 1899), p. 163.

[41] Ramón Fernández, "L'Art de Conrad", *Nouvelle Revue française*, XXIII (Décembre 1924), p. 734. In the same memorial issue of the *NRF* André Chevrillon wrote, apropos of the final scenes of *Victory*, that "figures, gestes, paysages, nous saississent par leur simplicité violente et hallucinatoire comme les silhouettes qu'un éclair fait brusquement surgir de la nuit et dont l'image persiste gravée sur notre rétine" (André Chevrillon, "Conrad", *ibid.*, p. 705).

[42] Flaubert, *Correspondance: Supplément (1864-1771)* (Paris, Louis Conard, 1954), pp. 92 f.

[43] *Ibid.*

to "hypnagogic" hallucination, and that he did not speak merely metaphorically when he invoked the term "hallucination" to characterize certain of his own visual experiences – as for example in his account of his first glimpse of the Eastern Archipelago, in the opening pages of *A Personal Record*. In any case his fiction betrays a chronic preoccupation with hallucinatory phenomena. In Flaubert both Emma Bovary and Frédéric Moreau experience hallucinated states, the latter on three distinct occasions; [44] but if we except *La Tentation de Saint Antoine*, which is a continuous fresco of hallucinated visions, such states are even more frequent in Conrad's fiction than in Flaubert's. Almayer distracted at sight of the corpse of the supposed Dain Maroola; Decoud stranded on the Great Isabel; Razumov on no fewer than four occasions in the course of his ordeal: these are only three of the most striking examples.[45] In few of his longer works is there wanting some description of a hallucinated vision, and in virtually all of his works the hallucinated (or somnambulistic) state is either directly attributed to one or other of his characters or evoked as a metaphoric referent – often with such frequency as to constitute a significant element in the metaphoric "undercurrent" of the novel.

Sharing as they did a highly developed optic faculty, neither writer relied for the communication of his vision exclusively on descriptive techniques and upon a Balzacian massing of minutiae. Indeed Fernández went so far as to say, with some exaggeration, that Conrad's art was the opposite of descriptive art, and notably of that of Balzac. Applying to Conrad's method the painter's term "impressionisme" (a term also applicable to Flaubert, but not current until late in his career and then applied rather to the Goncourts than to him), Fernández declared, in the course of an analysis of great subtlety, that the images in Conrad form the very tissue of the text ("le tissu même du texte"). The images, he added, contain the event in their immaterial substance – "il y a équiva-

[44]   Flaubert, *Madame Bovary*, p. 432; *L'Education sentimentale*, pp. 140, 183, 516. The account of Emma's state corresponds closely to Flaubert's account of his own hallucinatory experiences in the letter to Taine quoted *supra*.

[45]   *Almayer's Folly*, pp. 99 f.; *Nostromo*, pp. 497 f.; *Under Western Eyes*, pp. 36 f., 84 f., 88, 302.

lence stricte".[46] Fernández spoke of images in the generic sense, not limiting the term to figurative expressions (verbal images). It may be said, however – in full recognition that more is involved in the matter [47] – that both Flaubertian and Conradian impressionism consisted in large part in the evocative employment of metaphor and simile, often as a sort of descriptive stenography, but always (by definition) involving a modification of the object presented with a view to some affective response. Precisely in the far greater use of the affective and evocative resources of figurative language lay one of their principal modifications of the older descriptive realism of Balzac and the analytical realism of Stendhal.

The imagination of Flaubert, on the evidence of the published works – and more particularly of the earlier correspondence, in which the metaphors proliferate uncurbed by the rigor of the stylistic ideal that governs the novels – would appear to have been even more naturally productive of figurative comparisons, and more prone to their elaboration, than that of Conrad. Flaubert's voluminous correspondence, also, gives evidence, wanting in Conrad's correspondence, of an awareness both of the function of figurative language and of the hazards of excessive indulgence in it. Demorest cited a litany culled from letters extending over a period of some twenty years, of which the earlier passages (through the period of *Madame Bovary*) complain of his metaphoric bent in the tone of one describing the symptoms of a besetting vice, and the later (dating from the period of *Salammbô*) proclaim his ascendancy over the vice. Flaubert's struggle to curb his metaphoric exuberance was so far successful that Thibaudet could find, or believe that he found, a progressive reduction in the frequency of figurative expressions (*"images"*) from *Madame Bovary* ("le seul qui fournisse une moisson d'images") to *L'Education sentimentale* and *Bouvard et Pécuchet*, of which he declared the former to be almost, and the latter entirely, bare of

[46] Fernández, *loc. cit.*, pp. 731 f.
[47] For an analysis of the nominal syntax (or "style substantif") generally identified with literary impressionism cf. the chapter on "Sentence-Structure in the Goncourts", in Stephen Ullmann, *Style in the French Novel* (Cambridge, The University Press, 1957), pp. 121-145.

images.[48] Demorest, upon the basis of his inventory of all figurative locutions in Flaubert's work (of which he found almost 10, 000), was able to refute Thibaudet: he maintained in fact that the verbal images in *Madame Bovary* are somewhat less frequent than in *Salammbô* and *La Tentation de Saint Antoine,* only slightly more frequent than in *L'Education sentimentale.*[49]

Thibaudet's error, though surprising, becomes at least intelligible, as a sort of optical illusion, in the light of the great restriction upon metaphoric development in the works following *Madame Bovary,* and of the virtual elimination of the metaphoric set-piece ("métaphore à longue queue"), frequently commencing with an expressed comparison and subsequently elaborated as metaphor through a number of lines or even paragraphs – expressions of the unrealized lyric poet in Flaubert which in a few instances (notably the famous "Russian steppe" image) might figure, detached from their context, in an anthology of prose-poems in the manner of Baudelaire. Demorest's numerical reckoning, in which the most summary notation and the most elaborated comparison count each as an integer in a simple sum, is not in fact very revealing of the actual stylistic development, which as he acknowledged was in the direction of bareness of statement. A formula truly revealing of Flaubert's stylistic development in this regard (assuming that such matters can be illuminated by statistical methods) would have to take account of the two factors of frequency and extension. For want of such a formula, and for want of any such comprehensive numerical reckoning as Demorest has made of Flaubert's images, quantitative comparisons between the two writers must be made with due reserve. Such data as I have compiled, however, make it evident to me that Conrad (whether or not his imagination was naturally as fertile of images as Flaubert's) was, in his published works, no less prolific of figurative expressions. Indeed, in the work produced about the turn of the century, and again in that produced in the early years of the second decade of the century, he attained to a metaphoric

---

[48] Thibaudet, *Gustave Flaubert,* pp. 252 f.
[49] Demorest, *op. cit.,* pp. 476 f.

frequency measurably beyond that reported by Demorest for any
of Flaubert's published volumes of fiction.

In a series of a dozen representative works, spanning Conrad's
career from *Almayer's Folly* (1895) to *The Rover* (1923) and
comprising ten novels and two extended stories ("Youth" and
"Heart of Darkness") I find a sharp rise in the average frequency
of metaphor from the first novel to the works produced just before
the turn of the century (*Youth* and *Lord Jim*), followed by a
decline in frequency through *Nostromo* (1904) to *The Secret
Agent* (1907). This downward curve is followed by a second rise
through *Under Western Eyes* (1911) to *Chance* (1913) and a
second decline through *Victory* (1915) and *The Shadow-Line*
(1917) to *The Rover*. In terms of this single criterion of metaphoric frequency Conrad ends at approximately the point he
started from, with a style which – soberer in other respects than
that of *Almayer's Folly*, being less adjectival and far less prone to
personification – is about equally restrained in the employment of
metaphor. Moreover the tendency to the extension or development of metaphor corresponds in a general way to the tendency to
frequency. Particularly interesting is the fact that the novels and
stories in which Marlow figures are not only the most prolific of
metaphoric expressions of all Conrad's works, but are, it would
appear, the most abundant in extended or developed metaphors.

The great proliferation of verbal images in *The Nigger of the
"Narcissus"*, and even more markedly in *Lord Jim*, is accompanied by a notable restriction on the verbiage – redundant modifiers, synonymous substantives running in tandem or in troika –
which characterizes much of the writing in the earlier novels and
in such a story as "The Lagoon". A close stylistic analysis would
show, I think, that there is not a perfect synchronicity between
these inverse trends: *An Outcast of the Islands* (1897) is both
more densely figurative and more verbose than *Almayer's Folly*.
Conrad was clearly stung by Wells's respectful mauling of that
book in the *Saturday Review*, in the course of which the reviewer,
starting off by acclaiming the novel as "perhaps the finest piece of
fiction that has been published this year", went on to declare that
the author wrote "despicably", and concluded with the verdict

that "only greatness could make books of which the detailed workmanship is so copiously bad, so well worth reading, so convincing, and so stimulating".[50]

It is likely that the review spurred Conrad in the direction of greater restraint and verbal economy. At all events *The Nigger of the "Narcissus"* shows a greatly sharpened awareness of the expressive resources of metaphor and simile, which in this work becomes an Ockham's razor for the pruning of verbiage, with salutary results for his style. Wells had drawn the moral plainly enough in his review of *The Outcast*, pointing out how a "finely expressive symbol" was lost in a "dust-heap of irrelevant words"; [51] and though Conrad did not immediately kiss the rod laid on him, the fact remains that the subsequent development of his style followed the indications of the review: he learned what Wells called "the great half of his art, the art of leaving things un-written" when he had acquired confidence in the art of evoking them in images. Moreover, the relative restriction on verbal imagery after 1900 involved no relapse into the verbiage of the early prose: by the time of *Lord Jim* he had learned to make the images, both verbal and objective, carry much of the expressive burden, and he could be more or less sparing of the purely verbal imagery in his subsequent works according to their expressive requirements and to the narrative conventions employed.

He could do so without a sense of deprivation because he had learned by then to get more out of his metaphors – on the one

---

[50]   H. G. Wells, review of *An Outcast of the Islands*, in *Saturday Review*, LXXXI (16 May 1896), p. 509 f. The letters to Garnett and Unwin provoked by Wells' review – expressive of puzzlement, insisting upon his stylistic independence of reviewers – are interesting. (Cf. *Letters from Joseph Conrad*, p. 53; John Dozier Gordan, *Joseph Conrad: the Making of a Novelist*, pp. 281 f.) Nevertheless, Conrad initiated a correspondence with Wells, in the course of which he mentioned the review of *The Outcast*, some two years later, declaring that it "compelled me to think seriously of many things till then unseen", and adding that Wells was "responsible for many sheets torn up" (*Life and Letters*, I, p. 248).

[51]   Wells, *loc. cit.* It is true that Wells's example was an objective rather than a verbal image: the only specimen of verbal image he cited was condemned as "needless" and "inappropriate". What is significant for the argument, however, is simply the opposition of image to verbiage.

hand by elaboration (in this respect reversing the tendency of Flaubert's figurative usage), and on the other hand by thematic recurrence. This latter sometimes took the form of repetition (simple or incremental); more often it involved the multiplication of images having a common or cognate motif, ordering themselves into a thematic series and constituting a significant strand in the symbolic texture of the novel. The tendency to metaphoric elaboration assumes significance only from the time of *Lord Jim*; the tendency to thematic recurrence, already appreciable in *The Nigger of the "Narcissus"*, becomes ubiquitous in *Lord Jim*.

From the time of the earlier of these two works, and much more conspicuously from the time of the later, Conrad's prose betrays a deliberate determination to "wring the neck of rhetoric" – although never to within more than an inch or so of its life. His genius and his brooding temperament required a modicum of the rhetorical element in which to breathe; and his original style, steeped in Latinity and haunted by Polonisms from his childhood and gallicisms from his Marseilles days, would have been denatured had it been entirely stripped of its verbal sonority and its panache. But a drastic restriction of the logorrhea evidenced in the climactic chapters of *An Outcast* was imperative if he was to do justice to the subtlety and complexity of his insights; and this he accomplished (as I have argued) by discovering – or rather by learning to rely upon – the properties of imagery both objective and verbal. By mastering this resource he achieved in his art an equilibrium between the plastic and the musical impulses of his nature. The equilibrium was attained by the substitution of image for the expressive (or would-be expressive) rhetorical flourish and the attendant organization of these plastic units in related series constituting a quasi-musical order within the order of events, a thematic "undercurrent" to the flow of narrative.

My examination of the relations between Conrad and Flaubert has carried me into the question of Conrad's figurative language. In the chapter to follow I shall undertake a synoptic view of his metaphoric usage, following this by detailed examination of the thematic or symbolic recurrence of images within several specific works. Flaubert – who in certain aspects may be seen almost as

Conrad's tutelary saint – will get back into the picture from time to time in the chapters on metaphor and elsewhere, but only marginally. Before closing this chapter on Flaubert and Conrad, however, I want to wrap up my theme in a small packet of nearly related images which will perhaps suggest better than pages of analysis the immediacy and intensity of Conrad's imaginative response to his great predecessor.

In citing these examples – of which I may say that I find fewer than might be expected in view of the metaphoric proclivity of both writers – I do not mean to suggest deliberate imitation on Conrad's part: the operation of unconscious memory seems to me by far the likelier assumption. Nor do I suggest that the metaphoric texture of his prose in general need be traced to the example of Flaubert: in the first instance it was the product of a native faculty, supplied with abundant resources by a retentive memory operating on an exceptional professional experience. One would expect however that this aspect of Flaubert's prose would not have escaped Conrad's devoted attention, and the following examples of counterpart images tend to enforce such a conclusion.

The most striking examples are to be found in *The Nigger of the "Narcissus"*, a work which, quintessentially Conradian as to both mythos and ethos, reflects Flaubertian influence as much as any of his novels in style, as in method and ordonnance. There is an interesting stylistic study to be made in this connection, involving among other matters Conrad's appropriation of the highly idiosyncratic Flaubertian use of the conjunction "but" as a mark of transition (a usage commented on by Thibaudet and Proust in their analyses of Flaubert's style). This is not the place to examine Conrad's conjunctival peculiarities; however it is not irrelevant to point out that in *The Nigger of the "Narcissus"* one finds examples of a no less idiosyncratic Flaubertian usage: a double comparison of which one branch expresses a superiority of tenor over vehicle, the other an equivalence of the two terms. A familiar example from Flaubert is the image of the triumphant Homais in his official regalia, "plus garrotté qu'un Scythe et splendide comme un mage".[52] *The Nigger of the "Narcissus"* furnishes two examples

[52]   Flaubert, *Madame Bovary*, p. 475. For an equally characteristic ex-

of this type of image – both referring to the stars – of which the second is a modified echo or recapitulation of the first: "more intense than the eyes of a staring crowd, and as inscrutable as the souls of men"; and some fifty pages further on the responsive image: "more pitiless than the eyes of a triumphant mob, and as unapproachable as the hearts of men".[53] Elsewhere in the same novel the pattern is modified to produce a sequence of two comparatives (e.g., "the shadows darker than the night and more restless than the thoughts of men"). This pattern was to recur two years later in "Youth", in an image which echoes the Homais image in unmistakable fashion: "kings more cruel than Nero the Roman, and more splendid than Solomon the Jew".[54]

Conradian in development, but with a Flaubertian precedent for its nuclear term, is the image of the sailing-ship men in the forecastle (of whom Singleton is the ideal type), "like stone caryatides that hold up in the night the lighted halls of a resplendent and glorious edifice".[55] We may see in this a much elaborated version of Flaubert's glimpse of Dussardier, in *L'Education sentimentale*, standing on the steps of Tortoni's in the moment before his murder by Sénécal during the *émeute* of December 2, "sans plus bouger qu'une cariatide".[56]

James Wait enveloped in his "black mist", emanating the "subtle and dismal influence" that oppresses his shipmates, might serve as shadow to the moonlit substance of Salammbô, whom something from the gods enveloped in a subtle vapor ("d'une vapeur subtile");[57] and Jimmy dying in the sight of Donkin, who

---

ample, cf. p. 338 (description of the "voiture à stores tendus" of the Rouen cab-drive): "plus close qu'un tombeau et ballottée comme un navire".

[53] *The Nigger of the "Narcissus"*, pp. 29, 77.

[54] *Youth*, p. 18. The double comparison was virtually dropped from Conrad's stylistic repertory following the period of *Youth* and *Lord Jim*.

[55] *The Nigger of the "Narcissus"*, p. 25.

[56] Flaubert, *L'Education sentimentale*, p. 599.

[57] *The Nigger of the "Narcissus"*, p. 34; Flaubert, *Salammbô*, p. 14. Richard Curle, who detected in the treatment of the sailors in the forecastle of the *Narcissus* resemblances to Flaubert's treatment of the barbarians in Hamilcar's gardens, reported that Conrad told him that he had been reading *Salammbô* just before sitting down to write his novel (Curle, *The Last Twelve Years of Joseph Conrad*, Garden City, Doubleday, Doran, 1928, pp. 104 f.).

"was just in time to see Wait's eyes blaze up and go out at once, like two lamps overturned together by a sweeping blow", recalls Emma Bovary *in extremis*, whose eyes, "en roulant, pâlissaient comme deux globes de lampes qui s'éteignent".[58]

In *Under Western Eyes* the recurrent comparison of Mme de S— to "a galvanized corpse" has its antecedent in the same scene of *Madame Bovary*, in which the dying Emma raises herself from the pillow "comme un cadavre que l'on galvanise"; but the first version of the Conradian image ("like a galvanized corpse out of some Hoffman's Tale") suggests the likelihood of a common source for both novelists – since Flaubert was well acquainted with Hoffmann and the Hoffmannesque literature current during his formative years.[59]

Another image from *Salammbô* is prototype of a half-dozen similes found in works extending over much of Conrad's writing career. The Hannon of Flaubert's novel is introduced to us in the following trope: "On aurait dit quelque grosse idole ébauchée dans un bloc de pierre." [60] Conrad's variations on this sculptural figure include (from "Heart of Darkness") Marlow's vision of Kurtz as "an animated image of death carved out of old ivory"; from *Lord Jim* the Captain of the *Patna* "like a clumsy effigy of a man cut out of a block of fat"; Doramin "like a figure of a man roughly fashioned of stone"; Jewel, whose "white figure seemed shaped in snow"; from *The Secret Agent* Winnie Verloc in the blackness of a fogbound London night "like a figure half chiselled out of a block of black stone"; from *Victory* the men and women who, in Heyst's vision, navigate the stream of life "like figures cut out of cork and weighted with lead".[61] One's persuasion that some of these images at least betray the operation of unconscious memory is strengthened by the fact that four of them (those de-

---

[58]   Conrad, *op. cit.*, pp. 154 f.; Flaubert, *Madame Bovary*, p. 448. Conrad's image is anticipated by an earlier image in which Flaubert's word "globes" is employed: "the fleshless head resembled a disinterred black skull fitted with two restless globes of silver in the sockets of eyes" (p. 139).
[59]   *Under Western Eyes*, pp. 215, 222; Flaubert, *op. cit.*, pp. 448 f.
[60]   Flaubert, *Salammbô*, p. 45.
[61]   *Youth*, p. 134; *Lord Jim*, pp. 23, 260, 348; *The Secret Agent*, p. 280; *Victory*, p. 175.

scribing Kurtz, the Captain, Doramin, and Winnie) conform very nearly as rhythmic units, allowing for differences in inflection and syllabic quantity between the two languages, to the imaged element (*viz.,* all that constitutes the object of the verb) in Flaubert's simile. One would expect that such a fragment as Flaubert's Hannon image would be thrown up by the unconscious memory *en bloc,* as a rhythmic, as well as semantic, unit. It has to be added, however, that if we postulate a Flaubertian echo in the first of the series (that from "Heart of Darkness"), we may for the subsequent examples as well postulate an unconscious recollection of Kurtz as of Hannon. From "Heart of Darkness" on Conrad may have been haunted by his own image.

The counterpart images just considered fall into a general class of figures drawn from the visual arts, of which examples could readily be multiplied from the work of both novelists. I shall have occasion in my seventh chapter to consider instances of their recurrent use in Conrad's later novels. Aside from the suggestive rhythmic relation between the Flaubertian prototype and several of the Conradian versions, the images considered above were chosen for comparison in view of the detailed particularity of the referent which all of them share. What is distinctive to the images in question is that in each instance the sculptural material is specified and the reference is not merely to the finished work, but to the process as well.

There is a conspicuous Flaubertian prototype also for a similar class of Conradian image applied not to the person but to the costume of a character: compare, for example, with the garments of the humbler guests at Emma Bovary's wedding ("habits-vestes . . . dont les pans semblaient avoir été coupée à même un seul bloc, par la hache du charpentier") [62] the "smart jackets" worn by the crew of the *Narcissus* on the London quays "that looked as if they had been shaped with an axe".[63]

The figure of Hannon (whom Flaubert depicted as a leper) generated another striking image which finds its Conradian

[62]   Flaubert, *Madame Bovary,* p. 36.
[63]   *The Nigger of the "Narcissus",* p. 168. Also particularized are "glossy trousers that seemed made of crumpled sheet-iron" (*ibid.*).

counterpart. Hannon is moved to tears, and we are told that "des pleurs coulaient sur sa face comme une pluie d'hiver sur une muraille en ruine"; [64] an "old sea-dog" in Conrad's story "A Smile of Fortune" is similarly moved, and his tears "trickled down his weather-beaten face like drops of rain on an old rugged wall".[65] Here again there is a close approximation of rhythm and syllabic quantity between the two images – the approximation in this case embracing the entire image, tenor and vehicle together.

It is difficult to avoid one of two conclusions with regard to the more striking of these examples of counterpart images: either that they are deliberate appropriations by Conrad, or that they represent the operation of unconscious memory. Of the two hypotheses the latter is perfectly congenial with Conrad's character and working habits, the former quite inconsistent with them. Aside from the rudimentary comparisons that comprise a principal ingredient of colloquial speech and thus find their way into the prose of all novelists in the tradition of realism (even of Flaubert to whom platitude was far worse than obscenity), I have no doubt that other examples of counterpart images might be adduced from among the many thousands of figurative expressions employed by the two writers. The examples given are not cited to demonstrate that Conrad was a sedulous ape of Flaubert, wanting in plastic imagination and without that genius which Aristotle situated in the metaphoric organ. They are cited as a final piece of evidence to demonstrate the degree of his early saturation with the Flaubertian element and to enforce my view of him as a direct inheritor and continuator of Flaubert in natural succession. They are of a piece with the internal evidence afforded by certain stylistic idiosyncrasies, alluded to above, which were sucked up into the digestive apparatus of his early style, later to be eliminated or – modified beyond any easy recognition – to be absorbed into the body tissue. They serve to validate the external testimony cited earlier in the chapter – testimony to which I may add here, as especially germane to our context, Jean-Aubry's report of his

---

[64] Flaubert, *Salammbô*, p. 153.
[65] *'Twixt Land and Sea*, p. 15.

friend's intense and detailed relish for Proust's brilliant parody of Flaubertian style.[66]

Given his saturation (in which we may see a necessary precondition of the development of his mature style), some occasional appropriation of the sort illustrated was inevitable. Moreover, in all of these appropriations there is a modification of the particulars, and in each – with the arguable exception of James Wait's enveloping black mist – the appropriation is complete. That is to say that Conrad has made the image his own by assimilating it into the tissues of his own work, so that he might name it (echoing Stein) "in gewissem Sinne mein". This may suggest that I reject Aristotle's dictum that metaphor "cannot be imparted to another"; but I have no intention of challenging its soundness as generalization. As to specific *metaphors* (as distinct from the metaphoric imagination operating throughout a writer's work), the history of poetry is full of appropriations and adaptations, more or less deliberate and more or less successful. The real interest of the case lies not in the particular instances of appropriation but in the evidence of an imaginative affinity – in which I am far from seeing a servile dependence of one writer on the other.

In the following chapters, in which the argument divests itself of Flaubert's mantle, I shall be considering the main body of Conrad's verbal imagery in various of its aspects. It is a body of imagery which emerges, in the ensemble – whatever specific indebtedness one may discover in isolated images, and however numerous the class of colloquial images that frankly confess their origins in the genius of the language rather than in that of the novelist – as the distinctive product of an individual temperament and an individual apprehension of the phenomenal world. Not all of the images to be considered "come off": there is a perceptible range in the quality and intensity of the plastic imagination at work on the material. Though I shall cite examples of Conrad's imagery at its imaginative best, I shall also have to deal with

---

[66] "Ah! c'est vraiment bon! Et cela ... et cela! ..." (Jean-Aubry, "Souvennirs (Fragments)", *Nouvelle Revue française*, XXIII, Décembre, 1924, p. 679). For Proust's parody see Marcel Proust, *Pastiches et mélanges* (Paris, Gallimard, 1919), pp. 19-23.

images that are mediocre – to say nothing of those that are simply figurative commonplaces, often proverbial, sometimes simply banal. Although I believe that Conrad belongs (as Thibaudet said of Flaubert) "to the race of great creators of images",[67] I shall not be principally concerned to demonstrate this proposition by compiling a florilegium. Without questioning the propriety of applying critical criteria to individual images and of judging them accordingly, as one judges any other compositional element, I shall be principally concerned to trace the thematic relations among images and their functional significance within individual works. What I want to develop, in short, is the evidence afforded by his metaphors of that collaboration in Conrad between the plastic and the musical imagination which has constituted the principal theme of this chapter on Conrad and Flaubert.

---

[67] Thibaudet, *Gustave Flaubert*, p. 252.

V

VERBAL ICONOGRAPHY

Le métaphorisme est une nécessité littéraire en même
temps qu'une nécessité de la vie ordinaire du langage.
Brunot, *La Pensée et la langue*

What I shall be finally concerned with in my dealings with
Conrad's figurative expressions may be defined as metaphor
symbolically (or thematically) employed – that is to say metaphor
as allusive to, or symbolic of, themes discoverable by analysis of
the purely discursive prose, explicit or implicit in the interplay of
character and the progression of event, but given a deeper "resonance" by the imagery, both objective and verbal. Concentrating
on the verbal imagery I shall have to consider the context of
objective imagery. Although I do not, with Caroline Spurgeon,
equate symbolic imagery with recurrent imagery,[1] or see repetition
as a *sine qua non* of symbolic effectiveness (which can also be
achieved by nuclear development, or for that matter by sheer
vividness, as in what Fernández called the "impression-éclair"), it
is obvious that, as with motifs in music, the recurrence of images
in simple or cumulative repetition is the normal means of investing
them with a more than merely local expressive function.

My interest, in any case, lies finally with what Gerard Manley
Hopkins, apropos of the lyric passages of the Greek tragic poets,

[1] Caroline F. E. Spurgeon, *Shakespeare's Imagery, and What It Tells Us*
(Cambridge, The University Press, 1935). Cf. especially the following: "By
recurrent imagery I mean the repetition of an idea or picture in the images
used in any one play. ... This secondary or symbolic imagery within
imagery is a marked characteristic of Shakespeare's art, indeed it is, perhaps, his most individual way of expressing his imaginative vision" (*op.
cit.*, p. 213).

saw as the second of "two [counterpointed] strains of thought running together" in their drama, and which he defined, in a letter of 1883 to Alexander Baillie, as

> the underthought, conveyed chiefly in the choice of metaphors etc. used and often only half realised by the poet himself, not necessarily having any connection with the subject in hand but usually having a connection and suggested by some circumstance of the scene or the story.[2]

This will take us into an area which, as Hopkins acknowledged, does not admit of "irrefragable" proof, and we shall (as he suggested) have to rely upon an "induction of examples". Strictly speaking, most of the examples will be rather of simile than of metaphor, since Conrad shares with most novelists a marked preference for this more deliberate figure; thus my use of the terms "metaphor" and "metaphoric" must (ordinarily, and except as otherwise indicated) be understood in the generic rather than in the specific sense.

I think it desirable, however, to preface my particular examination of thematic imagery in a number of Conrad's major novels with a synoptic view of his figurative usage indicating, within a framework of empirical categories, certain salient characteristics and tracing certain lines of development from his earliest to his latest productions. The present chapter, largely descriptive and classificatory, will thus be concerned rather with stylistics than with symbolics and will require a certain degree of abstraction (necessarily partial) of the image from its context. This is preliminary work which does not aim at a comprehensive taxonomy, but which will provide a background for the examination of thematic imagery to follow. These pages also will require an

---

[2] The first strain, the paraphrasable or abridgeable content, Hopkins termed the "overthought". Hopkins develops his thesis with specific illustrations from Aeschylus' *Suppliants*. He employs musical analogies (counterpoint, "canons and repetitions"). At one point (apropos of certain of the New Testament Epistles, in which he finds "this same principle of composition") he speaks of "an *undercurrent* of thought governing the choice of images used". (My italics.) Gerard Manley Hopkins, *A Hopkins Reader*, selected and with an introduction by John Pick (New York, Oxford University Press, 1953), pp. 114 f.

"induction of examples", aimed at an over-all view of Conrad's verbal imagery.

Metaphor is so pervasive a feature of Conrad's style that a writer undertaking a synoptic view of his figurative usage confronts a rather daunting task. I can perhaps best broach the subject by recalling the discussion of metaphoric frequency in the foregoing chapter and refining somewhat on the general observations made in that context.

The first thing to be noted is the variation in frequency within individual works. From first to last, in the most densely as in the most sparsely figurative novels, there are marked variations of density, with pages or entire episodes of almost entirely non-figurative prose (ordinarily expository; sometimes, but by no means always, involving dialogue) alternating with pages or episodes densely metaphoric in their texture. One might trace these variations throughout Conrad's production, from *Almayer's Folly* (in which the unfigured account of Dain's audience with Lakamba is in marked contrast to the metaphoric profusion lavished on Dain's tryst with Nina in chapter XI) to *The Rover*, in which the near-abstention from metaphor in a number of scenes (e.g., Bolt's report to the commander of the *Amelia* on the conduct of his landing-party) is in no less striking contrast to the highly figurative prose devoted to Peyrol's encounter with Symons in the tartane (chapter IX). They are traceable even in the work produced from 1897 to about 1903, in which Conrad's verbal imagery frequently attained to a pitch that suggests Flaubert's hyperbolical account of his imaginative state during the composition of *Madame Bovary*: "one hundred thousand images exploding at once, like fireworks". In "Youth" itself, the climactic episode of which – from Marlow's backward vision of the burning *Judea* to his dialogue with the captain of the *Celestial* – is probably more prolific of metaphors than any comparable tract of prose in the entire range of his work, another crucial scene (the *Judea*'s collision with the steamer in Tynemouth and Captain Beard's rescue of his wife) is managed in a perfectly bare expository prose, entirely without benefit of metaphor. So also with "Heart of Darkness", in which the average frequency of metaphor approaches that of "Youth", and with *Lord Jim*, in which metaphor figures more prominently than in any other of the full-length novels.

The question arises: apart from the apparent effect of Marlow, as a narrative device – an orifice through which Conrad's voice acquired a greater metaphoric license than when he spoke as omniscient author – what particular types of material most incited his metaphoric faculty? An examination of *Lord Jim*, with side glances elsewhere, suggests the possibility of one or two tentative generalizations.

Structurally *Lord Jim* falls into two distinct parts comprising what may be called "the matter of the *Patna*" and "the matter of Patusan". Although these are annealed together far more closely than Conrad seems to have realized,[3] the line of transition, falling at dead-center in chapter XX (Stein-Marlow), is perfectly distinct. If we compare the first two hundred with the last two hundred pages – e.g., the *Patna* chapters (pages 3-203) with the Patusan chapters (pages 218-417) – we find a somewhat greater density of metaphor in the earlier chapters. If we look for the regions of greatest metaphoric density within the first half of the novel, we find them occurring in chapters V, IX, and XI. They give us clues to certain types of material and certain kinds of imaginative pressure that (so to speak) innervated Conrad's metaphoric organ.

The twenty-one pages of chapter V, containing some sixty-five figurative expressions, focus chiefly on two persons, the two principal grotesques of the novel: the elephantine captain and the delirious chief engineer of the *Patna*. The ten pages of chapter IX, in which the metaphoric frequency approaches four to a page, contain the climax of Jim's recital to Marlow, in the Malabar House dining room, of the crisis on the *Patna*, culminating with Jim's leap. Here again the grotesques – and principally the captain – occupy the center of the stage; indeed an appreciable number of images (e.g., "funny enough to make the angels weep"; "fit for knockabout clowns in a farce"; "a joke hatched in hell")[4]

---

[3] Cf. Conrad's remark to Garnett on "the division of the book into two parts" (*Letters from Joseph Conrad*, p. 171).
[4] *Lord Jim*, pp. 101, 104, 108. The motif pervades the entire chapter,

are devoted precisely to conveying a generalized impression of the element of the grotesque which, throughout the episode, exists in solution with the tragic. Moreover in the following chapter (the voyage in the lifeboat), in which the imagery, though less dense, is above the norm for the entire book, the grotesquerie of captain and crew again accounts for an appreciable proportion of the figurative expressions.

There is here another imaginative link with Flaubert who, in early youth, defined one of his primary temperamental and artistic biases when he professed his taste for "le grotesque triste". It may be said that the sense of the *grotesque triste* – spilling over on the one hand into the absurd, on the other into the sinister – sometimes imbues Conrad's imagery in contexts not in themselves either grotesque or triste. Meanwhile I note as evidence of the imaginative bent in question – apart from the recurrence of characters and situations partaking of the quality of the grotesque – the sort of hyperactivity of the imaging faculty induced in him by material of this sort, as illustrated above. Further evidence may be found throughout "Heart of Darkness" and (for a later example in a work appreciably more abstemious of metaphor) in the treatment of the "Russian Egeria", Madame de S–.[5]

---

infecting the vocabulary as well as the imagery: cf. such words and phrases as "antics", "capers", "burlesque", "funny grimaces", "scenes of low comedy".

[5] Over half of the verbal images employed in the scene of Razumov's interview with Madame de S— and Peter Ivanovitch are devoted to the grotesquerie of this lady (*Under Western Eyes*, pp. 214-225). Cf. the suggestive image applied to another of the sinister grotesques of this novel (Nikita), who is described as a creature "so grotesque as to set town dogs barking at its mere sight" (*ibid.*, p. 267). Aspects that set dogs barking set Conrad imaging. Conrad's penchant for *le grotesque triste* found frequent expression in objective as well as in verbal imagery. Cf., e.g., the twice-employed device of presenting a bearded man disfigured and discountenanced by the loss of half his beard – as image, one may say, of the disruption of human order and the abasement of human pretension at a moment of crisis. Don Juste Lopez has half his beard "singed off at the muzzle of a trabuco loaded with slugs" during the Monterist uprising, with a resultant impression as of "two men inside his frock-coat, one nobly whiskered and solemn, the other untidy and scared" (*Nostromo*, pp. 234 f.). Burns receives the news of the empty quinine bottles half-way through a depilatory operation with scissors, leaving him "grotesque be-

It is obvious, however, that the category of the *grotesque triste* (as I have called it, after Flaubert) does not define the total impact of the chapters cited from *Lord Jim*, and certainly not of "Heart of Darkness" considered in its entirety. Much of the imagery in chapter IX of *Lord Jim* arises from the physical and emotional pressures of the situation itself and conveys various modes of action (and of appalled inaction) at a time of crisis. In the chapter of the life boat most of the imagery (since captain and crew are quiescent during much of this episode) arises from Jim's reflections and inner convulsions. Moreover, in the brief chapter that follows (chapter XI), Marlow as chorus, observing Jim and wrestling with the moral aspects of his case, throws up (with an occasional contribution from Jim) an even denser thicket of metaphor than that found in the previous chapter.

From these observations we may derive one or two other tentative generalizations regarding Conrad's metaphoric usage. Scenes of concentrated or accelerated action or, simply, of emotional or moral crisis are apt to incite his metaphoric faculty. Interesting in this connection is Marlow's remark: "All this happened in much less time than it takes to tell, since I am trying to interpret for you into slow speech the instantaneous effect of visual impressions." [6] The remark follows, and comments on, his account of the captain's decampment in the gharry, a page and a half of prose that bristles with figurative locutions. Indeed the verbal images comprise about one-sixth of the words employed to describe the captain's departure, so that there is room to question my assertion in an earlier chapter that metaphor functions in Conrad stenographically. Given his expressive requirements, however, and particularly the determination "to make you *see*", with all that phrase implies in the way of affective and kinesthetic response to the things seen, one has to grant that the metaphoric tissue of the prose serves the purpose more economically than would a passage of strict, non-figurative description.

---

yond the fantasies of mad dreams, one cheek all bushy as if with a swollen flame, the other denuded and sunken, with the untouched long moustache on that side asserting itself lonely and fierce" (*The Shadow-Line*, p. 90).
[6] *Lord Jim*, p. 48.

Finally, when we consider the preponderance of images in chapter X devoted to the graphic presentment of inner states – of the affective or ideal contents of consciousness – and when we further note that virtually all of the twenty or so metaphors in chapter XI are of this inner-directed sort, we have another and perhaps the most significant clue to Conrad's figurative usage. For convenience' sake I shall speak of this type of image as "interior", in contradistinction to the "exterior" images aimed at rendering "the highest kind of justice to the visible world".[7]

Here, then, we have another important clue which accounts for many regions of metaphoric density throughout Conrad's fiction, particularly during the years in which the figure of Marlow took shape in his imagination and received his earlier incarnation in the fiction. Marlow has, like his creator, an eye for external appearances, and he produces his share of sensory images; but his characteristic role is either that of reflection and comment upon the inwardness of the events he describes (akin to the role of the Greek chorus), or else it is that of psychopomp, of guide through an inner landscape (his own or another's) and delineator of its features. In the present context he leads me to several generalizations, *viz.*, that the special efflorescence of interior imagery following the introduction of Marlow accounts in large part for the density of metaphor during these years; that it is, in large degree, this imagery of the inner world that is symbolically operative in Conrad's work, supplying most of those thematic links and references of which I have spoken, and which I shall presently illustrate; and finally that it is this type of imagery (the interior) even more than the exterior imagery, directed at the communication of sensory impressions, that defines Conrad's characteristic style in the works subsequent to *The Nigger of the "Narcissus"*. In this respect Conrad's imagery differs from Flaubert's, in whom, as Thibaudet and Dumesnil declared and Demorest demonstrated, the visual or, more generally, the sensory images predominate.

[7] I avoid the use of the contraposed terms "subjective" and "objective" in this connection, since I have reserved the term "objective image" for the non-figurative presentment of visibilia – and because, in any case, the normal function of the interior image is precisely the objectification, or quasi-objectification, of subjective contents.

I do not, of course, intend to attribute solely to Marlow's colloquial faculty the tendencies noted in Conrad's metaphoric usage. As Conrad's creature, Marlow came into being in response to certain expressive urgencies; and these, when Marlow was set aside, found other conduits – though none, it appears, equipped to carry quite so heavy a current of metaphor. But the preponderance of interior imagery discernible in "Heart of Darkness" and *Lord Jim* continues as a feature of style in the works that follow.

Demorest heroically undertook to measure the "interior" against the "exterior" imagery throughout Flaubert's production – a feat which I have not attempted to emulate. I have, however, established a sufficient number of bench marks to permit a tentative generalization.

Before advancing the generalization, however, I should point out that we are dealing with a factor which offers some resistance to a rigorous classification, given the complexity of a large proportion of Conrad's images and given the radical ambiguity of even some of the simpler images, with respect to the quality to be distinguished. The ambivalent image that, like *Janus bifrons*, seems to face both ways, ostensibly conveying a visual aspect or physical impression but in such terms as to convey unmistakably, and perhaps more significantly, a psychological state, is frequent enough in Conrad to frustrate any hope of inclusiveness or unfailing precision in distinguishing between these two categories.[8] When all exclusions have been made, however, there is still evidence of a rather portentous stylistic development.

What the evidence chiefly does is to emphasize the particular significance (or at any rate *a* particular significance) of *The Nigger of the "Narcissus"* as a crucial station on that Via Dolorosa Conrad traveled in pursuit of a prose style adequate to his artistic insights. I find, from an examination of five works with publication dates extending over the period 1895 to 1913, that Conrad, starting in *Almayer's Folly* with an approximately equal balance

---

[8]   Cf., e.g., the presentment of Wamibo "with the face of a man marching through a dream" (*The Nigger of the "Narcissus"*, p. 16), or of Razumov "pale like a corpse obeying the dread summons of judgment" (*Under Western Eyes*, p. 303).

of exterior and interior imagery, produced in *The Nigger of the "Narcissus"* (1897) a work of which the visual and sensory imagery is in an overwhelming proportion to the imagery of mental and moral states. Thereafter, the balance shifts sharply: already in "Heart of Darkness" (1899) the interior imagery exceeds the exterior; and the increment becomes significantly greater in *Under Western Eyes* (1907) and remains so in *Chance* (1913), though with some lapse from the relative level attained in *Under Western Eyes*.

The stylistic curve here adumbrated suggests at least one aspect of Conrad's intention when he remarked to his friend Helen Watson that *The Nigger of the "Narcissus"* contained "certain qualities of art that make it a thing apart".[9] It was in this context that he spoke of his effort to "get through the veil of details to the essence of life"; but one of the ways in which *The Nigger* may be distinguished from its predecessors is precisely in the shimmer he gave to the "veil" of surface detail, the glancing, vivid light with which his imagery, and particularly his metaphor, suffuses the surface of things. One does not have to insist upon the juxtaposition of shadow with the light in this novel, which heralds – in an appreciable proportion of its imagery, as in its basic symbolic conception – the dark inwardness of many of the later novels and stories. It is nevertheless true that, to a degree unexampled in his work, both the light and the shadow are concentrated on the visible aspects of things, illuminating them or throwing them into relief. There is no rhetorical ingredient in *The Nigger of the "Narcissus"* that one would say is not legitimately Conradian; but the proportions in which the metaphoric ingredients are mixed depart sharply from the pattern of earlier Conrad, nor are they typical of later Conrad – of what I think of as Marlovian and post-Marlovian Conrad.

To what degree we may attribute this stylistic development to "the lesson of Flaubert" may remain conjectural; but there can be little doubt that his example is implicated. In any case I see in *The Nigger of the "Narcissus"* ("not the sort of thing that can be attempted more than once in a life-time") [10] a sort of "wager" (as Baudelaire wrote of *Madame Bovary*) that Conrad made with himself, a heroic effort towards a cleansed and sharpened perception of phenomena, towards the mastery of a *sensory* impressionism. With the advent of Marlow as intermediary or alter ego and the period of experimentation in narrative technique that he portends, Conrad's imagery and the texture of his style generally settles into a more characteristic equilibrium between the two tendencies here roughly discriminated under the terms "inwardness" and "outwardness". But he was to profit throughout his career from the stylistic effort of *The Nigger of the "Narcissus"*, drawing upon the image-hoard laid up in that work not only for the rendering of objective sensory impressions but also for the expression, in terms of symbolic equivalences, of subjective states and intellectual operations. It was the latter, however, that would be preponderant in the major works to follow.

When Conrad wrote to Garnett that Stephen Crane was "the *only* impressionist and *only* an impressionist",[11] he meant, I suspect, to suggest (whether justly or not is open to question) that Crane's impressionism was largely a matter of surface rendering.[12] In any case, it is with the advent of Marlow and what he signifies in the way of the graphic presentment of interior states that Conradian "impressionism" assumes its own distinctive character – a character which, in accord with current terminology, contains as much of *ex*pressionism as of *im*pressionism – and it is chiefly in the works produced from the time of "Heart of Darkness" that Ramón Fernández' pronouncement on Conrad's method justifies itself: "Sa grande originalité est d'avoir appliqué cet impression-

---

[10]   So Conrad declared in the prefatory note he wrote for the American edition of 1914 ("To My Readers in America").
[11]   *Letters from Joseph Conrad: 1895-1924*, p. 118. Cf., in this connection, Garnett's praise of Crane's "unique and exquisite faculty of disclosing an individual scene by an odd simile". Conrad quoted this with approval in his preface to Beer's *Stephen Crane* (cf. *Last Essays*, p. 98).
[12]   The supposition would seem to gain support from a remark in a letter to Cunninghame Graham, written a month after the letter to Garnett: "The man [Crane] sees the outside of many things and the inside of some" (*Life and Letters*, I, p. 220).

isme à la connaissance des êtres humains." [13] Fernández, by the way, chose a Marlovian image (he termed it an *impression-éclair*) to illustrate this crucial sentence. He could, of course, have found examples in other quarters; but I take it as symptomatic that he turned to Marlow for the purpose.[14]

The precise degree of Conrad's originality in this respect is no doubt debatable. The term "impressionist" is one that Demorest, coupling it with the term "symbolist", applied to Flaubert in the concluding pages of his work; and it is apparent that he had in mind more than the rendering of external impressions. Certainly there are anticipations in Flaubert and (among English novelists) in Dickens of the sort of impressionism Fernández defined. But Flaubert's images of inner states are generally wanting in the concision and the *prime-sautier* quality essential in Fernández' account of Conradian method. (Consider, e.g., the "châteaux abandonnés" image in *Madame Bovary* cited by Faguet for its "symbolic" efficacy [15] – to say nothing of the "steppe de Russie" in the same novel.) One can of course find many less deliberate and less elaborated examples, but relatively few, I think, among Flaubert's interior images to which one would apply the term *impression-éclair*. In any case we are in touch here with a characteristic feature of Conrad's style, and one with significance for the symbolics of the novels and stories. Moreover, the stylistic development in the direction indicated runs counter to the tendency discerned in some critical quarters where it is held that

[13]   Fernández, *Nouvelle Revue française*, XXIII (Décembre 1924), p. 732. Cf. also, in the contribution to this same memorial issue of the *NRF* by the novelist Edouard Estaunié ("admirateur passionné de Conrad"), the tribute to "cette manière intérieure de faire surgir les êtres" (*ibid.*, p. 703). The formula is of particular interest in view of Estaunié's self-proclaimed role as novelist of "la vie intérieure".

[14]   "Conscious of being reprehensibly dense I groped in the darkness of my mind: De Barral, de Barral – and all at once noise and light burst on me as if a window of my memory had been suddenly flung open on a street in the City" (*Chance*, pp. 68 f.). Fernández' term "impression-éclair" might be even more vividly illustrated by the simile applied to Captain Whalley's evocation of the past as he paces the streets of the Eastern port: "swift and full of detail like a flash of magnesium light into the niches of a dark memorial hall" (*Youth*, p. 195).

[15]   *Madame Bovary*, p. 171 (cf. Faguet, *Gustave Flaubert*, p. 156).

"Flaubertian" influence (construed narrowly in terms of "phano-poeia", *viz.*, the graphic rendering of visibilia and of sensory impressions in general) set in most strongly in Conrad's prose during the years of the Ford collaboration and largely as a product of that collaboration.[16] I need not labor the point, since I have sufficiently demonstrated in my foregoing chapter the extent to which the Flaubert-imago was present to Conrad's conscious-ness (and to his unconsciousness) prior to the collaboration with Ford – which was initiated in October-November, 1898, subse-quent to the publication of *The Nigger of the "Narcissus"* and to the magazine publication of "Youth", and which was still in its exploratory stages during the weeks (mid-December, 1898, to early February, 1899) devoted to the composition of "Heart of Darkness".

My remarks on the frequency of metaphor in Conrad's fiction, and more particularly in the works written about the period of Marlow's first incarnation, suggest a more alembicated style than one actually finds. Even during the period in question, Conrad's prose – though certainly not without its calculated bedazzlements – is actually a soberer organ, and more efficient for narrative and expository purposes, than the metaphoric statistics would suggest. For two reasons: first because of the characteristic brevity and compactness of his figurative expressions (with notable exceptions, to be sampled presently); and secondly, because a substantial proportion of them are either involved so intimately with the tissue of the language as to retain only vestiges of their metaphoric identity or are given to us frankly, not as original products of artistic insight, but as productions of the national mind – pro-verbial or colloquial expressions of a figurative cast.

From first to last Conrad's prose style, however consciously

---

[16] Cf. especially Kenner, *The Poetry of Ezra Pound*, pp. 266 f. The Conrad-Ford collaboration has been explored in detail by John H. Morey in a still unpublished doctoral dissertation, "Joseph Conrad and Ford Madox Ford: A Study in Collaboration" (Cornell University, 1960). All that need be said here is that the most generally accessible testimony on the collaboration is found in Ford's various memoirs, and that his testi-mony cannot be accepted, as Kenner accepts it, uncritically. In any case the conclusions drawn in the passage cited are largely invalidated by an erroneous chronology.

elaborated, was more hospitable than Flaubert's to the proverbial and colloquial – and even to the conventional and commonplace. Flaubert's lifelong aversion to the "expression toute faite" – as attested repeatedly in the correspondence and systematically in the *Dictionnaire des idées reçues* – has a morbid intensity unexampled among major prose writers. In intention Flaubert restricted such expressions to direct or indirect discourse, where they serve as a deliberate device of ironic characterization. Homais' dialogue (a sort of oral *Guide Michelin des lieux communs*) is the most obvious example. In Conrad's prose the readymade expression (often metaphorical) spills over rather liberally from the dialogue into the recital itself – especially so in the works in which Marlow serves as narrator, converting the entire work into interrupted monologue. It would be interesting to speculate here upon the temperamental difference reflected by the stylistic difference in question, and particularly upon the consequences of the different relation in which the two writers stood to their respective linguistic media. In any case the line of distinction between live and dead metaphors of which Fowler speaks was very differently drawn by the two writers: throughout his writing career Conrad clearly found a savor in everyday expressions (seeing in them no doubt precious revelations of national character and temperament) which an English Flaubert, and perhaps an English-born Conrad, would have employed more sparingly.

This is particularly so where Marlow is narrator. A sampling from his discourse (including the dialogue he reports) in the first half of *Lord Jim* will suggest the range of repertory: "that's where the shoe pinches" (p. 63); "Why eat all that dirt?" (p. 65); "feathered his nest pretty well" (p. 66); "a penny in his pocket to bless himself with" (p. 66); "the cap fitted" (p. 81); "cutting the ground from under one's feet" (p. 82); "funny enough to make angels weep" (p. 101); "like chaff before the wind" (p. 104); "as easy as falling off a log" (p. 167); "made my blood boil" (p. 168). One can find such locutions throughout the range of Conrad's work, but nowhere so thickly strewn as in the Marlow volumes, in which, by converting narrative into monologue, he invested it with something of the freedom of dialogue. They serve as a counterweight to the Marlovian sonorities of diction and the Marlovian subtleties of distinction, as Sancho's earthy proverbs to the rhetorical flights of his master.[17] Cliché apart (and Conrad did not entirely avoid banalities of diction unredeemed by colloquial savor),[18] his want of inhibition in the matter of popular expressions enabled him to combine to a remarkable degree deliberate artistry of style with an impression of colloquial ease and pungency recalling Sterne and Smollett or the Cervantes he so greatly admired.

Most writers of original linguistic talent (apart from Cervantes one thinks of Rabelais and the Elizabethans, of Swift, of Joyce and Faulkner among others in this century) are rather attracted than repelled by the venerable commonplaces of the language, turning them into grist for their own verbal mills; and Conrad, without Joyce's deliberate virtuosity or instinct for linguistic transformation, has his own way of availing himself of the "lieu commun". Although the symbolic metaphors will ordinarily be found to be those which present themselves as products of unaided intuition, Conrad could often extract unlooked-for significance out of the verbal commonplace. I am reminded of Edwin Muir's assertion about him that "only a profound mind could have given such fundamental meaning to platitude".[19] Here I shall give only an example or two, in anticipation of a later phase of my inquiry.

One of the metaphoric commonplaces I have in mind is the figure of the drowning man clutching a straw; and to do justice to all aspects of this topic I preface my example (from *Lord Jim*) by

[17]   One could fill several pages with phrases of the sort from either *Lord Jim* or *Chance*. It may be added here that the anonymous mariner-narrators share, in less pronounced degree, Marlow's colloquial gift. But Conrad carefully restricts the colloquial range of the language teacher in *Under Western Eyes*, and he garnishes Decoud's epistolary style with Gallicisms.

[18]   "Silence" (or "stillness", or sometimes "darkness") "reigns" rather frequently in Conrad's fiction. Cf., e.g., *Youth*, p. 225; *Nostromo*, pp. 207, 377, 519; *The Secret Agent*, pp. 203, 205, 280; *Chance*, p. 308.

[19]   Muir, *Latitudes*, p. 55. Cf. Las Vergnas' remark: "S'il a touché tant de lecteurs par la jeunesse de ses images, c'est que, libéré des routines d'une langue maternelle, il a su, en raison même de ses tâtonnements et de ses ignorances, vitaliser les clichés" (Raymond Las Vergnas, *Joseph Conrad: Romancier de l'exil*, Lyon, E. Vitte, 1959, pp. 15 f.).

a later occurrence of the same figure, in which it is not, to my mind. redeemed from banality. In the final pages of *Nostromo* Conrad employs the figure to close a chapter and climax an episode – the revelation of the unlawful love between Gian' Battista (affianced to Linda) and Giselle: "the magnificent Capataz clasped her round her white neck in the darkness of the gulf as a drowning man clutches at a straw". Conrad turns to other matters in the following chapter, leaving his ill-starred lovers involved in one another's arms and in the toils of a metaphor which is not equal to the occasion, cannot convey the tragic intensity of the relation.

We can write this off as a characteristic weakness vis à vis what Thomas Moser, on dubious grounds, has called "the uncongenial subject" of romantic love; or we can attribute it to imaginative fatigue under the breaking-strain Conrad experienced during the final weeks of composition of *Nostromo*. For whatever reasons, there are pages in the final chapters of that massive work which fall below the sustained magnificence of the rest – though whatever fatigue he experienced did not prevent him from rounding out the "grand design" of the book and closing it with full authority. All this is by the way, however: the point is that the figurative commonplace, in the context cited, seems inadequate. But worked into the fabric of dialogue or of Marlow's inner dialectic, such locutions may be reinvested with something of their original significance, acquiring an increment of energy by contiguity or context.

In *Lord Jim* he uses the same figurative commonplace. It is thrown up to the surface of Marlow's consciousness in his reflections upon Jim (in relation to Chester's offer of employment as a guano-gatherer on Walpole Reef): "There was the Walpole Reef in [the ocean] – to be sure – a speck in the dark void, a straw for the drowning man." [20] Here the image strikes us not only as a characteristic product of Marlovian reflection, but as appropriate to the context, both of event and of imagery. This first occurrence of the image follows upon Marlow's first formulation of his recurrent vision of Jim as standing "on the brink of a vast obscurity,

[20] *Lord Jim*, p. 173.

like a lonely figure on the shore of a sombre and hopeless ocean". Marlow returns to his metaphor in the further course of his reflections ("If I spoke, would that motionless and suffering youth leap into the obscurity – clutch at the straw?"); and in the following chapter, during his interview with Jim (and during the deluge of a monsoon rain), it is recalled in another key, so to speak, in the derisive comment upon Jim's emotional stress offered by a leaky rain-pipe ("The perforated pipe gurgled, choked, spat, and splashed in odious ridicule of a swimmer fighting for his life").[21]

A more vivid example from the same context of this characteristic operation by which the latent suggestions of a metaphoric commonplace are turned to imaginative account and the figure redeemed from banality occurs when Jim, in gratitude to Marlow for his letter of introduction, stammers out that he "always thought that if a fellow could begin with a clean slate. . . . And now you . . . in a measure . . . yes . . . clean slate". Ingested into Marlow's reflective apparatus, Jim's banal metaphor yields one of the memorable pronouncements of the book, the resonance of which remains with the reader to the end: "A clean slate, did he say? As if the initial word of each our destiny were not graven in imperishable characters upon the face of a rock." And indeed the image cited is itself resonant of an earlier image which stands to it in ironic counterpoint: Marlow's statement, apropos of Brierly, that "the sting of life could do no more to his complacent soul than the scratch of a pin to the smooth face of a rock".[22]

Conrad had, then (in part, perhaps, because he was a late comer to it), a respect for the genius of the language which could embrace even those commonplace metaphors presumed by many writers to be dead or moribund. If his tolerance of the commonplace could betray him into occasional banality, it could also, and more characteristically, lend a deceptive impression of ease to the carefully modulated texture of his style, and it could, particularly through the agency of Marlow, provide a colloquial groundwork to support the sophisticated verbal structures erected upon it.

[21] *Ibid.*, pp. 174, 181.
[22] *Ibid.*, pp. 185, 186; 58. Readers of *Lord Jim* will recall the final sentence of the paragraph: "He committed suicide very soon after."

Before proceeding to a partial classification of verbal images by referent, I want to supplement my discussion of metaphoric frequencies by a consideration of the tendency toward the elaboration of images observable in the work of Conrad's most productive years – since this is an essential aspect of the stylistic tendency under review.

We may take as a bench mark *The Nigger of the "Narcissus"* – that effort of a highly deliberate art to which Conrad affixed his aesthetic credo, and in which, as we have seen, the resource of verbal imagery was laid under much heavier contribution than hitherto, becoming an unmistakable feature of the mature Conradian style which now begins to assume its definitive characteristics. In this work, moreover, the recurrence of metaphoric themes, that is to say the multiplication of metaphors having identical or related reference, establishing what I call a thematic series, becomes a significant feature of style and a definable element of symbolic structure. However, in contrast to the major works to follow, two things are notable about the imagery of *The Nigger of the "Narcissus"*. One of these – the exceptionally high ratio of visual and sensory images to those defining inner states – has already been remarked. The second is this: that, except for certain extended descriptive passages marked by a continuous vein of personification (chiefly implied in the choice of verbs and modifiers rather than stated as a direct comparison or an equivalence), not more than two or three images in the entire work are developed beyond two or three lines of text. It is these images that I want to glance at here, leaving for a later context our consideration of the thematic series that I discern in this work. The images that follow illustrate that associative or reflexive process of the imagination (noted in the foregoing chapter as characteristic of Flaubert, in *Madame Bovary* particularly) whereby a metaphor, introduced into the text with an appearance of casualness, is subsequently developed as simile, or vice versa – a process, or principle, that will express itself in recurrence from page to page, from chapter to chapter, and even from section to section of extended works. Here we see it on a restricted scale, within the limits of a single sentence or paragraph.

The first example (near the beginning of chapter II) is a personification of the tug that escorts the *Narcissus* out of the harbor; it follows, with vividness of contrast, the image of the ship as "a high and lonely pyramid, gliding, all shining and white, through the sunlit mist".[23] Reproducing (conjecturally) the imaginative process involved in what follows, I should say that the verb of motion ("gliding") applied to the ship evoked an antithetic verb for the tug – "crawling" – from the implicit metaphoric suggestion of which was engendered the following simile:

Twenty-six pairs of eyes watched her low broad stern crawling languidly over the smooth swell between the two paddle-wheels that turned fast, beating the water with fierce hurry. She resembled an enormous and aquatic black beetle, surprised by the light, overwhelmed by the sunshine, trying to escape with ineffectual effort into the distant gloom of the land. She left a lingering smudge of smoke on the sky, and two vanishing trails of foam on the water. On the place where she had stopped a round black patch of soot remained, undulating on the swell – an unclean mark of the creature's rest.[24]

Here the expressed comparison in the second sentence (itself deriving from the metaphoric verbal "crawling") emerges in metaphor in the final phrase of the paragraph.

The second example occurs in the first paragraph of the final chapter. It is one of those images objectifying mental impressions or psychic contents which, as I have said, will become increasingly characteristic of Conradian imagery. Aiming at a graphic present-ment of the dying Jimmy's presence to the consciousness of his

---

[23] *The Nigger of the "Narcissus"*, p. 27.
[24] *Ibid.* Cf., in "Heart of Darkness", the extended similitude between Marlow's river-boat and "a sluggish beetle crawling on the floor of a lofty portico" (*Youth*, p. 95). It may be mentioned here that Vernon Young sees the antithesis between the "high and lonely pyramid" of the *Narcissus* and the "enormous and aquatic black beetle" of the tug as "unquestionably a sidelong glance at the Egyptian figure of the pyramid, prime-symbol of direction and sun-worship, and of the scarab, symbol of creative energy" (Vernon Young, "Trial by Water: Joseph Conrad's *The Nigger of the Narcissus*", *Accent*, XII, Spring 1952, pp. 67-81. Reprinted, Stallman, *op. cit.*, p. 120). This is an agreeable conceit; and for all I know Conrad may have had it in mind – but if so it must remain a puzzle why he did not do more with it. In any case the critic's "unquestionably" strikes me as over-confident.

shipmates, it furnishes a sort of pendant to the image of the emanating black mist in the opening scene:

> And in the confused current of impotent thoughts that set unceasingly this way and that through bodies of men, Jimmy bobbed up upon the surface, compelling attention, like a black buoy chained to the bottom of a muddy stream.[25]

Here the genetic process seems no less apparent: the "congealed" metaphor "current of . . . thoughts", decongealed by the narrator's imagination, engenders the (uncongealed) metaphor "bobbed up upon the surface", which is extended and particularized by the following simile.

We can see in these isolated instances examples in miniature of the sort of imaginative operation that engendered from Decoud's recollection of a phrase of Bolivar's a sequence of marine images extending through much of the Casa Gould reception-scene and contributing an appreciable eddy to the metaphoric undercurrent of *Nostromo*.[26]

When we come to the earlier Marlow works – "Heart of Darkness" and the more spaciously designed *Lord Jim* – we find for the first time a significant number of figurative expressions elaborated in this way, many of them at much greater length than any discoverable in *The Nigger of the "Narcissus"*. This tendency to seize upon certain figurative expressions for detailed development will outlive Marlow and become a stylistic feature of a number of the works to follow, resulting in a few instances in a metaphoric development approaching that of the more extreme examples in *Madame Bovary* or in the later Henry James.

I shall confine myself to a handful of illustrations, commencing with *Lord Jim*. The earliest conspicuous example I find is, fittingly, the development of a figurative colloquialism – one of an exceptional number of images in this novel having a zoological referent. The germinal image is, in this case, not Marlow's own, but the extension of it is a characteristic Marlovian product. When the delinquent captain of the *Patna*, pajama-clad, reports to the Port Office on the eve of the inquiry he presents himself to

---

[25] *The Nigger of the "Narcissus"*, p. 138.
[26] *Nostromo*, pp. 186-205 (cited *supra*, ch. IV).

Archie Ruthvel, the principal shipping-master, who promptly thrusts him – hanging back and snorting "like a frightened bullock" – into the private office of Captain Elliot, the Master Attendant. The dimensions of the ensuing "row" are expressed by Archie's ruthful declaration to Marlow that "he felt as though he had thrown a man to a hungry lion". The recollection of Ruthvel's simile, colliding in Marlow's mind with a related metaphor current about Elliot, elicits from Marlow, at the end of a half-page of reminiscence about the redoubtable Elliot, the following summarizing word on the captain's interview:

His three daughters were awfully nice, though they resemble him amazingly, and on the mornings he woke up with a gloomy view of their matrimonial prospects the office would read it in his eye and tremble, because, they said, he was sure to have somebody for breakfast. However, that morning he did not eat the renegade, but, if I may be allowed to carry on the metaphor, chewed him up very small, so to speak, and – ah! ejected him again.[27]

To proceed from the circumference to the center of Marlow's concern, consider the well-known "new sovereign" image a few pages farther on:

He [Jim] looked as genuine as a new sovereign, but there was some infernal alloy in his metal. . . . How much? The least thing – the least drop of something rare and accursed; the least drop! – but he made you – standing there with his don't-care-hang air – he made you wonder whether perchance he were nothing more rare than brass.[28]

There is an image of comparable extension applied to the suicide Brierly (". . . the scratch of a pin to the smooth face of a rock . . . presented to me and to the world a surface as hard as granite"). There is Marlow's long elegiac excursus on the Wanderer and *Heimkehr* themes with its recurrent evocations of "the spirit of the land".[29] As for Jim himself, he is, from beginning to end of the book, the subject (or focus) of a series of metaphors that one may confidently say is unexampled in Conrad's work for frequency, extension and ramification of reference; and indeed one may add,

[27]   *Lord Jim*, p. 39.
[28]   *Ibid.*, pp. 45 f.
[29]   *Ibid.*, pp. 58; 222 f.

with not much less confidence, that only in Proust or James might one expect to find a fictional character exposed over so long a period to so deep a metaphoric penetration. But the imagery Marlow devotes to Jim is, for the most part, linked in a continuous series of cross-references, and must be reserved for a later phase of our inquiry. Here I shall cite only two isolated images of moderate extension (approximately fifty words each), illustrating two rather different aspects of Conradian imagery at this period. The first proceeds, with a distinct suggestion of imitative form in its fragmented rhythms, by verbal accumulation to develop a single metaphoric vehicle, of which the tenor (itself a metaphor) is Jim's mind flying "round and round the serried circle of facts that had surged up all about him to cut him off from the rest of his kind". Which engenders in Marlow the following simile:

... it was like a creature that, finding itself imprisoned within an enclosure of high stakes, dashes round and round, distracted in the night, trying to find a weak spot, a crevice, a place to scale, some opening through which it may squeeze itself and escape.

The second example illustrates with exceptional concision the linkage of nearly related images, one growing out of another by verbal suggestion in a sequence initiated by an all-but-imperceptible metaphor. The metaphor is of the type ordinarily thought of as "dead" – and like the Accountant in "Heart of Darkness" Marlow "toys architecturally with the bones":

He had passed these days on the verandah, buried in a long chair, and coming out of his place of sepulture only at meal-times or late at night, when he wandered on quays all by himself, detached from his surroundings, irresolute and silent, like a ghost without a home to haunt.[30]

I have multiplied instances from *Lord Jim* with a view to suggesting not simply the profusion of extended verbal images in this work, but the radically metaphoric texture of Conrad's style at this period. However, the examples quoted have been of only moderate extension. Before turning to *Nostromo* I want to identify, without quoting, a composite image which, viewed as a single whole, is

[30]   *Ibid.*, pp. 31; 82.

the most extended in Conrad's fiction and perhaps one of the longest in prose fiction before Proust. This is the paragraph comprising the entire first page of chapter XXI, the opening chapter of the second part of the novel, in which Marlow introduces his audience to Patusan under the likeness of "a star of the fifth magnitude" in an unfamiliar heaven. It is not the unitary and monolithic simile that Flaubert produced in the Russian steppe image; but it incorporates an all but unbroken thread of metaphor, with a single referent, visible in almost every element of the paragraph. Apart from its compositional function as prelude to the second portion of the novel this paragraph, which may appear in isolation as a rhetorical set-piece, forms a link, by virtue of its astronomical reference, with a continuous chain of cosmic imagery running from beginning to end of the book. It is the product of a Marlow temporarily disengaged from his material – a "conceit", quite different in tonality from most of the cosmic images in the book; but its thematic relation to these is unmistakable.

Perhaps the most consummately visualized of Conrad's more extended works, replete with landscapes of the greatest vividness and of objective imagery in general, *Nostromo* – wanting the metaphor-breeding apparatus of Marlow – is less prolific of figurative expressions than *Lord Jim*, and specifically of those extended images which we might describe (adapting Henry James's account of Conrad's method in the last of the Marlow novels) as a prolonged hovering flight over the outstretched ground of the similitude exposed. But there are notable exceptions to the prevailing succinctness of imagery in the novel. I have already cited an extended image with musical referent; also the closely connected sequence of marine images in the reception scene, none of which singly is developed beyond about thirty words, but which in the ensemble coalesce into an extended image-cluster dispersed over thirteen pages. I shall add to this example only the "cord of silence" image from the final section of the book (Part Third) – one of the most "metaphysical" images to be found in all of Conrad's production and (even though without benefit of Marlow, and for all its discontinuities) one of the most prolonged and hovering flights Conrad ever made in a single metaphoric vehicle. It is not a continuously elaborated metaphoric set-piece, but a series of incremental repetitions upon Decoud's hallucinated vision, during his isolation on the Great Isabel, which is expressed in the form of a simile:

On the tenth day, after a night spent without even dozing off once (it had occurred to him that Antonia could not possibly have ever loved a being so impalpable as himself), the solitude appeared like a great void, and the silence of the gulf like a tense, thin cord to which he hung suspended by both hands, without fear, without surprise, without any sort of emotion whatever.[31]

The image – a hallucinatory presentment of the colloquial metaphor "strung up" [32] – is reverted to four times on the next page, twice more on the following two pages, the final recapitulation occurring in the sentence reporting Decoud's plunge into the Gulf. The cord vibrates "with senseless phrases"; Decoud sees it "stretched to breaking point"; he wonders whether "I would hear it snap before I fell"; he decides that it will never snap on the island, that "it must let him fall and sink into the sea"; from the boat he sees it again, stretched taut; in the end he rolls overboard "without having heard the cord of silence snap in the solitude of the Placid Gulf".

Another discontinuous development of a single image, comparable in its extension to the one just considered, occurs in Conrad's next published novel, and the referent is curiously related. I have in mind the "tight-rope" image in *The Secret Agent*, introduced into the text as a symbol of the rather precarious virtuosity with which Chief Inspector Heat discharges his functions. The theme is broached in simile, at a length of over eighty words, to mark a turning-point in the long dialogue between Heat and the Assistant Commissioner. The conviction grows in Heat that his chief knows more of his *modus operandi* than he (Heat) had suspected. "He felt at the moment", Conrad tells us, "like a tight-rope artist might feel if suddenly, in the middle of the performance, the manager of the Music Hall were to rush out

[31] *Nostromo*, p. 498.
[32] An expression applied, e.g., to Razumov: "secretly strung up but perfectly sure of himself" (*Under Western Eyes*, p. 255).

of the proper managerial seclusion and begin to shake the rope." [33] After eight pages, during which the Assistant Commissioner's unflagging persistence has further defrosted Heat's *sang-froid*, the figure is reintroduced in metaphor at scarcely less length: Heat is declared to be unafraid at the prospect of "getting a broken neck", but full of indignation at having his performance spoiled. On the following page the Assistant Commissioner, in unruffled pursuit of his line of questioning, is said to administer "another shake to the tight-rope"; and after another half-page of dialogue and of morose reflection on Heat's part, "the Chief Inspector, who had made up his mind to jump off the rope, came to the ground with gloomy frankness".[34]

The only other verbal image of comparable extension in this work – the "stream of life" image – is isolated in the novel, a metaphoric set-piece without reprises or recapitulations. It is a rather conventional flight, developed as strict metaphor (with no expressed comparison) over almost half a page and in the ironically elegant diction characteristic of much of the prose of this novel. It has a sort of coda in the appended metaphor of Winnie's "domestic feeling, stagnant and deep like a placid pool".[35] It has, no doubt, a certain symbolic fitness since Winnie Verloc, a fugitive from the domestic pool, finds her end in the sea. But I chiefly see in it, as I see in all the other rhetorical elegances of *The Secret Agent*, the effect of ironic contrast to the squalor, fatuity, and desperation of the lives embalmed in a quasi-Augustan prose like flies in amber. Fowler remarked that "the present fashion is rather to develop a metaphor only by way of burlesque". But Conrad shows, notably in these two examples from *The Secret Agent*, that extended metaphor can also serve the purposes of irony.

In *Chance* we find, as we should expect – since the thread of

[33] *The Secret Agent*, p. 116. (It is perhaps Conrad's most dubious distinction to have anticipated the current adverbial use of "like"; and it is one of the puzzles of his relations with his publishers and their readers that none of them ever set him right about this abusage. This is not to say that he regularly committed the solecism; but the grammatical distinction between "like" and "as" seems never to have been fully settled in his mind.)

[34] *Ibid.*, pp. 124 f.

[35] *Ibid.*, p. 243.

discourse is spun out by an avatar of the earlier Marlow – an impressive number of developed similes and metaphors, many of them of popular origin. In the course of his confabulations with the Fynes over Flora's disappearance Marlow, "by a sudden and alarming aberration" that interestingly anticipates Eliot's "dance like a dancing Bear", becomes "mentally aware of three trained dogs dancing on their hind legs". Mrs. Fyne's aggressive response to a question he had put her breaks up the dance and provokes a sequel to the image: "In an instant I found myself out of the dance and down on all-fours so to speak, with liberty to bark and bite." [36] The grotesquerie of the de Barral empire and its collapse incites Marlow's imaging faculty at several points, as when an angling metaphor suggests itself to his mind and evokes an appendage of cognate terms, several of which are bunched close behind the initiating image, with the final item of the series dangling a half-page farther down.[37] So one might continue, especially through the first part of the novel; but I shall conclude with a final example recalling in its insistence and its dispersion through ten pages of text some of those cited from earlier novels. I have in mind the Carlylean metaphor of Fyne's solemnity as a garment, damaged by his unsuccessful parley with Anthony in the East End hotel:

"It must have been most distasteful to him; and his solemnity got damaged somehow in the process, I perceived. There were holes in it through which I could see a new, an unknown Fyne."

The image is three times reverted to before the final reprise, in which Marlow abandons it with the notation that "the rents and slashes of his solemnity were closing up gradually but it was going to be a surly solemnity".[38]

---

[36]   *Chance*, pp. 57 f.
[37]   "I don't think that a mere Jones or Brown could have fished out from the depths of the Incredible such a colossal manifestation of human folly as that man did." Cf. in the sentences that follow the terms "rising to the bait", "rise to a naked hook", "lure", and finally the summarizing term for de Barral's multitude of victims: "all sorts of very small fry" (*ibid.*, pp. 69 f.).
[38]   *Ibid.*, pp. 242-251. But the entire sequence had been anticipated at the

In *Under Western Eyes* there had been relatively little of the sort of extension or development of individual images that I have been illustrating. Perhaps Conrad's language teacher-narrator was inhibited by an acquaintance with Fowler on metaphor. However this may be, there are few exceptions in that work to the characteristically concise format of the Conradian verbal image; and there are, so far as I find, fewer still in the works that follow Marlow's reincarnation in *Chance* (1913). In Conrad's last completed novel (*The Rover*) the rule of concision is virtually unbroken.

Before proceeding to the examination of image-sequences which constitutes the principal agenda of the next chapter I want to distinguish some of the more conspicuous classes or families of Conradian metaphor. A number of these – notably those falling under the general heading of "interior" imagery – will be amply illustrated in the following chapter and need only be identified here. Of these are the extensive classes having their source in the realms of mortality, of disease and narcosis, of dream and hallucination, of enchantment and possession. Endowed with an inescapable affective content, these images will be found repeatedly in a symbolic nexus with objective episode and psychological analysis. Equally prominent (one might well say "obsessive") are related strains of cosmic and meteorological imagery which provide a sort of metaphoric undercurrent to the descriptive presentment of nature, reënforcing the symbolic role of the natural milieu in Conrad's fiction. Like the related marine imagery, and what I would term the imagery of the abyss, these are products, in large part, of that "oceanic feeling" which coexists in Conrad with artistically more amenable impulses – his irony, his narrative élan, his sensory impressionism – accounting for much of his early rhetorical excess, but accounting equally for much of the symbolic impact of such works as *Lord Jim* and "Heart of Darkness". The impulse behind this vein of imagery was expressed at its highest rhetorical pitch in a dictum which follows immediately upon the well-known paragraph in *A Personal Record* setting forth his

---

end of the preceding chapter, in the notation of Fyne's "native solemnity which flapped about him like a disordered garment" (*ibid.*, p. 195).

doctrine of a "spectacular" universe: "The great aim is to remain true to the emotions called out of the deep encircled by the firmament of stars . . ." [39] The conversion of those emotions, unquenchable in Conrad, into impression, into image, constitutes one of the most unmistakable features of his style and one of the recurrent symbols or symbol-complexes in his fiction, endowing it with that aspect of the "metaphysical" which has sometimes tempted critics to search his pages for hidden meanings or for the outlines of philosophic systems.

The symbolic or thematic suggestions implicit in sensory imagery are normally more casual and local, of the type defined by Austin Warren (apropos of Henry James's sensory imagery) as "an emblematic perception, or symbolized intuition" of a fictional character or motif. Examples of local reference, with a rather elementary propriety, are Marlow's image of the Sidiboy fireman in *Lord Jim*, "whose black face had silky gleams like a lump of anthracite coal", or his account of Mrs. Beard's face as "all wrinkled and ruddy like a winter apple" – an image which introduces a savor of the Essex countryside into the mariner's world of "Youth".[40] Elsewhere such images or epithets may serve as elementary devices of characterization, as when the "impenetrability" of Winnie Verloc is conveyed by repeated imagery of rock, stone, and adamant. Other substances, evoked in metaphor or epithet, may, like silver in *Nostromo* or ivory in "Heart of Darkness", carry a more generalized significance, enforcing the symbolic role which we attribute to the material itself, in its objective existence in the novel or story.

We need do no more than touch upon these "emblematic" images, in the interests of inclusiveness, since they are of a type almost universal in imaginative literature. Nor do we need to pause here over the class of animal images, the normal function of which, in literature as in heraldry, might also properly be defined

[39] *A Personal Record*, p. 93.
[40] *Lord Jim*, p. 171; *Youth*, p. 7. The latter image has an approximate antecedent in *Madame Bovary*: the thin visage of Catherine Leroux (recipient of the award at the *Comices*), "plus plissé de rides qu'une pomme de reinette flétrie" (*op. cit.*, p. 208).

as emblematic. There are instances, however, to be considered in
the following chapter, in which (as in the conspicuous case of the
insectile imagery in *The Brothers Karamazov*) metaphors with
animal referent serve a symbolic function involved with, but
transcending, their characterizing function.

Conrad's images drawn from the realm of the arts and of
artifacts have already been illustrated in the preceding chapter. In
illustrating further I wish to do no more than to indicate, first, the
way in which the "emblematic" suggestions implicit in various
material substances are incorporated into his sculptural imagery,
and secondly the frequency with which such images are made
portentous by contexts that evoke disease or death. The morbid
suggestions that cling to the image that presents Omar's face "with
the immobility of a plaster cast" are made explicit in the later
image of Ossipon "with a face like a fresh plaster cast of himself
after a wasting illness".[41] The presentment of Kurtz like "an
animated image of death carved out of old ivory", and of Singleton
"like a statue of heroic size in the gloom of a crypt", may serve
as examples of a rather numerous subclass of images referring to
mortuary or funerary sculpture.[42] We shall find more of these in
the one novel (*The Arrow of Gold*) in which metaphors referring
to works of art constitute an unmistakably significant image-
sequence; and we shall see how evocations of funerary sculpture
conjoin with the other mortuary imagery in the most sustained
symbolic image-sequence in *The Nigger of the "Narcissus"*.

One sees again from these examples the way in which the
ostensibly sensory and impressionistic imagery tends often in
Conrad to merge its identity with the expressionistic imagery of
inner states. As the interior imagery objectifies mental contents or
operations, so the exterior imagery typically endows sensory impressions with affective or intuitible content. The two types tend
in Conrad toward a common center of imaginative apprehension,
which in each instance may be referred back to the goal announced in the Preface to *The Nigger of the "Narcissus"* – the

---

[41]   *An Outcast of the Islands*, p. 100; *The Secret Agent*, p. 293.
[42]   *Youth*, p. 134; *The Nigger of the "Narcissus"*, p. 129.

effort, by "an impression conveyed through the senses", to "reach the secret spring of responsive emotions".

When Conrad wrote of the face of a bride, self-glimpsed in a mirror: "In the greenish glass her own face looked far off like the livid face of a drowned corpse at the bottom of a pool",[43] he not only betrayed an imagination as haunted by mortality as the imaginations of the Jacobean dramatists; he also exemplified (hyperbolically, no doubt) the affective impulse that lay behind his sensory impressionism. Indeed one might almost see the mirror in this image as a "magic mirror", itself symbolic of Conrad's habitual impulse to "interiorize" his visual and sensory imagery, to make it a vehicle of "magic suggestiveness", symbolic of moral states or premonitory of the moral vicissitudes of his drama.

But the example, however arresting, is extreme; and it will be better to close this consideration of the suggestive or affective range of Conrad's sensory imagery by a glance at a less "Gothic" example, more typical of his normal pitch. In the following extended simile from *Under Western Eyes*, Razumov's features, presented in terms of process, as well as of result, of the sculptor's art, convey an impression the deliberate ambiguity of which we may well feel to be significant of Razumov's character and destiny:

His good looks would have been unquestionable if it had not been for a peculiar lack of fineness in the features. It was as if a face modelled vigorously in wax (with some approach to a classical correctness of type) had been held close to a fire till all sharpness of line had been lost in the softening of the material.[44]

The image bears some resemblance to the more extended image Henry James employed to introduce Miss Birdseye in *The Bostonians* [45] but the suggestions implicit in James's image contain none of the ambiguity of Conrad's image, in which the two antithetic impressions of vigor and softness are, so to speak, held in solution. It is arguable that Conrad had no more in mind than to present to the reader's view a characteristically blunt-featured

---

[43] *Chance*, p. 384.
[44] *Under Western Eyes*, p. 5.
[45] Henry James, *The Bostonians* (London, Macmillan, 1886), pp. 26 f.

Muscovite type, on the Tolstoy pattern; but by analyzing the result into process he achieved a symbolic image of one of the most complex of his creatures, in whom, as in so many of the characters of Russian fiction, strength and weakness of soul seem indissoluble.

VI

THE DEMON OF ANALOGY

> [L'analogie] précise l'écho mystérieux des choses, et leur
> secrète harmonie, aussi réelle, aussi certaine qu'un rapport
> mathématique à tous esprits artistes.
>
> Valéry, Letter to Mallarmé

I undertake in this chapter to characterize the figurative texture
and to survey the principal thematic strains or currents of metaphor in the following novels, with publication dates extending
from 1895 to 1904: *Almayer's Folly, The Nigger of the "Narcissus", Lord Jim, Nostromo.* In the next chapter I shall consider
the following novels published from 1907 to 1923: *The Secret
Agent, Under Western Eyes, The Arrow of Gold, The Rover.* Of
the six (completed) novels omitted from this survey one – *The
Shadow-Line* – is treated at length in a later chapter. My point of
departure in all cases will be, in Sperber's terminology, from the
centers of metaphorical "expansion" rather than from those of
"attraction"; [1] that is to say that the material will be organized
according to the source rather than to the "relatum" of the images,
since it is the source of imagery that largely determines the flow of
the thematic undercurrent. The survey that follows is not exhaustive; from it, however, the reader may derive an approximate notion, comprehensive in scope if not in detail, of the range of
repertory and the relative frequency of metaphors drawn from the
major sources of Conradian imagery.

---

[1] Hans Sperber, *Einführung in die Bedeutungslehre*, 2nd ed. (Leipzig,
1930), chs. IV-X. Cited in Stephen Ullmann, *The Image in the Modern
French Novel: Gide, Alain-Fournier, Proust, Camus* (Cambridge, The University Press, 1960), p. 168.

ALMAYER'S FOLLY (1895)

To focus upon the verbal imagery of Conrad's first novel, in abstraction from other aspects, is not an exhilarating experience. Only in occasional flashes does one find reflected in it the great talent discernible in the ordonnance of the book, in the firm delineation of the principal characters, in much of the expository prose, and in a number of admirably conducted individual episodes – of which I mention only the collapse and death of Almayer and the excellent comic passage between Lakamba and Babalatchi (chapter six), foreshadowing the treatment of certain of the politicos of Costaguana. It is as though a specific imaginative faculty remained latent, as though his sensory apprehension of the physical world – evident enough in a number of non-metaphoric descriptive passages – could not, or could only rarely, grasp the object through a figurative medium. With the notable exception of personification, however. Appreciably over ten percent of all the figurative locutions in *Almayer* are of this species; and whatever we may think of the pathetically fallacious (or fallaciously pathetic) in fiction, the personifications in this novel, most of them applied to the vegetation of the tropical forest and concentrated in two episodes, constitute almost the only distinctive feature in its metaphoric texture. I should say that they also comprise the only image-group that has a thematic significance and contributes to the "underthought" of the novel. (Only one critic, so far as I find, has specifically denied thematic significance to the vegetation imagery in *Almayer*;[2] but few have concerned themselves with the question and those do not agree on the theme signified. Since I deal with this matter in a later chapter I shall say no more about it here.)

Of the remaining figures of speech in the novel half at least come from the *Capharnaum* of the "ready-made expression" (to

---

[2] *Viz.*, Vernon Young, who declared that "the recurrent underlining of parasitical death in the surrounding jungle is gratuitous throughout, not attributed to the projections of a character as it is in *An Outcast of the Islands* (or in 'Heart of Darkness')" (Vernon Young, "Lingard's Folly: The Lost Subject", *The Art of Joseph Conrad: A Critical Symposium*, ed. R. W. Stallman, Lansing, Michigan State University Press, 1960, p. 100).

adopt an expression ready-made from Flaubert); and of these, few have the colloquial sap that many of Marlow's commonplace expressions reveal, and none is exposed to the dialectical play that in later Conrad will often extract meat from the oldest chestnut. They are rarely pretentiously literary, but they are sometimes awkwardly mixed, and when unmixed they are, for the most part, inert.[3]

The original metaphors on the other hand – and particularly those which undertake to image affective states – are sometimes pretentious and they are only rarely illuminative. We can see in *Almayer* that the impulse toward imagery of interior states (which after *The Nigger of the "Narcissus"* was to preponderate over the external imagery) was strong in Conrad from the first: the interior images in this novel have approximately the same frequency as the exterior (slightly greater, in fact, by my reckoning). But their quality is another matter; and of this I shall only say that the writer of *Almayer* is a long way from the "impression-éclair" that Fernández praised and in which he detected Conrad's originality. There is no need to illustrate: it is sufficient to refer the reader to Dain's response to Nina's "look of surrender" – with the assurance, however, that this is the least successful (largely because it is the most prolix) passage of the sort in the novel.[4] That passage

---

[3] Two examples will serve to illustrate: "Almayer looked vainly westward for a ray of light out of the gloom of his shattered hopes" (p. 28); "the decision issued from the fog-veiled offices of the Borneo Company darkened for Almayer the brilliant sunshine of the Tropics, and added another drop of bitterness to the cup of his disenchantments" (p. 34). In the first example Almayer's shattered hopes give "convulsive twitches" (Fowler) in the face of his attempts to extract light out of their gloom. The second example is composite and illustrates a change rather than a mixture of metaphors; expressively considered, however, one feels that the decision referred to presents an aspect of metaphoric ambiguity at odds with its practical aspect, which is unambiguous. But this is perhaps a quibble – since the conventionality of both terms of the metaphor discourages any reflection upon its expressive function.

[4] *Almayer's Folly*, pp. 171 f. The passage is cited by both Thomas Moser (*Joseph Conrad: Achievement and Decline*, Cambridge, Harvard University Press, 1957, p. 52) and Albert Guerard (*Conrad the Novelist*, p. 75) as an instance of confusion of purpose. I mention it here for its confusion of diction and because, at considerable verbal expense, it fails to coalesce into a convincing image.

anticipates the straining toward expressiveness by verbal accumulation rather than by sharpening of the image which will mark extensive stretches of prose in the climactic chapters of the *Outcast* and which will flaw that ambitious book more seriously than its predecessor is flawed by its inexpressive metaphors.

I should not want to give the impression that Conrad produced nothing but mediocrity or worse in the expressed comparisons of his first novel. The personifications apart – and these, if excessive in their affectivity, betray the sort of excess in which Guerard justly saw the promise of later stylistic achievement [5] –, there is a handful of verbal images which anticipate the vividness he was later to achieve: e.g., the atmospheric evocation of "a film of dark, thread-like clouds, looking like immense cobwebs drifting under the stars", the rather ornate but undeniably vivid glimpse of an "islet which lay bathed in sunshine, the yellow sands of its encircling beach shining like an inlaid golden disc on the polished steel of the unwrinkled sea" – this latter the only simile in an extended paragraph of visual presentment (describing the entrance of Almayer's canoe into the Straits) which, in its entirety, would not dishonor any of its author's later novels.[6] Moreover there is at the other end of the novel a metaphor with animal reference (one of a small garner of animal images in *Almayer*) that anticipates Conrad's, and particularly Marlow's, later exploitation of the suggestive resources of the animal kingdom. I have in mind the succinct evocation of Hudig and Lingard disputing in the private office of Hudig's godown: "two mastiffs fighting over a marrowy bone".[7]

THE NIGGER OF THE "NARCISSUS" (1897)

But consideration in the ensemble of the verbal imagery of *Almayer* (and of its successor) impresses one not simply with the

---

[5] Cf. Guerard's remark apropos of a "purple patch" in "The Lagoon" that the passage "suggests that the true Conradian style was, like certain other great styles, achieved through the disciplining of initial excess" (Guerard, *op. cit.*, pp. 67 f.).

[6] *Almayer's Folly*, pp. 175, 186.

[7] *Ibid.*, p. 8.

great advance made in the third novel, but with the importance to Conrad's development of the sort of discipline he imposed on himself in writing *The Nigger* – which with respect to imagery, as in some other respects, may be viewed as the author's diploma-piece. To attain to the sort of impressionistic vividness he was later to achieve in his interior imagery he had first to direct his gaze strenuously outward upon the visible surfaces of things and acquire that spontaneous mastery of the imagery of direct sensuous impression which was later to furnish an example to a poetic movement. Here, as I have indicated, he found his own example in Flaubert: and most of the images I have already cited from *The Nigger* were cited in this connection. But those apparent echoes or adaptations of his great predecessor count quantitatively for very little in the totality of this densely figurative book, of which the general texture, much as it undoubtedly owes to Flaubert, is still distinctively Conradian. It is, however, to be distinguished from the imagery of the works to follow in several respects: in the quite exceptional preponderance of sensory over psychological or interior images; in the continued frequency of personifications; in the virtual absence of "nuclear" development of single images; and in the relative paucity of recurrent or thematic imagery.

Here I recall some of the images from *The Nigger* already cited: the rhetorical image of the stars, repeated in modified form but with an unmistakable echoing effect, the metaphor of Wait's "black mist", the simile of the sailing-ship men "like stone caryatides" and that of the jackets of "crumpled sheet iron" (cited in the fourth chapter, where I pointed out their Flaubertian prototypes); the images of the tug like an aquatic beetle, and of Jimmy rising "like a black buoy", the only examples that I find in this book of that "nuclear" development of a verbal image that will become so striking a feature of style in *Lord Jim* and the works to follow (cited in the foregoing chapter).

The repetition of the rhetorical similitude of stars and the hearts of men is echoed by a later similitude of shadows and the thoughts of men, completing a dispersed triad; [8] and this is matched by

8 "the shadows darker than the night and more restless than the thoughts

another triad: the repeated seasonal imagery, in which portions of
the ship's day are likened to seasons of the year.[9] Add to these
the evocation, in the final paragraph, of "the dark River of the
Nine Bends", and the muster on that "forlorn stream" of a quasi-
Vergilian "crew of Shades", and consider also the conventional
epithets (*epitheta ornantia*) sprinkled through the work,[10] and one
sees that there is a velleity of epic patterning in this novel, distinguishing it from the major works to follow, of which the typical
structure (though never without evidences of deliberate calculation) appears in its main features to have been empirically evolved
and suggests rather a principle of organic growth than of
architectonics.

There is an exceptional frequency of images with animal
reference, about half of which refer to mammals (including bat
and porpoise), and over half of the remainder to birds. There are
about six times as many of these as in *Almayer's Folly* – as many
as D.L. Demorest reported for Flaubert's much longer *Salammbô*.
Like most of the similes in this book, they arise from the immediate occasion and discharge their function in lending vividness.
With the exception of a single series they do not organize into
systems for purposes of consistent characterization or evocation.
Few are elaborated beyond the addition of a single modifier or so.
Many are colloquial and commonplace, part of the small change
of forecastle conversation, though sometimes occurring in narration: "strong as a horse", "mute as a fish", "gentle as lambs", "die
alone like a dog", "comin' at me like a mad bull", "caught like a
bloomin' rat in a trap". As commonly with Conradian animal
similes most are specific (in the strict terminological sense) but a
significant number are, not generic, but general – examples of that
deliberate refusal of the explicit which, early and late, will
characterize an appreciable number of Conrad's figurative locu-

---

of men" (*The Nigger of the "Narcissus"*, p. 145. Cf. pp. 29, 77).

[9]   *Ibid.*, pp. 31, 132, 145. Conrad's patterning cannot be said to be rigid:
he omits one season and scrambles the sequence of the remaining three.

[10]   Cf., e.g., the phrase "sleep, the consoler" (p. 24) and the various
epithets applied to the sea: "the mysterious sea" (pp. 25, 26), "the immortal sea" (p. 155), "the insatiable sea" (p. 157), "the heartless sea"
(p. 159), "the immortal and unresting sea" (p. 162).

tions. The range is for the most part Aesopian: with rare exceptions Conrad confines himself, here and elsewhere, to the *lieux communs* of the animal kingdom. The single out-of-the-way animal referent (springbok [11]) strikes one as an exotic among the other creatures of Conrad's metaphoric bestiary.

The more significant zoological references are avian. The ship is imaged repeatedly as a "great sea-bird", a "great tired bird", her sails as "white wings".[12] The single case of the Dickensian (and later-Conradian) device of characterization by repeated reference to a class of animals is the presentment of Donkin as a bird. Imaged in his first introduction to the scene with shoulders "peaked and drooped like the broken wings of a bird", Donkin assumes a definitively avian aspect half-way further on in the book, at the time of his attendance on the dying Wait, when he flourishes "a hand hard and fleshless like the claw of a snipe", displays "a conical, fowl-like profile", jerks "his bird face down at [Wait] as though pecking at the eyes". Meanwhile Wait confers upon him avian epithets: "a screechin' poll-parrot", "a dirty white cockatoo". In a later scene he is imaged as "hanging a peaked nose", like a "sick vulture with ruffled plumes".[13]

Since I shall speak briefly of the personifications in *The Nigger* in a later chapter, I need not linger over them here, except to point out that Conrad is prodigal of these as of all other figures of speech in this book, and that a significant proportion of the personifications are objectively conceived. When the narrator tells us that "the ship tossed about, shaken furiously, like a toy in the hand of a lunatic" or speaks of the rush of a "big, foaming sea" that "looked as mischievous and discomposing as a madman with an axe", we are aware of an aesthetic distancing, a play of the author's imagination over his material, that we do not feel in

[11] "... absurd little Belfast ... with both feet leaped straight up like a springbok" (*ibid.*, p. 68).
[12] *Ibid.*, pp. 57, 161, 163.
[13] *Ibid.*, pp. 10, 105, 110 f., 128. One should perhaps add in this connection, ignoring Linnaean distinctions, that Donkin's "big ears stood out, transparent and veined, resembling the thin wings of a bat" (p. 110). With the avian images in *The Nigger* cf. the feline similes applied to Ricardo in *Victory* – the most insistent example of this sort of characterization in all of Conrad's work.

connection with the vegetation imagery in *Almayer* and *Outcast*.[14]

The coruscating visual similes imaging aspects of sea and sky and ship tempt one to quotation at length, but I content myself with a few illustrative examples with related reference, which, taken together with certain images already quoted (the ship as pyramid and the tug as black beetle, the ship as sea-bird, Donkin as vulture), will suggest that one of the ways to read *The Nigger* is as an extended exercise in the Imagist mode: "It towered close-to and high, like a wall of green glass"; "the moonlight clung to her like a frosted mist, and the white sails stood out in dazzling cones as of stainless snow".[15]

But if a quite exceptional proportion of the verbal imagery of this novel is aimed at an enthralment of the inner eye and at a continuous quickening of the imaginative faculties, in the strictest sense, the novel is, of course, much more than a succession of magic-lantern slides. It has its theme and its mythos; and there is one family of images in the book that points, with an iteration as unmistakable as one can find in any metaphoric sequence in his work, toward the central crisis of the novel. *The Nigger* has been much interpreted, and perhaps over-interpreted. A reinterpretation of the novel "in depth" does not fall within the scope of the present study. For purposes of this chapter it is, in any case, only necessary to remind the reader of Conrad's declared intention to make James Wait "the centre of the ship's collective psychology and the pivot of the action".[16]

In this intention he succeeded. And whatever else we see in Jimmy – he has been seen as a Jonah figure, as a Jungian shadow-archetype, as a Satan attended by Donkin as Mephistopheles – we may say that he is moribund, and that his long dying, his final demise (following the episode of the storm and his rescue), and his subsequent sea-burial are essential determinants both of action and of "collective psychology". I would propose as the other

[14]   *Ibid.*, pp. 53, 57.
[15]   *Ibid.*, pp. 57, 103, 145. Guerard found in the last-quoted passage and the imagery surrounding it, evoking the ship "under the cold sheen of the dead moon", an "appeal to the reader's recollection of *The Ancient Mariner*" (Guerard, *op. cit.*, p. 119).
[16]   "To My Readers in America", *The Nigger of the "Narcissus"*, p. ix.

major motif of the work the theme of initiation: the initiation, in stress and peril, of the seamen into the values of their craft.[17] Allegorical suggestions cling to Jimmy – the "emanating black mist", the repeated references to his "veiled familiar" – but these are metaphoric locutions, registering affective impressions. Wait is not a "collective representation" but a seaman like the others, with a human history and antecedents. Nevertheless, as focus and pretext of the crew's unrests and apprehensions he is, in a proper sense of the word, a symbolic figure; and about his moribund frame, looming up with the head in shadow or reclining stiffly, a "black idol" in a "silver shrine", is waged a sort of Manichaean conflict between the life-sustaining and the life-sapping forces, the latter sophistically disguised as pity and comradely devotion ("The latent egoism of tenderness to suffering appeared in the developing anxiety not to see him die" [18]). It does not appear that Conrad intended Wait as a projection of the specific horror of death (*timor mortis*): though he speaks of "scared looks" during the storm (and retrospectively of "our horrible scare") he does not present the crew as demoralized by fear during the crisis.[19] The term *Daseinsangst* proposed by Johanna Burkhardt to characterize the anxieties of the crew (responding to – and finding their symbolic focus in – Wait's *Todesangst*) is perhaps as suggestive a term as any for the purpose.[20] But however we define the psycho-

[17] "Haven't we, together and upon the immortal sea, wrung out a meaning from our sinful lives?" asks the narrator in the last paragraph of the book (p. 173). Earlier the theme of initiation had been sounded, but in a contrary sense, crystallizing about the demoralizing figure of James Wait: "we had the air of being initiated in some infamous mysteries; we had the profound grimaces of conspirators, exchanged meaning glances, significant short words. We were inexpressibly vile and very much pleased with ourselves" (p. 139). For a development of this theme cf. James E. Miller, "*The Nigger of the 'Narcissus'*: A Re-examination", *PMLA*, LXVI (December 1951), pp. 911-918.

[18] *The Nigger of the "Narcissus"*, p. 138.

[19] *Ibid.*, pp. 87, 100.

[20] Johanna Burkhardt, *Das Erlebnis der Wirklichkeit und seine Künstlerische Gestaltung in Joseph Conrads Werk* (Marburg, H. Bauer, 1935), p. 40. Miss Burkhardt emphasized the symbolic significance of the crew's forgetfulness of Wait during the crisis (*Grenzsituation*) of the storm, in which the *Daseinsangst* is, as it were, dissolved: "In dieser höchsten Gefahr die blosse Daseinsangst plötzlich schwindet und jeder seinen Mann steht

logical nexus that exists between Wait and the others, Jimmy's death and the process of his dying must figure as a major theme against which other discoverable themes are counterpointed.

It was of this novel that Conrad asserted: "I tried to get through the veil of details at the essence of life"; but if we concentrate on the figurative undercurrent of the novel we may well think that he was no less concerned to distil a sort of metaphoric essence of death. A number of the mortuary images relate directly, as we would expect, to James Wait, that collective shadow-figure who from the first is himself shadowed by death as a "veiled familiar". His first fit of coughing, symptom of his illness, resounds in the forecastle "like two explosions in a vault"; trapped in his cabin during the storm, he is heard "screaming and knocking below us with the hurry of a man prematurely shut up in a coffin"; three pages later we are told that "he was as quiet as a dead man inside a grave; and, like men standing above a grave, we were on the verge of tears".[21] Much later, as his agony approaches, his flesh-less head is likened to "a disinterred black skull, fitted with two restless globes of silver in the sockets of eyes"; under the glare of Donkin, come to torment him for the last time, he moves "no more than a recumbent figure with clasped hands, carved on the lid of a stone coffin"; his smile in his last moments is already as "frightful . . . as the sudden smile of a corpse".[22]

The metaphoric influence of Jimmy's "veiled familiar" extends beyond his own person. Until the moment when death has actual-ly claimed its victim it imposes its presence throughout. The bodies of the crew are lost in the gloom of the berths "that resembled narrow niches for coffins in a whitewashed and lighted mortuary"; again, "the double row of berths yawned black, like graves tenanted by uneasy corpses"; the forecastle is "quiet as a sepulchre". Much later we see Singleton looming in the smoky

---

für das Ganze" (*ibid.*). Cf. Guerard who, in the course of a very close and suggestive scrutiny of *The Nigger*, has also noted the importance of this forgetfulness of Wait during the storm and of "the pattern of Wait's presences and absences" generally (Guerard, *Conrad the Novelist*, p. 111).
[21]   *The Nigger of the "Narcissus"*, pp. 18, 66, 69. Wait offers his own version of the grave image in reporting his sensations to Donkin (p. 106).
[22]   *Ibid.*, pp. 139, 147, 149.

forecastle "like a statue of heroic size in the gloom of a crypt".[23] Nor is the figure confined to the enclosed areas of cabin or forecastle. Captain Allistoun rises at night "out of the darkness of the companion, such as a phantom above a grave".[24] The ambiguity of a nautical term suffices to evoke the image, as when, at the height of the storm, a sudden gust catches the men in the rigging and pins "all up the shrouds the whole crawling line in attitudes of crucifixion". Recumbency and the stillness of sleep evoke the dominant image: Mr. Baker in the dark, on all fours among the dormant men, resembles "some carnivorous animal prowling amongst corpses".[25] As Donkin emerges from the cabin in which Jimmy has expired, the image of the grave defines his first impression: "Sleeping men, huddled under jackets, made on the lighted deck shapeless dark mounds that had the appearance of neglected graves." [26] Inanimate objects are affected by the contagion, and the image takes on an aspect of violence and mutilation: "Hung-up suits of oilskin swung out and in, lively and disquieting like reckless ghosts of decapitated seamen dancing in a tempest" (p. 54).

The method of simple enumeration, all but divorced from the nexus of narration, description, reflection in which the images have their being, may suggest on Conrad's part a too deliberate and calculated intent. Certainly we may detect in the mortuary imagery of this novel, as in a number of the image-sequences to be examined further on, evidence of that "rich passion for extremes" which Henry James demanded of the novelist and which Conrad's ideal of artistic discipline never entirely bred out of him. Whether, in the particular instance, the passion was indulged to the enrichment of the novel can only be judged in context. I think that it was; but my quotations can do no more than establish the

---

[23]   *Ibid.*, pp. 8, 22, 24; 129.
[24]   *Ibid.*, p. 30. The unidiomatic "such as" – more common in early than in later Conrad – may be viewed as a Gallicism ("tel que") or, as Professor Ludwig Krzyżanowski has pointed out, as a Polonism.
[25]   *Ibid.*, pp. 56; 78.
[26]   *Ibid.*, p. 155. Against this, in the same paragraph, the sea presents itself to Donkin's eyes as "the image of life, with a glittering surface and lightless depths".

theme of mortality as a metaphoric *Leitmotiv* of the novel, functioning in intimate relation with its discursive themes.

LORD JIM (1900)

When we come to *Lord Jim* we enter country in which the metaphoric growth is denser even than that of *The Nigger of the "Narcissus"*. Moreover the individual specimens often reach a greater spread and reveal to the inquiring eye affiliations that are both more numerous and subtler. In their figurative texture alone, without regard to other aspects, *Lord Jim* and the novels to follow suggest the Baudelairean "forest of symbols". In dealing with them – and particularly with *Lord Jim*, the most densely figurative of all Conrad's novels – I can do no more than indicate some of the principal threads in the fabric, illustrate their linkages, and suggest their relation to dominant themes and to certain objective images.

I start with what is perhaps simplest, the images with zoological reference. Though not more frequent than those in *The Nigger of the "Narcissus"*, *Lord Jim*'s zoological images are, I should say, the most significant ensemble of animal images in Conrad's fiction – even though they include many frank colloquialisms largely deprived by usage of their imaging function. In several instances they contribute by recurrence to individual characterization. In several episodes – particularly in the account of Marlow's interview with the chief engineer, in whose batrachian visions centipedes figure as well as "millions of pink toads as big as mastiffs", and in the narrative of the night in the boat – they contribute measurably, together with the related vocabulary of epithet that clusters around them, to our affective response.[27] And in one instance animal epithets serve, discreetly but unmistakably, as a *ficelle,* harkening back from one crisis to an earlier crisis to which it is dramatically or psychologically related.

It ought to be added here that in *Lord Jim* (as not in *The Nigger*,

---

[27] For the chief engineer's visions cf. *Lord Jim*, pp. 51-55. The night in the boat comprises chapter X of the novel.

in spite of the pig-sty on board the *Narcissus* [28]) the metaphoric animals have their evoked being within a context that accommodates a fairly significant representation of objective animal life. There is no non-human creature in *Lord Jim* so insistently pressed on our attention as Fyne's dog in *Chance.* or the "steed of apocalyptic misery" in *The Secret Agent,* or even perhaps Tekla's cat in *Under Western Eyes;* but there is a greater variety of objective (i.e., non-figurative) animal reference in *Lord Jim* than in any other Conrad novel. Apart from a number of allusions (the devotion of Brierly's retriever, the passing reference to a buffalo in the overheard testimony in the assault case that follows the *Patna* inquiry) [29] in which I see no more than the novelist's feeling for his milieu and his instinct for objective specification of its characteristic elements, there is one episode whose contribution both to event and to characterization is unmistakable. I have in mind the "yellow-dog" incident following the inquiry, which occasions the first spoken communication between Marlow and Jim. Finally, there are Stein's preserved specimens – his butterflies and beetles. [30]

Of Stein and his collection, and especially of his Celebes butterfly, I shall have something to say in the ninth chapter. Here I want only to indicate two rather particularized, but highly illustrative, effects that they have on the subsequent verbal imagery of the novel. Our recollection of Stein's butterflies – in addition to the more metaphysical implications one may intuit in them – lends intensity to the later evocations of Jewel and her "tenderness" under the aspects of unfolding and fluttering wings. [31] And Marlow's account of the beetles ("horrible miniature monsters, looking malevolent in death and immobility" [32]) supplies a prospective context for the insectile epithets later to be applied to

[28]   *The Nigger of the "Narcissus",* p. 32.
[29]   *Lord Jim,* pp. 58-64 (*passim*), p. 71.
[30]   The "yellow-dog" episode, prospectively mentioned on p. 34, is recounted on pp. 70-74; Stein's collection is introduced on p. 203, referred to throughout chapter XX, reverted to occasionally thereafter, and especially in the last sentence of the book.
[31]   "Her tenderness hovered over him like a flutter of wings" (p. 283); "two wide sleeves uprose in the dark like unfolding wings" (p. 308).
[32]   *Ibid.,* p. 203.

Cornelius. Cornelius' first introduction to the scene under his emblematic sign is sufficiently hair-raising of itself; [33] but it derives an increment of energy from our recollection of Marlow on *Buprestidae* and *Longicorns*.

The yellow-dog episode is one of Conrad's strokes of purely novelistic resourcefulness, admirably contrived to open communication between the two central characters in circumstances revelatory of Jim's temperament and of the defensive-aggressive stance he has adopted ("Who's a cur now – hey?" [34]). But although this episode would requre no other *raison d'être*, it lends a resonance to a number of colloquial dog references, seemingly casual: to Jim's evocation of the captain and the chief engineer in the boat, "yapping before me like a couple of mean mongrels at a tree'd thief", and the dog imitations that follow ("Yap! yap! Bow-ow-ow-ow-ow! Yap! yap!"); to his muttered "go to the dogs as likely as not", in response to Marlow's inquiry as to his plans at the end of Jim's recital at the Malabar House; and to Marlow's responsive reflection: "But he was too interesting or too unfortunate to be thrown to the dogs, or even to Chester." [35]

In speaking earlier of Conrad's sense of "le grotesque triste" (Flaubert's term) and of the stimulus provided by matter of this sort to his image-making faculty, I have noted the abundance of figurative expressions accreting to the persons of the *Patna*'s crew. Here I need only add that animal imagery in particular proliferates in the episodes in which the grotesques figure, and that it is especially in this connection that the contagion of the imagery is, so to speak, evident in the vocabulary. What I have in mind is the

[33] "His slow laborious walk resembled the creeping of a repulsive beetle, the legs alone moving with horrid industry while the body glided evenly" (p. 285). Cf. on p. 286: "can one imagine a loathsome insect in love?" and on p. 323: "he bolted out, vermin-like, from the long grass. ..."

[34] *Ibid.*, p. 73.

[35] *Ibid.*, pp. 117 f., 155, 177. Before leaving the dog imagery in this book, it may be mentioned simply as a descriptive item that Conrad is exceptionally specific about the reference of a number of the canine similes in *Lord Jim*. These include – aside from mastiffs and mongrels – a greyhound, retrievers, a spaniel, a "well-bred hound", and the "two china dogs on a mantel-piece" in whose likeness Marlow and the French lieutenant confront each other at the abrupt end of their interview (pp. 13, 32, 372, 248, 148).

application to human subjects or agents of animal epithets, and of terms originally, or characteristically, applied to animals. I have no doubt that one could duplicate all, or almost all, of the following words from other sources in Conrad, but I seriously doubt that any other of his novels, with the sole exception of *Victory*, employs such a vocabulary with such insistence. Virtually all of the following words are applied repeatedly to characters in *Lord Jim*, many of them with marked frequency; and most of them occur in connection (*inter alia*) with the *Patna*'s crew, or with the insectile Cornelius:

Verbs: creep, crawl, grub, hawk, nestle, prowl, ruffle, shepherd, slink, trample, wag, wriggle; bark, bellow, bleat, cackle, crow, growl, grunt, howl, screech, snarl, snort, yap.

Nouns: ass, beast, brute, cattle, cur, hound, hyaena, insect, owls, popinjay, puppy, skunk; carcase, claw, gullet, shanks, tentacle; game, prey, spawn, specimen; flutter, yelp; cock-pit, humbug, scarecrow.

Modifiers: beastly, cocky, dogged, fishy, mulish, shrewish, sluggish, wolfish; mangy, venomous.[36]

The nouns listed are those employed in epithet, though a number of them are also employed in simile or metaphor. Add to them the vehicular terms from the eighty zoological images, accounting for almost ten per cent of all figurative locutions in the novel, and one has an evoked bestiary of considerable diversity and range, in which are mirrored the acts and gestures of the human characters. In certain areas of the prose there is something approaching saturation, of both imagery and vocabulary, constituting one of the rhetorical modes of the novel, and also, scarcely less conspicuously than in Shakespeare's later plays, one of its significant symbolic modes. Without attempting to catalogue the imagery in all its variety, I shall leave the topic with a brief identification of an instance in which two successive animal

---

[36] Phrasal referents in similes, other than the animal specimens themselves, include ant-heap, cage of beasts, disturbed hive, dumb pack, poultry yard, sheep-pen, spider's web. And cf. such metaphors as "feathered his nest", "licked their chops", "singeing your wings", and Chester's "piece of ass's skin".

references (a colloquial simile and a slang epithet) awake reson-
nances, and serve in collaboration both as *ficelle* and as a
contributory determinant of action – or, more strictly, of *in*action.
The scene in question is the parley across the creek between Jim
and Gentleman Brown, in which Brown – by luck, by instinct, by
a sort of sixth sense – touches the nerve of recollection in Jim,
evoking, in a succession of inspired references, "a sickening suggestion of common guilt", with the consequence that Jim gives him
the "clear road" he asks for. In a context of more explicit references to Jim's disgrace Brown uses the epithet "fishy": "He asked
Jim whether he had nothing fishy in his life to remember"; and we
recall (though perhaps only on a rereading of the novel), and know
that Jim recalls, that this was the formula ("something fishy") in
which Jim had expressed, during his recital to Marlow at Malabar
House, his sense of the suspicions aroused on board the *Avondale*
after that ship had picked up the four derelicts from the *Patna*.[37]

Moreover Brown's earlier identification of himself with "a rat
in a trap" – a simile developed in dialogue with Jim and emerging
finally in Brown's plea (as reported to Marlow): "I would have
thought him too white to serve even a rat so"[38] – harkens back to
the formula with which Egström had expressed his bafflement at
Jim's abrupt throwing up of his job:

" 'What is it you're running away from?' I asks. 'Who has been getting
at you? What scared you? You haven't as much sense as a rat; they
don't clear out from a good ship. . . . This business ain't going to sink,'
says I. He gave a big jump." (p. 195)

The implicit reference back to the abandonment of the *Patna*, via
the exchange with Egström, is unmistakable. In these two instances we may see telling examples of the seriousness of Conrad's
engagement with the vocabulary of his adopted language, his
instinct for "revitalizing clichés" (as Las Vergnas put it) and
resuscitating the buried metaphors of vulgar speech. For it is
through these verbal echoes (enforced, as we shall see, by others
more sonorous) that Jim's susceptibility to the "sickening suggestion of common guilt" is made actual to the reader.

[37]   *Lord Jim*, pp. 387, 82.
[38]   *Ibid.*, p. 381.

The "cosmic image" – understood as a variant of a basic trope in which a fragment of human reality is suddenly envisaged within a framework of cosmic events – is recurrent in Conrad, not so much a device of style as an ineluctable modality of his vision of the human, as it was with the Elizabethan and Jacobean dramatists.[39] The image of ship as planet, first evoked in the early pages of *The Nigger of the "Narcissus"* ("The ship, a fragment detached from the earth, went on lonely and swift like a small planet") and re-evoked twenty years later in *The Shadow-Line*, may be taken as the type-image, symbolizing the cosmic perspectives evoked in related metaphors in perhaps a dozen novels and stories.[40] It is in *Lord Jim*, however, that such imagery is most insistent and most unmistakably symbolic. The planetary image applied to the *Patna* sounds the first note of this metaphoric *sostenuto* which, in a sort of canonic relation to the meteorological imagery, will continue to sound throughout the novel:

The ship moved so smoothly that her onward motion was imperceptible to the senses of men, as though she had been a crowded planet speeding through the dark spaces of ether behind the swarm of suns, in the appalling and calm solitudes awaiting the breath of future creations. (pp. 21f.)

The close relation between cosmic and meteorological imagery in the novel is typified by the final sentence in the paragraph of description devoted to the dining-room of the Malabar House:

The riding lights of ships winked afar like setting stars, and the hills across the roadstead resembled rounded black masses of arrested thunder-clouds. (pp. 78f.)

The most insistent and imposing objective image in the novel is that of Jim's "lunar spectacle", the repeated rising of the moon between the twin peaks of Patusan, to which Marlow devotes three dispersed paragraphs of description and reflection.[41] I shall not

[39] Cf. Ford on Conrad: "*Homo europaeus sapiens*, attuned to the late sixteenth century" (Ford, *Joseph Conrad, A Personal Remembrance*, p. 11).
[40] *The Nigger of the "Narcissus"*, p. 29. "My command might have been a planet flying vertiginously on its appointed path in a space of infinite silence" (*The Shadow-Line*, p. 74). And cf. Marlow on the stir aboard the *Ferndale* as it prepares to weigh anchor: "like the awakening to life of a world about to be launched into space" (*Chance*, p. 274).
[41] *Lord Jim*, pp. 220 f., 245 f., 322.

illustrate here the verbal images embedded in them, since I quote the passages at length in a later chapter; but they must be held in mind here as major symbolic items in the novel's system of cosmic imagery. They set up resonances throughout the book. The kinesthetics of the image (the moon floating up "like an ascending spirit out of a grave" [42]) may recall for us Marlow's image – evoked by Jim's recital – of the sunrise following the abandonment of the *Patna*: "the tremble of a vast ripple running over all the visible expanse of the sea, as if the waters had shuddered, giving birth to the globe of light" (p. 123). It can evoke also the counter-image in which Jim's last apocalyptic glimpse of the *Patna*'s yellow mast-head light had been communicated: "high up and blurred like a last star ready to dissolve" (p. 112). Marlow's analysis of the properties of moonlight, his metaphysical contrast of moon to sun, the presented chiaroscuro of the passages in question, recall in their varied aspects several antecedent passages of verbal or objective imagery. They recall the sustained chiaroscuro of the first Stein-Marlow scene, with its profoundly ambiguous evocations ("a charming and deceptive light, throwing the impalpable poesy of its dimness over pitfalls – over graves"; "its crepuscular light, overshadowed in the centre, circled with a bright edge as if surrounded by an abyss full of flames"; "the flicker of two flames . . . stealing silently across the depths of a crystalline void"; "the sudden revelations of human figures stealing with flickering flames within unfathomable and pellucid depths" [43]). They recall Marlow's reflections on "that side of us which, like the other hemisphere of the moon, exists stealthily in perpetual darkness, with only a fearful ashy light falling at times on the edge" (p. 93). And the sun-moon antithesis (moonlight "like the ghost of dead sunlight. . . what the echo is to the sound" [44]) recalls, or is recalled by, images of Jim under solar illumination: aft in the brigantine at his departure for Patusan, "detached upon the light of the western-ing sun, raising his cap high above his head", while Marlow watches, his eyes "too dazzled by the glitter of the sea below his

[42] *Ibid.*, p. 245.
[43] *Ibid.*, p. 215 f.
[44] *Ibid.*, p. 246.

feet to see him clearly"; in Patusan during Marlow's visit, "high in the sunshine on the top of that historic hill of his", a figure "set upon a pedestal", dominating "the forest, the secular gloom, the old mankind", with Marlow's recollection of "the incident which had given a new direction to his life" figuring (in the final sentence) as "a shadow in the light"; or again Marlow's final glimpse of Jim on the shore in the twilight of a setting sun, "white from head to foot", at last "a speck, a tiny white speck, that seemed to catch all the light left in a darkened world".[45]

This light-dark imagery links in turn with the climatic and meteorological imagery repeatedly applied to Jim. ("You know", Marlow remarks, "that sailor habit of referring to the weather in every connection." [46]) Marlow's phrase, "under a cloud",[47] repeated throughout the second half of the book with characteristic Marlovian iteration, and recurring at the very end, is the emblematic image here; but Jim's affinity for this sort of imagery has been evidenced much earlier in several of the most arresting examples in the novel of ostensibly visual imagery bent to purposes of characterization – or perhaps one had better say (having regard to the inenarrably metaphoric nature of the operation) to the purpose of evoking an "interior landscape". The first registers Marlow's impression of Jim on their first encounter (the "yellow-dog" episode):

to watch his face was like watching a darkening sky before a clap of thunder, shade upon shade imperceptibly coming on, the gloom growing mysteriously intense in the calm of maturing violence. (p. 71)

The second images Jim's expression as he recalls the moments in the boat following his jump:

[45] *Ibid.*, pp. 241, 265, 336. Marlow's final view of Jim is anticipated much earlier in his evoked image of him outlined dimly against the night in the window of the Malabar House. With the Walpole Reef in mind (the site of Chester's guano deposit) he sees Jim as standing "on the brink of a vast obscurity, like a lonely figure by the shore of a sombre and hopeless ocean" (p. 173). The image is recapitulated with minor verbal changes on p. 177.

[46] *Ibid.*, p. 122.

[47] *Ibid.*, pp. 276, 339, 342, 411, 414, 416. Jim's familiar cloud links also, in another of its aspects, with Marlow's repeated evocation of his opportunity "veiled at his side like an Eastern bride" (pp. 243 f., 336, 416).

The muscles round his lips contracted into an unconscious grimace that tore through the mask of his usual expression – something violent, short-lived, and illuminating like a twist of lightning that admits the eye for an instant into the secret convolutions of a cloud (pp. 118f.)

The third expresses Marlow's intuition of Jim at a later point of his recital:

He heard me out with his head on one side, and I had another glimpse through a rent in the mist in which he moved and had his being.[48]

It is not necessary to urge the relationship of these three meteorological images to the recurrent imagery of the abyss that sounds the tonic metaphoric chord, preluding or echoing the basic trope supplied to Marlow by Jim's own tormented eloquence when he defines the terminus of his jump from the *Patna* as "an everlasting deep hole".[49] Around this as node Marlow's evocations of the abyss vibrate. The word "abyss" itself is the nuclear term in no fewer than six similes and metaphors dispersed throughout the *Patna* and into the Patusan chapters, of which the first two belong to the preliminaries of the novel, prior to the *Patna*'s collision: "an abyss of unrest" (defining Jim's state after his injury by a falling spar on the training ship); "the days ... as if falling into an abyss forever open in the wake of the ship". The others follow: "one abyss of obscurity"; "the souls of men floating on an abyss"; "surrounded by an abyss full of flames"; "as if into an abyss".[50] Marlow finds other formulae to evoke the image: "as if poised on the brow of yawning destruction" (p. 26); "felt the ground cut from under his feet" (p. 82); "on the brink of annihilation" (p. 97); "cut off ... by a chasm without bottom" (pp. 103f.); "like being swept by a flood through a cavern" (p. 112); "a network of paths separated by chasms" (p. 130); "bellow to a man you saw about to walk over a cliff" (p. 155); "melted into shapeless gloom like a cavern" (p. 204); "across the depths of a crystalline void" (p. 216); "a

---

[48] *Ibid.*, p. 128. This image is deveolped on the same page and in the pages immediately following; cf. pp. 129, 133.
[49] *Ibid.*, p. 111. The image is picked up by Marlow on the following page and is reverted to later. It links with Brierly's "Let him creep twenty feet underground and stay there" (*ibid.*, p. 66; recalled by Marlow on pp. 202, 219).
[50] *Ibid.*, pp. 11, 16, 102, 121, 215, 264.

jump into the unknown" (p. 229); "plunge your gaze to the bottom of an immensely deep well" (p. 307). One might continue, citing "indefinite immensities", "indefinite open spaces", "the dread of the unknown depths". But the examples cited, taken together with the evocations of celestial immensities, of convoluted clouds, of diminishing perspectives on the shores of darkening seas, suffice to suggest that we have, most densely in the earlier portion of the book, but awakening responses throughout, a sort of saturation of imagery and vocabulary, a rhetorical soaking in a solution that might as accurately be termed "metaphysical" as metaphorical. It is an unmistakably Conradian mixture of a "palpable obscure" and an "intense inane", that is somehow intended, we feel, to afford perspectives upon Jim and his clouded case, and that in any event constitutes the principal metaphoric undercurrent in the novel and perhaps the most insistent and conspicuous in any of Conrad's novels.

I have no notion of defining with precision or adequacy the symbolic operation performed by this cumulus of imagery and epithet. Many of the images may be said, however, to sound overtones on a tonic chord, or variations on a central theme – the theme of a man who, having jumped into a hole, tries to get out, refuses the abyss. Strategically they may be said to prepare us for the scene that precipitates the catastrophe – specifically for the terms of Brown's appeal to Jim as "a man trying to get out of a deadly hole by the first means that came to hand", and for Jim's fatal response to the appeal.[51]

Beyond this they contribute a sort of "pathos of distance", in a sense not intended by Nietzsche. Abstractly viewed, the cosmic perspectives interjected into the human narrative might be expected to shrink the theater of action and its protagonists to minuscule size; and one can, indeed, find in Conrad (in a sentence spoken by the Marlow of *Chance*) an explicit expression of just this sense of the diminution of the creature vis-à-vis the infinite.[52] But the

[51] *Ibid.*, p. 387.
[52] "It was one of those dewy, clear, starry nights, oppressing our spirit, crushing our pride, by the brilliant evidence of the awful loneliness, of the hopeless obscure insignificance of our globe lost in the splendid revelation of a glittering, soulless universe. I hate such skies" (*Chance*, p. 50).

illuminative effects of the heavenly bodies may confound the suggestions of perspective, as Marlow recorded in his account of a sunset over Patusan, noting that "the sun, whose concentrated glare dwarfs the earth into a restless mote of dust, had sunk behind the forest, and the diffused light from an opal sky seemed to cast upon a world without shadows and without brilliance the illusion of a calm and pensive greatness".[53] Much of the meteorological imagery in particular, rather than diminishing the human characters, serves (like that in *King Lear* and other Elizabethan dramas) the function postulated by Baudelaire of "correspondance", symbolizing the human predicaments, motives, psychological states dramatized in the narrative, thus extending the function of landscape (*paysage*) as defined by Mallarmé and illustrated by Flaubert.

Scarcely less prominent is the vein of spectral imagery – metaphoric evocation of ghosts, shades, phantoms, apparitions, wraiths. Obsessive with Conrad, like the cosmic and meteorological imagery, it is, like them, at its highest intensity in *Lord Jim*. The motif is first announced impersonally in the image of the *Patna*'s wake, "like the phantom of a track drawn upon a lifeless sea by the phantom of a steamer". It is sustained by the evocation of the audience at the inquiry as "staring shadows" and the "court peons" flitting "as noiseless as ghosts", of the chief engineer in flight from the inquiry haunted by his "spectral alarms", of Jim awaiting the inquiry as "a ghost without a home to haunt", and of Jim, after judgment has been pronounced, as one who "lived surrounded by deceitful ghosts, by austere shades". It achieves a sinister and unmistakably symbolic intensity in Marlow's suggestion that the *Patna* had been crippled by "a kind of maritime ghoul on the prowl to kill ships in the dark".[54] The Marlovian elaboration of this metaphor, with references to "wandering corpses", sinister gales like "vampires", and "aimless ... devilry", bringing home the implication of possession by "dark powers" latent in the motif of haunting by spectre or shade,

[53]   *Lord Jim*, pp. 305 f.
[54]   *Ibid.*, pp. 16, 29, 32, 50, 82, 154, 159.

suggests a symbolic identification between the "maritime ghoul" and some dangerous unassimilated portion of Jim's psyche.[55]

I need not cite in detail the recurrence of the image as applied to Jim – in metaphors that identify him with the evoked spectre or apparition or, alternatively, that show him as accompanied by, or grappling with, the spectres of imagination and introspection. They culminate in the insistent imagery of Marlow's account of his interview with Jewel (when he "stood up, like an evoked ghost, to answer for [Jim's] eternal constancy" [56]) in which, in a half-dozen or so distinguishable images embedded in a continuous vein of reference to the contrapuntal themes of haunting and exorcism, Marlow conjures up a tableau of two Vergilian shades beside a river "as black as Styx" – in colloquy concerning an absent brother shade ("my brother from the realm of forgetful shades").[57] Brown and his crew are touched by the contagion of Marlow's ghostly reference, "fading spectrally without the slightest sound" when they float away on the fog-shrouded river following the parley with Jim. And the image emerges at the end, in company with the related images of Jim's enveloping cloud and his veiled opportunity, in that final recapitulation of metaphoric and symbolic themes with which Marlow wraps up his narrative:

and yet upon my honor there are moments, too, when he passes from my eyes like a disembodied spirit astray amongst the passions of this earth, ready to surrender himself faithfully to the claim of his own world of shades. (p. 416)

[55]   *Ibid.*, pp. 159 f. On this point cf. Dorothy Van Ghent, "On Lord Jim", *The English Novel: Form and Function* (New York, Rinehart, 1953), p. 234. We may, with Miss Van Ghent, define the symbolic indication here as a form of "collusion" between outer nature and "the hidden portion of the soul", or we may simply call it a "correspondence". Or we may discern no symbolic velleity here at all – but the relation in series of the metaphor to images of haunting and possession applied to Jim seems unmistakable. For allusions to the "Dark Powers" (both capitalized and uncapitalized), cf. *Lord Jim*, pp. 121, 246, 354, 409. In the first context they are introduced in suggestive relation to "the irrational that lurks at the bottom of every thought, sentiment, sensation, emotion". In the third context Brown is identified as their "blind accomplice".
[56]   *Lord Jim*, p. 416.
[57]   *Ibid.*, pp. 312-319. For other imagery with spectral reference applied to Jim, cf. pp. 180, 197, 215, 251.

There is imagery focussing on others among Conrad's obsessive metaphoric themes, mortuary imagery, for example, and imagery of perdition; but one finds that the more arresting images in these classes are apt to be assimilated to the dominant theme of spectral haunting or malevolent enchantment, as in Marlow's assertion that he "listened [to Jim's account of the abandonment of the *Patna*] as if to a tale of black magic at work upon a corpse" (p. 109), or his statement that "the corpse of his [Brown's] mad self-love uprose from rags and destitution as from the dark horrors of a tomb" (p. 383), or (far back toward the beginning of the book) his first formulation of his reaction to "the facts" of the *Patna* affair, following Jim's first appearance before the board of inquiry, when he tells his audience that "they made a whole that had features, shades of expression, a complicated aspect that could be remembered by the eye, and something else besides, something invisible, a directing spirit of perdition that dwelt within, like a malevolent soul in a detestable body" (pp. 30f.). Only in the extended image of "the sword of his country's law" – a characteristic Marlovian elaboration on a metaphoric theme, in which Jim's plight is presented, with reference to the "bowed neck" and the "condemned man", to the "ceremony of execution" and the "fall of the axe", to block and scaffold [58] – is death evoked at length in metaphor without attendant circumstances of spectral haunting or malevolent possession.

These, then, together with imagery of the abyss and the related cosmic and meteorological imagery, are the obsessive metaphoric motifs that bear on Marlow's narration of Jim's history and that do much to determine, at the subliminal and suggestive level, our affective response to the events recorded. But there is also, of course, a wealth of sensory imagery which I have largely omitted from this survey; and this, together with the animal imagery, serves to anchor in a familiar and palpable element a system of metaphor that is in the ensemble perhaps the most disquieting to be found in any major work of English fiction.

[58]   *Ibid.*, pp. 151 ff., 156 ff.

NOSTROMO (1904)

Before dealing with the more inwardly oriented imagery of *Nostromo* I want to devote a paragraph or so to the range of historical and classical reference, only occasionally conveyed in figurative locutions, but nevertheless serving like metaphor a suggestive or evocative function, though one directed largely to the "public" themes of the novel. There is a comparable system of allusion (particularly classical) in the two novels of conspiratorial intrigue that followed *Nostromo*.

The Bolivar reference identified in an earlier chapter [59] is one of a number of allusions to the Liberator, who in turn is one of over a dozen modern historical figures (including conquistador and pirate, monarchs and chiefs of state, revolutionaries and politicos) whose names and deeds, cast up in conversation or reflection, serve to give not so much a local as a continental and epochal habitation to the characters and events of the novel. Rarely has a novelist created so extraordinary an illusion of historical perspective with so marked an economy of means.

The recurrent classical references – the majority of them Roman – extend the historical perspective and evoke (with a total effect of irony, though the specific intention is only occasionally evident) a sense of the sort of optical illusion whereby the founders of the American republics North and South saw themselves (and were upon occasion so portrayed in effigy) as Roman tribunes and dictators and the establishers of new Roman republics. The most conspicuous classical reference is that conveyed in the names of the O.S.N. fleet, several of whose Olympian bottoms play their roles in the action: *Juno* as scene of the company *convité* which serves as recurrent focus of the synoptic early chapters of the book, *Ceres* as conveyor of the Gould's San Francisco guests "off into the Olympus of plutocracy", *Minerva* as vehicle of Ribiera's flight from the Monterists, *Hermes* as conveyor of the Goulds back to Sulaco from their post-revolutionary world tour.[60] Some of the references are conveyed in a phrase (Don José's "Imperium

[59] *Supra*, p. 100.
[60] *Nostromo*, pp. 9 f., 68, 117 f., 227, 505.

in imperio"; Decoud's "Pro Patria!" and his reflections on the dementia of those whom the gods would destroy; Mrs. Gould's paraphrased reflections, in her thoughts of her husband, on the "fiat justitia" theme [61]); others in epithet (Don José as "Nestor-inspirer of the party", Decoud's "vir Romanus" applied to Don José, the "stentorian" voice of Hernandez' emissary, Viola as "the old Spartan" [62]); still others in simile. Thus Gould, we are told, rides "like a centaur"; Holroyd has "the profile of a Caesar's head on an old Roman coin"; Decoud, having evoked "the Great Pompey" on the eve of Barrios' engagement with the Monterists, proceeds in a counter-simile to reject the identification of Montero with Caesar and thus to lay the spectre of another Pharsalia. [63] All these verbal allusions link with Pedrito's pompous allocution on Caesarism, [64] and with a number of objective images dispersed through the book, notably the marble vase in the Marchesa's palazzo, "ornamented with sculptured masks and garlands of flowers, and cracked from top to bottom", upon which Charles Gould fixes his gaze during his recital to Emilia of his father's death, and which (apart from the symbolic anticipation that we may well sense in it of the flawed union between Charles and Emily Gould) serves prospectively as ironic commentary on the apparatus of classical allusion – and the rhetoric of neo-classical illusion – in the book. Other items, more frankly ironical, in this series are the marble medallion "in the antique style" commemo-rating Decoud; the Cavaliere Parrochetti's preposterous design for a "bronze Justice" to replace the equestrian statue of Carlos IV; the New Custom House "with its sham air of a Greek temple". [65]

[61]   Ibid., pp. 111 (and passim), 158, 200, 379 (repeated on p. 402).
[62]   Ibid., pp. 144 (and passim), 169, 353, 516.
[63]   Ibid., pp. 48, 76, 168 f. The train of reference to Caesar and Pompey is touched off by Decoud's muttered version of the Caesarian Alea jacta est. Cf. pp. 165 ff.: "Mrs. Gould ... heard him mutter to himself in French, as he opened the carriage door, 'le sort en est jeté'."
[64]   Ibid., pp. 404 f.
[65]   Ibid., pp. 61 f., 478, 482, 530. More than one commentator has seen in the cracked marble vase of the palazzo an anticipatory symbol of the flawed personal relations of the Goulds (cf., e.g., Leo Gurko's comment in his Joseph Conrad: Giant in Exile, New York, Macmillan, 1962, p. 128n.). This seems to me an inescapable suggestion of the image, which – if it arrests the reader's attention at all – can hardly help recalling to mind the

This system of historical and classical imagery illuminates the public themes (with a peculiarly dry light) and helps to establish the illusion of a historical continuum. Abetted by a dense array of visual and tactile imagery, it serves as ballast to the novel, functioning like the animal imagery in *Lord Jim* as counterpoise to the "metaphysical" strain of the more obviously thematic imagery. Largely wanting in the imposing cosmic and meteorological imagery found in its predecessor, *Nostromo* shares with *Lord Jim* an insistent vein of metaphoric reference to the motifs of haunting and enchantment, of possession and diabolism; and it is this imagery that largely conducts the thematic "undercurrent" of the novel.

The metaphoric evocations of the theme of possession and malign enchantment, by spectre or devil or evil spirit, recurrent from beginning to end of the novel, have their objective correlative in the quasi-legendary treasure of gold in Azuera, haunted by the gringos who perished in quest of it. Here again, as in *Lord Jim*, we come to a linked system of reference so ubiquitous that a full identification of particulars would produce a small catalogue. The key image of the "two gringos, spectral and alive", the "tenacious gringo ghosts" of Azuera, is evoked in the opening pages, where their legend is set forth, and is five times re-evoked by Nostromo: twice dead-center in the novel – in discourse with the dying Teresa Viola on the eve of his departure with the silver, and in colloquy with Decoud during their first moments in the lighter; much later, in discourse with Monygham in the Custom House following his return from the Great Isabel; twice in self-communion in the closing chapters of the book when, confirmed as the faithful "slave of the San Tomé treasure", engaged in the process of "growing rich very slowly", he contemplates his servitude.[66]

The unlawful treasure is a "shining spectre", a "curse" or

---

golden bowl of James's novel. But the classical ornamentation, no less than the flaw, is intrinsic to the imaged vase – in which I see a striking instance of Conrad's instinct, at work throughout, for welding the public and private themes of the novel into an imaginative unity.

[66] *Nostromo*, pp. 4 f., 255, 263 f., 460, 526, 531.

"spell" cast on Nostromo. The "spirits of good and evil" that
hover over it, like the "ghosts and devils" of Azuera, hover also
over its source in the Rincon Gorge, the mine – imaged by Gould
as "vampire" or "ghoul" or "Old Man of the Sea" fastened upon
his father's shoulders – by which, under the son's management,
Sulaco prospers, "growing rich swiftly on the hidden treasures of
the earth . . ., torn out by the labouring hands of the people".[67]

For Nostromo such locutions are more than metaphor, they
express a conviction of occult powers practically operative. These
powers conspire, in his imagination, with Teresa Viola's death-bed
prophecy of his end in "poverty, misery, and starvation", in which
he feels "the force of a potent malediction", and with the vengeful
intention he attributes to Decoud ("to cast a spell") in absconding
with the four ingots from the treasure of the Great Isabel. They
are enforced by the spell cast by Giselle Viola – "a spell stronger
than the accursed spell of the treasure".[68] The "Ya-acabo" of the
owl drifting across his path (as he leaves the fort after his swim in
the Gulf) is testimony to him of Teresa's death and of the judgment upon him by "unseen powers" for his refusal to fetch a priest
to her.[69] The account of his tranced moment in the dinghy of the
lighter, when expression returns to his empty stare "as if an outcast soul, a quiet, brooding soul, finding that untenanted body in
its way, had come in stealthily to take possession", affects us less
as simile than as psychic experience.[70] Like the batrachian and
spectral visions of the chief engineer in *Lord Jim*, Nostromo's
repertory of popular beliefs functions as a peculiarly practical
(and highly characteristic) link between the metaphoric current of
the novel and the experiential reality it explores: what in other
contexts is presented as evocation or imaginative construction
becomes in his case vital conviction, just as the chief engineer's
fantasies were presented as optic vision, however hallucinated.[71]

Drawn into the vortex of this imagery of evil enchantment that

---

[67] *Ibid.*, p. 504.
[68] *Ibid.*, pp. 469, 502, 504 f.
[69] *Ibid.*, pp. 418 f.
[70] *Ibid.*, p. 493.
[71] Cf. the more aggravated case of Burns's illusions in *The Shadow-Line*,
considered in my chapter on that work.

clings to treasure and mine is the imagery evoking the devil and his minions – this also for Nostromo corresponding to an apprehended reality. The legendary "ghosts and devils" of Azuera are doubled by a less remote "king of the devils" who, to Nostromo's apprehension, sends Monygham to the Custom House to meet him and tempt him with proposals appealing to his vanity.[72]

Reënforcing the imagery of enchantment and diabolism is the recurrent imagery of treasure and mine as burden or instrument of bondage, illustrated in Gould's epithet "mine-ridden" and objectively symbolized by Decoud's plunge into the Placid Gulf weighted by the four ingots from the treasure of the Great Isabel. Thus the Capataz speaks (to Decoud in the lighter) of the treasure as "tied for safety round Nostromo's neck", he feels it "growing heavy upon my back"; implored by Giselle to carry her off from her "grave of clouds" on the island he feels "the weight as of chains upon his limbs", comes in the end to imagine his movements accompanied by an audible "clanking of . . . silver fetters".[73] Like the gringos of Azuera "bound down to their conquest", he sees himself as "a slave set on guard" over the spoils of his theft; and in the closing pages of the book his slavery is placarded to him in epithet, largely replacing the resounding formula of "Magnificent (or Illustrious) Capataz de Cargadores" by which he had hitherto been identified.[74]

Responding to the image of Nostromo's treasure as burden or bondage are the images, evoked in the solitary reflections of Emily Gould, of the mine as burden ("and now the fetish had grown into a monstrous and crushing weight") and as prison – a "circumvallation of precious metal", a "wall of silver-bricks, erected by the silent work of evil spirits".[75]

In these linked images of haunting, enchantment, and possession, of encumbrance and claustration, the principal undercurrent

---

[72] *Ibid.*, p. 462. Cf. the popular conviction that the devil had carried off the body of Guzman Bento (p. 47), the popular image of the passage of the silver-train through the Alameda and the Calle, "as if chased by the devil" (p. 114).

[73] *Ibid.*, pp. 265, 268; 539,546.

[74] *Ibid.*, pp. 526; 495; 533, 539, 542, 544 f.

[75] *Ibid.*, pp. 221 f.

of the novel, expressing the impact of treasure and mine, is conveyed, with an iteration which it is not fanciful to compare to the iteration of the Rheingold motif in Wagner's "Ring". They are enforced occasionally by other motifs, having their source in the realm of disease and narcosis; but these are incidental, and ancillary to the motifs traced – to which their functional relation is evident.[76]

Before leaving *Nostromo* I want simply to point to the countersymbolism implicit in the "good fairy" image applied to Emily Gould. Evoked in the early chapters of the novel and briefly re-evoked thereafter, it is reverted to in a minor key at the end, immediately following Emily's conversation with Monygham in the garden, in a series of reflections in which her isolation is summarized. "A fairy posed lightly before dainty philtres dispensed out of vessels of silver and porcelain": [77] so Mrs. Gould is presented to us in the early years of her Sulacan residence, in an image to which the following image responds forlornly across a tract of almost 500 pages:

Small and dainty, as if radiating a light of her own in the deep shade of the interlaced boughs, she resembled a good fairy, weary with a long career of well-doing, touched by the withering suspicion of the uselessness of her labours, the powerlessness of her magic.[78]

There are other traceable metaphoric motifs – among them a recurrent imagery of dream and somnambulism to which a generalized symbolic function may be imputed; a system of allusions to gambling (the mine as stakes, decisions made on the throw of dice); imagery of "the abyss" under the figure of a "black" or "sombre" cavern, applied to seaboard and Gulf, enforcing the

---

[76]   Cf., e.g., Nostromo's assertion that "this thing has been given to me like a deadly disease" (p. 264); the author's observation (apropos of Nostromo) that "a transgression, a crime, entering a man's existence, eats it up like a malignant growth, consumes it like a fever" (p. 523); Gould's reflection on the "weapon of wealth, doubled-edged with the cupidity and misery of mankind, steeped in all the vices of self-indulgence as in a concoction of poisonous roots. . . ." (p. 365).

[77]   *Ibid.*, p. 52; and cf. on p. 112: "gracious, small, and fairy-like, before the glittering tea-set".

[78]   *Ibid.*, p. 520.

physical impression descriptively conveyed in the superb pages devoted to the night on the Gulf.[79] Moreover the expressive value of such extended local images as those of the political tide and of Decoud's "cord of silence" (examined in the preceding chapter) should not be minimized. But it is in the complex of motifs traced above that I discern the principal undercurrent of metaphoric suggestion in *Nostromo*.

[79] Cf., e.g., pp. 6, 552.

VII

THE DEMON OF ANALOGY
(continued)

L'éternel coup d'aile n'exclut pas un regard lucide scru-
tant l'espace dévoré par son vol.
Mallarmé, "Les Poëmes d'Edgar Poe"

THE SECRET AGENT (1907)

In *The Secret Agent*, as in *Nostromo*, a system of dispersed
references to classical antiquity, metaphoric or merely allusive,
serves a generalized symbolic function, more emphatically ironic
than that in *Nostromo* by force of contrast with the moral squalor
of the presented events – so much so, in fact, as to suggest Eliot's
classical evocations in the Sweeney poems. In this respect the
classical allusion and imagery may be considered as a logical
exfoliation of the heavily latinized diction, at times almost
Augustan in its formality, as if with deliberate intent of the author
to shield himself from contamination by his subject. An examination of the rhetorical texture of the novel would not be irrelevant
here, since it has a function that may warrantably be termed
symbolic; but this may be left for separate treatment elsewhere.

The classical allusions need only be indicated, with the preliminary observation that they are, on balance, more mythological
in their reference than those in *Nostromo* and less allusive to *res
publica*. As in *Nostromo* they are presented in epithet (Verloc's
"Hyperborean manners" and "Hyperborean swine", apropos of
Mr. Vladimir; the Professor's "Capua!" flung out in contempt for
the England that allows him to remain at large; Heat's "basilisk"
stare in face of the Assistant Commissioner's impracticability;

Ossipon's "Apollo-like ambrosial head" [1]); in quoted phrase (Mr. Vladimir's "Vox et . . . ." in dialogue with Verloc, clearly a fragment of the Plutarchian "Vox et praeterea nihil"; the author's version of *genius loci* – "the genius of the locality" [2]); and in metaphor or simile. A number of similes with classical reference provide good examples of what Kenneth Burke has called "perspective by incongruity", e.g.,

A butcher boy, driving with the noble recklessness of a charioteer at Olympic Games, dashed round the corner sitting high above a pair of red wheels (p. 14).

His [the cabman's] jovial purple cheeks bristled with white hairs: and like Virgil's Silenus, who, his face smeared with the juice of berries, discoursed of Olympian Gods to the innocent shepherds of Sicily, he talked to Stevie of domestic matters and the affairs of men whose sufferings are great and immortality by no means assured.[3]

Winnie . . . talked evenly at him the wifely talk, as artfully adapted, no doubt, to the circumstances of this return as the talk of Penelope to the return of the wandering Odysseus. (p. 183)

This is the normal pitch of the classical images in this novel, sustained in one or two other examples (as in the image of Verloc's London walks with Stevie as the strolling of "a peripatetic philosopher" in subtle discourse with a disciple [4]), modified in still others – as in the author's comparison of the Professor with Caligula (p. 83), or the Chief Inspector's mental reference to the Roman arena (p. 114), or the Professor's own Archimedean fantasy of moving the world with the lever of "madness and despair" (p. 309), in all of which the intent is grimmer and the perspective less incongruous than in the examples earlier cited.

It may be added here that Biblical reference and allusion, occasional throughout Conrad's work, is somewhat more frequent in this work than in most. It can scarcely be termed frequent in any absolute sense, comprising only a half-dozen or so scattered allusions; but some of these, though casual, are telling, and in the

---

[1] *The Secret Agent*, pp. 25, 212; 73; 125; 310 (and cf. 309).
[2] *Ibid.*, pp. 24, 147.
[3] *Ibid.*, p. 166. Cf. the name of the anarchist's rendezvous: the Silenus beer-hall (p. 78 and *passim*).
[4] *Ibid.*, p. 230.

ensemble they may be said to contribute to the vein of ironic counter-symbolism discernible in the more conspicuous classical references. As the classical images range from the cabman's Golden Age to the Professor's evoked cataclysm, so the Biblical allusions range from Genesis to Revelation.[5]

The more immediately thematic images may be classified into two composite series, in one or two instances impinging upon each other through some particularity of reference: a series of images referring to disease, narcosis, torture, and death; a series principally directed at evoking the atmosphere of the city, referring to forest or jungle, or to some variously defined abyss of damp darkness.

The systems thus loosely defined may be said to converge in the early image evoking the site of Michaelis' "solitary reclusion" and breeding-ground of his visionary faith: "the sepulchral silence of the great blind pile of bricks near a river, sinister and ugly like a colossal mortuary for the socially drowned" (p. 44). It is, I should say, the one fully memorable mortuary metaphor in the novel, the other imposing evocations of death deriving their force rather from objective presentment than from metaphoric reference. So with the macabre "cortège" of cabman, apocalyptic steed, and "waddling" cart – like "the Cab of Death itself"; [6] and so also with Winnie's evoked images of execution ("the drop given was fourteen feet") with its contrasted tableaux of an archaic gallows "erect against a black and stormy background, festooned with chains and human bones, circled about by birds that peck at dead men's eyes", as in old illustrative woodcuts, and

---

[5]   Cf. p. 266 (Stevie "blown to fragments in a state of innocence"); p. 246 (Winnie mentally assumes "the biblical attitude of mourning"); p. 250 ("men whose flesh is grass"); p. 120 ("Michaelis' 'Autobiography of a Prisoner' which was to be like a book of Revelation in the history of mankind", and which – as we learn later (p. 303) – is divided into three parts, apostolically entitled "Faith, Hope, Charity"); p. 167 (the cabman's "steed of apocalyptic misery"). And cf. the references to absent "handwriting" on the whitewashed wall following Verloc's revelation to Winnie of Stevie's demise (pp. 240 f.).

[6]   Ibid., pp. 168, 170. The image finds an echo in the subsequent metaphor of Verloc leading "a cortège of dismal thoughts along dark streets. . . ." (p. 177).

of the contemporary actuality, "within four high walls, as if into a
pit, at dawn of day . . . amongst a lot of strange gentlemen in silk
hats who were calmly proceeding about the business of hanging
her by the neck".[7]

Linked with the mortuary imagery is imagery of disease and
narcosis, ranging in tone from the jocularly sinister ("Mr. Verloc
. . . generally arrived in London (like the influenza) from the
Continent, only he arrived unheralded by the Press; and his
visitations set in with great severity" [8]) to the sinister *tout court*
("The shadow of his evil gift clung to him yet like the smell of a
deadly drug in an old vial of poison, emptied now, useless, ready
to be thrown away upon the rubbish-heap of things that had
served their time" [9]). The presentment of Ossipon's face in the
likeness of "a fresh plaster cast of himself after a wasting illness"
(p. 293), cited in an earlier chapter, follows shortly upon an
indication of the identity of the illness metaphorically referred to.
The suppliant Winnie, "twined round him like a snake", inspires a
terror that becomes "a sort of intoxication", acquiring "the
characteristics of delirium tremens".[10]

To these metaphors of disease, narcosis, and death one should
add some mention of the "eloquent imagery" of Karl Yundt on the
theme of the law under the similitude of a "pretty branding
instrument invented by the overfed to protect themselves against
the hungry". Provoked by Ossipon's reference to Lombroso,
Michaelis' metaphor, developed with particulars of "red-hot
applications" and the burning and sizzling of human "hide",
culminates in an evocation of cannibalism, with further graphic

---

[7] *Ibid.*, pp. 267 f. Most of the remaining verbal images with mortuary
referent are succinct: e.g., Verloc's reflection that "a prison was a place
as safe from certain unlawful vengeances as the grave" (p. 235: an image
perfunctory in itself, but one that re-evokes the more imposing metaphor
of Michaelis' "colossal mortuary"); Winnie in dialogue with Verloc: "It
was as if a corpse had spoken" (p. 247); Winnie with her veil down,
"black as commonplace death itself, crowned with a few cheap and pale
flowers" (p. 295).
[8] *Ibid.*, p. 6.
[9] *Ibid.*, p. 48. (The character described is Karl Yundt.)
[10] *Ibid.*, p. 291.

particulars.[11] Yundt's images, which have an immediate effect (as of "swift poison") on Stevie's nerves, anticipate, in their particulars, the equally graphic imagery in which Stevie's remnants will be presented to our view ("an accumulation of raw material for a cannibal feast") and that which Winnie, much later, will devote to Stevie's diaspora: "bits of brotherly flesh and bone, all spouting up together in the manner of a firework".[12]

Enforcing the more explicitly thematic imagery of morbidity, violence, and death, the atmospheric imagery – devoted to evocation of the "monstrous town" as a palpable moral and physical envelope for the characters and events of the novel – is no less crucial to the symbolic structure of the work. Like the landscape and other visual imagery of "Heart of Darkness", it contributes to the "sinister resonance" Conrad strove for, composing in fact into an apocalyptic image of the city hardly to be matched since Dickens.[13] I shall say something in my next chapter of the presented image of the second-hand furniture store (combining references to cavern and forest, with particulars of "undergrowth tangle" and woodland pool) which provides the setting for the first encounter between Heat and the Professor.[14] The forest motif in this image is preluded by the Professor's reflection upon his "hermitage" (a single room, "lost in a wilderness of poor houses"); and an increment of suggestion adheres to it from the insectile similes in the previous paragraph, in which the city's multitudes present themselves to the Professor's imagination swarming "numerous

---

[11] *Ibid.*, pp. 47 f., 51.
[12] *Ibid.*, pp. 86; 260. Cf. also Ossipon's catastrophic vision in the basement of the Silenus during the Professor's discourse on detonators (p. 67).
[13] Cf. the "Author's Note": "Then the vision of an enormous town presented itself, of a monstrous town more populous than some continents and in its man-made might as if indifferent to heaven's frowns and smiles; a cruel devourer of the world's light. There was room enough there to place any story, depth enough there for any passion, variety enough there for any setting, darkness enough to bury five millions of lives" (p. xii). And cf. Conrad on "Heart of Darkness" (in the "Author's Note" to *Youth*): "That sombre theme had to be given a sinister resonance, a tonality of its own, a continued vibration that, I hoped, would hang in the air and swell on the ear after the last note had been struck" (p. xi).
[14] *The Secret Agent*, p. 82.

like locusts, industrious like ants".[15] It evokes echoes later in the
book – in the Assistant Commissioner's impression, as he approaches the Brett Street shop, of being "ambushed all alone in a
jungle many thousands of miles away from departmental desks
and official inkstands"; in Winnie's impression that her house is
"as lonely and unsafe as though it had been situated in the midst
of a forest"; in the effect of the green silk shades in Sir Ethelred's
room, imparting to it "something of a forest's deep gloom".[16] All
these figurative references to forest and jungle come to ironic focus
in the objective references to the "Explorers' Club", of which Mr.
Vladimir and Sir Ethelred's secretary are fellow members.[17]

Allied to the evocations of forest or jungle is the imagery of the
abyss repeatedly applied to the fog-bound city. Fog penetrates the
city during much of the action of the novel and imagery of the fog
interpenetrates with other imagery. Thus the image of Stevie's
remains as they appear to Heat's inspecting eye ("an accumulation
of raw material for a cannibal feast") follows immediately upon
the image of Heat's swallowing "a good deal of raw, unwhole-
some fog in the park" (p. 86). This strain of imagery finds its
definitive expression in the "aquarium" simile which, near the
center of the book, evokes the atmosphere of the Assistant
Commissioner's pedestrian mission to Brett Street. I cite the
passage in full, with its appendage of descriptive particulars
following the controlling original figure:

His descent into the street was like the descent into a slimy aquarium
from which the water had been run off. A murky, gloomy dampness
enveloped him. The walls of the houses were wet, the mud of the
roadway glistened with an effect of phosphorescence, and when he
emerged into the Strand out of a narrow street by the side of Charing
Cross Station the genius of the locality assimilated him. He might have
been but one more of the queer foreign fish that can be seen of an
evening about there flitting round the dark corners. (p. 147).

This central symbolic image of the city as aquarium is echoed in
various figures of abyss, immensity, trench, well. The Assistant
Commissioner advances "into an immensity of greasy slime and

15   *Ibid.*
16   *Ibid.*, pp. 150; 201; 217.
17   *Ibid.*, pp. 216, 228.

damp plaster interspersed with lamps" (p. 150); Winnie, after the murder, throws open a window, contemplating suicide, but recoils "from the depth of the fall into that sort of slimy, deep trench" (p. 254); London presents itself to her vision as a town "sunk in a hopeless night", resting "at the bottom of a black abyss from which no unaided woman could hope to scramble out" (p. 271); Brett Place under the falling mist appears to her "a triangular well of asphalt and bricks, of blind houses and unfeeling stones" (p. 276). The evocations of well and abyss in this primarily sensory imagery devoted to the city are echoed in a number of interior images, as for example in the representation of Ossipon as fearful of "losing his footing in the depths of this tenebrous affair".[18]

But it is the aquarium image that sounds the tonic chord of this image-sequence, and that simile, which borrows a resonance from the earlier metaphor of the "socially drowned", is linked in a chain of ironic allusion to the Fisheries question that preoccupies Sir Ethelred and that provokes the exchange of grim pleasantries between the Assistant Commissioner and Toodles on the subject of Vladimir and his complicity in the bomb plot – exchanges conducted in terms of a sinister reference to sprats and sardine canneries, to dog-fish and whale.[19] Here, as in *Lord Jim* (through the agencies of the "yellow dog" incident, of Stein and his collection) and as so often elsewhere, Conrad brings the "underthought" of imagery into practical contact with the "overthought" of exposition, ironically abetting by references from

---

[18]   *Ibid.*, p. 279. An image of the abyss in a more metaphysical context is evoked by the clock on the landing which counts off – immediately before the second putting out of lights in the Verloc house – "fifteen ticks into the abyss of eternity" (p. 181). The reprise of this image follows the murder, when blood drips on the floor-cloth "with a sound of ticking growing fast and furious like the pulse of an insane clock" (p. 265).

[19]   *Ibid.*, pp. 145, 215 f. Sir Ethelred is pressing for passage of a Bill for the Nationalization of Fisheries. It might be added here that Michaelis' picture of "the great capitalists devouring the little capitalists" (p. 49) would seem to contain a concealed piscine allusion, since its prototype can scarcely be other than the Hobbesian "big fish devouring the little fish". We may have here an authentic example of "cryptographic" writing (Stallman's term for the Conradian method) – though from a professional standpoint one could scarcely claim very much for the impenetrability of the cipher employed.

the sphere of objective event the symbolic operation of metaphor.

There is a hint of this interchange of potency between metaphor and objective image or narrative datum in the retrospect of Winnie's aborted romance with the jolly butcher ("a fascinating companion for a voyage down the sparkling stream of life"). This fragment of urban pastoral, placed in the text immediately after Winnie learns of Stevie's explosive end, evokes for the reader a recollection of Heat peering at a table "with a calm face and the slightly anxious attention of an indigent customer bending over what may be called the by-products of a butcher's shop with a view to an inexpensive Sunday dinner".[20]

There are other metaphoric strains in the novel that might be traced, notably the animal images which, though relatively infrequent, have a special propriety in the jungle-aquarium world of this novel.[21] But in tracing the major image-sequences of the novel I have, I believe, sufficiently suggested the intensity with which verbal imagery focusses upon the themes and enforces, by expressive evocation or by ironic counter-suggestion, the dominant impression of moral squalor and imbecility, of violence and desperation, which one derives from the presented action. Flaubert declared (in a harsh vein that scarcely expressed the complexity of his feeling for his heroine) that he had tried to evoke in *Madame Bovary* something of the impression of moldiness (*moisissure*) associated with the existence of wood-lice. Conrad might have found such an image for *The Secret Agent*, though it would have been pitched, one suspects, in an even more sinister key. Coming back to the work twelve years after its

[20] *Ibid.*, p. 243; p. 88.
[21] Some of these are perfunctory, mere *façons de parler*; others – e.g., the repeated image of the gas-jet purring "like a contented cat" (p. 231; and cf. p. 195) – have an ironic "counter-symbolic" function. However, most of the principal characters, and several of the incidental ones – e.g., the Gampish charwoman Mrs. Neale, "a sort of amphibious and domestic animal" (p. 184) – are sooner or later adorned with animal similes or epithets; and there is a sort of summarizing force in the image of Verloc snarling with vexation at his wife in the moments preceding his murder, with an effect suggesting "a reflective beast, not very dangerous – a slow beast with a sleek head, gloomier than a seal, and with a husky voice" (p. 257).

composition he saw it as "a grisly skeleton" clothed in "a literary robe of indignant scorn".[22] It would be impertinent to suggest that he misapprehended the sentiments with which his material inspired him; but the fact is that it is the scorn more than the indignation, which shows through the ironic mask with which he shielded himself from the contagion of his material.

Out of his scorn and his irony (which did not exclude certain carefully controlled impulses of compassion, as in the treatment of Stevie and his mother or the account of Winnie's suicidal despair) he fashioned a work to which one might apply, under a more sinister aspect, Thibaudet's accolade of *Madame Bovary*: "comédie de la bêtise humaine". The "grisly skeleton" of the novel – that is to say the ordonnance of event and episode, the masterly "progression of effect" – counts for much in its impact. But it is the quality of the prose, both in its brilliant rhetorical aspects and in the intensity and resourcefulness with which the imagery is brought to bear on the dominant themes, that lifts the novel above the realm of a mere "entertainment" and gives it a distinguished if isolated position in the Conrad canon, and thus in the canon of English fiction in this century, making it in fact the most impressive production in English prose since Swift in the vein of "l'humour noir".

UNDER WESTERN EYES (1911)

In this novel most of the dominant metaphoric motifs of the three novels preceding it (*Lord Jim, Nostromo, The Secret Agent*) are again in evidence. There is little to correspond to the cosmic and meteorological imagery of *Lord Jim*, or to the atmospheric saturation of *The Secret Agent*; but there is significant mortuary and spectral, or phantasmal, imagery (the latter chiefly related to Razumov's hallucinatory visions), imagery from the areas of disease, narcosis, physical torture, and from the realms of possession and evil enchantment. There are also representatives of what I have termed Conrad's imagery of the abyss; and there is, finally,

[22]   Cf. the Familiar Preface (*ibid.*, pp. xivf.).

a significant sequence of verbal images, and a related sequence of objective items and of non-figurative allusions, bearing upon the ambiguous theme of "vision" implicit in the title of the novel.

I have considered in some detail the operation of most of the above classes of imagery in other contexts; however, in view of the importance of the novel and in view of the distinction of its imagery, I shall not treat it as summarily as I might otherwise be disposed to do. (On this point I might say in passing that in my own hierarchy of Conrad's full-scale works *Under Western Eyes* stands on a summit at approximately the level of *Nostromo* and *Lord Jim*.)

Before turning to the distinctively thematic imagery I may mention that in this novel, as in its two predecessors, the public themes – which may be captioned the State and Revolution – accrete to themselves a patina of historical and classical (and some Biblical) paraphrase and allusion, occasionally expressed in metaphor. I have ventured some tentative generalizations as to the function of such allusions in the two previous contexts, and shall not pause over the examples in *Under Western Eyes*. The most suggestive of them falls into one of the principal image-sequences of the novel and will be identified presently.

The imagery with explicit and uncomplicated mortuary reference is relatively infrequent and apt to be perfunctory: e.g., the "grave-like silence" of Razumov's room, Haldin "rigid with the immobility of death", Razumov "pale like a corpse obeying the dread summons of judgment", Mikulin after his fall turned "civilly into a corpse".[23] In Razumov's evocation of Russia as "a sullen and tragic mother hiding her face under a winding-sheet" the mortuary phrase is an incidental item in a personification of more general reference;[24] and in the repeated cadaverous and skeletal epithets applied to Mme de S– (e.g., "grinning skull", "ancient painted mummy", "death's-head smile"), the death-motif is complicated – the "undercurrent" of reference as it were contaminated – by implications of the ghoulish, linking this imagery with that of evil enchantment and possession. This is made most

[23]   *Under Western Eyes*, pp. 46 (image anticipated on p. 43), 55, 303, 306.
[24]   *Ibid.*, pp. 32 f.

explicit in the simile of "a galvanized corpse out of some Hoffman's tale".[25]

The motif of enchantment is more generally evoked in connection with Russia and the Russian people, as in the narrator's mental vision of Mrs. Haldin keeping vigil "under the evil spell of an arbitrary rule" – an image anticipated by a passage in the narrator-Razumov dialogue at the center of the book ("under a curse . . . an evil spell") – and by Sophia Antonovna's graphic image of life in Russia: "lapped up in evils, watched over by beings that are worse than ogres, ghouls, and vampires".[26]

One need not insist upon the relation of these metaphors to the more frequent imagery of diabolism, nor upon the thematic relation of this entire complex to the aspect of "perdition" (Razumov's own summarizing word, in his confession to Natalia) presented by the protagonist's career. As in *Nostromo* this imagery is rooted in a soil of popular conviction, if only in the single context of the Razumov-Ziemianitch encounter (the latter's conviction that the beating administered by Razumov was the work of the devil). Sophia Antonovna's remark on Ziemianitch's belief ("there are plenty of men worse than devils to make a hell of this earth" [27]) puts the devil-damnation imagery in metaphoric perspective for the more sophisticated characters in the novel; but we see at the end that popular convictions about "the personal Devil of our simple ancestors" retain an imaginative actuality for Razumov. The devil archetype is evoked in casual epithet: Sophia's "Mephistophelian" eyebrows, Razumov's temptation to "Mephistophelian" laughter at Haldin, his "satanic" enjoyment at the scorn he feels for Peter Ivanovitch, Sophia's remark at the end on "the devil work of Razumov's hate and pride".[28] It is exposed to the narrator's philosophic commentary, in a paragraph of reflection on the Razumov-Mikulin interviews, with reference to "old

[25]   *Ibid.*, pp. 215, 224. This lady is also imaged under the style of "a witch in Parisian clothes" (p. 215).

[26]   *Ibid.*, pp. 335, 194, 254.

[27]   *Ibid.*, p. 281. Sophia Antonovna, in her dialogue with Razumov on this question, adopts the view that the beating was the work of "some police-hound in disguise".

[28]   *Ibid.*, pp. 245 (and *passim*), 60, 228, 380.

legendary tales where the Enemy of Mankind is represented holding subtly mendacious dialogues with some tempted soul", to which is added the suggestion that "the Evil One, with his single passion of satanic pride for the only motive, is yet, on a larger, modern view, allowed to be not quite so black as he used to be painted".[29] It receives its most explicitly thematic treatment in Razumov's two confessions to Natalia. In his oral confession he evokes the archetype in the figure of "the old Father of lies – our national patron – our domestic god, whom we take with us when we go abroad", and recalls "the atrocious temptation in the garden of that accursed villa". In the written confession he identifies his former state as one of possession, confesses to "the unpardonable sin of stealing a soul".[30]

Like the imagery of enchantment and damnation, imagery of disease and narcosis has both general and particular reference, i.e., to Russia and the Russians and to Razumov specifically – and in the present connection to the conspiratorial circle of Geneva as well. Harboring Haldin, Razumov thinks of himself as "harbouring a pestilential disease", a metaphor which he develops in interior dialectic, arriving at a Biblical conclusion suggested by the metaphoric context:

Yet we combat a contagious pestilence. Do I want his death? No! I would save him if I could – but no one can do that – he is the withered member which must be cut off.[31]

The motif is echoed in various contexts in conjunction with other metaphoric motifs: Razumov's awakening is "the awakening of a man mortally ill, or of a man ninety years old"; the narrator, in discourse with Razumov, sees him as a "secret refugee from under the pestilential shadow hiding the true, kindly face of his land"; he supposes Razumov to look at his narrative journal "as a threatened man may look fearfully at his own face in the glass,

---

[29]   Ibid., pp. 304 f. One may well surmise that Thomas Mann, rereading this novel during the gestation-period of Doctor Faustus, found the passage cited – and the colloquies it refers to – peculiarly suggestive for his purposes (cf. Thomas Mann, Die Entstehung des Doktor Faustus, Amsterdam, 1949, pp. 168, 186).
[30]   Ibid., pp. 350, 354; 359 f.
[31]   Ibid., p. 36 (and cf. p. 32).

formulating to himself reassuring excuses for his appearance marked by the taint of some insidious hereditary disease".[32]

In this novel, as in its immediate predecessor, imagery of morbidity is doubled by imagery of narcosis and related imagery of chemical decomposition or corrosion. Of the more imposing metaphors in this sequence, one, relating to poisonous fungi, links also with a strain of vegetation imagery which I shall identify presently. I have in mind Razumov's reference, in discourse with Peter Ivanovitch, to "the poisonous plants which flourish in the world of conspirators, like evil mushrooms in a dark cellar" (p. 206). The second, incorporating an implicit classical allusion, describes Razumov's relation to his fellow-students at the University following the Haldin affair: "It was there that the dark prestige of the Haldin mystery fell on him, clung to him like a poisoned robe it was impossible to fling off." [33] The narcotic element is conceived in diverse modes, enters the system through various orifices. Referred to the "accumulated bitterness" of her existence as *dame de compagnie* in the Château Borel, it enters into Tekla's veins ("bitterness . . ., like some subtle poison, had decomposed her fidelity to that hateful pair" [34]); tainting the atmosphere in the form of "choking fumes of falsehood", it takes Razumov "by the throat" (p. 269); and in the moments following Razumov's oral confession to Natalia the poisonous element dispersed throughout, taking on a wider reference, becomes – in another of the more pregnant images of the novel – an atmosphere imperilling the soul:

[32]   *Ibid.*, pp. 68; 184; 214.
[33]   *Ibid.*, p. 299. I should suppose that Conrad had in mind the figure of Hercules clad in "the shirt of Nessus". One cannot press the analogy in detail: Natalia would seem to resist any attempt to assimilate her into the orbit of the image in the role of Deianira. But there is symmetry in the fact that the poison that destroys the mythological hero is transmitted to the garment by the blood of Nessus, itself poisoned by the arrow with which Hercules has slain him. So Razumov is morally poisoned by the blood of the man whose death he has taken upon himself.
[34]   *Ibid.*, p. 235. The components of the "hateful pair" are, of course, Peter Ivanovitch and his Egeria, Mme de S.—. The interior chemistry of the metaphor cited has its objective correlative in Tekla's apparel: "In the sunlight her black costume looked greenish, with here and there threadbare patches where the stuff seemed decomposed by age into a velvety, black, furry state" (p. 231).

Shadows seemed to come and go in them [Natalia's eyes] as if the steady flame of her soul had been made to vacillate at last in the cross-currents of poisoned air from the corrupted dark immensity claiming her for its own, where virtues themselves fester into crimes in the cynicism of oppression and revolt. (p. 356)

Still later, in Razumov's written confession, it is imaged – again with particular reference to Razumov's duplicity – as a potion ("the poison of my infamous intention"), drunk in Natalia's presence.[35] Cognate with the motif of narcosis is that of chemical decomposition or corrosion, implicit in one of Razumov's mental pronouncements on the Russian people ("Better that thousands should suffer than that a people should become a disintegrated mass"), explicit in the narrator's reflection on "Russian simplicity, a terrible corroding simplicity in which mystic phrases clothe a naïve and hopeless cynicism".[36]

There is a slight but significant strain of imagery of the abyss employed alternatively with frankly metaphysical reference (e.g., the narrator to Razumov: "Those that are lost leap into the abyss with their eyes open") and to convey a mental impression of a sensory datum, as in the notation of the sudden disappearance of Nikita and Yakovlitch at the foot of a wall in the grounds of the Château Borel, "as if the earth had opened to swallow them up".[37] In at least one instance the image, introduced ostensibly to convey a physical impression, is developed with explicit reference to the novel's revolutionary theme: "her eyes rested upon him, black and impenetrable like the mental caverns where revolutionary thought should sit plotting the violent way of its dream of changes".[38]

The theme of the abyss, evoked ordinarily to define mental or physical impressions, finds its way into the dialectical fabric of the novel. The images cited above, and the evocations of the

[35] *Ibid.*, p. 360. Cf. Razumov to Kostia (p. 82): " 'My ideas may be poison to you'."

[36] *Ibid.*, pp. 34, 104.

[37] *Ibid.*, pp. 185; 23, 239. With the last cited simile cf. Razumov's outburst to the narrator in the course of their dialogue in the Bastions: " 'You spring up from the ground before me with this talk. Who the devil are you? . . .' " (p. 186).

[38] *Ibid.*, p. 261 (colloquy between Razumov and Sophia Antonovna). Cf. the antecedent notation of Razumov "plunging his glance into the black eyes of the woman" (p. 260).

"subterranean" which are linked with them (the "long cavernous place like a neglected subterranean byre" in which Ziemianitch is beaten by a presumed devil and in which he hangs himself; the "dark cellar" in which the evil mushrooms of conspiracy sprout; and we might even add Peter Ivanovitch's "subterranean voice" [39]), are reverberant in, or are themselves reverberant of, the "sinister jocularity" of Peter Ivanovitch's metaphoric thesis "that for us at this moment there yawns a chasm between the past and the future. It can never be bridged by foreign liberalism. . . . Bridged it can never be! . . . Do you understand, enigmatical young man? It has got to be just filled up." [40]

A vein of imagery developed throughout in dialectic conveys a current of allusion to vegetation. The motif is first succinctly evoked in Haldin's metaphoric allusion to the deceased Mr. de P–: "He was uprooting the tender plant." It is developed in a contrary sense, but with a still honorific inflection, by Razumov in the first of his self-communings. Razumov turns the metaphor against Haldin: "The seed germinates in the night. Out of the dark soil springs the perfect plant. But a volcanic eruption is sterile, the ruin of fertile ground." [41]

The counter-imagery of "evil mushrooms" is obviously implicated in this sequence, as in those relating to the motifs of narcosis and of the subterranean.[42] So also is Sophia Antonovna's indignant outburst to Razumov in which she denies the appellative "life" to a "subservient, submissive" existence: "Life? No! Vegetation on the filthy heap of iniquity which the world is." [43] But in its final reprise the vegetation-motif is reinvested with the honorific sense

---

[39]   *Ibid.*, pp. 29, 206, 129. One might also adduce in this connection the graphic presentment of the Laspara daughter when she admits Razumov into her father's quarters following his confession to Natalia: "looking more than ever like an old doll with a dusty brown wig, dragged from under a sofa" (p. 363). In some of the imagery of this novel of a conspiratorial underground the concept of a metaphoric "undercurrent" is invested with a peculiarly literal significance.

[40]   *Ibid.*, p. 211.

[41]   *Ibid.*, p. 34. The aptness of allusion in the final sentence to Haldin's crime requires no commentary.

[42]   *Ibid.*, p. 206.

[43]   *Ibid.*, p. 260.

it bore in its original versions. The narrator, in the final sentence of the narrative proper, immediately preceding his summarizing afterword, envisages Natalia Haldin as

wedded to an invincible belief in the advent of loving concord springing like a heavenly flower from the soil of men's earth, soaked in blood, torn by struggles, watered with tears. (p. 377)

There are other strains of imagery, minor but expressive, which might be traced – e.g., the strain of reductive simile and epithet applied to the world of Geneva's "petite Russie", typified by the repeated presentment of the Laspara daughters as "old dolls", and involving a variety of grotesque disparities – between Laspara's megalomaniac ideas and his diminutive size, between Nikita's monstrous proportions and his doll-like "piping" voice (the "falsetto of a circus clown"), between Peter Ivanovitch's immense pretensions and legendary fame and his infantile dependence on Mme de S–.[44] This imagery, enforced by the reductive imagery applied to the physical setting (the "painted cardboard" of the Petit Lac and its "toylike jetties"), functions at once as characterization and commentary – less explicit, but hardly less telling, than Marlow's image of Kurtz (in "Heart of Darkness") as a "papier-mâché Mephistopheles".[45] But I want before leaving this densely metaphoric novel to identify several additional strains of unmistakably thematic imagery which arise out of, or focus upon, Razumov's hallucinated visions.

There is, first, an image-sequence evocative of modes of torture (and in one instance of self-torture), of which the nodal point is the third of Razumov's hallucinations – the vision, experienced during the first Mikulin interview, of "his own brain suffering on

[44] Cf., e.g., pp. 266 (Nikita); 268 (the Laspara daughters resembling "old dolls", the dwarfish Julius descending from his three-legged stool as "from the heights of Olympus"), p. 363 f.

[45] *Youth*, p. 81. It is not amiss to note in this connection Conrad's enduring passion (which he shared with Flaubert) for the theater of marionettes, in whose "rigid violence" and "impassibility in love, in crime, in mirth, in sorrow" he found an aesthetic satisfaction he did not find in the conventional theater (*Life and Letters*, I, pp. 212 – letter addressed to Cunninghame Graham in 1897). Punch and Judy serve as vehicle for more than one Conradian similitude (cf., e.g., *The Nigger of the "Narcissus"*, p. 16); and an old French nursery rhyme about marionettes supplied the epigraph to *A Set of Six*.

the rack", as in "some dark print of the Inquisition". Anticipated in the opening pages, in the narrator's observation that "the words and events" of the evening with Haldin "must have been graven as if with a steel tool on Mr. Razumov's brain", it is evoked with still more precise reference to the central image in the notation that Razumov, "on the borders of delirium" following Haldin's departure, "heard himself saying, 'I confess', as a person might do on the rack". It reverberates in the simile in which Sophia Antonovna's "slowness of utterance" as she hovers, in her conversation with Razumov, about the question of Haldin's betrayal is likened to "the falling of molten lead drop by drop". It is again recalled in the narrator's impression of Razumov's demeanor during his final interview with Natalia: "It was as though he had stabbed himself outside and had come in there to show it; and more than that – as though he were turning the knife in the wound and watching the effect." [46]

There is frequent evocation of states of trance and somnambulism, first with reference to Haldin ("the quiet impersonal voice of a man in a trance"), subsequently – and repeatedly – with reference to Razumov.[47] These culminate in the objective presentment of the trance-like state the latter experiences during the illness that attacks him as he awaits word from Mikulin; they have what may be called their discursive correlative in Razumov's reflection as he paces the little island, "all alone with the bronze statue of Rousseau", in an interval between entries in his notebook: " 'Perhaps life is just that. . . . A dream and a fear'." [48]

There is a vein of imagery having its source in that realm of the spectral and phantasmal in which the hallucinations themselves originate, which finds many of its occasions in Razumov's mental or visual recall of his first hallucinated vision of Haldin in St. Petersburg on the night of the betrayal ("on the snow, stretched on his back right across his path . . ., solid, distinct, real, with his inverted hands over his eyes, clad in a brown, close-fitting coat

---

[46] *Under Western Eyes*, pp. 88; 24, 65; 270; 350 f.
[47] *Ibid.*, pp. 24, 317, 336.
[48] *Ibid.*, pp. 298; 316. Razumov's pronouncement summarizes a page of reflection on the "vida es sueño" theme.

and long boots" [49]). The phantom is eidetically re-evoked for Razumov, in another posture, and is repeatedly alluded to in discourse or reflection.[50] All these evocations and allusions bear thematically upon the underlying vision of Russia and things Russian which informs the book – if one can affix that predicate to a subject so expressly wanting in definition. That vision is articulated by the narrator early in his recital when he speaks of "Russia, the land of spectral ideas and disembodied aspirations".[51]

There is, finally, a sequence of imagery, allusion and epithet focussing on the theme of vision itself, in which (as in the title of the novel) optic vision functions as symbol or surrogate for intellectual or moral perception. This current becomes more evident with each rereading of the novel; but though it is widely diffused throughout, I limit myself in the present context to a few notations. First, I would advance the suggestion that it pivots on the distinction Razumov draws, in his final interview with Natalia, between "the blind" (i.e., the "visionaries" of an earlier pronouncement, made in audience with Mikulin) and the "clear-eyed", and that it involves many ironies and ambiguities (as in Razumov's recollection, in the very context referred to, of the "amazing and un-

---

[49]   *Ibid.*, pp. 36 f.

[50]   *Ibid.*, pp. 84; 55, 61 (in conversation with Haldin: "what it needs is not a lot of haunting phantoms that I could walk through – but a man!"); pp. 224 f. (in conversation with Mme de S—: " 'There are phantoms of the living as well as of the dead'."); p. 246 ("the event appeared as a featureless shadow having vaguely the shape of a man"); pp. 299 f. (in reflection on Haldin: "a moral spectre infinitely more effective than any visible apparition of the dead").

[51]   In writing the above I am aware that the narrator is a narrator only, not the author *in propria persona*, and I recognize that there are other embracing formulae for things Russian in the novel – among them that of "cynicism" (cf., e.g., p. 104). But though there are also occasional indications of a less desperate view of the case (e.g., "the shadow hiding the true kindly face of the land") it seems to me that the total impact of the book supports the narrator's metaphorically expressed judgment. In this connection I refer the reader to Conrad's own characterization of Russia in his essay entitled "Autocracy and War" (originally published in the *Fortnightly Review* in 1905): "the Russian phantom, part Ghoul, part Djinn, part Old Man of the Sea" (*Notes on Life and Letters*, p. 113). Cf. with this, in addition to the narrator's formula cited in text, Sophia Antonovna's "watched over by beings that are worse than ogres, ghouls, and vampires" (*Under Western Eyes*, p. 254).

expected apparitions" he has seen).[52] Aside from reference throughout to the narrator's condition of spectatorship, to "the observation of my Western eyes",[53] this image-cycle comprises in its orbit many particular references (largely ironical) to the optic endowments of individuals : e.g., the "goggle" eyes of General T–; Mikulin "like an idol with dim, unreadable eyes"; Peter Ivanovitch "with his dark glasses like an enormous blind teacher"; Mrs. Haldin's eyes which "could not support either gas or electricity"; Peter Ivanovitch's accolade of his Egeria: "Nothing can remain obscure before that – that – inspired, yes, inspired penetration, this true light of feminity." [54] One should add to these the "trustful" eyes of Natalia Haldin, alluded to throughout the book.[55]

The motif of vision is embodied in the episodic structure of the novel by the device of Mikulin's fixing his rendezvous with Razumov – to discuss the conditions of his employment as an agent for " 'European supervision' " – at the address of an oculist, following which Razumov adopts the rather sinister affectation of a green shade over his left eye.[56] It is allied with the light-dark imagery dispersed through the book (as, for discursive example, in Razumov's reflection that "obscurantism is better than the light of incendiary torches" [57]) – an imagery that comes to a particularly intense focus in the "revelation" scene between Razumov and Natalia.[58] It is, of course, inextricably involved with the spectral

---

[52]   " 'One must look beyond the present' ", Natalia tells Razumov in a tone of "ardent conviction". To which Razumov replies: " 'The blind can do that best. I have had the misfortune to be born clear-eyed....' " (p. 345). The sentence parenthetically referred to is Razumov's "Visionaries work everlasting evil on earth" (p. 95).

[53]   These are particularly frequent in the final chapters of the book: cf. on pp. 339, 345, 346, 374, 381.

[54]   *Ibid.*, pp. 45 f.; 95; 329; 338; 213. Cf. also on Peter Ivanovitch: "the impenetrable earnestness of the blue glasses meeting his [Razumov's] stare" (p. 213).

[55]   *Ibid.*, pp. 22, 102, 349, 377.

[56]   *Ibid.*, pp. 304, 309 f. " 'Eye better?' " Razumov's visitor asks him, receiving in reply a succinct " 'Nearly well now' " (p. 309).

[57]   *Ibid.*, p. 34.

[58]   "The light of an electric bulb high up under the ceiling searched that clear square box into its four bare corners, crudely, without shadows – a strange stage for an obscure drama" (p. 342; and cf. on p. 355: "the searching glare of the white anteroom"). The light of this antechamber is

and phantasmal imagery that, deriving from Razumov's repeated hallucinatory visions, focusses on the continually re-evoked phantom of Haldin – as we see, for example, in the scene of the final Razumov-Natalia interview, where the allusion to the weakness of Mrs. Haldin's eyes is followed within a few pages by Natalia's distressed cry to Razumov (in allusion to her mother's grief over Victor Haldin's death): " 'She expects now to *see him!*' " [59]

More could be said about the verbal imagery of *Under Western Eyes*. The animal imagery, for example, though by no means comparable in frequency to that in *Lord Jim*, is not without significance in the total pattern, as one might gather from Conrad's characterization (in his "Author's Note") of Peter Ivanovitch and Mme de S– as "apes of a sinister jungle".[60] But I have traced in sufficient detail a sufficient number of thematic strands to suggest that, if it is not the most densely metaphoric of Conrad's novels, it is the one which reveals, perhaps, the most complex and closely woven texture of thematic imagery. With no great exaggeration one might say of the Conrad whose imagination spun out the figurative texture of this novel, in the words applied to de Barral by the Marlow of *Chance*: "Everything was fly that came into his web." [61]

I pass over *Chance*. It is a distinguished work, of extraordinary compositional interest, and one that reveals a marked metaphoric concentration on its central themes. But I have considered in some detail the thematic imagery of the first (and I think the greater) of the two Marlow novels, so that the second becomes more dispensable for my purposes than any of the intervening works. *Victory* and *The Rescue* I omit as works whose verbal imagery, though certainly not without its felicities, and even its brilliant local successes, does not, as I apprehend it, present the same degree of thematic patterning as that discoverable in the four

---

contrasted with the "semitransparent gloom" of the big room, with blinds drawn and "lighted only by a shaded lamp", in which Mrs. Haldin sits, "lost in the ill-defined mass of the high-backed chair" (p. 338 f.).

[59] *Ibid.*, p. 348.
[60] *Ibid.*, p. ix.
[61] *Chance*, p. 75.

works last examined, nor does it have the developmental interest of the imagery in *Almayer's Folly* and *The Nigger of the "Narcissus"*.[62]

I shall close this chapter with a glance at *The Arrow of Gold* and *The Rover* more cursory than my inspection of the greater and more complex works of Conrad's early and middle periods. *The Arrow of Gold* I select as an example (the most conspicuous, if not the only example in the Conrad canon) of sensory imagery employed sequentially and with an unmistakably thematic significance; it is only the sequence of imagery drawn from the realm of art and artifact that I shall trace. *The Rover* I select for its chronological position in the series of the novels. As Conrad's last completed novel it marks a logical terminus for the inquiry undertaken in this chapter. Though I find it an abler and more attractive production than do a number of contemporary critics, there can, I think, be no serious question of its taking rank in the company of the four works just considered. It falls measurably, in fact conspicuously, below them in all those attributes invoked by Conrad himself when he defined for Barrett Clark the operancy of the symbolic in art: i.e., "in complexity, in power, in depth and in beauty".[63] But it is not devoid of these qualities. Moreover, it has the special interest for Conrad scholarship of standing as its author's final completed artistic statement.

THE ARROW OF GOLD (1919)

The weaknesses of this late work have been canvassed as thoroughly as those of *The Rover*, and perhaps more so. Undoubtedly it is vitiated by a tendency to rhetoric in the Yeatsian sense of the word (the will attempting to do the work of an imagination that shows some signs of fatigue), and by a misconceived attempt to impose upon the reader by the mere repetition of certain epithets or verbal stereotypes. The word "fatal" is repeatedly hung upon

---

[62]   The most conspicuous metaphoric sequence in *Victory* is provided by the animal imagery, enforced (as in *Lord Jim*) by epithet.
[63]   *Life and Letters*, II, p. 205.

Blunt like a placard; of Rita we are too often informed that she is "enigmatic", "mysterious", "symbolic", that she is "as old as the world", with something in her of "the women of all time". These somewhat factitious formulae, recalling those with which Pater wove his glamor about la Gioconda, cannot of themselves convey the mythic quality aimed at. Fatality, mystery, *das Ewigweibliche* – these are categories in which mere statement, however well it served Conrad in other contexts, can accomplish little. Repeated statement becomes merely fatiguing. Marlow's "one of us" in *Lord Jim*, embodying a rational concept, summarizes a complex of social and ethical values. We make of it what we can, but we do not feel that we are being exposed to a "hard sell" when Marlow reiterates it, as he does throughout the novel. This, I think, is what we do feel with regard to some of the verbal stereotypes of *The Arrow*. As Miss Bradbrook trenchantly remarked of the novel, "the butter's spread too thick".[64] However, the butter is spread unevenly; and there are portions of the novel – chapters and episodes – in which its quality, if not that of the very best butter, is very good indeed. If Conrad's imagination showed signs of fatigue in *The Arrow of Gold*, it was not played out. One of the ways in which he redeemed his too facile reliance upon verbal formulae was by a succession of images drawn from the visual arts, effective as the verbal stereotypes are not in conveying to the reader, as felt experience and not simply as an arbitrary *donnée*, something of the beglamored state of the narrator-protagonist, and also in evoking the myth of a sort of modern Galatea, a peasant girl who becomes a painter's model and mistress and is fashioned by her protector into a *grande dame*.

The Conradian images graphically project the contrast between Rita de Lastaola, about whom is evoked a symbolic ambience of pagan antiquity at once luminous and mysterious, and the other figures of the novel who (except for the narrator and Dominic, linked by epithet and image to the world of the *Odyssey*) inhabit metaphorically a rather morose world of bourgeois Catholic art or of peasant handicraft. The antique is evoked in the likening of

---

[64] M. C. Bradbrook, *Joseph Conrad, Poland's English Genius* (Cambridge, University Press, 1941), p. 70.

Rita's face to "the faces of women sculptured on immemorial monuments"; [65] and again in a glimpse of her, "rosy like some impassive statue in a desert in the flush of dawn".[66] "A head like a gem", a bared neck "round like the shaft of a column", suggest the classic or the classicizing renaissance.[67] And when M. George dreams of Rita, she appears to him in a *décor* from Ovid, as Titian or Claude might have rendered it, "with white limbs shimmering in the gloom like a nymph haunting a riot of foliage".[68]

Rita's sister Therese evokes by turns the notion of a severe proletarian and utilitarian art ("a hard hollow figure of baked clay . . . an achievement in unglazed earthenware") and of an ascetic Catholic art, looking "as though she had come out of an old, cracked, smoky painting . . ." or, more particularly, reminding the narrator of "a strange head painted by El Greco".[69] Elsewhere she is imaged, in contrast to the roseate Rita, as "flat without detail, as if cut out of black paper" (p. 154).

So with the other figures. Allègre, "like a severe prince with the face of a tombstone Crusader" (p. 27), suggests antecedents dis-

---

[65] *The Arrow of Gold*, pp. 66 f. Cf., on p. 146, the view of Rita "as if carved six thousand years ago in order to fix for ever that something secret and obscure which is in all women" – which, if it embodies the too facile stereotype, at least presents it to our inner eye as image rather than as mere assertion.

[66] *Ibid.*, p. 101. Cf. with this the Rita of p. 303: "Rosy all over, cheeks, neck, shoulders, she seemed lighted up softly from inside like a beautiful transparency."

[67] *Ibid.*, pp. 134, 92. The classical evocations of the imagery are enforced by classical reference – e.g., Blunt's reference to Rita of the Danaë myth (p. 37).

[68] *Ibid.*, pp. 255 f. It should be said for Rita that she is not entirely content to be regarded as an *objet d'art*. She expresses her gratitude to Mills for approaching her – as her lover Henry Allègre had approached her – as a human being, and not "as if I had been a precious object in a collection, an ivory carving or a piece of Chinese porcelain" (p. 84). Only at the end of the book does the narrator arrive at this frame of mind.

[69] *Ibid.*, pp. 121, 138 f., 157. The particularity of the El Greco reference is highly uncharacteristic of Conrad's similes in this realm, resembling rather the practice of Proust or of Henry James in his later novels, in which one may find metaphoric evocations of canvasses by Titian and Bronzino, Van Eyck and Memling, and various others. The image cited is, so far as I find, the only metaphoric reference to the work of a particular artist in Conrad's fiction.

tinguished enough, but stylistically remote from those of his mistress, belonging to a different epoch, a soberer art. As for the posturing Blunt, he also evokes a mortuary reference, but from an age of debased art, and hardly honorific: through Rita's eyes he is seen with "a funereal grace in his attitude so that he might have been reproduced in marble on a monument to some woman in one of those atrocious Campo Santos: the bourgeois conception of an aristocratic mourning lover" (p. 212). This system of aesthetic reference, embracing even quite minor characters, is ubiquitous. Blunt's mother is presented as "a perfect picture in silver and grey, with touches of black here and there" (p. 180); the Italian father of M. George's fellow lodgers has "silvery locks curling round his bald pate and over his ears, like a *barocco* apostle" (p. 239); even the nameless guests at Rita's supper are shown, after the intrusion of the Paris journalist, sitting "rather like a very superior lot of waxworks . . . with that odd air wax figures have of being aware of their existence being but a sham" (p. 69).

There are local echoes of some of the old "metaphysical" motifs that, obsessing Conrad's imagination, saturated his imagery in the great series of works commencing with *Lord Jim* and "Heart of Darkness" – e.g., a few graphic images of damnation and torment referred to Ortega – but most of the successful imagery of this novel is of the visual and tactile order. Indeed, except for a sequence, not very extended, of images evoking the mood of fairy tale and nursery tale, there would seem to be no other conspicuous image-sequence than the one traced above.[70]

THE ROVER (1923)

The imaginative fires remain banked in *The Rover*; indeed one is almost disposed to feel, confronted with the great majority of the figurative expressions in this novel, that Conrad's image-

---

[70] The most conspicuous of the legendary references is perhaps the King of Thule simile in the final paragraph; but this (occurring in the "Second Note") falls outside the story proper. The characteristic mode of this strain of imagery is pictorial, so that it links with the major strain of

making faculty (whatever we may say of the other imaginative capabilities revealed in the work) has come full circle to the unresponsiveness betrayed in *Almayer's Folly*. Certainly there is no longer any question of similes and metaphors exploding like "fireworks". A handful of the old expressionistic veins are tapped (the spectral in a half-dozen or so contexts, the mortuary once or twice), but perfunctorily and to no great expressive effect. There is a recrudescence, psychologically interesting, of animal imagery, a class as densely represented in this novel as in *Lord Jim* itself; but all but a handful of the locutions in this class – images only in a Pickwickian sense – are the merest notations, of the sort reduced by usage to an almost tautological status (e.g., "blink like an owl", "bolt like a hare", "shoot [down] like dogs", "a snail's pace"). They do not in the aggregate have anything approaching the suggestive significance of the zoological imagery in *Lord Jim*.

But if the Conradian fires are quiescent, a stubborn plastic quality of imagination persists to the end, less memorably operant than in *The Arrow* or than in almost any other of the novels from *The Nigger of the "Narcissus"* on, but not at any rate extinguished. Moreover, the inveterate instinct toward thematic reference is still traceable, however attenuated its operacy. As in *The Arrow of Gold* the most conspicuous strain of verbal imagery (or at any rate one of the two most conspicuous strains) is from the realm of art, but with the significant difference that here the images all are sculptural, presenting by turns Peyrol, Catherine, Scevola, Symons under the aspects of masks, carvings, effigies of stone and clay, in one instance a medal. This strain of imagery compounds with a continuous strain of epithet and simile attributing to various of the characters of the novel, including the fisherman's dog, the immobility of stone or rock. On two occasions an expressly "enchanted" immobility is evoked.[71] To these more conspicuous sequences may be added the several evocations of the sea in

---

imagery examined above. Cf. especially the following: "But the picture I had in my eye, coloured and simple like an illustration to a nursery-book tale of two venturesome children's escapade, was what fascinated me most" (p. 149).

[71] *Ibid.*, pp. 119 ("Peyrol, turning suddenly into stone as by enchantment"); p. 223.

terms of stone, of gem, of metal.[72] I should say that, although none of these veins of imagery could be called thematic in any full and unimpeachable sense of the term, they all contribute to an encompassing mood and tempo which we may identify – as a number of critics have done – with the author's physical and mental fatigue, but which is felt in the novel as precisely the sense of enchanted immobility mentioned above. In this sense they have their symbolic value.

Of those mentioned, only the sequence of sculptural images need detain us; of these there are only two – both profile presentments – that may be said to be independently memorable: the succinct but expressive "immobility of a head struck on a medal", said of Peyrol; and the "sharp carving of an old prophetess of some desert tribe" evoked expressly to communicate the hardness of Catherine's features.[73] But more of course is suggested in these images than the mere substantive and graphic qualities (hardness, incisiveness of contour). We find that in other contexts the second image is divested of its sculptural component and that Catherine is presented alternatively as "chieftainess", "peasant-priestess", and "prophetess" of "sibylline aspect" – a motif elaborated at one point (during one of her parleys with Peyrol) in the image of "an old sibyl risen from the tripod to prophesy calmly atrocious disasters".[74]

In this sequence of sibylline images we sense, I believe – apart from their obvious aspect of the "portentous" in the strict sense – an intention that has to do not so much with the definable themes of the novel as with a generalized atmosphere or aura of the

---

[72] In addition to "flint" and "a slab of black lead", the Mediterranean is imaged with a "gemlike surface perfectly flawless in the invincible depth of its colour"; in the likeness of "a plaque of mother-of-pearl" under a veiled sun "like a silver disc"; and (in the scene of the tartane's immolation) as "a hard blue gem" beneath a sunset sky "clear like a pale topaz" (pp. 30, 144, 280).

[73] *Ibid.*, pp. 107; 174.

[74] *Ibid.*, pp. 169, 228, 282; 170. There is also an interesting simile in another vein, in which Catherine is presented – with a curious implication of transvestism – in the likeness of "a senator in his curule chair awaiting the blow of a barbarous fate" (p. 247).

legendary. They may be said, in any case, to link in an associative bond with a series of images (having reference to Peyrol or attributed to Peyrol) in which is evoked, in similitudes of shipwreck and exploration, of strange tribes and idols, something of the adventurousness of Peyrol's roving, Odyssean past. And they serve also to prepare us for his quasi-legendary end – in which one may discern a suggestion, deliberate or otherwise, of that of the Dantean Ulysses.[75] The motif is announced in the opening paragraphs, in the expression of Peyrol's feeling as he is about to set foot on French soil at the Port of Toulon ("like a navigator about to land on a newly discovered shore"). It is developed in the following chapter in the notation of his setting out on mule-back from the inn-yard on the outskirts of Hyères, "as calmly as though setting out to explore the mysteries of a desert island".[76] The second of these similes finds its echo near the end of the book when Peyrol, on board the tartane as it sails on its final voyage to encounter the *Amelia*, tells Michel: " 'If I had gone away by myself, I would have left you marooned on this earth like a man thrown out to die on a desert island' " (p. 253).

Elsewhere the motif of discovery and exploration, of the geographically remote and isolated, takes on a freight of ethnological reference: Peyrol listens abstractedly to Michel's talk of the Revolution "as if to the tale of an intelligent islander on the other side of the world talking to the rest of mankind" (p. 94); to Réal he discourses "with gusto of Englishmen as if they had been a strange, very little-known tribe" (p. 110). Later this strain of ethnological allusion links again, as in the image of Catherine as carved prophetess, with the sculptural imagery, in Peyrol's reflective evocation (apropos of Réal) of the figure of an Indian idol:

[75] *Inferno*, xxvi. Cf. John Lehmann: "Was it not Odysseus returning at last to Ithaca, with all his fabulous doings in the Trojan War and his fabulous adventures on the homeward journey, that Conrad's drawing of Peyrol suggested?" ("On Rereading 'The Rover' ", in John Lehmann, *The Open Night*, New York, Harcourt, Brace, 1952, p. 58). But Lehmann's essay limits its references to Homeric sources (the *Iliad* as well as the *Odyssey*), without mention of the medieval Ulysses of *Inferno*, whose legend I suspect to be implicated in *The Rover*, as in Tennyson's poem.
[76] *The Rover*, pp. 2, 14.

"She sat and stared at him as if he had been gilt all over, with three heads and seven arms on his body" – a comparison reminiscent of certain idols he had seen in an Indian temple. (p. 179)

These metaphoric evocations are enforced by a recurrent strain of recollective allusion to scenes, properties, episodes of Peyrol's adventures as a Brother of the Coast – to the Cape of Storms and the Gulf of Tonkin; to Chinese vermilion and Madapolam muslin; to "the shores of Mozambique Channel, the coral strands of India, the forests of Madagascar"; to a period of enslavement by an Arab sheik and a fight in which he (Peyrol) "had received a wound which laid him open and gushing like a slashed wine-skin".[77]

One may, of course, regret that Conrad, failing to retain to the end the full imaginative vigor of his prime, did not leave as artistic testament a more full-blooded and imposing work. But we take from our artists what they give us: and there is reason to "take" *The Rover* rather than to reject it – to take it not merely in a spirit of piety but as a serious, and in some degree successful, attempt by a major artist in the decline of his powers to evoke a resonance of the legendary out of a theme that was deeply and intimately felt. Not many commentators on this novel have succeeded in striking a reasonable balance between the almost ludicrously contrary evaluations that have been advanced by such critics as Ford and Miss Bradbrook on the one side, Guerard and Moser on the other. When an acceptable balance is struck one may hope that the *consensus criticorum* will take into account the verbal imagery of the novel. It does not, as in the major works, constitute an imposing and inescapable feature of style. Greatly attenuated from the robust metaphoric growth in that series of earlier and greater works explored above, it contains only a few expressions of undeniable evocative power. Nevertheless we can find in it traces, slight but artistically effective, of the old strategy of quasi-musical reference and the old obsessive instinct of symbolic saturation – in which, as I have tried to illustrate in this chapter, a significant portion of the imaginative power and authority of Conrad's fictional art resides.

[77] *Ibid.*, pp. 15, 36, and *passim.*

VIII

THE TEMPLE OF NATURE

> Tout l'univers visible n'est qu'un magasin d'images et de
> signes auxquels l'imagination donnera une place et une
> valeur relative; c'est une espèce de pâture que l'imagi-
> nation doit digérer et transformer.
>
> Baudelaire, "Salon de 1859"

Apostrophizing Almayer in *A Personal Record*, Conrad speaks of
wrapping round his unhonoured form "the royal mantle of the
tropics".[1] Though the metaphor has the air of a rhetorical flourish,
it suggests in fact a salient aspect of his fictional art, one that
Daniel-Rops expressed with some precision when he wrote:

> En réalité, un homme, décrit par lui, ne prend complètement sa vie
> que placé dans un cadre, dans un milieu, dans une atmosphère. ...
> L'ambiance, chez Conrad, complète le héros mieux que ne saurait
> faire un commentaire psychologique.[2]

In this matter as in so many others Conrad learned early the
lesson of Flaubert, so much akin to the precept and example of
Baudelaire; or if he did not learn it from these sources he had,
from the time he set pen to paper, arrived at it intuitively.

The significance in Flaubert's novels of the landscape, and the
role of imagery in evoking an "inner landscape", have been
studied in detail by Demorest, but we may turn to an earlier and
more casual critic for a concise statement of one of the functions
of natural imagery in Flaubert. Commenting on a famous image

---

[1] *A Personal Record*, p. 88. It is interesting to compare this with Flaubert's assertion "qu'il voulait entourer Salammbô de voiles mystérieux et
vagues" (quoted, Demorest, *L'Expression figurée* ..., p. 518*n*.).
[2] Daniel-Rops, *Carte d'Europe*, p. 79.

from *Madame Bovary*, Emile Faguet defined its *modus operandi* in terms unexpectedly recalling Mallarmé:

La comparaison a ici toute la valeur d'un symbole, c'est-à-dire de cette figure par laquelle on représente un état d'âme par un paysage, ou plutôt par laquelle un état d'âme *se représente à lui-même* par un paysage.[3]

The reference here is to a verbal image, but the statement defines as well Flaubert's intent in much of his objective presentment of landscape. "Il n'y a point dans mon livre une description isolée, gratuite; toutes *servent* à mes personnages et ont une influence lointaine ou immédiate sur l'action": [4] so he wrote in the "apologie de *Salammbô*" which he addressed to Sainte-Beuve in 1862, and one may suspect that he expressed there the intention underlying much of the descriptive detail, and specifically of the landscape, in all his novels.

Whether the implied intention was as unfailingly operative as he would have had his correspondent believe may be doubted – since in even so deliberate a strategist of the novel as Flaubert one must postulate a creative *élan* that did not always wait upon his calculations. But one must also postulate – for Flaubert as for other nineteenth-century novelists – a concept of the novel as "microcosm", in a rather strict material sense: as three-dimensional model or construct of an intuited "actual" world. When Henry James declared the novelist's primary task to be "solidity of specification" he stated as a principle what for him, and for most novelists of his own and the preceding generations, was originally instinct. In imputing a generalized significance to "solidity" itself – independent of any particular significances attributable to the

---

[3] Emile Faguet, *Flaubert (Collections des grands écrivains français)* (Paris, Hachette, 1899), p. 156. The italics are Faguet's. The image in question, from the opening paragraph of chapter 7, part 2, of the novel, is as follows: "Le lendemain fut pour Emma une journée funèbre. Tout lui parut enveloppé par une atmosphère noire qui flottait confusément sur l'extérieur des choses et le chagrin s'engouffrait dans son âme avec des hurlements doux, comme fait le vent d'hiver dans les châteaux abandonnés" (Flaubert, *Madame Bovary*, p. 171).
[4] Flaubert, *Correspondance*, V, p. 60 f. The letter, written in response to Sainte-Beuve's friendly, but frequently dense, strictures on the novel, occupies over fifteen pages in the Conard edition.

items specified – James expressed the nineteenth century's aspiration to make of the novel a total symbol of an actual world apprehended as solidly material and abounding in meaningful specifics.

The traces of this aspiration are strong in Conrad. In this connection we may recall his assertion in *A Personal Record* (p. 92) of the "fond belief" that the object of the universe is "purely spectacular" – a profession of faith which, as Jean-Jacques Mayoux has shrewdly suggested, may be taken to imply a Berkeleyan metaphysic.[5] We may set aside the question whether Conrad – whose ultimate concern did not, of course, lie in the way of metaphysics – would actually have subscribed to the Berkeleyan *Esse est percipi*, as an ontological principle. As aesthetic principle, however, some such formula could, with no great extravagance, be derived from the Preface of 1897, which declares in substance that the work of art can be communicated only through the way of sensory perception – can, in short, have no *being* as a work of art except as it is sensuously *perceived*. Clearly a work aspiring to represent or symbolize a reality conceived of as spectacle must itself contain the elements of spectacle.

We may infer, then, that for Conrad as for James solidity of specification, particularity of reference to the material environment (and specifically to the objects and elements of created nature), subserved a generalized symbolic function transcending any account we may give of the specific function of isolated particulars. In a significant sentence of the paragraph just cited from *A Personal Record* he declared: "The unwearied self-forgetful attention to every phase of the living universe reflected in our consciousness may be our appointed task on this earth." In proposing such a task for the human species generally, and *a fortiori* for the artist, Conrad may be said to imply just such a generalized justification of the descriptive element in his fiction – a justification that one may well suspect to be more candid than Flaubert's defensive assertion of a specific intent behind every descriptive particular. The sentence is not far, indeed, from implying that

---

5   Quoted in Raymond Las Vergnas, *Joseph Conrad: Romancier de l'exil* (Lyon, Vitte, 1959), p. 143.

much in the way of descriptive particularization is to be accepted "because it is there". It is there in the novel, that is to say, because it was in the novelist's mind, a feature in his imaginative land-scape, an integral element of his created world, as reflected back upon the artist's consciousness from that "living world" which furnishes the *Grundstoffe* of his creation. And indeed Flaubert himself, further on in the course of that apologia to Sainte-Beuve from which I have quoted (in which one may suspect that his candor grew with his confidence as he warmed to his task), im-plied much the same thing when he wrote:

Ce n'est pas ma faute non plus si les orages sont fréquents dans la Tunisie à la fin de l'été. Chateaubriand n'a pas plus inventé les orages que les couchers de soleil, et les uns et les autres, il me semble, appartiennent à tout le monde.[6]

But if the concept of the novel – at any rate of the nineteenth-century novel – implies a measure of autonomy in the novelist's descriptive particularizations, we have still to reckon with the sense we derive from a number of the most imposing novelists in that tradition (among whom I include Conrad as well as Flaubert and James) that much of the descriptive detail bears the stamp of a particular fitness. After the generality of the statement just quoted, Flaubert fell back upon an *ad hoc* defense having to do with the mythology of his novel; and we may suspect that he could, if pressed, have found a specific *raison d'être* for many like phenomena throughout his fiction. In Conrad too we may assume – with support from the author in several specific connections – that his deployment of landscape and of the natural elements had frequently, indeed characteristically, a specific suggestive or symbolic function. The artist's consciousness in which are reflected those "phases" of "the living universe" of which he wrote in *A Personal Record* was a consciousness saturated with the specific issues and involvements of the world of its own creation; and these in turn reflected back upon the image or spectacle of the living universe discriminated in his creation. Thus that reciprocal process identified by Conrad in the work of another novelist as

6 Flaubert, *Correspondance*, V, p. 64.

an "interpenetration" of the human agents and their physical milieu, so that we may say of much of his work (as Goethe said of Shakespeare's) that "even the inanimate world takes part; subordinate things have their rôle, the elements, the phenomena of the heavens, the earth and the sea, thunder and lightning".[7] In this sense, as in his metaphoric usage, he brought to the novel a poetic apprehension of reality.

Conrad was not a metaphysician, and we need not take his obiter dictum on the meaning of the universe with entire seriousness. It was posited in opposition to an ethical view which he found irreconcilable with his novelist's sense of the way things happen in the only world his skepticism admitted – the world of material and organic creation. Of his own artistic universe, the world of his novels, there can be no doubt that he intended an ethical as well as a "spectacular" content. One suspects, in fact, that much of his chronic irritation at being stereotyped in the popular mind as a writer of sea tales – at having always dangling behind him "that infernal tail of ships and the sea" – originated in his well-founded suspicion that much of his public responded to his work on no higher level than that of spectacle. Yet the spectacle was essential, the indispensable vehicle of the ethical insights and ideal values; and the "spectacular" elements of his art – notably the presentment of nature as spectacle – are indissolubly related to the moral and psychological involvements in the novels and stories. Nature in Conrad provides an ambience, a translucent material envelope through which the moral complications of the drama are refracted or in which they are reflected.

If Conrad cannot in any proper sense of the word be called a mystic, his work nevertheless affords evidence that he was accessible to that residue of primitive feeling which (self-consciously articulate in English poetry since Wordsworth and the first romantics, and in French poetry in such notable examples as

---

[7] "Shakespeare und kein Ende"; quoted by Wolfgang Clemen, *The Development of Shakespeare's Imagery* (New York, Hill & Wang, 1962), p. 174. In the original text the sentence contains an appended reference, omitted by Clemen, to the role of the evoked animal life ("... wilde Tiere erheben ihre Stimme, oft scheinbar als Gleichnis, aber ein wie das andere Mal mithandelnd").

Hugo, Baudelaire, and Valéry) emerges in the form of a felt reciprocity between psychic events and the natural processes taking place in the environment. In the earlier works this sense of reciprocity often expresses itself in the elementary mode of personification (Ruskin's "pathetic fallacy") – i.e., in the direct projection upon the natural phenomena of the states and feelings the author wishes to communicate. Though it remains an appreciable feature of style through the *Youth* period, it is in the early Malay novels and stories and in *The Nigger of the "Narcissus"* that personification of the natural environment is most conspicuous. I have already cited examples of personification in *Almayer's Folly*, and shall presently have occasion, in a special context, to illustrate more fully. Whatever the limitations on Ruskin's argument as applied to poetry, I should say that personification in *Almayer* and its successor, too facilely applied, must count, on the whole, as a blemish of style, as evidence of a sensibility still too deeply engaged with its material for artistic detachment.[8]

Personification of nature is scarcely less conspicuous a feature of style in *The Nigger of the "Narcissus"* than in the two Malay novels that preceded it; but, more coolly handled, it in no sense constitutes a blemish on that work. It accords with the epic suggestions that hover about the novel (conveyed, for example, in such quasi-Homeric epithets as "sleep, the consoler" and "the immortal and unresting sea", or in such devices as the three formal similes spaced through the body of the novel in which various portions of the ship's day are likened to seasons of the earth).[9] Moreover, it is less importunately "pathetic", does not make such peremptory affective demands upon the reader as are made in the earlier works. There is nothing like the "caress of infinite pity" with which, in the first novel, a breath of air touched Almayer's cheek. In particular the homecoming passage off the coast and up

[8] Conradian personification, together with such other early stylistic idiosyncrasies as his postpositioned modifiers, was neatly parodied by Max Beerbohm in "The Feast", in such passages as the following: "The roots of the congested trees, writhing in some kind of agony private and eternal, ..." (Max Beerbohm, *A Christmas Garland*, London, Heinemann, 1938, p. 125).

[9] *The Nigger of the "Narcissus"*, pp. 31, 132, 145.

the river, from the first entry into "the chops of the Channel", in which all is personified – the *Narcissus* herself and the craft she meets in her passage, as well as the clouds and the land and the structures on it, lining the shores of the river – has at first a buoyancy and a kinesthetic vigor ("The coast to welcome her stepped out of space into the sunshine"), later a gravity and rhetorical magnificence, that make it one of the memorable descriptive passages in early Conrad.[10]

From the first, Conrad employed simile and metaphor as adjuncts to his direct personifications. He was never entirely to abandon the more primitive figure (which for him as for Dickens responded to something permanent in his mode of apprehending the universe), but more and more he came to rely upon his growing mastery of the direct presentment of visibilia, with the aid of metaphor or simile only.

By the time of *Nostromo* – although the ambience of the natural setting is as omnipresent and as symbolically effective in that novel as in anything Conrad produced excepting only "Heart of Darkness" – the direct personification of nature is conspicuous for its rarity. To consider only one of a score or so of masterly landscapes dispersed through the book, the great panoramic view of Campo and Cordillera that comprises the long opening paragraph of chapter six, part third, with no fewer than seven metaphoric locutions (chiefly similes), contains no personification of nature, and none of any sort other than the hint conveyed in the epithet "crouched" applied to the ranchos.[11] Indeed, though a search will yield a number of examples of this figure in *Nostromo*, there is, I should say, only one – the popular conceit of the Golfo "asleep under its black poncho", repeated at intervals throughout the novel – that remains vividly in the reader's imagination.[12]

In the earlier works, and in *The Rescue*, of which much of the prose dated from Conrad's first half-dozen professional years, the

[10]   *Ibid.*, pp. 161-165.
[11]   *Nostromo*, pp. 394.
[12]   I may say here in passing that I have found no landscape in any work of Conrad's between *Youth* and *The Rescue* comparable for the density and explicitness of its personifications to the famous Forest of Fontainebleau scene in *L'Education sentimentale* (*op. cit.*, p. 466).

reciprocity of man and nature was occasionally made explicit in similes in which the normal relation of vehicle to tenor is reversed – i.e., in which the psychic state is the term of comparison for the natural object or element. In *Outcast* we are told of Lingard's love of "the narrow and sombre creeks, strangers to sunshine: black, smooth, tortuous – like byways of despair" (p. 201); in "The End of the Tether", the "concentrated calms" of the equator are likened to "the deep introspection of a passionate nature" (*Youth*, p. 244); in *The Rescue* Edith Travers, in a hallucinated moment, imagines herself enveloped by a "shadow, that like a suspicion of an evil truth darkens everything upon the earth on its passage" (p. 151). Or consider such a passage as the following (also from *The Rescue*) in which Lingard, in a boat with Mrs. Travers skirting the reefs of the Shore of Refuge, identifies himself with the conflict between sea and shore:

The struggle of the rocks forever overwhelmed and emerging, with the sea forever victorious and repulsed, fascinated the man. He watched it as he would have watched something going on within himself. (p. 245)

The image just quoted suggests an instructive comparison with the passage which links parts second and third of *Under Western Eyes*. Razumov, following his first interview with the narrator in the Bastions, leans over the parapet of a bridge above the swiftly-flowing Arve:

He hung well over the parapet, as if captivated by the smooth rush of the blue water under the arch. The current there is swift, extremely swift; it makes some people dizzy; I myself can never look at it for any length of time without experiencing a dread of being suddenly snatched away by its destructive force. Some brains cannot resist the suggestion of irresistible power and of headlong motion..
It apparently had a charm for Mr. Razumov. (p. 197)

With this image (followed only by a few concluding lines of reflection on the part of the narrator) Conrad closes his second part. Part third opens with Razumov still hanging over the parapet:

The water under the bridge ran violent and deep. Its slightly undulating rush seemed capable of scouring out a channel for itself through solid granite while you looked. But had it flowed through Razumov's breast, it could not have washed away the accumulated bitterness the wrecking of his life had deposited there.

"What is the meaning of all this?" he thought, staring downwards at the headlong flow so smooth and clean that only the passage of a faint air-bubble, or a thin vanishing streak of foam like a white hair, disclosed its vertiginous rapidity, its terrible force. (p. 198)

The post of observation has shifted in this third part: with the narrator off the scene Razumov is omnisciently viewed and his thoughts are directly presented. Nevertheless, there is no explicit self-identification of Razumov with the river. The negative metaphor in the first paragraph is a conceit, a play of the imagination about the object and the observer.

As in the memorable image of Haldin's descent of the stairs on his departure from Razumov's quarters (the descending footfalls, the "fleeting shadow", the "wink of the tiny flame", the ensuing stillness [13]) so here, in a passage evoking the earlier one, Conrad lets the sensory impression do its own work. The affective force of the image lies in its objective presentment and in the objectively reported fixity of Razumov's regard. If the river is correlative to "something going on within" Razumov, or to something intuitible in the current of his destiny, it is the reader who must make the correlation: the image is presented as symbol, not as express surrogate. The method here is characteristic of Conrad's handling of the natural milieu during the period of his greatest achievement.

But if the method becomes less explicit and less insistent, the instinct for symbolic identification of psychic states with the aspects of created nature – or, more generally, for symbolic interpenetration of one with the other – remains inveterate, so that when he turns to the city for the locale of *The Secret Agent* he finds, among other "ecological" images (that of the aquarium, for example), a metaphor that evokes the ominous secrecy and density of the forest. Inspector Heat encounters the Professor by night in the premises of a second-hand furniture store,

---

[13] *Under Western Eyes*, p. 63. Although auditory rather than visual impression is primary in this earlier image, Razumov's post of observation – hanging over a railing gazing into depths below him – is identical in both.

where, deep in the gloom of a sort of narrow avenue winding through a bizarre forest of wardrobes, with an undergrowth tangle of table legs, a tall pier-glass glimmered like a pool of water in a wood. (p. 82)

Here the express metaphoric nexus is merely between the clutter of the second-hand store and the evoked forest. Again there is no explicit representation of a moral state; but the evoked landscape (like the *selva oscura* of *Inferno I*) stands in a metaphoric relation to the world of the novel, serving, like the drained aquarium, as symbol of an intuited moral universe.

So characteristic a feature of style is natural imagery in Conrad's work that at least one critic (Johanna Burkhardt) has seen in his symbolic presentment of nature (*sinndeutende Naturdarstellung*) the most direct approach to the experience of reality (*Wirklichkeitserlebnis*) communicated in his work. In the development of her thesis Miss Burkhardt relied rather heavily on the earliest works, citing, for example, the simultaneity of the sun's setting with the first appearance of James Wait on the deck of the *Narcissus*.[14] As I suggested earlier, in considering its possible Flaubertian antecedent, the imagery here, with its particulars of "black mist" and "mourning veil", wears its symbolic intent with a certain obviousness; and it is not made less obvious by the collaboration of the sun in producing the symbolic chiaroscuro. Indeed we seem for the moment to be in a fictional world in which, as in that of Melmoth the Wanderer and the Gothic romances, the experienced "reality" is liable to dilution with some other element. If the entire treatment of Wait were pitched in this key we might feel that the strictures of Marvin Mudrick had some basis.[15]

We may follow Miss Burkhardt's lead, however, for a still earlier example of the natural symbol which is not subject to the

---

[14] *The Nigger of the "Narcissus"*, p. 34; Johanna Burkhardt, *Das Erlebnis der Wirklichkeit und seine künstlerische Gestaltung in Joseph Conrads Werk*, pp. 98-100. Miss Burkhardt's definition of this Conradian device ("einer engen Verstrickung, eines wechselseitigen In-sich-Hineinziehens von Natur und Mensch") is simply a more generalized version of Conrad's remark on the "interpenetration of the sea and of life" in Cooper's tales.

[15] "Claptrap symbolism" is Mudrick's term for Conrad's handling of Wait (Marvin Mudrick, "The Artist's Conscience and *The Nigger of 'The Narcissus'* ", *Nineteenth-Century Fiction*, XI, March, 1957, pp. 288-297).

same sort of strictures. The instance in question is implicit in the forest imagery of two separate passages in *Almayer's Folly*. Containing substantial fragments of "pathetic fallacy", they illustrate the rather importunate affectivity of Conrad's early treatment of nature. But they also contain much vigorous objective presentment, they evoke an atmosphere, and however much one may prefer the cooler and more "distancing" evocations of, say, *Nostromo*, these early landscapes have their own character, and a special interest as revelatory of the original impulse that lay behind his more mature handling of landscape. Moreover, though their affective appeal is obvious enough (indeed all too obvious), the thematic suggestion implicit in them is apparently less so – they have, at any rate, been variously construed by qualified readers. Thomas Moser's view of the symbolism of these passages from *Almayer* is quite different from that of Miss Burkhardt.[16] The difference points up what seems to me the obligation of the interpretative critic towards the author's text – an issue sufficiently important to justify a more prolonged scrutiny than I should otherwise devote to these specimens of earliest Conrad. The conclusion which will emerge from the next half-dozen pages of text is of importance for the view of the symbolic implicit in this study.

Moser instances two descriptive passages in *Almayer's Folly*, almost identical as to content and closely related as to context. The first passage supplies the *mise-en-scène* of the first assignation of Dain Maroola and Nina Almayer; the second, of the meeting preceding their flight from Nina's island home. About to part after their first rendezvous, the lovers float side by side on the Pantai,

---

[16] Distinct from both, and from each other, are the views of Adam Gillon that "the wilderness . . ., in Conrad's work, is always a symbol of moral corruption", and of John H. Hicks that "unmodified passion (in any form) is consistently represented in the novel as a decaying forest of parasitic growth, dark and impenetrable" (Adam Gillon, *The Eternal Solitary: Joseph Conrad*, New York, Bookman Associates, 1960, p. 64; John H. Hicks, "Conrad's *Almayer's Folly*: Structure, Theme, and Critics", *Nineteenth-Century Fiction*, XIX, June, 1964, p. 24).

while above, away up in the broad day, flamed immense red blossoms
sending down on their heads a shower of great dew-sparkling petals
that descended rotating slowly in a continuous and perfumed stream;
and over them, under them, ... the intense work of tropical nature
went on: plants shooting upward, entwined, interlaced in inextricable
confusion, climbing madly and brutally over each other in the terrible silence of a desperate struggle towards the life-giving sunshine
above − as if struck with sudden horror at the seething mass of
corruption below, at the death and decay from which they sprang
(p. 71)

The motif is reintroduced and elaborated immediately before the
dénouement of the novel, as Dain, a fugitive now, awaits in a
clearing the appearance of the mistress who is to join him and flee
with him to his own country:

... the big trees of the forest, lashed together with manifold bonds by
a mass of tangled creepers, looked down at the growing young life
at their feet with the sombre resignation of giants that had lost faith
in their strength. And in the midst of them the merciless creepers clung
to the big trunks in cable-like coils, leaped from tree to tree, hung in
thorny festoons from the lower boughs, and, sending slender tendrils
on high to seek out the smallest branches, carried death to their
victims in an exulting riot of silent destruction. (p. 165)

The theme is reiterated a page later, in the image of the generations of trees, "entombed and rotting", of the trees still unfallen,
"immense and helpless, awaiting their turn", of the "sinuous rush
upwards into the air and sunshine" of the parasites,

feeding on the dead and the dying alike, and crowning their victims
with pink and blue flowers that gleamed amongst the boughs, incongruous and cruel, like a strident and mocking note in the solemn
harmony of the doomed trees. (p. 167)

We may take these descriptive splendors as *gratia sua*, as revelatory (in John Bayley's phrase) only because "they are what they
are". But if we ask why they are what they are, and where they
are − as backdrop for lovers' meetings − then it seems to me, as it
did to Miss Burkhardt, that the answer lies unmistakably to hand:
the images anticipate Nina's revolt against paternal authority, her
deception of her father, her flight with Dain from Sambir,
Almayer's collapse and disintegration. One need not be a
Darwinian, or saturated as Conrad was in the descriptive works

of Alfred Russel Wallace, to see in these images the triumph of young and vigorous life – struggling for self-assertion, flowering out of decay – over the declining life from which it drew its sustenance.

Moreover if we turn back to the opening pages of the novel, in which we are made aware of the gulf between the actual squalor and futility of Almayer's life and the scope of his dreams of wealth and status, we may find a like suggestion in the images of the tree uprooted by the monsoon, at the mercy of the river's "brutal and unnecessary violence" (p. 4).

If we scrutinize this imagery in the light only of the given context – in the light, that is, of themes explicit or implicit in the work itself – and not with a view to detecting symptoms of the author's own psychological perplexities, then, as I have said, the suggestions are evident. Moser, however, assigning a feminine gender to the vines and creepers, by implication refers the dead and decaying trees to Dain. Consistently with his general thesis of "the uncongenial subject" (*viz.*, sexual love), rather than with the specific text, he sees in this imagery a sort of Strindbergian fantasy of sexual strife, with the lethal female strangling the helpless male. "Although Conrad intends marital bliss for Dain", he declares, "the imagery of a less conscious and more persuasive Conrad speaks only of death"; and further on Moser speaks of "the life of the forest producing death and equated with woman".

Moser's a priori interpretation of the imagery in question has the serious inconvenience of rendering it (in the critic's words) "inappropriate" and symptomatic of a "serious confusion" subversive of Conrad's alleged artistic intentions. Somehow the intrusion of a sombre tonality into the love-trysts of Dain and Nina disappoints his expectations: he is persuaded – though on what grounds is not apparent, since the ominous image in question is from the first an accompaniment of the Dain-Nina theme – that this love is "meant to be an idyllic romance", suffused in glamor.[17]

Now it is perfectly true that the more persuasive Conrad speaks, in this novel, of decay and ignominious death. Almayer's decline is the subject of the novel (which clearly owes something to

[17] Thomas Moser, *Joseph Conrad, Achievement and Decline*, pp. 52-57.

Madame Bovary, and something also, I suspect, to *Père Goriot*); his collapse under the weight of his collapsed illusions is its *terminus ad quem*; and these things are undoubtedly more persuasive than the Dain-Nina relationship, idyllic or otherwise, or than any foreshadowed marital bliss – of which the author has, in any case, little to say. Construed in Moser's sense, the vegetation imagery neither supports nor is supported by anything in the discursive texture of the novel. Almayer and his folly are, as we would know from the book itself, even without the testimony of *A Personal Record*, the *raison d'être* of the novel. The lovers are there, we may assume, primarily for the light they throw upon Almayer's case and the complications they contribute to its working out. What, after all, could have afforded a more workable vehicle for the nullification of Almayer's caste- and race-proud dreams of social rehabilitation than the marriage of his adored daughter to a "native"? Whatever we may think of the handling of the erotic complication, the imagery of these passages affords no grounds for Moser's charge that the artist is here "at war with his intentions". Rather it is evidence of the strict subordination of the minor to the major theme – of the persistence in the novelist's imagination of the primary intention in the face of any temptation to abandon himself to irrelevant glamor. We may, as some of his contemporaries did, find Conrad's intentions ruthless and abhorrent; but we cannot warrantably, in the given instance, see his treatment as subversive of his intentions.

Moser supported his view of the vegetation imagery in *Almayer* by referring back from the imagery of *An Outcast of the Islands*, in which there is an identification (explicitly apprehended as such by Willems, the "outcast" of the novel) between the woman Aïssa and the "intensity" and perfidious beauty of the tropical life (instinct with "poison and death") that surrounds him.[18] It may appear to be axiomatic that, in these two novels so close to one another in the Conrad canon, identical in setting and certainly related in theme and tonality – growing, indeed, out of a common stock of lived experience and having in common several of their

[18] Moser, *op. cit.*, p. 57. The Conradian passage cited is from *An Outcast of the Islands*, p. 70.

central characters – the imagery of tropical vegetation should afford a common denominator, bear an identical freight of reference. Such a conclusion would be specious, however, and for several reasons.

First, the passage cited from *An Outcast of the Islands* is presented through the sensorium of Willems, as an express datum of a particular consciousness: the responses (bafflement, repulsion, almost fright) are his own, by him identified with his attitude to the woman – "the very spirit of that land of mysterious forests" (p. 70). In his apprehension of the forest Willems experiences a sort of revelation: "the mystery is disclosed", and its lineaments are identical with those of the woman. There is nothing of the sort in relation to the images quoted from *Almayer's Folly*. Moreover the woman who is thus mysteriously revealed to Willems is not simply woman, innately perfidious and baffling to the male; it is the specific woman, Aïssa, the indigenous child of the forest with which she is identified. If mystery and danger inhere in her mere femininity, the passage does not tell us so. It implicitly suggests that for Willems the mystery and danger inhere in Aïssa's existence as a native woman, a creature of the tropic forest, vis-à-vis himself, the "civilized" European. And the suggestion is confirmed by his more explicit reflections in the following chapter:

He, a white man whose worst fault till then had been a little want of judgment and too much confidence in the rectitude of his kind! That woman was a complete savage, and . . . he tried to tell himself that the thing was of no consequence. It was a vain effort. The novelty of the sensations he had never experienced before in the slightest degree, yet had despised on hearsay from his safe position of a civilized man, destroyed his courage. He was disappointed with himself. He seemed to be surrendering to a wild creature the unstained purity of his life, of his race, of his civilization.[19]

In *Almayer's Folly* the situations of the two lovers are quite otherwise – they are all but reversed. There it is the Malayan male rather than the half-caste woman who is the more unequivocally the creature of the tropic forest. To insist upon an identical significance of the forest imagery in the two novels is to be misled

[19] *Ibid.*, p. 80. The ellipsis occurs in Conrad's text.

by an imperfect analogy and to do violence to the implicit indications of the earlier text.

If I have prolonged the analysis here, devoting what may appear to be undue space to early works which stand far below the peak of Conrad's achievement, it is largely because the case in point affords an exceptional occasion for affirming two fundamental principles. The first may be condensed into the precept that in dealing with the symbolic in literature the meaningful is to be preferred to the meaningless construction, or to the construction subversive of meaning. Expressed less tautologically, this is to say that a construction which vindicates the coherence of a given item with an apprehended whole is, if not intrinsically absurd, to be preferred to a construction which has the converse tendency. The second principle, less self-evident, is no less fundamental, at least from the point of view adopted in this study. It is this: that the symbols and images of literary art are not fixed counters or the vehicles of constant values and significances. As in music identical motifs can evoke disparate or even diametrically opposed feelings in diverse contexts,[20] so with the images and intuited symbols of imaginative literature, and particularly, I should say, with the radically ambiguous contents of that "warehouse of images" which Baudelaire discerned in nature. Although the artist, when he deals with the more public symbols of his culture, tampers with the reader's normal expectations at his own risk, he is bound by no laws and no precedents (including his own) – he is bound only by the inherent properties of the objects he evokes and by his own imaginative limitations – in the use of his symbols, which derive their significance through the relations actualized within the given work of art.

From the rather schematically employed vegetation imagery of the first two novels – univocal in its reference (so far as I can determine) if we consider it in each context separately – I turn to the densely metaphoric *Lord Jim*, of which the natural imagery is more richly suggestive, being for the most part resistant to confi-

[20] This principle (attributed to Hanslick by the musicologist E. A. Lippman) can perhaps be most readily confirmed in the compositions of the Baroque.

dently assigned "meanings". I have suggested in an earlier chapter
some of the connotations I discern in the sea – its relation, in
particular, to the imagery of "the abyss" – and in the cosmic and
meteorological imagery. The natural images that dominate the
second half of the novel – the Patusan half – are the two-headed
mountain and, in conjunction with the mountain, the manifestations of the moon.

The two-headed mountain of Patusan (or twin mountains –
Conrad's equivocation in the matter is doubtless deliberate) is one
of a number of geographic eminences in various of his works
which, with more or less of practical significance, suggest a
symbolic intent. One thinks of Higuerota, dominating the Sulacan
Campo of *Nostromo*, remote, lofty, gleaming "like a frozen
bubble", evoked from time to time to give (one may say) a sort of
"pathos of distance" to the human turmoil in the city and plain.
Or of Koh-ring, symbolically effective in *The Shadow-Line* as a
looming presence, expressing in its fixedness the corresponding
immobility of the becalmed ship; both practically and symbolically effective in the earlier "Secret Sharer", as the target of the ship's
approach to the land in the climactic scene in which the mountain
figures as a feature in an evoked landscape of Erebus. Or of the
indolent and portentous volcano of *Victory,* puffing equivocally
like the end of a gigantic cigar on Samburan.

The cleft mountain of Patusan is described by Marlow at the
time of our first introduction to Jim's realm. Here and in a later
episode, equally arresting from a visual standpoint, it is associated
with the rising of the moon. I quote the earlier passage in full, with
the comment that follows:

At a point on the river about forty miles from the sea, where the first
houses come into view, there can be seen rising above the level of the
forests the summits of two steep hills very close together, and separated
by what looks like a deep fissure, the cleavage of some mighty stroke.
As a matter of fact, the valley between is nothing but a narrow ravine;
the appearance from the settlement is of one irregularly conical hill
split in two, and with the two halves leaning slightly apart. On the
third day after the full, the moon, as seen from the open space in
front of Jim's house (he had a very fine house in the native style
when I visited him), rose exactly behind these hills, its diffused light at

first throwing the two masses into intensely black relief, and then the nearly perfect disc, glowing ruddily, appeared, gliding upwards between the sides of the chasm, till it floated away above the summits, as if escaping from a yawning grave in gentle triumph. "Wonderful effect", said Jim by my side. "Worth seeing. Is it not?"

And this question was put with a note of personal pride that made me smile, as though he had had a hand in regulating that unique spectacle. He had regulated so many things in Patusan! Things that would have appeared as much beyond his control as the motions of the moon and the stars. (*Lord Jim*, pp. 220f.)

The image introduces us to a physical feature which will be the scene of an action of critical importance in the development of the "Tuan Jim" legend in Patusan – Jim's placement of a battery, under cover of night, on the summit of one of the hills, and his reduction of the insurgent Sherif Ali's fort on the other hill. It is thus not a gratuitous feature in terms of action. Beyond this, however, one is likely in retrospect to find oneself associating the twin mountains, which dominate the scene of his new life and which to the eye appear as a single cleft peak, with the split in Jim's consciousness between the ideal and the actual, and with the corresponding cleavage effected in his life by his leap from the *Patna*. John Dozier Gordan, who closely examined five major works concerned with the career of Rajah Brooke of Sarawak, discovered a series of correspondences with the events and characters of *Lord Jim* which leave no doubt that Brooke's career made an "incalculable appeal" to Conrad's imagination and furnished him with source material. Among the corresponding items Gordan mentions "Sarambo, a high detached mountain . . . with a notch in the center",[21] from which Brooke blasted a fortified rebel post during an uprising. But if Conrad borrowed the detail, we need not therefore assume that it was borrowed casually; on the contrary, we may rather assume that it made some particular imaginative appeal, commended itself upon some definable artistic ground.

It was, in short, a particularly suggestive item from nature's warehouse of images offered to him by the "Brookiana" in which

[21] Gordan, *Joseph Conrad: the Making of a Novelist*, p. 66.

he had immersed himself; [22] and though as symbol it must be self-validating, since it does not explicitly declare its intent, we get, I believe, an indication of this in a later passage (a reprise, in a different tonality, of the moonrise) when Marlow tells us:

> He had a mind to try a coffee-plantation there. The big hill, rearing its double summit coal-black in the clear yellow glow of the rising moon, seemed to cast its shadow upon the ground prepared for that experiment.[23]

But clearly the moon and the quality of the light it sheds are implicated with the configuration of the mountain in any symbolic or suggestive function attributable to this image. Here a remark of Conrad's written four months after completion of the novel is itself suggestive. Lamenting, in a rather desperate letter to Garnett, the "want of power" in the book, he assured his correspondent that he did "not mean the 'power' of reviewers' jargon. I mean the want of illuminating imagination. I wanted to obtain a sort of lurid light out [of] the very events." [24] One of the events out of which (in a memorable display of the sort of "illuminating imagination" which he claimed to be wanting in the novel) he obtained a sort of light, "lurid" or otherwise but in any case profoundly suggestive, was precisely this repeated spectacle of the moon rising between the twin peaks. It suggests to my mind, in the first instance, the light of imagination itself – the mental function sometimes associated with the moon (as, for example, in Coleridge and in Yeats) – and I associate it with Marlow's repeated characterization of Jim as an "imaginative beggar". But it may be argued that the imaginative in art is the illusory in life:

[22] Or, alternatively, by his recollections of Berau and the campong of Captain William Lingard, in the Bornean hinterland, at the junction of the Segah and the Kelai rivers. Cf. the interesting article by Jerry Allen, "Conrad's River", *Columbia University Forum*, V (Winter, 1962), pp. 29-35. Miss Allen has established that Lingard's campong was called "Patusan" from the Malay *putus*, meaning split or broken off, and that it stood "at the base of a split hill" (p. 35). Actually there is no need of an "either/or" here: the reasonable assumption is that Brooke's Samburan enforced for Conrad the imaginative impression made by the "split hill" of Berau.

[23] *Lord Jim*, p. 322.

[24] *Letters from Joseph Conrad*, pp. 171 f.

Jim is also "romantic", and the romantic is a creature of illusions. Is the image to be taken then as a symbolic judgment on Jim?

Our response to the image is modified by an extended paragraph of Marlovian reflection on its implications, and by a later reënactment of Jim's lunar spectacle. The reprise of the rising-moon image, from which I have just quoted, is witnessed by Marlow alone on the last night of his final visit to Patusan; and it has, by virtue of its different context, a different emotional tonality from that of the original announcement of the motif. Its rising coincides with Marlow's reflection that "nothing on earth seemed less real now than his [Jim] plans, his energy, and his enthusiasm". Continuing, Marlow describes the moonrise:

and raising my eyes, I saw part of the moon glittering through the bushes at the bottom of the chasm. For a moment it looked as though the smooth disc, falling from its place in the sky upon earth, had rolled to the bottom of that precipice: its ascending movement was like a leisurely rebound; it disengaged itself from the tangle of twigs; the bare contorted limb of some tree, growing on the slope, made a black crack right across its face. It threw its level rays afar as if from a cavern, and in this mournful eclipse-like light the stumps of felled trees uprose very dark, the heavy shadows fell at my feet on all sides, my own moving shadow, and across my path the shadow of the solitary grave perpetually garlanded with flowers.[25]

The two following sentences which close the paragraph, the first evoking a realm of the dead, the second likening the lumps of white coral that shine around the dark mound of the grave (it is the grave of Jewel's mother) to "a chaplet of bleached skulls", compound the disquieting impression, reflexively modifying our impression of the earlier image.

Dorothy Van Ghent (who has also seen in the cleft peak of Patusan an evocation of Jim's inner division) juxtaposes these two passages, proposing that we see in the recurrent image of moonlight "a figure of the ego-ideal", with "its illusionariness, and the solitude implied by illusion".[26]

Quoting from a passage of Marlovian reflection – a passage in which the moonlight is likened to "the ghost of dead sunlight",

[25]   *Lord Jim*, p. 322.
[26]   Dorothy Van Ghent, *The English Novel: Form and Function* (New York, Rinehart, 1953), p. 237.

and related to the sunshine ("which – say what you like – is all we have to live by") as the echo to the sound, misleading and confusing, giving "a sinister reality to shadows alone" – Guerard took up the question where Mrs. Van Ghent left it, developing the theme of "illusionariness". "The moonlight of Patusan", he declared, "is certainly associated with immobility and isolation, and with times when Jim is seriously entranced by his pride and illusion of success." [27] There are useful insights in Guerard's treatment of these passages. Certainly "isolation" and "pride" define, to a degree, Jim's posture throughout the book. Moreover the passage illuminated by the second of these moonrises is portentous of Jim's final "immobility" in the face of disaster. And yet if we turn back to the passage first quoted, registering Marlow's impressions on his first visit, we can hardly find grounds for referring the entranced immobility of the scene to the Jim of this period – unless we are to think of Jim as an "unmoved mover". The hint of irony in Marlow's comment on his talent for "regulating" things contains no implication that the reported vigor and efficacy of Jim's administration of Patusan is to be viewed as itself illusory.

Moreover, if Jim is by nature a solitary (like all Conradian heroes), if isolation is his fundamental condition and his ultimate destiny, it is precisely on Patusan, at the time of Marlow's first visit, that this condition is *least* to the fore, is most mitigated by his human contacts and his self-imposed responsibilities. No doubt Jim – like the Brooke whom his situation, in some respects, resembles – is a charismatic leader, whose relations with his people, marked as they are with "a sort of fierce egoism, with a contemptuous tenderness",[28] are wanting in the full degree of "togetherness" which modern Western taste prescribes; but there are more than hints, there are explicit statements, to show that his relations as administrator-general of Doramin's realm involve a genuine sense of solidarity, a degree of identification (limited certainly, but unmistakable), so that the pattern of almost total

[27] Guerard, *Conrad the Novelist*, p. 163.
[28] *Ibid.*, p. 248.

isolation that dominates the first half of the novel is radically modified in the Patusan chapters, to reëmerge only at the end.

This proposition could be demonstrated at large, but two citations, widely spaced and associated respectively with Marlow's two visits, will serve the purpose.[29] Immediately following Marlow's extended reflections on the first moonrise, there is a passage of visual impression that culminates in the image of houses crowding the river-bank "like a spectral herd of shapeless creatures pressing forward to drink in a spectral and lifeless stream". But the tonality of the scene is at once modified by the "red gleam" of twinkling lights "warm, like a living spark, significant of human affections, of shelter, of repose". At this point Marlow tells his audience:

He confessed to me that he often watched these tiny warm gleams go out one by one, that he loved to see people go to sleep under his eyes, confident in the security of tomorrow. "Peaceful here, eh?" he asked. He was not eloquent, but there was a deep meaning in the words that followed. "Look at these houses; there's not one where I am not trusted. Jove! I told you I would hang on. Ask any man, woman, or child . . ." He paused. "Well, I am all right anyhow." (pp. 246f.)

Here I want to make myself fully understood. Unquestionably there is irony (on the author's part), and unquestionably there is illusion (on Jim's part), in that last line. The illusion involves Jim's pride (or hybris), and there is nothing to prevent us from referring these qualities to the moonlight. But if Jim is admittedly not "all right", it does not follow that he is "all wrong", that his pride has "entranced" him out of his sense of waking reality, or that the palpable practical success of which he speaks, even if it is the product of a "life-illusion", is itself an illusion, his claims mere boastfulness. The tragic irony of the catastrophe derives precisely from the fact that Jim is trusted and that there is every evidence that the trust has been earned. No further instance need be adduced than that provided by the visitation of the head-man and

[29] But cf. also Gordan's citations in demonstration of his proposition that "Conrad had Jim find his own rehabilitation in the rehabilitation of Patusan" (Gordan, *op. cit.*, pp. 72 f.), especially Marlow's assertion that Jim had taken "the leap that landed him into the life of Patusan, into the trust, the love, the confidence of the people" (*Lord Jim*, p. 380).

his son-in-law, embroiled with Tunku Allang over "a lot of turtles' eggs" (pp. 332f.), which is woven into the scene of Marlow's final leavetaking, on the morrow of the second enactment of Jim's lunar "spectacle" (thus immediately following Marlow's final excursus on the moonlight motif). Jim postpones a hearing on the case until Marlow's boat has pushed off; then:

The two half-naked fishermen had risen as soon as I had gone; they were no doubt pouring the plaint of their trifling, miserable, oppressed lives into the ears of the white lord, and no doubt he was listening to it, making it his own, for was it not a part of his luck – the luck "from the word Go" – the luck to which he had assured me he was so completely equal? (p. 336)

Here I touch upon my most serious reservation about Guerard's subtle and very able chapters on *Lord Jim*. Ultimately it involves nothing less than the proper relation of critic to text; proximately, it involves our view of the relations of Marlow to his creator. Guerard, like William Y. Tindall, insists that we must not identify the two, not consider Marlow as a mere author-surrogate, and in so far he is undoubtedly right.[30] The reader who "puts his trust in Marlow", he tells us (putting the risks of contemporary readership in a suitably "lurid light"), "does so at his peril".[31] The reader "must attend, eagerly yet skeptically, to everything": the reading of the novel is "a combat: within the reader, between readers and narrators, between reader and the watching and controlling mind ultimately responsible for the distortions".[32] Guerard sustains the combat with skill and courage, attending to more in the novel than perhaps any critic before him had attended to. But his citations are selective (must be selective, of course: ideally the reader must attend to everything; practically the critic cannot without greatly exceeding his text in length); and certain of his omissions,

[30] William Y. Tindall, "Apology for Marlow", *From Jane Austen to Joseph Conrad: Essays Collected in Memory of James T. Hillhouse*, ed. Robert C. Rathburn and Martin Steinmann, Jr. (Minneapolis, University of Minnesota Press, 1958), pp. 274-285. Cf. Especially, on p. 275: "It requires little critical awareness, however, to discover that Marlow, in spite of monocle and beard (if, indeed, he wears them), is a creature distinct from his creator."
[31] Guerard, *op. cit.*, p. 152.
[32] *Ibid.*, p. 153.

though doubtless not deliberate, are significant. Both citations and omissions have their bearing on the question of when one may warrantably risk the "peril" of accepting Marlow as Conrad's *porte-parole*. Guerard, declining the risk when Marlow affirms that Jim had "achieved greatness",[33] accepts it in relation to Marlow's excursus on moonlight. "Whatever their sympathies in the matter", he tells us, "Marlow and Conrad clearly believe that we shall be saved by the sunlight of action and that deceptive half-lights are menacing." Finally, Guerard adds that "all this (if we are to trust Marlow at all) has an important bearing on Stein's ambiguous advice".[34]

Now it is Stein's ambiguous advice, abetted by his active agency as *deus ex machina*, that takes Jim to Patusan and flings him into his active role there, not only as legendary figure but as practical administrator and justiciary; and it is precisely in this connection that Guerard's analysis seems to me unsatisfactory. Having in effect denied actuality to Jim's career (in the formulae "immobility" and "illusions of success"), he nevertheless later speaks of "successes and physical dangers overcome" and of "Jim's period of success".[35] But Conrad's attention to "the Patusan background" he finds "disproportionate", the chapters devoted to it (22-35) less rewarding and authentic than the rest of the book, Jim's success imagined at a lower "level of intensity and belief" than his failure and death.[36] That the chapters in question do not constitute the strongest and most memorable portion of the novel may be granted; but that Conrad has been "bemused by his sources" and by the "appalling success of the historic Brooke" is not at all evident.[37] The fact is that the chapters in question have their own magnificence, and in any case betray no relaxation of Conrad's grasp of his material or of his subject.

There is a certain (doubtless inadvertent) sleight-of-hand here: in questioning Conrad's proportioning of his material and his distribution of accent Guerard is not exceeding his critical func-

[33] *Ibid.*, p. 152.
[34] *Ibid.*, p. 164.
[35] *Ibid.*, pp. 168, 171.
[36] *Ibid.*, p. 171.
[37] *Ibid.*, p. 168.

tion, but (as though by the contagion of Conrad's, or Marlow's, example) his focus has shifted without warning. It is no longer a question of arriving at Conrad's view of Jim by sorting it out from Marlow's. In suggesting that the chapters of action are disproportionately developed, Guerard (who omits from his citations the view of Jim with Marlow, "high in the sunshine on the top of that historic hill of his" [38]) seems to suggest that Jim has no business under that alien light, that he should get back where he belongs, under the moonlight of immobility and illusion. But this, of course, would be to suggest that it is neither Marlow's Jim nor Conrad's that we should attend to, but Guerard's.

Doubtless Guerard does not intend this; but it is evident that here he is no longer "with" Conrad – who we have every reason to believe did not see Brooke's success as "appalling", and who clearly did not see Jim's active career in Patusan, whether in its epic or its administrative aspect, as irrelevant to the story he had to tell or to the destiny it unfolds.[39] It is part of the "case exposed", and though the critic may find the exposure too prolonged at this point, he cannot reconstruct the text. He must interpret every detail in the light of all the relevant context; and he is not warranted in dismissing as irrelevant any part of the context on grounds that it falls short of the imaginative level of the rest or that it deals with aspects (e.g., "physical perils" rather than "perils of the soul" [40]) other than those which he has decided are the essential aspects.

[38]   *Lord Jim*, p. 265.
[39]   Here it may be in order to recall Wallace's view of the first Rajah Brooke, as expressed in the book (*The Malay Archipelago*) with which Conrad was saturated and which was a prime source for all the Malay novels. Wallace reported that Brooke had established equal justice, protected the Dyaks, harried the pirates, and banned slavery; and that in so doing he had "secured the affection and good will" of both Dyaks and Malays (Alfred Russel Wallace, *The Malay Archipelago*, London, Macmillan, 1869, I, 145 f.). However appalling to mid-twentieth-century sensibilities, there are no grounds for thinking this would have shocked Conrad.
[40]   Guerard, *op. cit.*, p. 168. "For a while the appalling success of the historic Brooke must have made Jim's introspections seem unimportant; the physical perils are emphasized, not the perils of the soul." In view of the fact that Jim's "soul" is imperilled as the outcome of a failure of nerve, a shrinking from physical peril, the suggestion here of a mutually

I return to Marlow and to the question of "trusting" him. The question for Guerard is when and in what connections one may trust him; and here I submit that we cannot warrantably single out Marlow's lucubrations on moon versus sun and ignore or dismiss his reflections on reality and illusion – and specifically the reflections that occupy his thoughts immediately following each of the two presented images of the rising moon. There are three crucial statements to be considered here. The first forms a thread in the extended evocation of "the spirit that dwells in the land", in which we are made to feel that in Patusan Jim has selected the spot on earth in which to root himself, from which to draw his life and strength. Here Marlow rejects any sharp distinction between truth and illusion ("there is so little difference, and the difference means so little"), declaring of Jim: "The thing is that in virtue of his feeling he mattered" (p. 222). The second occurs immediately following, near the end of the chapter of Marlow's meditation on his first visit to Patusan. Affirming that Jim had "achieved greatness", he harangues his auditory: his tale will be "dwarfed . . . in the hearing" because they have chosen the "respectable" course of living without illusions (p. 225). The third passage, following immediately upon the recapitulation of the moonrise image, expresses the suspicion that "our illusions" are in fact only "visions of remote unattainable truth, seen dimly", and closes with the much-quoted formula in which Marlow attempts to capture the essence of Jim's story as he apprehends it: "the truth disclosed in a moment of illusion" (p. 323).

To summarize: if moonlight equals "illusion" or "illusionariness" in these scenes we cannot therefore interpret it as merely condemnatory in intent. So equated it is involved in the "psycho-moral ambiguity" (Guerard's term) of the entire novel, and in our view of Jim's case and our evaluation of Jim's (and Stein's) romanticism – which in turn is involved with our views of the value and the danger of life-illusions. As readers we are not obliged to accept the *Weltanschauung* of the author (or of the

---

exclusive relation between the two kinds of peril seems to me singularly misplaced.

Marlow who may or may not be his *porte-parole*); but as critics
we are obligated to weigh all relevant indications of the author's
own evaluation of his characters and events – and Marlow's discourse has an evidential value which cannot, I think, be dismissed
except for demonstrated cause. Nor can we, as readers, concentrating upon the symbolic essence of moonlight, ignore the repeated notation of a triumphant rise from depths: "as if escaping from
a yawning grave in gentle triumph"; "like an ascending spirit out
of a grave"; "its ascending movement was like a leisurely rebound".[41] These indications are, or should be, inextricably implicated in our response to the images in question: the kinesthetics of
the scene are part of the "wonderful effect", no less relevant than
any symbolic properties with which we invest the moon and its
spectral light, and more relevant than any associated chaplets of
bleached skulls or other images of death, in which we may see
simply a foreshadowing. That soaring flight from chasm or
yawning grave appears to me to be an unmistakable counter-
symbolism to the repeated imagery of the abyss in the earlier part
of the book, as resumed in Jim's phrase: "an everlasting deep
hole", and in Brierly's prescription: "Let him creep twenty feet
underground and stay there".

Here I think it worth noting that Guerard does not remind his
readers – nor does Mrs. Van Ghent remind hers – of Marlow's
haunting apprehension for Jim before Patusan, conjured up immediately following his assertion that "in virtue of his feeling he
mattered". "The earth is so small that I was afraid of, some day,
being waylaid by a blear-eyed, swollen-faced, besmirched loaf-
er . . ." (pp. 223f). This was Marlow's forecast for a Jim endowed
with feeling but without the courage of his illusions, without the
"romanticism" (and the intervention of the romantic Stein), which

---

[41] *Lord Jim*, pp. 221, 245, 322. I do not want to insist unduly on what
seems to me obvious; but it may be useful to the reader to evoke for
himself Jim's spectacle in reverse, and to dwell on the different affective
response elicited by a recurrent setting or dropping of the moon into that
yawning gravelike chasm. No doubt a resourceful criticism might discover
a symbolic fitness in a spectacle so arranged, but it is not the spectacle
arranged for Jim by his creator – and I think we may take it that in this
instance Conrad "knew what he wanted to do", even though the intention
may only have been consciously formulated subsequent to the conception.

led him to Patusan. One might say of course, that Marlow's vision did not exhaust the alternatives. Marlow recognizes this: "It might even come to something worse, in some way it was beyond my powers of fancy to foresee" (p. 224). And of course a Jim without feeling, or without an "ego-ideal" to pursue, could have followed Brierly's advice to "creep twenty feet underground and stay there" (pp. 66, 202, 219), could have nested comfortably in his "everlasting deep hole" (p. 111). He might have lived longer; but then he would not have "mattered" – to Marlow, to Conrad, or for that matter to Guerard.

What I see in Guerard's handling of the imagery of moonlight is a projection back upon it of views otherwise based, followed by an attempt to make the imagery, so interpreted, enforce the views. To a degree it does so: but in abstraction from its kinesthetic aspects and from Marlow's testimony on the undefined frontiers between illusion and truth, the imagery, deprived of ambiguity, suffers a loss of evocative power. Undoubtedly there is a critique of the romantic temperament in this novel – with *Madame Bovary* it is probably the most accomplished since Cervantes. But it is not the critique of an Irving Babbitt turned novelist, it is the critique of Joseph Conrad, for whom the term *homo duplex* had "more than one sense", who was obsessed with the interpenetration of life and the dream, of illusion and reality, and who produced in *Lord Jim* a work as radically ambiguous, as insusceptible of any unitary formula, as *Don Quixote* itself.

Jim departs from us "under a cloud, inscrutable at heart", and the imagery cannot pluck out the heart of the mystery for us. Discursively Guerard recognized this when he wrote that "imagery also leaves us in provisional and perhaps lasting uncertainty"; [42] practically, however, by making the moonrise image all but univocal, he attempted, I think, to make it more explicit and demonstrative than it can be. But it is not the function of imagery – even of univocal and unambiguous imagery – to "prove". The simpler types of "emblematic" imagery (e.g., animal imagery) can do no more than imaginatively enforce our impressions of character and event. The thematic reference of the vegetation imagery in

[42]   Guerard, *op. cit.*, p. 161.

Almayer is, if I am correct, unmistakable; but though it can affect our imaginative apprehension, it cannot of itself control our moral evaluation, of the human entanglement we take it to symbolize. A natural process is presented, at once ruthless and superb – productive on the one hand of vigorous beauty, on the other of decay and death. It can only have meaning – beyond its intrinsic value as spectacle – in a reciprocal relation to action and event and discursive context. When these are ambiguous the imagery, in so far as we see it as symbolic, must partake of the ambiguity – and so much the more when (as in the image we have been considering) its presented aspects are multiple or complex.

In Jim's lunar "spectacle" we encounter a natural image which in its radical ambiguity answers, perhaps as closely as any isolated image in Conrad's work, to the ideal type of the "insight symbol" and which, by virtue of its suggestive range and what one may reasonably call its "metaphysical" implications, engages the reader closely with an entire spectrum of intuited meanings – with the inconvenience that a treatment at once concise and adequate to the complexities of the issues raised becomes impossible. However, the case just considered – which has the sort of ambiguity more characteristically associated with thematic verbal imagery in clusters or series – is, I think, exceptional. Much of Conrad's natural and cosmic imagery, particularly that which serves rather unmistakably as foreshadowing ("ominous" in the strict sense) or, somewhat in the manner of incidental music, as thematic accompaniment to a dramatic crisis, offers less incentive to discursive elaboration. With the general caveat that one should never rest too comfortably on a unitary formula, I shall deal much more briefly with my remaining examples of natural "correspondences".

I have mentioned, in one or two earlier connections, Conrad's instinct for "foreshadowing". It is an instinct common enough in narrative and dramatic art and the Conradian examples need not detain us long. It employs various agencies, not confined to the realm of natural manifestations: e.g., classical reference (the evocation of the Parcae in the persons of the knitting women of "Heart of Darkness"), or, as in "Youth", the actualization of a proverbial commonplace (the departure of the rats from the *Judea* in Falmouth harbor). But like Plutarch and Livy and the Elizabethan dramatists who went to them for subjects, it is to the manifestations of the heavens and of the elements that Conrad most frequently turns for ominous purposes: if he gives us no showers of meteors he gives us portentous sunsets and gravid skies, storms and (as in *Outcast* or *Victory*) their antecedent calms.

Perhaps the best-known sunset in Conrad is the unconsummated sunset that accompanies Jim's leavetaking of Jewel immediately before his immolation. It may figure in our minds as a sort of pendant to the moonrise scenes; but it is in any case the symbolic prefiguring of Jim's end – another "spectacle" such as Jim might himself have arranged, but a spectacle that does not equivocate:

The sky over Patusan was blood-red, immense, streaming like an open vein. An enormous sun nestled crimson amongst the treetops, and the forest below had a black and forbidding face.

Tamb' Itam tells me that on that evening the aspect of the heavens was angry and frightful. I may well believe it, for I know that on that very day a cyclone passed within sixty miles of the coast, though there was hardly more than a languid stir of air in the place.[43]

The counterpart to this is the sunset over the Golfo Placido in part third of *Nostromo*, which serves, depending upon our perspective, as a foreshadowing or an aftershadowing, a prefiguring or a postfiguring:

In the face of the open gulf, the sun, clear, unclouded, unaltered, plunged into the waters in a grave and untroubled mystery of self-immolation consummated far from all mortal eyes, with an infinite majesty of silence and peace. Four ingots short! – and blood! [44]

Here the event (Decoud's suicide) has occurred; it is the recital of the event, to follow immediately, which the image preludes.

It is in the imagery of storm and calm that Conrad suggests most clearly a sympathetic relation between the universe and the

---

[43] *Lord Jim*, p. 413. Cf. Titinius in *Julius Caesar* (V, iii, ll. 60-63): "O setting sun,/As in thy red rays thou dost sink to night,/So in his red blood Cassius' day is set,/The sun of Rome is set."
[44] *Nostromo*, p. 495.

"little world of man". The variety and frequency of meteorological disturbances in his fiction is scarcely surprising in view of his first profession. Nor does he in any work, ôther than the "storm-piece" *Typhoon*, rival *Wuthering Heights* in the density of this sort of imagery. There is, of course, no want of significant storms in English and American fiction – the squall in Salem on the night of Judge Pyncheon's death, the autumnal rain in Venice that serves as accompaniment to Lord Mark's final interview with Milly Theale, to name only two that come to mind.[45] In his storm-scenes Conrad worked within a well-recognized convention, but he availed himself of the convention more frequently than most "realistic" novelists.

Hardy was characteristically earnest about this matter, in a passage from *Tess* which makes explicit the impulse behind much early-Conradian personification:

On these lonely hills and dales her quiescent glide was of a piece with the element she moved in. Her flexuous and stealthy figure became an integral part of the scene. At times her whimsical fancy would intensify natural processes around her till they seemed a part of her own story. Rather they became a part of it; for the world is only a psychological phenomenon, and what they seemed they were. The midnight airs and gusts, moaning among the tightly wrapped buds and bark of the winter twigs, were formulae of bitter reproach. A wet day was the expression of irremediable grief at her weakness in the mind of some vague ethical being whom she could not class definitely as the God of her childhood, and could not comprehend as any other.[46]

Conrad's normal method is simply to present, without analysis or explication, the elemental phenomena, as atmospheric medium of the drama, leaving to the imagination of the receptive reader the discovery of a psychological equivalence or reference, except for such explicitness as might be achieved by metaphor. It is true, however, that these are sometimes perfectly explicit and leave no doubt that he proceeded deliberately; and our persuasion of this is

[45] Cf. *The House of the Seven Gables*, ch. 18; *The Wings of the Dove*, ch. 30. Dickensian examples may be supplied by the reader for himself.
[46] Thomas Hardy, *Tess of the D'Urbervilles* (New York, Harper, 1921), pp. 93 f.

strengthened by such passages in his correspondence as the following in which he declared to Garnett, apropos of his second novel:

In the treatment of the last scenes I wanted to convey the kind of
placidity that is caused by extreme surprise. You must not forget
that they are all immensely amazed. That's why they are so quiet –
(At least I wanted them to be quiet and only managed to make them
colourless). That's why I put in the quiet morning – the immobility of
surrounding matter emphasized only by the flutter of small birds.[47]

In *Outcast,* calm is followed by storm, the elemental accompaniment of the climactic scene of reckoning between Captain Lingard
and Willems,[48] and the first example of that "Conradian tempest"
(as we may call it) which will provide the orchestral background
for the climactic scenes of two later novels. I do not speak of the
disturbances in *Typhoon* and *The Nigger of the "Narcissus",* the
classic storm-pieces from the standpoint of descriptive presentment, not only in Conrad's work but perhaps in the entire range of
English fiction. Though it would be an error to see in either novel
a *mere* storm piece, neither could exist as a coherent structure
without its storm. Remove the tempest and the edifice would
collapse.

The storms in *Victory* and *Under Western Eyes,* on the other
hand, are dispensable from the standpoint of the plot: their significance is thematic, like the storms in *King Lear* and *Macbeth* or the
thunder at the climax of *Doctor Faustus* or of *The Revenger's
Tragedy.* They are, in a double sense, purely "atmospheric"
disturbances.

In *Victory* (1915) the sequence discovered in the much earlier
Outcast – of oppressive calm in which, as in a thunderhead,
tensions accumulate, followed by the discharge of these tensions
during an episode of storm – is repeated; and the relation of these
meteorological events to the human events of the drama is made
explicit by metaphor. As Heyst elaborates his ineffectual plans for
meeting the challenge of his antagonists, "the sense of the heavy
brooding silence in the outside world seemed to enter and fill the
room – the oppressive infinity of it, without breath, without light.

[47] *Life and Letters,* I, p. 182.
[48] *An Outcast of the Islands,* pp. 255, 283.

It was as if the hearts of hearts had ceased to beat and the end of all things had come" (p. 373). When Heyst keeps his rendezvous with Ricardo, we are told that "the great cloud covering half the sky hung right against one, like an enormous curtain hiding menacing preparations of violence" (p. 374). As events unfold to a climax we hear recurrently the growl and rumble of the thunder; the report of Jones's shot which, aimed at Ricardo, lodges in Lena's breast, is "detached on the comminatory voice of the storm" (p. 401). Finally, as Lena approaches death: "Over Samburan the thunder had ceased to growl at last, and the world of material forms shuddered no more under the emerging stars" (p. 406).

All of this is theatrical, in the strictest sense – and the metaphor of the curtain betrays the author's awareness of its theatricality (and perhaps a recollection of Villiers' *Axël*, which also had its climactic storm). If we approach the episode in a spirit of sophistication we cannot but find Conrad's notations of calm and storm too apt, too punctual; nothing is wanting but that, as in *The Revenger's Tragedy,* the dramatis personae should invoke the "comminatory thunder", peal by peal. But *Victory*, though not without its own sophistications, must be confronted from a somewhat different stance than that from which we confront novels in the main stream of the English tradition. Whatever the relation of Conrad's work as a whole to the "great tradition" of F. R. Leavis, *Victory*, at any rate, is a kind of sport. Considered in other terms its catastrophe can only be seen – as Albert Guerard saw it – as crude melodrama.[49]

I have mentioned the latent affinities of the novel with Villiers' *Axël*; and I may mention here that some years ago a writer on Goethe found in it affinities with *Faust*.[50] With its intimations of pastoral and of the satanic, one could also find in it resemblances to various of the exemplars of that American tradition of the "romance-novel" which Richard Chase differentiated from the

[49] Cf. Daniel-Rops, who wrote of the novel: "On ne peut plus même admettre que cela soit véridique. Il est en dehors de l'humain" (*Carte d'Europe*, p. 78).
[50] Alice Raphael, "Joseph Conrad's Faust", *Goethe the Challenger* (New York, Jonathan Cape & Robert Ballou, 1932), pp. 39-83.

predominant English tradition. And we might look beyond these modern analogues to Elizabethan drama, and beyond that to the medieval drama vestigially present in the Elizabethan. We are likely, in any case, to find the storm of *Victory* acceptable to the degree that we find acceptable the conception of the novel as a whole. If we accept it, it is as we accept similar parallelisms of human and cosmic events in *Macbeth* and *King Lear*, because Conrad's art in *Victory* – though not allegory in any proper sense of the word – nevertheless approaches, more than in any other of his works, that of the medieval morality or mystery.[51]

I say more than anywhere else, but indeed something of this atmosphere is not wanting to others of the novels, and among them to *Under Western Eyes*, even though that novel (clearly influenced by Dostoevsky) is firmly rooted in a soil of social and psychological realism and embodies a continuous dialectic on the state and revolution that makes it in other respects one of Conrad's most emphatically contemporary novels.[52] But the cosmic accompaniment to the peripety of the novel, though scarcely less apt than that of *Victory,* is, I should say, less restricted in its function. Though here also the storm is clearly intended to create an "atmosphere", to suggest the discharge of accumulated tensions, its manifestations are related with some precision to the aspects of Razumov's moral and psychological crisis. There is, first, the premonitory thunder-clap, "like a gun fired for a warning of his escape from the prison of lies" (p. 363) – a sort of symbolic reversal of the traditional thunder of *Doctor Faustus* and of the

[51] Cf. Conrad's remark to Symons: "The earth is a temple where there is going on a mystery play, childish and poignant, ridiculous and awful enough, in all conscience" (*Life and Letters*, II, p. 83).
[52] *Under Western Eyes* is one of the novels (together with *Chance* and *The Rover* but not, curiously, *Victory*) which Raymond Las Vergnas singled out in illustration of his general remark that Conrad's novels "évoquent un peu l'atmosphère d'un mystère médiéval, d'un drame en quelque sorte allégorique, où se jouerait la passion de l'homme sous l'aspect progressif de la tentation, de la possession, et de la perdition" (Las Vergnas, *Joseph Conrad*, 1938, p. 174). If we take it as reservedly as it is proffered – i.e., if we do not take it as an assertion that Conrad was an allegorist *tout court* – the remark seems to me just in its application to *Under Western Eyes*, though it scamps the question of an ultimate redemption.

various versions of the Don Juan legend. Equally explicit is the evocation of the cleansing and consecrating (baptismal) function of the rain. " 'You've got very wet' ", the landlord remarks as Razumov enters, out of the streaming night, the shop below his quarters. " 'Yes, I am washed clean', muttered Razumov, who was dripping from head to foot" (p. 357). The suggestion is as perfunctory as Frederick Henry's reflection after his plunge into the Tagliamento; [53] the symbol is a universal one, it requires no elaboration, and I would maintain that it performs – with no attempt at subtlety, but without pretension or fuss – its thematic function.

Conrad introduces a third manifestation of the storm (lightning) following Nikita's assault upon Razumov; but here we can scarcely discern a symbolic function, unless we wish to see it as a parody of divine judgment – perhaps parodying Raphael's "flaming brand" in the expulsion scene of *Paradise Lost*. What the lightning vividly and resourcefully does (and it is all that we need ask of it) is to convey as a sense-experience, in all its physical immediacy, the awareness of Razumov's deafness – since the lightning, as apprehended by Razumov, is followed not by a thunder-clap but by silence. It is one of those eloquent "absences" that Conrad, like Mallarmé, sometimes gives us – which does not prevent it from commending itself to us as a stroke of authentically novelistic tact.[54]

That flash of silent lightning and that evocation of absent thunder serve usefully to remind us, at the close of this synoptic, and by no means exhaustive, inquiry into Conrad's dealings with the images in nature's "warehouse" and some of the correspond-

---

[53]   Ernest Hemingway, *A Farewell to Arms* (New York, Scribner's, 1929), p. 248.
[54]   Karl, for somewhat different reasons, finds the storm of *Under Western Eyes* no more satisfactory than Sainte-Beuve found the storm of *Salammbô*: "As a psychological comment the storm is senseless, . . . and as a physical medium of expression, the storm forces the obvious" (Frederick R. Karl, *A Reader's Guide to Joseph Conrad*, New York, Noonday Press, 1960, p. 227). Consideration of that superb effect of the absent thunder-clap ("l'absent de tous tonnerres"), which in itself could be said to justify the entire storm, would, I suspect, have modified so distempered a view of the matter.

ences latent in them, that he started always from a sensory awareness of the objects and elements in question – as acute perhaps as any English novelist has been endowed with. That he often, indeed characteristically, intended more in his presentment of landscape and natural image than the mere spectacle is attested in many ways; and his human agents and their predicaments often gained an increment of suggestive meaning from the "atmospherical medium" (to use Hawthorne's phrase). But that medium is before all else a *material* envelope, to be apprehended and valued as such. The vividness of the sensory impression, and the physical presence or imminence of the phenomena described, remain paramount: if we lose contact with these the landscape becomes backdrop to an allegorical charade, the references we may make, the correspondences we may establish, become mere bloodless abstractions, *vox et praeterea nihil*. If Conrad's landscapes and natural images are evocative it is in part, no doubt, the result of a deliberately allusive method; but it is in the first instance attributable to the intensity of his visualization and of his apprehension of the sensory world. To these existential aspects of the novelist's art we do well, I think, to return from all our ventures into the realm of symbolized meanings.

IX

THE RELEVANT IRRELEVANT

> Upon the episodes, after all, the effect of reality depends
> and as to me I depend upon the reader *looking back* upon
> my story as whole.
>
> Conrad, Letter to Meldrum

"The Informer" is a slight tale of thirty pages, competently done, but significant in the corpus of Conrad's work less for its own sake than as a preliminary foray into the underworld of revolutionary conspiracy and intrigue that was to furnish the material of the two major novels – *The Secret Agent* and *Under Western Eyes*.[1] One may find in it preliminary sketches of Michaelis' protectress (the "Lady Amateur" of the story) and of the "Professor", dedicated to the development of a more nearly perfect detonator, both elaborated in *The Secret Agent*. Moreover the narrator's angle of vision has some affinity with that of the narrator of *Under Western Eyes,* and the relations of the informer Sevrin with the Lady Amateur adumbrate the more complex relations between Razumov and Natalia Haldin in that novel. Touching as it does upon certain deep-seated preoccupations of Conrad's middle years, it is not (as Conrad morosely characterized one of its companion-pieces in the same volume), a mere "magazine fake"; but since my concern with it here is limited to a single detail, I need do no more than identify its theme: the suicide of a double agent, following upon his exposure of a bomb plot and the

---

[1] The story, one of the collection entitled *A Set of Six* (1908), was written in December 1905, immediately before Conrad commenced work on *The Secret Agent*.

consequent apprehension of the conspirators with whom he had ostensibly identified himself.

The facts in the case are supplied to the narrator in a London restaurant by a "Mr. X", identified as an anarchist. During the course of his narration Mr. X. orders a *bombe glacée*, the remnants of which melt in the dish as he discourses.[2] The device of interjecting into the tale this insubstantial confection with the sinister name has a certain obviousness; as an "emblematic perception" or a sudden illumination of the theme we need take it no more seriously than, say, an acrostic in a ballade stanza of Villon. The reference to the *modus operandi* of anarchist politics is essentially verbal; the item has the effect of an embodied pun. It is, nevertheless, an *object* that is introduced – though introduced, one assumes, rather for the sake of its name than for any existential quality. It nevertheless illustrates with a peculiar neatness, if on an exceedingly elementary level, Conrad's habit (or instinct) of weaving into the texture of his fiction elliptical references to, concretions or foreshadowings of, his major themes – objective as well as verbal, episodic as well as metaphoric. We have seen evidence of this in our examination of his treatment of the natural milieu. In this chapter I want to consider from the entire body of his fiction the ways in which his imagination, playing upon the objective instrumentalities of his action, or hovering over episodes all but irrelevant to the action, pressed them into the service of theme or tonality, achieving by their aid a thematic coherence that supplements on another level the machinery of plot.

For the most part I have set aside the question of intention in my discussion of Conrad's use of metaphor and of the natural environment, though not suppressing evidences of deliberate intent when these lay to hand. We need not greatly concern ourselves with the question here. There can be no doubt that the *bombe glacée* of "The Informer" (though we may not accord it the dignity of a symbol) embodied an intentional reference to the plot. The same is evidently true of the house of cards which Lingard builds for the small Nina Almayer (in *An Outcast of the Islands*) while he beguiles the girl and her father with tales of gold

[2] *A Set of Six*, p. 82.

and visions of future grandeur.[3] In these instances we can scarcely doubt that "Conrad knew what he wanted to do".[4]

Moreover, we have testimony, in a more important connection, to the deliberateness with which he sometimes sought to give emblematic expression to a theme, to "incorporate" it in some material object or substance, thereafter bending both language and episode to the end of symbolically reenforcing the theme thus objectified. In a letter to E. Bendz of March 7, 1923, he wrote of *Nostromo*:

Silver is the pivot of the moral and material events, affecting the lives of everybody in the tale. ... I struck the first note of my intention in the unusual form which I gave to the title of the First Part, by calling it "The Silver of the Mine", and by telling the story of the enchanted treasure on Azuera, which, strictly speaking, has nothing to do with the rest of the novel. The word "silver" occurs almost at the very beginning of the story proper, and I took care to introduce it in the very last paragraph, which would perhaps have been better without the phrase which contains that key-word.[5]

Here Conrad articulates the instinct for thematic linkage of part to part – and in this case of beginning to end – whose operation I have already examined as it is revealed in his metaphoric usage. It was the same instinct or principle (and I suggest that it was instinct later erected into principle) that prompted him on the first page of his first published work to the image of the "glowing gold tinge on the waters of the Pantai" [6] – though the explicitness of

[3] *An Outcast of the Islands*, pp. 195 f. The house of cards collapses in the breath of the child's contented sigh.

[4] Cf. the assertion to Davray, in a letter of January, 1908: "Quand je ne serai plus là si on parle de moi devant vous, vous pourrez toujours dire 'qu'au moins Conrad savait ce qu'il voulait faire' " (*Lettres françaises*, p. 87).

[5] *Life and Letters*, II, p. 296. This passage, in part or in whole, has been frequently quoted – e.g., by Tindall in his valuable chapter on "Supreme Fictions" in which some of the principal images and symbols of a number of major and minor works of fiction (including *Madame Bovary, A Portrait of the Artist*, "Heart of Darkness", novels of Henry Green and Malcolm Lowry) are examined in their fictional context and in a context of scholarly and critical awareness to which this study of Conrad is much indebted (cf. Tindall, *The Literary Symbol*, pp. 68-101).

[6] *Almayer's Folly*, p. 3. The passage continues: "and Almayer's thoughts were often busy with gold; gold he had failed to secure; gold the others

the following passage is far removed from the suggestiveness with which the motif of silver is handled in the opening pages of *Nostromo*, and though there is no responding echo of the motif in the final pages of *Almayer's Folly* as there is in *Nostromo*.

When Conrad remarked that "strictly speaking" the story of the enchanted treasure had "nothing to do with the rest of the story", he clearly equated story with plot, with the bare narrative bones of his novel. But as he had remarked in a much earlier letter to his friend Mrs. Sanderson, "the apparently irrelevant is often the illuminative".[7] How he worked the metaphoric theme of enchantment into the fabric of his prose, with repeated recollections of the haunted treasure of Azuera, I have already considered; in the present context I need only insist upon the role of the objective non-verbal components – the actual episode of the gringos on Azuera, the actual silver of the mine, and the symbolic values attached to them. The associations with the Rheingold motif in *The Ring of the Nibelungen* are so close (the precious metal as pivot of action, the aura of legend and enchantment surrounding it) that it is difficult not to feel that the example of the Wagnerian *Leitmotiv* is implicated in the conception of *Nostromo*.

As for the verbal occurrence of the "key word" at the beginning and its recurrence at the end, Conrad might have found examples of that in Mallarmé, and he might have found in Mallarmé's correspondence an explicit statement of intention in this regard. I have in mind a letter of 12 January 1864 to his friend Henri Cazalis in which – with an acknowledgment to "mon grand maître Edgar Poe" – Mallarmé declared of *L'Azur*:

Je te jure qu'il n'y a pas un mot qui ne m'ait coûté plusieurs heures de recherche, et que le premier mot qui revêt la première idée, outre qu'il tend lui-même à l'effet général du poème, sert encore à préparer le dernier.[8]

---

had secured – dishonestly, of course – or gold he meant to secure yet, through his own honest exertions, for himself and Nina".

[7]   *Life and Letters*, II, p. 116.

[8]   Quoted in Mondor, *Vie de Mallarmé*, p. 104. Examples of this strategy could be multiplied: cf., e.g., Valéry's *Cimetière marin*. A subtler example of a link between first and last lines (a thematic link without verbal repetition) is that between "Paphos" and the "antique Amazone" in Mallarmé's great sonnet *Mes bouquins refermés*. . . .

I shall have more to say about the silver of *Nostromo* in connection with other items – substances, implements, objective agencies of various sorts – to which I think symbolic as well as practical values are attached. First, however, I want to follow up the suggestion afforded by the story of Azuera – an avowedly irrelevant intrusion into the "rest of the story" which is nevertheless knit firmly into the thematic texture of the novel – by consideration of a comparable instance, differing greatly in its proportion to the whole, but illustrating the same instinct for objectifying his themes and the same principle, which we may identify as that of the "relevant irrelevant".

The story of the enchanted treasure of Azuera, if we discerned in it a mere irrelevance, with no symbolic or premonitory value, would figure as so slight a detail on the vast canvas of *Nostromo* as to cause us no serious aesthetic discomfort. On the other hand if, in "A Smile of Fortune", we were to dismiss as superfluous the five-page account of the funeral and the conversation that grows out of it, we should have to acknowledge in this brief recital of eighty-five pages a somewhat substantial blemish on its artistic unity.[9] Neither of the bereaved captains who figure in the episode appears again, nor is either's grief again referred to. If the episode has an artistic *raison d'être*, if it is there as anything more than a fragment of recollected experience which Conrad, under the tyranny of his prodigious memory, could not bring himself to omit, it must be for some thematic relation implicit in it. The relation is there; but since it is anticipatory it may (like many meaningful items in Conrad's work) impress itself upon our conscious minds only upon a rereading, or at any rate upon a recollection of the tale as a whole.[10]

---

[9] *'Twixt Land and Sea*, pp. 15-20. Though the episode contributes nothing to the plot, it must be acknowledged that it affords a perspective on the character of Jacobus. Cf. the outburst of the captain of the *Hilda*, whose ship has lost her figurehead, and for whom Jacobus has offered to procure a replacement: " 'Procure – indeed! He's the sort of chap to procure you anything you like for a price' " (p. 19).

[10] In this connection Thomas Mann's plea in favor of the rereading of *The Magic Mountain* is to the point – though it betrays a more emphatic self-consciousness and a more cordial note of self-appreciation than Conrad permitted himself in addressing his public: "Only so can one really

The story is, whatever else it may be, the narrative of a loss. At the end of the story the narrator's occupation, like Othello's, is gone. The loss is perhaps not permanent – this we are not told; but the narrator has thrown up his command and gravely imperiled his professional future. The practical loss is symptom of a moral loss, a loss of the sense of dedication; fortune has smiled, but grace has abandoned him, his life has lost its focus. It is in the perspective of this loss that the episode of the funeral – the narrator's first social occasion upon debarking, his lugubrious initiation to the "Pearl of the Ocean" – comes into focus for the reader, and with it the narrative of the captain of the *Hilda*, for which a chance meeting at the funeral offers the occasion. Ostensibly sharing the grief of his bereaved colleague (who had lost an infant son at sea), this second captain is in fact mourning the *Hilda's* figurehead – "a woman in a blue tunic edged with gold" [11] – lost at sea after twenty years' service. Jacobus, the ship's chandler who in the body of the tale serves as agent of the narrator's disenchantment, has offered to procure for the *Hilda* a fiddlehead as substitute for the lost emblem. The captain, however, can see in this sensible commercial proposal only insensitivity and greed: to purchase a replacement for the loved object would be for him (we are made to feel) scarcely less a profanation than for the other captain to procure a replacement for his lost child. The youthful narrator is amused at so excessive a reaction to the loss of a mere figure of wood; for the captain of the *Hilda*, however, the figurehead is clearly the repository of the ideal values of the seaman's calling, independent of and higher than the practical interests that calling subserves.

The narrator is amused; but we have nevertheless learned, at the very beginning of his narration, that for him too there are

---

penetrate and enjoy its musical association of ideas. The first time, the reader learns the thematic material; he is then in a position to read the symbolic and allusive formulas both forwards and backwards" (Thomas Mann, "The Making of 'The Magic Mountain'", *Atlantic*, 191, January, 1953, p. 44). The statement follows a discussion of the author's employment of Wagnerian *Leitmotiv*.

[11] Cf. the Madonna of the Casa Gould, in blue robes with a gilt crown (*Nostromo*, p. 234 and *passim*).

ideal values of the craft that are menaced by the prudential considerations of commerce:

Ah! These commercial interests – spoiling the finest life under the sun. Why must the sea be used for trade – and for war as well? Why kill and traffic on it, pursuing selfish aims of no great importance after all? [12]

The figurehead had become for the captain of the *Hilda* all but a creature, the symbol of a life's devotion: its loss (as in *Walden*, Thoreau's loss of the hound, the bay horse, and the turtle dove) the symbol of all irretrievable losses. In the perspective of the narrator's achieved experience we feel the episode as an integral strand in the web, an anticipatory announcement of the dominant theme; the two elder seamen with their separate losses dwell in our minds in inextricable association with the figure of the narrator, correlatives of his more inward and complicated bereavement.

An apparently irrelevant episode at once longer and (as I see it) more difficult to justify as "illuminative" or thematically suggestive is the opening chapter of *Chance*, recounting in detail the succession of adventitious circumstances that resulted in Powell's procuring a berth on the *Ferndale* and following with his wharfside adventures when he goes to claim his berth. Since Powell, though not without significance as a character in the drama and as a link in the chain of indirect narration (being Marlow's principal informant), is peripheral to the central embroilment explored in *Chance*, it can scarcely be said that the thirty or so pages devoted to his encounters at shipping office and wharfside are organically justified by such illumination as they may throw on his character. If one could accept at face value the implication of Conrad's title and could actually see the workings of chance as the organizing theme of the novel there would be no difficulty. Conrad's ostensible intention appears manifest in the chapter title ("Young Powell and his Chance"), which echoes the title of the book. One thinks of a lecturer who, before settling down to the demonstration of his thesis at large, offers an illustrative example. In this perspective Powell's adventure, portending

[12]   *'Twixt Land and Sea*, p. 6.

the role of the fortuitous in the action to follow, could be said to discharge the same thematic function – illuminative, as well as illustrative – that I have attributed to the episode of the funeral in "A Smile of Fortune". But since the work of chance seems to me entirely too general and speculative a concept to constitute the real theme of the novel – just as the smile of fortune does not seem to me to be the real theme of the story of that name – I find, after a number of rereadings of the novel, that the first chapter of *Chance* still figures to my mind as a sort of prior appendage, admirably fashioned but rather tenuously attached to the parent organism.[13] I do not press the matter here: *Chance* is otherwise a highly self-coherent and integrated novel, in fact one of the most striking examples of structural involution Conrad has given us; and it is arguable – from the critical standpoint that finds too great a degree of structural rigor oppressive, and contrary to the character of the novel – that the opening chapter justifies itself precisely because it introduces a degree of *disinvoltura* into the work. The point is that it is not justified (at least so far as I am able to detect) in the same way that the treasure of Azuera is justified in *Nostromo* or the funeral episode in "A Smile of Fortune". It does not fall under our musical analogy; it does not plunge us *in medias res* either practically or thematically. In this respect it seems to me exceptional among Conrad's opening episodes.

As a major theme may be prefigured by an apparently adventitious episode, so Conrad's imagination tends repeatedly to seize upon concrete instrumentalities of action, focussing on them, pressing them upon our attention, in ostensibly casual contexts, in anticipation of the moment of crisis when they will be pressed into service for the performance of their destined function. One recalls Chekhov's counsel to the playwright: if you have a gun hanging on the wall be sure it is fired in the course of the play. The dictum

---

[13] My evaluation of this matter involves the persuasion that Goethe's apophthegm, "Character is destiny", expresses the operative conviction of most dramatists and novelists – including Conrad – and that the interest in the operations of chance, however lively (as frequently with Hardy, and no doubt with Conrad in the novel in question), is always involved, in a subordinate relation, with the interest in character.

seems to imply its converse – if you want to fire a gun in the play be sure you anticipate by producing the weapon beforehand. Some such instinct is at work in *The Secret Agent*, in which Conrad finds repeated occasion to focus attention upon the knife which, wielded by Winnie Verloc, will find its lodging-place in her husband's breast. F. R. Leavis, noting the device as "an illustration of the economy of form and pattern that gives every detail its significance", has instanced the premonitory allusions to the knife in the chapter (ch. XI) which culminates in the murder; [14] but a more liberal citation from the context, and a reference to a significant earlier allusion will illustrate more fully the ironic values Conrad derives from the knife. Following Inspector Heat's visit to Verloc's shop, in the course of which he has acquainted Winnie Verloc with her husband's responsibility for her brother Stevie's violent death, Verloc (in a long passage in which all the proliferating ironies of the book achieve their sharpest focus) moves about the house in an ecstasy of self-commiseration at the collapse of his plans, while his wife's horror and fury swell to a climax. Famished after the hazards and exertions of the day he attacks with the carving knife the cold beef which Winnie's "wifely forethought" has provided.[15] Brooding upon the outrageousness of his master Vladimir, he expresses his sense of his employer's treachery and reveals the fears that dog him in his outburst to Winnie:

A man like me! And I have been playing my head at that game. You didn't know. Quite right, too. What was the good of telling you that I stood the risk of having a knife stuck into me any time these seven years we've been married? I am not a chap to worry a woman that's fond of me. (p. 238)

Spent with his emotions he again assaults the roast beef:

The sensations of unappeasable hunger, not unknown after the strain of a hazardous enterprise to adventurers of tougher fibre than Mr. Verloc, overcame him again. The piece of roast beef, laid out in the likeness of funeral baked meats for Stevie's obsequies, offered itself

[14] F. R. Leavis, *The Great Tradition: George Eliot, Henry James, Joseph Conrad* (New York, George W. Stewart, 1948), p. 215.
[15] *The Secret Agent*, p. 231.

largely to his notice. And Mr. Verloc again partook. He partook raven-
ously, without restraint and decency, cutting thick slices with the sharp
carving knife, and swallowing them without bread. In the course of
that refection it occurred to Mr. Verloc that he was not hearing his
wife move about the bedroom as he should have done. (p. 253)

At the end of the chapter, when the knife has been put to its
definitive use, we may perhaps recall the passage at the end of
chapter three in which (coincident with the first ominous putting
out of the light) the carving-knife had first been presented to our
view:

"I had to take the carving knife from the boy", Mrs. Verloc continued, a little sleepily now. "He was shouting and stamping and sob-
bing. He can't stand the notion of any cruelty. He would have stuck
that officer like a pig if he had seen him then. It's true, too! Some
people don't deserve much mercy." Mrs. Verloc's voice ceased, and
the expression of her motionless eyes became more and more con-
templative and veiled during the long pause. "Comfortable, dear?"
She asked in a faint, far-away voice. "Shall I put out the light now?"
    The dreary conviction that there was no sleep for him held Mr.
Verloc mute and hopelessly inert in his fear of darkness. He made a
great effort.
    "Yes. Put it out," he said at last in a hollow tone.[16]

More characteristic in its obliquity than these direct allusions to
the murder-weapon, and at the same time more direct in its
implicit commentary upon the subject of the novel, is the way in
which Conrad prefigures Stevie's own fate. In the course of our
first introduction to Stevie, the boy's emotional instability finds
expression in the act of letting off fireworks on the staircase of the
office in which he is briefly employed:

He touched off in quick succession a set of fierce rockets, angry
catherine wheels, loudly exploding squibs – and the matter might
have turned out very serious. An awful panic spread through the
whole building. Wild-eyed, choking clerks stampeded through the
passages full of smoke, silk hats and elderly business men could be

16   *Ibid.*, p. 60. Cf. Dostoevsky's premonitory allusion in *The Idiot* (ch.
III, part II) to the knife with which Rogazhin will murder Nastasya.
Edwin Muir has remarked on this in *The Structure of the Novel* (London,
The Hogarth Press, 1954), pp. 75 ff. The device is somewhat differently
handled in *The Idiot*, in which the premonitory quality is felt by the char-
acters themselves as attaching to the knife.

seen rolling independently down the stairs. Stevie did not seem to derive any personal gratification from what he had done. His motives for this stroke of originality were difficult to discover. It was only later on that Winnie obtained from him a misty and confused confession. It seems that two other office-boys in the building had worked upon his feelings by tales of injustice and oppression till they had wrought his compassion to the pitch of that frenzy.[17]

The episode affords the paradigm, at once pathetic and farcical, for Winnie's mental image of her brother's death during the last fatal colloquy with her husband:

Smashed branches, torn leaves, gravel, bits of brotherly flesh and bone, all spouting up together in the manner of a firework. . . . Mrs. Verloc closed her eyes desperately, throwing upon that vision the night of her eyelids, where after a rainlike fall of mangled limbs the decapitated head of Stevie lingered suspended alone, and fading out slowly like the star of a pyrotechnic display. (p. 260)

The episode of the fireworks not only foreshadows the mode of Stevie's demise – the appropriate mode of martyrdom for the victim of a twentieth-century political crime; it provides also in its senselessness and barrenness the fitting analogy to the incendiarism (the attempted blowing-up of Greenwich Observatory) which stands at the center of the novel.[18]

Certain images (significant acts or events) recur in like contexts in different works. An example is the unveiling, found in both *The Secret Agent* and *Under Western Eyes*, the two novels of political intrigue in which the element of discovery is peculiarly prominent. When Mrs. Travers, in *The Rescue*, loses her sandal outside Belarab's stockade, she thinks of the loss as "symbolic as a dropped veil" (p. 396). In his two novels of underground conspiracy, Conrad presses into service the symbolism of the veil

---

[17] *The Secret Agent*, p. 9.
[18] We are not surprised to find, in this novel in which there is so much of the premonitory, that death by drowning is also prefigured – this time in metaphor, and with overt intent since Winnie Verloc has already determined upon this mode of self-destruction ("This entrance into the open air had a foretaste of drowning; a slimy dampness enveloped her, entered her nostrils, clung to her hair", p. 269). The image links up with the entire metaphoric complex relating to the fog, the symbolic importance of which I have considered in an earlier chapter.

dropped or removed (*revelatio*) as accompaniment to a crucial scene of revelation, in which the truth of one human soul is first revealed to another. The first instance is in the same eleventh chapter of *The Secret Agent* from which I have quoted above, the chapter that culminates in Verloc's murder by his wife.

Made desperate by her discovery of Stevie's death through her husband's agency, Winnie's first impulse is simply to get out of the house. She dresses for the departure, but fearful of Verloc's intervention she sits irresolute, "under her black veil, in her own house, like a masked and mysterious visitor of impenetrable intentions".[19] Exasperated by the wall of silence she has thrown up between them, Verloc drags off the veil, "unmasking a still unreadable face, against which his nervous exasperation was shattered like a glass bubble flung against a rock".[20] The significance of the act is symbolic rather than practical: for Verloc there is no revelation in this unveiling. Impervious in his obtuseness and fatuity, he fails to the end to fathom his wife, reading no more in her features than he had read in her silence. He is, indeed, in the act of wooing her (it is the climactic irony in the novel) when the truth of her feeling is at last revealed to him by the sight of the shadow of the knife and the arm that wields it upraised above his recumbent body (p. 262). Verloc's revelation comes only with his death; insensitive to symbolic values he does not avoid his fate, since unmasked or masked his wife remains impenetrable to him to the last. This first unveiling has, indeed, an expressive value that, being essentially ironic, might be termed "counter-symbolic".

Winnie Verloc resumes her veil following the murder. She wears it into the slimy London night and during her desperate flight with Ossipon. The obscurity of the veil doubles the obscurity of the fogbound night: at one point the visual effect is emphasized by the double image which presents Ossipon "looking thoughtfully at her face, veiled in black net, in the light of a gas-lamp veiled in a gauze of mist".[21] Before and after the murder the veil

[19] *The Secret Agent*, p. 256.
[20] *Ibid.*
[21] *Ibid.*, p. 280. I have suggested in the previous chapter the extent to which the London atmosphere, together with the imagery evoking it,

is mentioned (with characteristic Conradian insistence) more than a dozen times, the last time in a second scene of unveiling, the revelatory impact of which is not this time lost on the beholder. When Winnie, moments before her abandonment by her "savior", uncovers "a face like adamant" from which the eyes burn out at him "like two black holes in the white, shining globes", Ossipon, invoking Lombroso, sees (or thinks he sees) the hereditary marks of the degenerate.[22]

Again in *Under Western Eyes* the removal of a veil preludes the major revelation of the novel: Razumov's confession to Natalia Haldin that he is not the selfless revolutionary patriot she has taken him to be but the informer who has betrayed her brother to the authorities. The two have met in an anteroom of the Haldin apartment, under the eyes of the narrator; and Conrad, who in the imagery as in the title and in the hallucinated visions of Razumov has touched repeatedly upon the theme of vision, of the opposition between the "visionary" and the clear-sighted,[23] is careful to put the crucial interview in a harsh and searching light.[24] In the course of the interview Natalia removes her veil; shortly afterward it drops to the floor. Again, immediately following Razumov's first outburst of candor, we see the dropped black veil lying on the floor between them. Finally, when the full enormity of the case has been laid bare to her, Razumov stands rooted to the spot while "at his feet the veil dropped by Miss Haldin looked intensely black in the white crudity of the light". He snatches it up, presses it to his eyes, carries it off with him out of the apart-

---

figures (like the fog in *Bleak House*) as a symbol of the moral and spiritual insulation of the characters in the novel.

[22]   *Ibid.*, pp. 296 f.

[23]   Cf. Razumov's remark to Mikulin: "Visionaries work everlasting evil on earth" (p. 95); and cf. the following interchange between Natalia and Razumov:

"One must look beyond the present." Her tone had an ardent conviction.

"The blind can do that best. I have had the misfortune to be born clear-eyed. And if you only knew what strange things I have seen! What amazing and unexpected apparitions! . . . But why talk of all this?" (p. 345).

[24]   "The light of an electric bulb high up under the ceiling searched that clear square box into its four bare corners, crudely, without shadows – a strange stage for an obscure drama" (p. 342).

ment. Later he sends it back to Natalia with his confession wrapped in it.[25]

Here the question may arise: can we see in Natalia's unveiling an appropriate or meaningful symbol of the episode in which it figures – since it is Razumov and not Natalia who stands "revealed", his character and motives "unveiled?" [26] If one requires representational strictness of the symbolic acts and gestures of fiction, one must conclude either that Conrad has missed fire, or (more reasonably) that the unveiling is a purely adventitious piece of business to which any attribution of a metaphoric intent is gratuitous, if not perverse. One might undertake to answer such an objection by arguing that, if the confessor stands revealed, the recipient of the confession experiences a revelation. But I do not think that the answer lies in a verbal or grammatical quibble. My position is rather that in the present instance, as characteristically in local symbolisms of this order, the suggestion is all, and that the suggestion is conveyed by association (of idea and image) and not by a detailed analysis of corresponding particulars. We may, ignoring Conrad's habitual reference to the veil in verbal metaphor, see in Natalia's veil an article of apparel and nothing more – as indeed we ought if it does not commend itself as metaphor, without taxing the author with failing to achieve what, on this view, he may be presumed not to have intended. In my own view the entire scene, with its physical particulars (the harsh light as well as the veil and its removal), is an instance of that "conaissance" of event and image which Fernández hypostatized and which I see as the characteristic mode of Conrad's fictional imagination. The searching light falls equally upon Razumov and Natalia – since this is not a scene of police interrogation. The veil (since Conrad, unlike Hawthorne in "The Minister's Black Veil", is not writing allegory) must be attached to Natalia and be removed by her. A strict actualization of the metaphor implicit in

[25] *Ibid.*, pp. 347 f., 349, 355 f., 362. Cf. with the examples from *The Secret Agent* and *Under Western Eyes* the scene in *An Outcast* in which Willems tears the veil from the face of Aïssa (*An Outcast of the Islands*, p. 139).

[26] The question is not entirely hypothetical: it has been put to me by a reader of considerable sophistication, and one well acquainted with Conrad.

the word "revelation" was not available to him; but for suggestive purposes it is sufficient that the veil which at the outset hangs between the faces of the two interlocutors, is removed in the course of the confession.

The image of the veil, the symbolic act of unveiling – these were readily available to Conrad in the *couture* of his day. The origins of another such recurrent image are accessible to us in his biography. I have cited Conrad's testimony to his deliberate concern to make silver "the pivot of the moral and material events" of *Nostromo*, "affecting the lives of everybody in the tale". Affecting lives, the silver of the mine also effects more than one death – notably that of Nostromo himself, the "faithful and lifelong slave" of his stolen treasure on the Great Isabel. But Decoud's death also is attributable to the Gould mine; and in the mode of his death the symbolic value that attaches to the silver throughout is clearly operative. A total skeptic, Decoud proceeds, via his attachment to Antonia Avellanos, and with no diminution of his skepticism, into total involvement in the politics of Costaguana. It is in his lucid mind that the Sulacan separatist movement is conceived and on his initiative that it is implemented. Stranded on the Great Isabel island, to which he and Nostromo have brought the treasure of silver which they have undertaken to secrete from Montero's mob, Decoud fails the test of solitude and of that silence which presents itself to his hallucinated vision as a tense and vibrant cord. Resolved upon suicide, he weights himself with four silver ingots from the concealed treasure to expedite his self-immolation in the Golfo Placido.[27]

Readers of *The Mirror of the Sea* will recognize the paradigm of Decoud's death, and at the same time will recognize the way in which Conrad reshaped the material furnished him by memory, suiting it to the needs of the novel. During his years in Marseilles, in the course of his service with Dominic Cervoni on the balancelle that smuggled guns to the Spanish Carlists, Conrad was witness to an obscure drama of treachery and avarice and (if we are to credit

---

[27] *Nostromo*, pp. 499 ff. The silver is contributory to the act only, an accessory after the fact, since Decoud has taken the precaution of shooting himself before collapsing over the gunwales into the Gulf.

his account) of their retribution. This episode he wove into the texture of "The 'Tremolino' ", the admirable narrative of his Carlist adventures that constitutes the penultimate chapter of *The Mirror of the Sea*. At the climax of the narrative – immediately before Cervoni, pursued by the French guardacosta, runs his craft aground and destroys it – his nephew, the wretched Cesar, is drowned. Cervoni has discovered that Cesar has betrayed them to the customs. Knocked overboard by a blow from his uncle's fist, the young man goes at once to the bottom, plummeted by the weight of gold in the money belt which (we learn from his uncle) he had stolen from Conrad and strapped beneath his clothing.[28]

Decoud's relation to the accessory agent of his death is not, of course, identical with Cesar's relation to his stolen gold: there is here no simple history of exemplary retribution for a personal offense, in the manner of Haman's fate. Decoud is the victim (in part, at least: one should not overlook the "soft spot" in him, the failure of temperament that leads him to despair) of the world and the epoch in which his lot is cast, and specifically of that nexus of "material interests" in which, through passion rather than conviction, he is implicated. His crime – to advert to the passage from Calderón which Conrad used as epigraph to *An Outcast of the Islands* – is to have been born, and born into a world for which he is by temperament unfitted. But the silver which plummets him to the bottom of the Gulf is no less symbolically appropriate to the event than the gold of Cesar's stolen money belt.

There is a counterpart to Decoud's suicide in the suicide of Captain Whalley, in "The End of the Tether". Whalley, his sight failing him, is prevented from retiring by the importunities of a

---

[28] *The Mirror of the Sea*, p. 181. Jocelyn Baines claims to have established, by examination of the records of the French merchant marine, that Cesar survived the episode. Accepting Baines's testimony, we may assume one of several things: that Cesar escaped drowning, unknown to Conrad; that Conrad's recollection, after thirty years, was at fault; or that he deliberately altered the fact in the telling. The facts in any case were such as to evoke (if they did not supply) the fatal consequence (Baines, *Joseph Conrad*, p. 47n.).

chronically needy daughter. Concealing his defect, he retains his post as pilot of the *Sofala*, relying upon the eyes of a Malay serang. Both the mate Sterne and Massy, the unscrupulous engineer-owner of the ship, discover the old man's secret. Massy exploits his knowledge in a plot to wreck the craft for the sake of the insurance. Whalley, in the certainty that he can find no further employment, resolves that he will not survive the ship. To weight him for his leap overboard he stuffs his pockets with the rusty iron scraps with which Massy, having gathered them up out of a rubbish-crammed storeroom above the boiler space, has deflected the compass and so destroyed the ship.[29]

Aside from their immediate and explicit function as agencies of the shipwreck, we may, I think, detect in these iron scraps a more symbolic relation to Whalley's downfall. For iron, in this tale, is vested with at least an aura of the generalized thematic significance that attaches to silver in *Nostromo*. Whalley is a survival of an age of wooden sailing-ships (his very name evokes the whaling-trade), to whom service on a steamship is a misfortune. His facile optimism about moral progress, ironically refuted by the events of the story, and skeptically regarded by his confidant Van Wyk, comes from the top of his head only: objectively he appears to us as a sort of Samson among the sordid Philistines of an iron age.[30] Like Samson he is in the power of a woman, has compromised his good repute for her. It does not do to sentimentalize over Whalley, who, lapsed from professional rectitude, is far from guiltless of his own fate.[31] Still, compromised as he is, he remains a

---

[29]   *Youth*, p. 333. The Flaubert allusion on p. 322 (where the storeroom is spoken of as a "Capharnaum of forgotten things") ought to be noted in passing. Massy's Capharnaum plays much the same role in the story as Homais' in *Madame Bovary*.

[30]   The reference is made explicit in Whalley's outburst to Van Wyk when, justifying himself for his imposture, he declares: "It seems to me that, like the blinded Samson, I would find the strength to shake down a temple upon my head" (p. 301).

[31]   Cf. Conrad's evaluation of Whalley in a letter to Meldrum: "The pathos for me is in this that the concealment of his extremity is as it were forced upon him. Nevertheless it is weakness – it is deterioration" (*Letters to William Blackwood*, p. 169). Ford said that Conrad "disliked the story as being too sentimental" (*Joseph Conrad*, p. 264), and some critics (among them Guerard) have found it so. That Conrad felt affection for

figure of archaic grandeur. Van Wyk has a vision of him as "an amazing survival from the prehistoric times of the world coming up to him out of the sea" (*Youth*, p. 287). With his legendary past as "pioneer of new routes and new trades" (p. 167), with his beard like a "silver breastplate" (p. 215), one feels that like the more fortunate Singleton he was, for his creator, a heroic type of the lost epoch of Conrad's own initiation into the life of the sea – the world of the *Tremolino* and the *Narcissus* – and that Massy is the type of a sordid age of iron and steam and overriding "material interests". Something of this is implicit in Whalley's feeling-reaction to his first encounter with the *Sofala*, laid up at its wharf:

A laid-up steamer was a dead thing and no mistake; a sailing-ship somehow seems always ready to spring into life with the breath of the incorruptible heaven; but a steamer, thought Captain Whalley, with her fires out, without the warm whiffs from below meeting you on her decks, without the hiss of steam, the clangs of iron in her breast – lies there as cold and still and pulseless as a corpse.[32]

This opposition between two maritime epochs is not greatly insisted on in the tale, and we cannot without critical distortion see in it the dominant theme of the work. It is there however, one of the figures in the carpet, and its existence gives a special fitness to the mode of Whalley's suicide. Like the less questionable case of Decoud's suicide, the episode attests to the primacy in Conrad's fictional economy of the concrete, the definite image, and to the resourcefulness with which he pressed into service, at crucial junc-

---

Whalley (as Balzac clearly did for Goriot) is attested in the final sentence of the "author's note" to *Youth*; but there is no sound evidence, either internal or external, that his affection caused him to lose his grasp of the moral bearings of the case. Cf. his letter of 22 December 1902 to Garnett, commenting on the story's critical reception: "Touching, tender, noble, moving. ... Let us spit!" and again: "the touching, tender noble Captain Newcome-Colonel Whalley thing" (*Letters from Joseph Conrad*, pp. 184 f.).
[32] *Ibid.*, p. 214. For an unmediated statement of Conrad's feelings in the matter of steam vs. sail, cf. his letter of January 1924 to a certain Captain Phillips, in which he declares: "I share to the full your sentiments about all kinds of mechanical propulsion. It changed the life entirely, and changed also the character of the men. There is not much difference now between a deck and a factory hand" (*Life and Letters*, II, p. 334. And cf. also the essay entitled "The Fine Art" in *The Mirror of the Sea*).

tures, the significant material elements of his imagined world as precipitants of action or of catastrophe.

Before leaving Whalley and Massy's iron scraps I may suggest the possibility of a more "metaphysical" symbolism, inhering in the magnetic property of the iron. In the deflection of the compass by the agency of the iron scraps may we perhaps see an objective correlative of the moral disorientation attendant upon Whalley's betrayal of trust, his swerving from the path of professional rectitude? [33] This would bring the item into direct symbolic relation with the principal moral crux of the story. There is, in any case, no conflict between the two interpretations advanced; neither need exclude the other, since it is the property of the symbol, rightly understood, that it works by suggestion and evocation, and not "cryptographically" by a one-for-one equivalence, addressing itself not to the discursive understanding but to the imagination.

The symbolic role of silver in *Nostromo* is so evident in the text that, even without Conrad's explicit acknowledgment of his intentions, it could scarcely have escaped critical notice. It would be superfluous at this date to trace its occurrences in detail through the novel or to try to extract a symbolic velleity from each of the innumerable references to silver or mine as a focus of interest or pivot of action. It is a public and inescapable symbol, and the meanings attaching to it are, for the most part, in the public domain.[34] It is ubiquitous throughout, figuring particularly about the person of Nostromo (in buttons and tassels, spurs, whistle, and the trappings of his silver-grey mare), figuring a score

[33]   I am indebted for this suggestion (which I find, tautologically speaking, a highly "suggestive" one) to Professor Daniel B. Dodson, who read an earlier draft of this study in manuscript.

[34]   Cf. Guerard: "The symbolism of 'Nostromo' is traditional, extraneous, and perhaps even Victorian: silver, 'the incorruptible metal', merely tightens the structure of the novel" (Albert J. Guerard, "The Heart of Conrad", *Nation*, CLXVI, 3 January 1948, p. 22). The word "extraneous" seems to me meaningless in the context: extraneous to what? certainly not to the novel – and if so how does it tighten its structure? But traditional, yes; and perhaps Victorian. Here, as always, much of Conrad's (as also much of James's) authority lay in his Victorian "solidity of specification", without which his experiments in the fictional medium would not have had the impact they have had. But here as elsewhere many of the solid specifics of his world are resonant of the intuited themes of the novel.

of times in metaphors applied to sky and sea, to the hair of a statesman, to the rolling eyeballs of a demagogue, to the tinkling of bells. It serves as a principal source of the proliferating ironies of the novel. Ironically, since it is the agency of corruption, Conrad plays repeatedly on the idea of its incorruptibility. Ironically, since it is the focus of those "material interests" to which Gould looks as the basis of justice and order, it becomes the source of moral bondage and anarchic strife. Thus Gould, the master of the mine, becomes its prisoner, dwelling, as Emily mentally remarks, within a "circumvallation of precious metal" (*Nostromo*, p. 222); and Nostromo — the "free agent", a man passionately independent of restrictions and ties — becomes, like the guardians of legendary hoards, the "faithful and lifelong slave" of his treasure, coming in the end to imagine himself accompanied by an audible clanking of "silver fetters" (p. 546).

These matters I have touched on in my discussion of the metaphoric texture of the novel. Here I shall add only the following suggestion: that there is, in the contraposition of the mine and the "paradisal" gorge (vividly imaged in the early pages of the novel and reëvoked by Emily Gould's water color sketch), or elsewhere of mine and patio or mine and garden, the suggestion of a counter-symbolism that appreciably amplifies the "resonance" of the central symbol. Generically speaking — and apart from the mythic suggestions attaching to Garden and Mine — I detect in this a counter-symbolism of the mineral versus the vegetative, of the inert substance silver against the vital and exfoliating substance wood. It would take too much space to trace the operation of this thematic contraposition through the ramifications of the novel ("cette énorme machine", as Conrad once called it), and I shall cite only our final view of Emily in company with Monygham, encircled by the trees and flowers of the garden and abandoned by her husband who has remained at the mine, isolated within his "circumvallation of precious metal" (pp. 519-522). In such episodes, in which the dramatized relations of character to character are enforced by the symbolic suggestions inherent in the physical environment and the material agencies, Conrad concentrates the tragedy of alienation that lies at the center of the novel, epitomizing the insufficiency of "material interests" as the focus of a life's endeavor.

The contraposition of mineral and vegetable in *Nostromo* suggests the absent member of the three "kingdoms" of the school-book natural histories. I shall close this chapter on Conrad's symbolic exploitation of material agency and objective image by turning back to the first Stein-Marlow scene in *Lord Jim* for a glance at some of the suggestions I see as implicit in Stein's butter-flies and beetles. The episode, of course, involves much more in the way of suggestion than can be derived from Stein's specimens alone – his lepidoptera and his buprestidae – and some pre-liminary excursus is required before we can usefully focus our attention upon these. But when we recall that the final words of *Lord Jim* present to us the image of Stein waving "his hand sadly at his butterflies" (p. 417), we can scarcely doubt that these had for Conrad some thematic significance. I have touched in an early chapter upon the episode of Marlow's first visit to Stein, consider-ing only the way in which the two men's candlelit passage through the dark room provides an image contributory to our imaginative sense of Marlow's inquiry. Here I want to consider the context of that image, to examine the art by which Stein himself, with his exceptional history and his dominant passion, by which the entire interview – that grave, elliptical, and richly suggestive consultation on Jim's "case" – serves to quicken our apprehension of the issues involved.

We may see Stein's function as that of a "lens" – the most sensitive of a series of informants and interlocutors (Brierly the suicide, the delirious chief engineer, the punctilious French lieutenant, the egregious Chester, the baffled Egström, the ag-grieved rice-mill owner are others) through whose diverse per-ceptions Jim's character and destiny are successively refracted, occasioning successive adjustments of Marlow's, and our own, angle of vision.[35] Nowhere, certainly, did Conrad more success-

[35] The term "lens" is one that E. K. Brown employed in a comparative essay on the methods of James and Conrad. Of Conrad's works it was in *Lord Jim* that he found the method most persistently and effectively used. Cf. the following: "Conrad sets in motion a highly intricate machine, and the ultimate purpose of every piece in that machine is the illumination of

fully exploit that characteristic, indeed obsessional, impulse which he shared with Henry James to multiply his "posts of observation", to make of a novel a great composite eye, with multiple facets successively focussing upon the aspects of the case exposed. So much so, indeed, that when Marlow's privileged auditor, who receives the packet containing his narrative of the final episode, looks out through the "clear panes of glass" in his lofty rooms, "as though he were looking out of the lantern of a lighthouse",[36] we feel this local and apparently casual image to be significant of the artistic method employed.

But if Stein is a lens, it is not through his words only that our vision is refracted. We make of his "diagnosis" of Jim's case what we can. It is – apart from the directness of his assertion that Jim is "romantic" – elliptical, metaphoric, designedly allusive in the way it enshrines in its Heideggerian image of the human condition ("A man that is born falls into a dream like a man who falls into the sea") [37] an oblique reference to the particularity of Jim's destiny. The passage containing that image is one of the great rhetorical passages in Conrad, perhaps more often quoted than any other; and it is radically ambiguous. Its appeal, which is ineluctable, is largely to the imagination rather than to the discursive understanding; and behind the imaginative appeal of Stein's pronouncements on man's destiny (which certainly contribute

---

the dark area in Jim. To vary the metaphor, he allows us to inspect those dark places in his hero through a succession of lenses, each of them irreplaceable because each penetrates a particular part, or else a particular kind of darkness, which eludes all the others" (E. K. Brown, "James and Conrad", *Yale Review*, XXXV, Winter 1946, pp. 265-285. The quoted passage is found on p. 271). Years earlier Louis Gillet, in a review of *The Arrow of Gold*, had employed a similar metaphor to characterize Conrad's method, remarking upon "ces narrations à double enveloppe, par lesquelles l'artiste se plaît à obtenir les effets de recul et de lointain, à créer l'atmosphère et à nous faire voir les objets comme par le jeu compliqué d'une jumelle à prismes" (Louis Gillet, *Revue des deux Mondes*, 6e période, LIII, 1 octobre 1919, pp. 676-685. The quoted passage occurs on pp. 678 f.).

[36] *Lord Jim*, p. 337.

[37] *Ibid.*, p. 214. I do not know whether it has been noticed that Stein's metaphor of the human condition has some congruity with Heidegger's concept of man's "*Entworfenheit*".

their own opaque glow to the "halo" that surrounds the novel) [38] are the images of Stein himself, with his collector's passion, and of the creatures to which his passion attaches.

Admitted to Stein's house, Marlow finds his friend rapt in contemplation of a butterfly of exceptional splendor and rarity; in the intensity of his absorption we recognize (it is, I think, the first thing we see) the model of Marlow's absorption in his human specimen. So far, indeed, Conrad takes us by the hand as though solicitous that sluggish imaginations shall not fail to make the connection:

> "The work", he began, suddenly, pointing to the scattered slips, and in his usual gentle and cheery tone, "is making great progress. I have been this rare specimen describing. . . . Na! And what is your good news?"
>
> "To tell you the truth, Stein", I said with an effort that surprised me, "I came here to describe a specimen. . . ."
>
> "Butterfly?" he asked, with an unbelieving and humorous eagerness.
>
> "Nothing so perfect", I answered, feeling suddenly dispirited with all sorts of doubts. "A man!" [39]

Possession of the butterfly is for Stein the fulfillment of an ideal aspiration, a thing dreamed of at the very height of prosperity and good fortune. His own long-delayed success is commentary upon his prescription for Jim: " 'That was the way. To follow the dream, and again to follow the dream – and so – *ewig* – *usque ad finem* . . .' " (pp. 214f.). And we feel too in his account of the events surrounding his discovery and capture of the butterfly (following an ambush foiled by his instinctive resourcefulness and intrepidity) a hint of the exigencies that surround Jim's own pursuit of the dream, even a "foreshadowing" – in a peculiarly literal sense, since Stein's first awareness of the creature's presence is his

---

[38]   The reference here is to Marlow's pronouncement on "the meaning of an episode", in "Heart of Darkness" (*Youth*, p. 48).

[39]   *Lord Jim*, pp. 211 f. The ellipses occur in the text. The passage has been prepared by an earlier exchange in which Marlow counters Stein's fervors ("This wonder; this masterpiece of Nature – the great artist") with the question, "And what of man?"; to which Stein replies: "Man is amazing, but he is not a masterpiece. . . . Perhaps the artist was a little mad. Eh? What do you think?. . ." (p. 208; my ellipses).

glimpse of its shadow crossing the face of one of his dead assailants – of the fatal outcome of Jim's quest.

In speaking of Jim's pursuit of "the dream" we have employed Stein's (and Conrad's) own vocabulary. But may we not, without impropriety, translate Jim's pursuit of the dream into a quest for the possession of his own soul, seeing in the two quests, the two passions (Stein's and Jim's), a symbolic identity? In fact, does not Conrad again (though more discreetly here) hint as much, suggest that we see in Stein's gorgeous quarry, winged and radiant as Psyche was imaged by the Greeks, with its color and markings enduring in death, an image of the soul of man, when he has Marlow tell us how he contained his impatience to broach the subject of Jim out of respect for

the intense, almost passionate, absorption with which he looked at a butterfly, as though on the bronze sheen of these frail wings, in the white tracings, in the gorgeous markings, he could see other things, an image of something as perishable and defying destruction as these delicate and lifeless tissues displaying a splendour unmarred by death.[40]

And if we have followed Marlow in apprehending the butterfly as image of man's soul, and Stein's impassioned absorption as image of man's concern with the soul, may we not see in the beetles that complement the butterflies in Stein's collection – "horrible miniature monsters, looking malevolent in death and immobility" (p. 203) – an adumbration of another and darker aspect of the soul, the aspect Plato in the *Phaedrus* imaged as the dark steed, which Marlow hinted at when he spoke of "the infernal alloy in his [Jim's] metal" (p. 45), and which he identified in another image when he remarked of Jim that

he appealed to all sides at once – to the side turned perpetually to the light of day, and to that side of us which, like the other hemisphere of the moon, exists stealthily in perpetual darkness, with only a fearful ashy light falling at times on the edge.[41]

[40] *Ibid.*, p. 207. Did Conrad recall when he conceived this scene that Psyche of the butterfly wings was, in some versions of her legend, imaged as the butterfly itself – or that she bequeathed her name to a family of lepidoptera? The question is an intriguing one; but it would, after all, make the imagery neither more nor less evocative if we knew the answer.
[41] *Ibid.*, p. 93. It may be worth noting that Conrad twice in *Lord Jim*

We are, in this great and moving scene that lies at the heart of *Lord Jim*, on quite another expressive level than that upon which Mr. X.'s *bombe glacée* reposed in full view of the most casual reader. It is true that Conrad hints, in the dialogue, at a symbolic nexus. Nevertheless, in verbalizing the intuited symbols of an art so discreet, so in command of its agencies, we run the risk of doing violence to the delicate fabric we handle. The suggestion, in particular, of a symbolic reference to the soul (a word not to be found in Marlow's and Stein's discourse) may be felt as supererogatory. Edwin Muir, praising Conrad's psychological acumen (which he likened to Dostoevsky's), denied to him any concern with the soul; [42] and indeed the term is not one that ordinarily imposes itself upon the critic of Conrad's fiction, as it does, for example, upon the critic of Dostoevsky's. The reference proposed cannot, certainly, be "proved" by invoking classic myth. We can demonstrate with some confidence that Wallace's *Malay Archipelago* was a contributory source for the conception of Stein and his master passion, and even for specific details of the episode in question (the configuration and markings of the butterfly, Stein's emotional reaction to its capture); [43] but we cannot find any such specific source in Greek literature. I can only indicate what I feel to be implicit in the symbolic pattern, without insisting upon the acceptance of particular verbal formulae, which can at best be only approximations. The symbol, as Cassirer remarked, "harbors the curse of mediacy; it is bound to obscure what it seeks to

---

employs metaphorically the image of an impaled beetle, once during the inquiry, with reference to the captain of the *Patna* ("I waited to see him overwhelmed, confounded, pierced through and through, squirming like an impaled beetle"); and once to evoke one of Jim's narrow escapes from death in Patusan (pp. 42, 270).

[42] "The soul he has not tried to know at all" (Muir, *Latitudes*, p. 48).

[43] Cf. Florence Clemens's assertion: "Never would Stein of 'Lord Jim' have told his wonderful story of capturing a Celebes butterfly if Wallace had not actually caught the original of that same gorgeous creature years before" (Florence Clemens, "Joseph Conrad as a Geographer", *Scientific Monthly*, LI, November, 1940, pp. 460-465). For a fuller account of Conrad's relation to Wallace's work see the same author's "Conrad's Favorite Bedside Book", *South Atlantic Quarterly*, XXXVIII (July, 1939), pp. 305-315. The creature Miss Clemens alludes to is described in Wallace, *The Malay Archipelago*, I, p. 341.

reveal"; [44] and we might add that it sometimes, in compensation, reveals more than it actively seeks to reveal. Its curse, however, is the secret of its fascination, and something is always risked when we attempt to render it immediately available to the discursive understanding. All that I can hope for in dealing with the clustered images of this chapter of *Lord Jim* is to have suggested their potency to engage the collaborative imagination of the reader, to enlist it in the "prolonged hovering flight" of Conrad's own initiating imagination over the facts and the latent significances that constitute his recital of Jim's case.

[44] Ernst Cassirer, *Language and Myth* (New York, Dover Publications, n.d.), p. 7.

X

HOMO DUPLEX: "THE SECRET SHARER"

"It was as if the ship had two captains to plan her course
for her."

Written in November, 1909, and first published in *Harper's
Magazine* in the summer of 1910, "The Secret Sharer" is the
second of the three long stories that comprise the volume *'Twixt
Land and Sea* (1912). Much more commented on than its two
companion-pieces, it seems to be firmly established, in spite of
one or two dissenting voices, as one of its author's principal
achievements in the genre.

The story is, like the later *Shadow-Line*, a record of initiation.
It shares with the latter work its locale (the Gulf of Siam, the
scene of Conrad's own first command on the *Otago* in 1888) and
its primary *donnée:* the coincidence of the objective ordeal of a
seaman's first command with an inner crisis of anxiety and self-
doubt. But this *donnée*, which we know to have an autobiographic
source, is here subjected to a bolder symbolic transformation than
in the later and longer *Shadow-Line*.[1] Out of the anxiety and
self-doubt comes, in both works, a self-confrontation; in the earlier
story, however, Conrad employs the fictional strategy of the
Doppelgänger, objectifying the alter ego, the other self that the
daytime self confronts. But in adopting the device of the *Doppel-*

---

[1] We have Jessie Conrad's testimony that the narrative content was an
invention. When she reproached her husband for never having spoken to
her of the episode of Leggatt, the "secret sharer", he (with "a hoot of
delight" at having hoodwinked his wife) exclaimed: " 'My dear, it is pure
fiction. I don't know where the idea came from ...' " (Jessie Conrad,
Joseph Conrad and his Circle, New York, Dutton, 1935, p. 77).

gänger he does not, like the German romantics, venture into the realm of the supernatural, nor like Dostoevsky ("The Double") into the realm of mental alienation, nor like Stevenson or Poe ("William Wilson") into some ambiguous realm combining the two. He remains, as always, faithful to his concept of the humanly possible.

The theme of psychic *dédoublement* is a recurrent – we may even say an obsessive – theme in Conrad's fiction. It is a critical commonplace that, in "Heart of Darkness", Marlow's confrontation with Kurtz implies a confrontation with self. The sense in which the one may be seen as the other's "double" is so restricted that it is perhaps better to suppress the term in this connection. Still, looking into Kurtz's "impenetrable darkness" (looking "as you peer down at a man who is lying at the bottom of a precipice where the sun never shines" [2]), Marlow feels that in that encounter a light has been thrown "on everything about me – and into my thoughts".[3] Viewed from a certain angle, Burns in *The Shadow-Line* and Gentleman Brown in *Lord Jim* appear as "double" figures, the projections of some dark psychic content which the protagonist confronts as though confronting a fragment of the self. But the motif of the double had been adumbrated much earlier, in each of the first two novels, by the device of dream or hallucination – i.e., through the projection, upon a mind on the threshold between sleep and waking, of a phantasm of the self whose detached movements remain under the scrutiny of the dreaming self. Almayer's vision is of a detached, or semidetached, Almayer who falls over a precipice but refuses to die; [4] Willems's, of another Willems "going away from him", who, though viewed in ever diminishing perspective, yet does not disappear.[5] There are many passages in Conrad in which this fissiparous quality of the self is

[2]   *Youth*, p. 149.
[3]   *Ibid.*, p. 51.
[4]   *Almayer's Folly*, pp. 99 f.
[5]   *An Outcast of the Islands*, p. 145. For a later example of the same device, cf. Renouard's vision of himself, "reflected in a long mirror", moving through the halls of an empty palace (*Within the Tides*, pp. 31 f.). And cf. Razumov's hallucination of "his own brain suffering on the rack" (*Under Western Eyes*, p. 88).

hinted at by the device of the man who confronts his image in a mirror.[6]

There are indications enough in his correspondence that this crisis of inner division and self-confrontation, recurrent in the fiction, responded to something in Conrad's own psyche. We find him writing to Kasimir Waliszewski in 1903: "Le 'homo duplex' a, dans mon cas, plus d'un sens. Vous me comprendrez. Je ne m'étends pas sur cette question." [7] And nine years earlier he had written to his Belgian relative, Mme Poradowska, who, complaining of a "dark gloom", had cried out against the transitoriness of life:

> But you are afraid of yourself; of the inseparable being forever at your side − master and slave, victim and executioner − who suffers and causes suffering. That's how it is! One must drag the ball and chain of one's selfhood to the end.[8]

Pole and Englishman, master mariner and master novelist, Conrad could find in the objective circumstances of his life "more than one sense" in which he could claim to be a double man, so that he had, in truth, no need to extend himself on the question; but the antinomies he postulates in his letter to Mme Poradowska point to more radical and inward divisions.

---

[6] E.g., Alvan Hervey in "The Return" (*Tales of Unrest*, p. 136), and the narrator in *The Shadow-Line* (p. 53). In the latter passage the captain scrutinizes the "quietly staring man" in the mirror "both as if he were myself and somebody else". Elsewhere the image of the mirror is used metaphorically, as in *Under Western Eyes* (p. 214), and in the story under consideration in this chapter (*'Twixt Land and Sea*, p. 101). Flora de Barral spies herself in a mirror − "distant, shadowy, as if immersed in water" − during her first inspection of the *Ferndale* (*Chance*, p. 265), anticipating the experience of the narrator in *The Shadow-Line*, and reminding us once again of the fundamental symbolic significance for Conrad of the Baudelairean metaphor enshrined in his 1906 title, "The Mirror of the Sea".

[7] *Lettres françaises*, p. 61.

[8] *Letters of Joseph Conrad to Marguerite Poradowska: 1890-1920*, p. 72. The passage cited furnishes one among several inconclusive suggestions that Conrad's acquaintance with Baudelaire dated from his early years. Cf. the sentence in *Mon cœur mis à nu*: "Il serait peut-être doux d'être alternativement *victime et bourreau*" (*Spleen de Paris*, p. 129; the marks of emphasis are mine).

This sense of inner division, reflected most commonly in the "doubling" of complementary characters mentioned above, perhaps also underlies the impression of "inconsequence" which French criticism in particular had discovered in some of Conrad's characters. This was stated with the greatest generality by Louis Gillet who – enforcing his attribution to Conrad of the "sense of mystery" – observed that

ses personnages si vivants nous donnent presque toujours l'impression de ne pas nous être entièrement connus; il leur échappe par moments des gestes, des sentiments qui ne concordent avec ce que nous savons de leur manière d'être; on dirait qu'un second personnage qu'ils ne connaissent pas eux-mêmes agît tout à coup à leur place.[9]

More limited in its reference but alike in its tendency is Gide's journal entry apropos of the "*parenté*" which he discovered between *Under Western Eyes* and *Lord Jim*, and which he defined (in terms recalling his treatment of Dostoevsky) as

cette inconséquence du héros, pour le rachat de laquelle toute sa vie, ensuite, est comme mise en gage. Car ce qui tire le plus à conséquence, ce sont précisément les conséquences d'une vie. "Comment effacer cela?" Il n'y a pas sujet de roman plus pathétique et qu'ait plus empêché, dans notre littérature, la croyance en la règle de Boileau, que le héros doive demeurer, d'un bout à l'autre d'un drame ou d'un roman "tel qu'on l'a vu d'abord".[10]

This complexity or duality of the author's nature, reflected repeatedly in the psychic makeup of his complex or dual characters and further projected through the many counterpart characters, finds its most unmistakable expression in "The Secret Sharer".

In availing himself of the device of the *Doppelgänger*, Conrad

[9]   Louis Gillet, *Revue des deux Mondes*, 6e période, LIII (1 octobre 1919), p. 677.

[10]   André Gide, *Pages de Journal (1929-1932)* (Paris, Gallimard, 1936), pp. 17 f. The passage cited illuminates, perhaps as much as anything he wrote about Conrad, the *parenté* that Gide felt with the older writer. Students of Gide will recognize this theme of "inconsequence", and recall the role it plays in Gide's critical appreciation of Dostoevsky and in his own fiction. Cf. especially his contrast between Dostoevskian psychology and the Balzacian ideal dominant in French fiction and French life (Gide, *Dostoïevsky (Articles et causeries)*, Paris, Plon, 1923, pp. 134-140 and *passim*).

remains, as I have said (unlike Gogol and Dostoevsky, Poe and Stevenson, Henry James and Oscar Wilde) within the confines of fictional naturalism and of normal psychology. Leggatt, the "double" or "other self" of the story (the epithets are the narrator's, repeated perhaps a score of times in the course of his narration), is presented neither as daemonic being nor as hallucinatory projection. Ostensibly the terms "double" and "other self" are simply metaphors, expressing a felt kinship between the narrator-captain of the tale and the fugitive Leggatt whom he secretly harbors in his cabin. Having said this, however, one must at once add that one has accounted for the story only at one interpretative level; for it is of the essence of this story of a man and his double that it must be read in a double perspective – as it were through bifocal lenses.

The epithets in question are offered as metaphors; take them as such, and the story stands up as narrative – of events remarkable enough, to be sure, but not transgressing the bounds of the possible and not, so far as the sequence of objective events is concerned, wanting in the verisimilitude that Conrad at all times strove to convey. (There is, I think, a distinct lapse from verisimilitude in the Captain's evaluation of his situation at the close; but that is another matter, to be considered later.) But the metaphors are organic metaphors; they summarize a felt identity – the imperfect identity of two aspects of the same nature – of which the story is the symbolic presentment. More circumstantially than "Heart of Darkness", the story objectifies a state of psychic division or duality; and it also, though not without ambiguity, projects the subsequent resolution of that state. We may think of it in terms of the confrontation of consciousness and the unconscious, or of the daylight self and the "shadow side", the side which – to revert to Marlow's metaphor in *Lord Jim* – is "turned away from the light".

The opening paragraph is dense in its symbolic suggestion on the one hand of isolation, on the other of division or duality: solitude of the ship in the gulf, of the captain on the ship's deck; division of sea and shore, bisection of the land by the river. The first sentence presents, on the narrator's right hand, "lines of fishing-stakes resembling a mysterious system of half-submerged tropical fishes . . ."; and to the left "a group of barren islets, suggesting ruins of stone walls, towers and blockhouses". The suggestions are multiplied throughout the paragraph, each succeeding detail of the firmly visualized scene reëmphasizing the motifs: "the straight line of the flat shore joined to the stable sea, edge to edge, with a perfect and unmarked closeness, in one ' levelled floor half brown, half blue under the enormous dome of the sky", the "two small clumps of trees, one on each side of the only fault in the impeccable joint", marking the mouth of the river Meinam. And finally the view inland, of the distant wooded and "mitre-shaped" hill of the Paknam pagoda, of the windings of the river with its "gleams as of a few scattered pieces of silver", and (recalling the central symbol of "Heart of Darkness", that earlier essay in inner exploration) of the tug that "steaming right into the land became lost to my sight, hull and funnel and masts, as though the impassive earth had swallowed her up without an effort, without a tremor".[11] The ship is becalmed, awaiting the favorable wind that will speed it on its way out of the gulf to the open sea.

We see the ship alone in the gulf, the captain alone on her deck:

In this breathless pause at the threshold of a long passage we seemed to be measuring our fitness for a long and arduous enterprise, the appointed task of both our existences to be carried out, far from all human eyes, with only sky and sea for spectators and for judges. (p. 92)

The parallel between ship and captain is extended a page later in the captain's admission that "what I felt most was my being a stranger to the ship; and if all the truth must be told, I was somewhat of a stranger to myself" (p. 93). The reflection prompts the captain to wonder "how far I should turn out faithful to that ideal conception of one's own personality every man sets up for himself secretly" (p. 94).

These doubts are apparently resolved in a sudden sense of complacency and security; the passage, and particularly the final phrase, is one of characteristic Conradian irony:

[11] *'Twixt Land and Sea*, pp. 91 f.

Only as I passed the door of the forecastle I heard a deep, quiet, trustful sigh of some sleeper inside. And suddenly I rejoiced in the great security of the sea as compared with the unrest of the land, in my choice of that untempted life presenting no disquieting problems, invested with an elementary moral beauty by the absolute straightforwardness of its appeal and by the singleness of its purpose.[12]

The adventure that follows is, in its narrative details, quickly summarized. The captain's sense of isolation, the "solemnity of perfect solitude" is dispelled by his discovery of another ship in the gulf, prelude to the apparition, off his own ship's side, of Leggatt, the stranger ship's fugitive mate. To the captain, who has himself taken the first watch (obeying an impulse which plainly strikes his officers as "queer"), Leggatt is manifested within the opaque belt of the ship's shadow in a flash of naked, as though phosphorescent, limbs, "appearing as if he had risen from the bottom of the sea" (p. 98). Recovered from his amazement, the captain secludes the stranger in his cabin and hears the whispered recital of his adventure. A storm at sea, threatening his ship, the *Sephora*, with destruction, has brought on a crisis of morale and discipline. In an access of general panic and near-mutiny only Leggatt, the first mate, has kept his head, but his very firmness has betrayed him. Adopting the only disciplinary measure available to him in the circumstances, he strikes a cowardly and insolent seaman (briefly portrayed for us as a counterpart of Donkin of *The Nigger of the "Narcissus"*) and then, temporarily beside himself in the melee that follows, he strangles the man in his attempt to hold him at bay. Charged with murder by his demoralized captain and placed under arrest, he escapes and strikes out for the distant lights of the narrator's ship.

Leggatt's story, and more particularly Leggatt himself, engage the confidence of his host. Prompted by a sympathy which, as I have said, expresses itself as a sense of identity, the captain adopts

[12] *Ibid.*, p. 96. Cf. also the reflection immediately above: "But I took heart from the reasonable thought that the ship was like other ships, the men like other men, and that the sea was not likely to keep any special surprises expressly for my discomfiture." Had the captain been a reader of Conrad his confidence would have been shaken by the ominous emergence from nowhere of the scorpion which, a week before, had bemused the chief mate (p. 94).

the perilous and quite unprofessional course of secreting his un-
bidden guest in his own cabin until the moment when he can
stand his vessel close enough to shore to offer Leggatt the chance
to reach land. As the anchored ship awaits the favoring wind there
follow successive crises of near discovery by the crew, aware of
an unaccountable tension in the captain's manner and a certain
inconsequence in his actions – an awareness fully shared by the
captain, whose situation engenders in him a dual consciousness.[13]

The ritual of deception and concealment, of sudden substitutions of one "self" for another, like the brusque alternations of a
schizoid's personality, are narrated with a Kafkaesque elaboration
of detail. There is a crisis of near-discovery when the captain of
the *Sephora* visits the still becalmed ship of the narrator in quest
of his fugitive mate. The wind rises, freeing the immobilized ship,
which commences its passage along the east coast of the gulf. The
adventure culminates in the captain's rash and, to his crew, unaccountable maneuverings off the threatening headland of Koh-
ring and the consignment of Leggatt to the water from which he
had emerged, but within reach now of land, and no longer naked,
being provided from the captain's purse and wardrobe against the
contingencies of life on land.

Douglas Hewitt was one of the first to stress the relationship of
"The Secret Sharer" to the theme of the fatal and demoralizing
bond explored earlier in *Lord Jim* (Jim-Gentleman Brown) and
"Heart of Darkness" (Marlow-Kurtz). We might put it that in all
three instances the moral orbit of the protagonist, apparently
secure (though not without eccentric inclinations), is invaded by a
wandering star, with disturbing consequences. Jim's case is
simplest; for him Brown is simply the unnerving reminder of a
humiliating personal past which he had falsely believed himself to
have expiated. Kurtz appeals to a more radical awareness in
Marlow of a racial past ("the night of Primeval ages"), of a

---

[13] "And all the time the dual working of my mind distracted me almost
to the point of insanity. I was constantly watching myself, my secret self,
as dependent on my actions as my own personality, sleeping in that bed,
behind that door which faced me as I sat at the head of the table. It was
very much like being mad, only it was worse because one was aware of
it" (pp. 113 f.).

something tainted in the sources of human life itself. In each there is a relationship of involuntary complicity, of a more or less obscure fellowship in guilt.

The narrator of "The Secret Sharer" [Hewitt remarks] is similarly faced by the realization of a bond between him and Leggatt, but he finds a solution; at the end of the story he frees himself from the haunting presence of his "other self".[14]

The statement, though unexceptionable, requires amplification; as it stands it falls short of defining the full impact of the story, and specifically of the dénouement. True, the captain's sense of release, of a difficulty surmounted, coincides with his successful solution of his self-imposed task, which in turn has involved his separation from Leggatt. This separation, this freeing of himself from the "haunting presence" of the other, provides the narrative climax of the story. Yet as symbol this "delivery" of the captain's is complex and ambiguous; it cannot be seen as simply an exorcism, and certainly not as the sloughing off of a "deadly incubus" (Hewitt's term for Kurtz and Brown). Inconvenient and complicating and "haunting" Leggatt's presence undoubtedly is, but (as Hewitt recognizes) he is not sinister as Kurtz and Brown are sinister.

If Leggatt, the involuntary homicide, embodies a dark potentiality of the self, this side is not presented as merely hostile to an evolved world of higher human values, as in the example of Kurtz, whose career has been a cynical degradation of value, a devolution from civilized standards and moral integrity. Leggatt, we are made to feel, has betrayed nothing; certainly it is by no relaxation of vigilance or slackening of morale that he comes to grief. Rather he has been betrayed: by an excess of his own virtue compounded of that fidelity and devotion which Conrad elsewhere celebrates in a succession of mariner heroes from the Captain Beard of "Youth" to Peyrol of *The Rover*. Such a betrayal suggests (as in the somewhat different but comparable instance of Billy Budd) a treason to our human values in the very nature of things, a "flaw in the universe".

[14] Douglas J. Hewitt, *Conrad: A Reassessment* (Cambridge, Bowes & Bowes, 1952), p. 70.

This is not to say that the presentment of Leggatt offers no handle for moral judgment. He has erred as Oedipus erred at the crossroads, though with greater provocation and from a less self-regarding impulse. His act was lawless in the formal sense that he took the law into his own hands; but his manslaughter is presented as the involuntary outcome of an original act of volition (the order to reef a foresail) which saves the ship – it is the tragic overplus of heroic impulse.[15] There is in him an excess of Plato's "spirited element", which we can (as the captain does, Leggatt acquiescing) call by the simpler word "temper". Now it is precisely at this point that the narrator sees Leggatt, metaphorically, as his mirror-image [16] – evidence enough that he sees him (in his capacity as alter ego) as an explosive and dangerous aspect of the personality. Nevertheless, the narrator does not pronounce against Leggatt's act; and I do not find that Conrad, by any device of irony or multiple perspective, implies any moral judgment beyond the judgment (or suspension of judgment) of the narrator. And indeed such a view is enforced by the portrayal of the spiritless and faintly absurd captain of the *Sephora*, whose visit in search of the fugitive occasions the first crisis of near-detection, and whose own admission to the narrator ("I don't mind telling you that I hardly dared give the order") makes it clear that without Leggatt's initiative the ship would have been lost.[17]

If we view Leggatt's case, and the atmosphere of complicity established between Leggatt and the narrator, in terms of implicit *Weltanschauung*, we may perhaps come up with some such formula as this: Our lives are at the mercy of contingent occasions;

[15] Cf. the narrator's view of Leggatt's act: "It was all very simple. The same strung-up force which had given twenty-four men a chance, at least, for their lives, had, in a sort of recoil, crushed an unworthy mutinous existence" (*'Twixt Land and Sea*, pp. 124 f.).

[16] "It was, in the night, as if I had been faced by my own reflection in the depths of a sombre and immense mirror" (p. 101).

[17] *Ibid.*, p. 118. For a hint at Conrad's own attitude toward Leggatt, cf. this from a letter of 1913 to Galsworthy: "I haven't seen many notices, – three or four in all: but in one of them he is called a murderous ruffian, – or something of the sort. Who are those fellows who write in the Press? Where do they come from? I was simply knocked over, – for indeed I meant him to be what you have seen at once he was" (*Life and Letters*, II, p. 143 f.).

we may be betrayed not simply (like Jim or Kurtz) by "what is false within", but by what is truest, not simply by a deficiency but by an excess of the most highly prized virtue – which, it would seem, is to be betrayed by life itself, by a universe indifferent or even hostile to our scheme of human values. For the narrator, Leggatt may be seen as embodying the malign potentialities inherent in the sort of responsibility imposed by his own position. "Untried as yet by a position of the fullest responsibility, I was willing to take the adequacy of the others for granted. They had simply to be equal to their tasks" (p. 93f.). But what if such confidence should prove to be ill-founded? One can, after all, rely only upon oneself. And yet, one may oneself keep faith, measure up to one's ideal conception of one's own personality, and still be betrayed.

I think that these are some of the implications latent in the story. Conrad's temperament inclined him at times to an attitude of root-and-branch pessimism. The vein has been remarked on before, with more or less of exaggeration (e.g., by Symons and H. L. Mencken), and we need introduce in evidence nothing more than the celebrated sentence of Calderón which he attached as epigraph to *An Outcast of the Islands*: "Pues el delito mayor / Del hombre es haber nacido." It is clear, however, that this does not summarize the final impression the story makes on the reader; rather the final note is one of affirmation, implying the resolution of the problems raised. The implications of a radical pessimism are dissipated in the dénouement of the tale, the suggestion of a flawed universe is not insisted upon to the end as in *Billy Budd*. This suggestion may remain as a rumor in the air, but it does not define the central theme of the tale.

Nevertheless, our final impression, if affirmative, contains an ambiguity. If the captain's inner ambiguities are resolved (as we are made to feel that they are), the ambiguities of the tale, as a work of fiction, are, I believe, inexpugnable; they cannot be fully resolved, but only examined and accepted. The focus of the closing paragraphs is dual, and in accounting for this duality we come back to the symbolic plane, to the implications of the narrator's metaphoric representation of Leggatt as his "double", his "other" or "secret self". In terms of outward event, the climax of the tale effects the separation of the two principals, which on the face of it we might reasonably see as symbol of the exorcism or splitting off of the troublesome "other self". In Stevenson's story, the final triumph of Hyde and the subversion of Jekyll mark unambiguously the victory (fatal in its consequences) of the lower over the higher self. So also, in Poe's tale, with the murder of William Wilson by his namesake. But we cannot define the climax of "The Secret Sharer" by a converse formula.

Conrad is not allegorizing as Poe and Stevenson allegorized; whatever the story "means", its meaning lends itself to no such unambiguous formulation. Here neither "self" is overcome or subverted: each in its different way is, in consequence of its brief alliance with the other, delivered from something which compromised its security. In the unforeseen communion the narrator – the "daylight" self – is delivered from the "strangeness" to himself which defines his psychological condition at the outset of his adventure, and which impairs his confidence. Leggatt, the "other" self, delivered from the destructive element of the sea, refreshed from the communion with the captain, departs with strength and confidence to confront his destiny. Moreover, the separation does not, we are made to feel, involve the termination of the captain's identification with Leggatt. Jocelyn Baines, contrasting Conrad's story with "William Wilson" and "The Double", has insisted that "there is no suggestion of a transcendental relationship between Leggatt and the captain",[18] and though he is doubtless right, in the ordinarily accepted sense of the term, there can be no doubt that the significance of the relationship, of the intimate communion established between Leggatt and the narrator, *transcends* the brief period of their actual communion.

To give Leggatt a chance for salvation the captain, at the risk of his ship, to say nothing of his reputation for sanity, is obliged to stand as near to shore as possible. The indications are, in fact, that he behaves compulsively here, standing in much nearer than is either reasonable or necessary. The peril of the situation is dramatized by the black mass of Koh-ring, towering above the

18 Baines, *Joseph Conrad*, p. 356.

ship "like a towering fragment of the everlasting night".[19] The ship is saved only by the appearance of the captain's white hat which he has in "sudden pity for his mere flesh" (p. 142) pressed upon Leggatt and which, floating upon the waters of the gulf, serves the captain at the critical moment as a mark to indicate that the ship, after the peril of its approach to Koh-ring, is making headway into the gulf.

The hat is another of those physical objects, palpable tokens – like Decoud's silver bars or Captain Whalley's pocketful of scrap iron – with which Conrad's novelistic tact bodies forth a moral issue or a system of relationships. I take it, not as a Freudian symbol, but as a token of the relation of reciprocity subsisting, beyond the term of their actual physical proximity, between the captain and his "other self". Bestowed in solicitude for Leggatt, it serves instead, and unexpectedly, the ends of the captain; that which was intended for the other or secret self inadvertently profits the conscious, daylight self.

Unexpectedly, irrationally, the captain's conduct toward Leggatt, his identification with his uninvited guest, which has until now involved him in so ambiguous and precarious a posture vis-à-vis his crew and his ship, has as its final consequence the establishment of a firmer and solider relationship between the captain and his command. So, at any rate, the narrator tells us, and so, we must believe, he evaluates his situation:

The foreyards ran round with a great noise, amidst cheery cries. And now the frightful whiskers made themselves heard giving various orders. Already the ship was drawing ahead. And I was alone with her. Nothing! no one in the world should stand now between us, throwing a shadow on the way of silent knowledge and mute affection, the perfect communion of a seaman with his first command.[20]

Certainly there is an implication of relief here, of a crisis surmounted, a difficulty resolved. But I do not think that this outcome is merely a function of the captain's success in disposing of Leggatt, in sloughing off the embarrassing double. The "shadow" that has stood between the captain and his command was em-

19   'Twixt Land and Sea, p. 139. Cf. the simile on p. 143: "like the very gateway of Erebus".
20   Ibid., p. 143. The "frightful whiskers" are the mate's.

bodied in Leggatt; we have only to recur to the opening pages, however, to remind ourselves that, metaphorically, the shadow was already there in the captain's feeling of strangeness and self-doubt. By being embodied in flesh it has become recognizable, manageable, disposable.

For Conrad the reality that counts, wrote Raymond Las Vergnas, is "la découverte, à l'instant-crise, de notre moi profond".[21] By way of self-recognition and self-knowledge the captain of "The Secret Sharer" is enabled to come to terms with his objective environment of ship and crew. Moreover, though Leggatt as embarrassing presence has been disposed of, we are, as I have argued, made to feel that the captain's sense of identification with him has not been abolished; rather, we feel, Leggatt has been annexed to, incorporated in, "le moi profond". He remains for the captain a significant "absence". The paragraph quoted above is not, as we might think fitting, the final, but only the penultimate paragraph. The final word lies with Leggatt, or with the captain's evocation of Leggatt:

Walking to the taffrail, I was in time to make out, on the very edge of a darkness thrown by a towering black mass like the very gateway to Erebus – yes, I was in time to catch an evanescent glimpse of my white hat left behind to mark the spot where the secret sharer of my cabin and of my thoughts, as though he were my second self, had lowered himself into the water to take his punishment: a free man, a proud swimmer striking out for a new destiny.[22]

For me the effect of the sequence of these final two paragraphs, with their equal distribution of accent, is analogous to the phenomenon of binocular vision, in which two impressions coalesce into a single image. What they seem symbolically to suggest is that the "other self", once it has been confronted, recognized, provided for, remains as a permanent accession to the personality. As a father may live in the life of his son, so the captain continues to share Leggatt's consciousness, to live in his imagined life. Domesticated in his professional world of ship and crew, he is at the same time himself the "free man, the proud swimmer striking out for a new destiny".

[21] Las Vergnas, *Joseph Conrad* (1938), p. 50.
[22] *'Twixt Land and Sea*, p. 143.

I have cited a number of figurative locutions in passing. I may add here, before going on to consider the relation of "surface" to "sub-surface" in this most deliberately symbolic of Conrad's shorter fictions, that the texture of the prose (characteristically for this period) is much less densely metaphoric than that of "Heart of Darkness", though appreciably more so than that of *The Shadow-Line*. It is by no means bare of figurative expressions, but the proportion of original metaphors is relatively low. The rather Dickensian synecdoche by which the mate is repeatedly presented as an expressive pair of whiskers,[23] popular metaphors like "taken down a peg or two", hyperboles like "he nearly jumped out of his skin", contribute to the colloquial ease and vigor that Conrad generally achieved in his narrated *récits*, but they do not contribute much in the way of symbolic evocation or thematic linkage. On the other hand several of the visual images in the opening paragraph, the imagery devoted to the first appearance of Leggatt off the ship's side, and particularly that devoted to the climactic episode (the ship's maneuvers off Koh-ring) have an evocative splendor recalling the stories in the *Youth* volume. But there is relatively little of the sort of resonance achieved in "Heart of Darkness" and in most of the novels considered in the earlier chapters by the recurrence of metaphoric themes: not much more than the once-repeated evocation of Erebus [24] (the only explicitly classical reference in the story) and the scattering of Biblical allusions focussing on the Cain-Abel story.[25] Like *The Shadow-Line* radically metaphoric in its conception, the story largely dispenses with thematic metaphor as a local feature.[26]

---

[23]   *Ibid.*, pp. 132 f. Cf. on p. 140: "deprived of the moral support of his whiskers".

[24]   *Ibid.*, p. 140; repeated in the final paragraph of the story, p. 143.

[25]   The first reference to "the brand of Cain" and to his punishment occurs in the course of Leggatt's narrative (p. 107), where it is elaborated in a contemptuous reference to Leggatt's victim as "an Abel of that sort". Leggatt reverts to it on p. 132 ("What does the Bible say? 'Driven off the face of the earth' ") as he prepares for his leave-taking. At the climax of the story the narrator recapitulates the theme as he watches the hat in the water (p. 142).

[26]   Cf. Goethe: "Es gibt eine Poesie ohne Tropen, die ein einziger Tropus ist" (*Maximen und Reflexionen*).

The adverse criticism of "The Secret Sharer" has tended to call in question either the significance of the symbolic pattern or the author's competence in the conduct of it. The rather insistent candor with which, by repeated use of such epithets as "double", "second self", and "secret self", Conrad seems in this story to invite "interpretation in depth", so incensed one critic that he took the story as a base of operations for a general offensive against both Conrad and Conrad criticism. Since his attack was mounted on a particularly foolish oxymoron – viz., that Conrad was at once "anticipating psychoanalysis" and trafficking in "popular-priced psychoanalytic terms" – it cannot be said to have made much impression on either of its targets.[27] Some years later Frederick Karl, seizing the stick by the other end, commended the surface of the story but found it "psychologically shallow", remarking that "the surface in this case *is* the story, and the surface is the arrival of the Captain at a degree of maturity in which he gains self-respect and confidence".[28] Karl was right to call attention to the surface of the story, which my own discussion has, until now, somewhat neglected in favor of the "sub-surface" indications. It is, in fact an admirable surface, firmly handled in the descriptive and expository details and sufficiently uncomplicated in its linear progression to have won acclaim from V. S. Pritchett as a good example of Conrad's "best manner", defined as the "straightforward daytime manner" proper to "the *Youth* class" – a manner that happily eschews "the famous Conrad atmosphere and mystification".[29] What I think Karl's verdict ignores is this: that,

[27]   Marvin Mudrick, "Conrad and the Terms of Modern Criticism", *Hudson Review*, VII (Autumn, 1954), pp. 419-426. It may be noted here that Conrad's story has been claimed for Jungian psychology as an example of the "shadow", "unerringly portrayed" (M. Esther Harding, "The Shadow", *Spring*, 1945). Conrad's only recorded encounter with psychoanalytical literature was in Corsica in the winter of 1921. He kept a volume of Freud overnight, returned it the following morning to the lender (H.-R. Lenormand) without comment, but "with scornful irony" ("avec une ironie méprisante").
[28]   Karl, *A Reader's Guide to Joseph Conrad*, pp. 234 f.
[29]   Otherwise termed by Pritchett "the Conrad fog" (V. S. Pritchett, *The Living Novel*, New York, Reynal & Hitchcock, 1947, pp. 144-147). I assume that Pritchett's "straightforward daytime manner" referred to "Youth" and not to the entire *Youth* volume, "Heart of Darkness" included.

viewed at the surface level, the captain's behavior is from beginning to end professionally exceptionable, and can in any case hardly be seen as involving a progression towards maturity. The original decision to conceal and shelter Leggatt is presented to us as the product not of mature judgment but of instinctive sympathy, operating without regard to the possible implications of the action for the captain's reputation, for the discipline of the crew, or for what may be called the morale of the service.

The history of the captain's relation to Leggatt is, then, one of steadfast and unquestioning adherence to his instinctive judgment and his impulsive decision regardless of the real risk to himself, his ship, and his crew; regardless also of the progressive alienation of crew from captain, as revealed throughout in a number of ways, of which the mate's repeated trick of tapping his forehead with his forefinger may be taken as a sample.[30] At the climax of the story we are, as I have already suggested, made distinctly to feel that there is something compulsive in his defiance of risk; his maneuvers off Koh-ring are in no sense conformable to the notion of mature professional judgment and awareness of professional obligation.[31]

In his encounter with Leggatt the captain, like Razumov when he found Haldin in his room, confronted the horns of a moral dilemma: in choosing his horn (which is the horn not chosen by Razumov) he chooses instinctively; but his instinctive choice, though professionally indefensible, is at least not patently in-

[30] 'Twixt Land and Sea, p. 128. And cf. those passages in which the mate's "terrible whiskers" express their criticism and concern (pp. 132 f.).
[31] The following passages sufficiently suggest the extent of the risk and the captain's frame of mind: "My heart flew into my mouth at the nearness of the land on the bow. Under any other circumstances I would not have held on a minute longer" (p. 139). "Was she close enough? Already she was, I won't say in the shadow of the land, but in the very blackness of it, already swallowed up as it were, gone too close to be recalled, gone from me altogether" (p. 140); "what would she do now? Had she way on her yet? ... It was impossible to tell – and I had not learned yet the feel of my ship" (p. 142). On the ethical crux here cf. Porter Williams, "The Matter of Conscience in Conrad's The Secret Sharer", PMLA, LXXIX (Dec. 1964), pp. 626-630. I am not in entire agreement with the author's evaluation; but his study is the most detailed examination of the question I have encountered.

defensible on more general moral grounds, if we accept his evaluation of Leggatt. But the moral bearings of his case are far more complicated than those of Razumov's case, since unlike Razumov ("as lonely in the world as a man swimming in the deep sea") the captain is not responsible to himself alone. And whatever we may make of his earlier behavior, his action in risking his ship and all hands (as we are made unmistakably to feel he does risk them) cannot by any license be said to illustrate a maturity of either professional or moral judgment; nor can it – still viewed in terms of the surface aspects of the event – be said to furnish him with valid rational grounds for "self-respect and confidence". In short, his self-respect and confidence are irrationally grounded; he has, as it were, made a wager – with himself, with "Fate" – and he has won it.

In terms of the "surface", of the external relationships actualized in the story, the captain's final reflection upon his own situation – his assurance of a "perfect communion" with his command – looks very much like self-delusion. Leggatt may be disposed of; but if one reflects on the matter one is obliged to conclude that the captain will find that he has to reckon with a considerable "shadow" on the way of a perfect communion with his command – a shadow cast by the distrust and apprehension of a mate and crew to whom he has appeared throughout as irresponsible, and at the last as a sort of desperado. One may imagine some involuntary admiration on the part of the crew for the technical qualifications displayed by their captain off Koh-ring, and more, perhaps, for his supernatural luck; but one feels that this would hardly be more cordial than the admiration felt for Ahab by the crew of the *Pequod*.[32]

If Conrad sensed any want of conformity between the objective reality of the captain's situation and his subjective feeling about it,

---

[32] Some such objection would seem to be implied (though not explicitly stated) in Carl Benson's interesting comparative study of "The Secret Sharer" and *The Shadow-Line*, in which he says that "the initiation of the captain of 'The Secret Sharer' was humanly abortive". For a brief discussion of Benson's views cf. the following chapter on *The Shadow-Line*.

he must have dismissed it as unimportant.[33] If so, it might be argued that he has been vindicated by success, since no critic, including even Carl Benson, appears to have pressed the question of what actually would be the captain's position vis-à-vis his command after the affair of Koh-ring. Once one has posed the question, however, a rather strenuous suspension of disbelief is required to accept the captain's view of his situation. The best that I am able to do in this direction is to suppose (as a "possible improbability") that his newly-won confidence may in time dispel the "shadow".

I think that this is a flaw in the surface conduct of the story, and even to a degree in its conception. Conrad's art is exposed here to the charge of resembling the art of the illusionist. But if it is a flaw that we have detected, the flaw will be seen as more or less serious to the degree that we accept Karl's verdict that "the surface in this case *is* the story". Here we can become enmeshed in semantic difficulties, since in a strict (non-metaphoric) sense the surface, in fiction as in painting, is all, and any impression of depth is an implied effect, corresponding to the effect of perspective in painting. But Karl's qualifying "in this case", and his remark that "The Secret Sharer" is "psychologically shallow", imply a metaphoric sense – another handling of the material would, we gather, have probed below the surface and given us psychological depth. My own response to the story is different, however, as I hope I have sufficiently conveyed. For me the surface – although the surface of a fiction can never be dismissed – is not in this case the story. The symbolic presentment of psychic division, latent (though not very latent) "below the surface", and translucent through it, is essential to the story, although our interest in it is by no means exclusive of an interest in the story "on the surface", without which the other story could not exist.

In dealing symbolically, rather than descriptively and analytical-

---

[33] Conrad's own satisfaction with the story, as revealed in a remark to Garnett three years after its composition, was unreserved – a case almost unique in his relations to his completed works: "On the other hand The Secret Sharer, between you and me, is *it*. Eh? Every word fits and there's not a single uncertain note. Luck my boy. Pure luck. I knew you would spot the thing at sight" (*Letters from Joseph Conrad*, p. 243).

ly, with psychic contents – material involving by definition much irrational impulse – a degree of ambiguity is unavoidable. In the present case – by an interesting and instructive paradox – the ingenuity with which the narrative *données* are made to objectify aspects or relations in the realm of "depth-psychology" recoils in the end on the surface and occasions an anomaly in the realm of a more everyday psychology. It is as though Conrad had been so drawn into his symbolized profundities that he lost touch, at a crucial point, with the surface actualities. The crux examined above (if it is indeed the anomaly I take it to be) imperils at the end our full acceptance of the story at the surface level – it imperils, that is, the delicate equilibrium of "manifest" and "latent" content, the refusal of any "split between appearance and reality", that characterizes fiction in the main stream of the European tradition – with whatever increment of symbolized meaning in individual works. Now this would be of little moment in terms of frank allegory – a mode which normally holds as irrelevant the novelist's criterion of verisimilitude, his concern for the way things happen in an "actual" world, as distinct from an intuited realm of essences or ideal concepts or objectified psychic contents. And it may be that in the present case the reasonable solution is simply to admit the term allegory, which a number of critics, with no apparent *arrière-pensée*, have accustomed their readers to apply at large to Conrad's work.

But my own view of Conrad, and my concept of his métier as he received it from such masters as Flaubert, Dickens, and Turgenev and as he normally practiced it, with whatever adaptations, make me reluctant to do so. My reluctance is augmented by my strong sense of the value of the critical distinction involved. The surface of the story is, to my mind, simply not the surface of allegory; if we define that term, as I think we should, with reference to the classical models of the genre: to *Le Roman de la rose* or *Piers Plowman*, to *The Faerie Queene* or *The Pilgrim's Progress*. I must acknowledge, however, that to define with confidence the mode of this story in terms of the Coleridgean distinction (which pivots on the genesis, the original germ, of the poem or story in the author's mind) we should need testimony that we do not have.[34] So that perhaps after all the simplest and most valid view is that we are here in touch with an instance where Coleridge's logical opposition between the two modes breaks down, and that we must see them here as empirically intermingled – by which view we would have an impressive story rather uncomfortably lodged in the symbolic mode, with one foot dangling over the edge into allegory; or, alternatively, an allegory of which the narrative surface, viewed from almost every angle, presents an "actuality" and a verisimilitude characteristic *not* of traditional allegory but of realistic fiction.

But if it is indeed a mixed mode that we are dealing with, and if this is betrayed by a flaw in the surface texture, then I should say that the flaw is venial to the degree that the underlying reality is able to transpire through the events at the surface. If we accept (as most readers have apparently done) the captain's exhilaration in the penultimate paragraph of the story, suppressing our reasonable doubts as to the actual posture of affairs, it is because we have been insensibly led to evaluate his situation in terms of its subjective components, responding rather to the sub-surface than to the surface relations.

Finally I want to consider briefly the possible relation of the duality objectified in "The Secret Sharer" to the conflict presumably occasioned by Conrad's discovery of his second vocation. To what extent does the story symbolically express the psychic split that we may hypostatize in the Conrad of the early 1890's, between the public Conrad, the dedicated master mariner, and the second Conrad, the nascent novelist, stirring behind the persona of the mariner? The question (like the question of Milton's self-identification with his blind Samson or Shakespeare's with the book-drowning Prospero) is a beguiling one; and it is inevitable that we should question the text for an answer. Certainly the

---

[34]   On this point cf. Conrad's reported statement to his wife, quoted at the beginning of the chapter. Jessie Conrad's testimony is not really refuted by Conrad's assertion in the "Author's Note" that "the basic fact of the tale I had in my possession for a good many years" (*'Twixt Land and Sea*, p. viii). The reference here is to the manslaughter on board the *Cutty Sark* – not to the central involvement of Conrad's tale, the clandestine harboring of a fugitive.

period in which, in the privacy of his cabin, in the intervals between watches, Captain Korzeniowski gestated *Almayer's Folly* is the period in which he presents himself most arrestingly to our contemplation as a "double man". It was the Conrad of this epoch that the dramatist Lenormand, who met him on Corsica in 1921, arrestingly evoked in a passage in his memoirs:

Joseph Conrad faisait son métier de marin et un autre lui-même, le double créateur de Joseph Conrad, était pourtant, en lui, la proie inerte et inconsciente du Dieu qui se plaît quelquefois à rendre immortel l'instant vécu par l'artiste.[35]

We know that *Almayer's Folly* was not commenced until some twenty months after that first voyage of his first command – the passage from Bangkok through the Gulf of Siam in the barque *Otago* – which provided the frame of external reference for "The Secret Sharer" (as it did for "Falk" and *The Shadow-Line*). *Almayer* was commenced in London lodgings and was written on land and sea during four and one-half years in which its author held no command except that of *Le Roi des Belges* on the Congo.[36] But these biographical data would not, of course, have prevented him from combining the two episodes (the experience of first command and the discovery in himself of the writer's vocation) by a sort of stereoscopic projection familiar enough in fictional creation. There are, in any case, no a priori grounds for rejecting the hypothesis that in Leggatt Conrad objectified the "double créateur" who accompanied him on a number of voyages in Eastern waters.

But R. W. Stallman went farther, claiming that the story contains (as one of its "concentric circles of meaning") an "allegory of the plight of the artist".[37] Since I am unconvinced by Stallman's

---

[35] Lenormand, *Les confessions d'un auteur dramatique*, II, p. 151.

[36] For Conrad's account of the inception of *Almayer's Folly* in rooms in Bessborough Gardens, see chapter IV of *A Personal Record*. Interesting in our present context is his account, if we can call it that, of the motivating factors: "The necessity which impelled me was a hidden, obscure necessity, a completely masked and unaccountable phenomenon" (p. 68). Jean-Aubry has fixed the date in September 1889 (*The Sea-Dreamer*, p. 151). Conrad announced the completion of the novel in a letter of 24 April 1894 (*Letters to Marguerite Poradowska*, pp. 65 f.).

[37] R. W. Stallman, "Life, Art, and 'The Secret Sharer' ", in William Van

assignment of significance to the L shape of the captain's cabin, and since this is the one arguably allegorical item adduced in his argument, I am obliged to reject his view. In rejecting it I do not intend to deny the speculative interest – which is ineluctable – in the autobiographic implications of an author's work. I think simply that this interest must be distinguished from the concerns of objective criticism. This is not to say that the two may not on occasion converge or that biographical data may not properly be used to establish certain presumptions as to the meaning of a text. The question is whether the presumption derived from the biographic data is confirmed by the text.

Here I want to put forward a private reference of my own. I suggest that if we look, with the above-mentioned associations in mind, at the casual anecdote of the scorpion, which the narrator – with no other ostensible intention than to illustrate the temperament of the mate – recounts in his opening pages, it is difficult not to see in the fate of the scorpion, drowned in the inkwell of the mate's writing-desk, the writer's private allusion to his trade, and specifically to the years in which he secretly practiced it. The passage is as follows:

His dominant trait was to take all things into earnest consideration. He was of a painstaking turn of mind. As he used to say, he "liked to account to himself" for practically everything that came in his way, down to a miserable scorpion he had found in his cabin a week before. The why and the wherefore of that scorpion – how it got on board and came to select his room rather than the pantry (which was a dark place and more what a scorpion would be partial to), and how on earth it managed to drown itself in the inkwell of his writing-desk – had exercised him infinitely.[38]

It is, fittingly, a desperate allusion, an allusion to "une pratique

O'Connor, ed., *Forms of Modern Fiction: Essays Collected in Honor of Joseph Warren Beach* (Minneapolis, University of Minnesota Press, 1948), p. 239. For a soberer treatment of the nexus between the "ordeal" of the typical Conrad hero and Conrad's own ordeal of composition, cf. Carlisle Moore, "Conrad and the Novel of Ordeal", *Philological Quarterly*, XLII (January, 1963), pp. 55-74. It is in *Lord Jim*, however, that Moore undertakes to trace what he calls "the pattern of ordeal by writing".
[38] *'Twixt Land and Sea*, p. 94. The casualness of this episode has hitherto (so far as I find) shielded it from critical comment.

désespérée", and the key to it is to be found in a rather desperate letter written to Davray six years before the composition of "The Secret Sharer", when the author was half-way into *Nostromo* and half-dead with fatigue and strain ("la moitié est faite, – et je suis à moitié mort et tout-à-fait stupide"), inhabiting a solitude, a tomb, a hell, a nightmare "ou [sic] il faut écrire, écrire, écrire", with a mind haunted by Dante's "lasciate ogni speranza".[39] And the image he finds, the comprehensive metaphor to express it all, is this:

Une stupeur de l'esprit, un invincible dégoût de la plume, une terreur de l'encrier, mon cher, comme si c'était un trou noir et sans fond où on pourrait se noyer.[40]

I have little doubt that the metaphor of 1903 is genetically related to the objective image of 1909, that we have to do here with a resonance set up in the echo-chamber of Conrad's mind, and that the echoing image retained for the writer some of the vibratory associations of the image it echoes. All of which is (for me at least) of the greatest psychological interest. But if we ask what it means for our critical dealings with the story, the self-contained object of our scrutiny, then I think the answer is that it means very little. If, within the context of the given, we see the episode of the scorpion as symbolic – if we see in it a value beyond its humor and its declared illustrative value – it can only be as an example, among many others in Conrad's work, of the author's inveterate instinct for "foreshadowing". In the unaccountable intrusion of the scorpion into the mate's cabin we may, if we wish, see an "emblem" of Leggatt's subsequent intrusion. To make anything of the inkwell (unless we find it significant that, like the sea, its contents are dark and fluid) we must go outside the frame of the text, we must extrapolate from Conrad's biography; and what the effort yields can have no more significance for the understanding of the story than as a private (and rather desperate) joke, an ingenious but irrelevant cipher painted into the canvas like one of Whistler's butterflies.

I conclude the foregoing considerations by reiterating my view

---

[39] *Lettres françaises*, pp. 50 f.
[40] *Ibid.*, p. 50.

that the story cannot properly be read – at least on the strength of any interpretative items so far put forward by its critics – as an "allegory of the plight of the artist", unless we choose to see the plight of the artist "allegorized" in every situation of isolation, alienation, and inner division. Moreover, acknowledging the strength of the solicitations to identify Leggatt with "le double créateur" who wrote *Almayer's Folly*, I see nothing in the text itself to enforce such an identification and no way to do so except by extrapolation from Conrad's biography. In any event the identification is in no sense necessary to an adequate response to what is given in the story itself. As Kenneth Burke wrote, apropos of Coleridge and "The Ancient Mariner": "Many of the things that a poet's work does for him are not things that the same work does for us (i.e., there is a difference in act between the poem as being-written and the poem as being-read)." [41] If "The Secret Sharer" functioned for Conrad as a symbol of the duality in himself of seaman and artist (and I have no doubt that this was involved in its meaning for him), he did not elect to make of this the substance of his story. We may be sure, in any case, that this dichotomy itself was symptomatic of more radical and generic divisions originating in the inmost depths of consciousness. These may be – and have been – formulated in various terms; [42] but no analysis of Conrad's inner divisions will suffice as exclusive formula for the relationship which we as readers intuit between the narrator of "The Secret Sharer" and the Leggatt whom he calls his "secret self".

The story unquestionably (to my mind) undertakes to objectify the contents of a divided psyche. Viewed in this perspective it is

[41] Kenneth Burke, *The Philosophy of Literary Form* (Baton Rouge, Louisiana State University Press, 1941), p. 73.

[42] Cf., for example, Guerard: "The great personal conflict of Conrad, or at least the great conflict in his fiction, was between a very strong natural sympathy for the dreamer, the rebel, the lawless individualist, and a very strong moral and intellectual commitment to society, order, tradition, custom, law" (Albert J. Guerard, "The Voyages of Captain Korzeniowski", *The Reporter*, XVI, 21 March 1957, p. 43). On the "strong natural sympathy" posited by Guerard, cf. Conrad's admission, in a letter of 1897 to Garnett, that the impenitent thief on the cross was "one of my early heroes" (*Letters from Joseph Conrad*, p. 99).

full of suggestion, precisely because its ambiguities resist any pat reduction to psychoanalytical categories. The division postulated is healed by the communion, the reciprocity of understanding and confidence, in the captain's cabin; but it is "doubled" so to speak by a division, a gap, in the structure of the story itself – a gap between the surface and the symbolized realities such as we do not find in "Heart of Darkness" and *The Shadow-Line*. This does not show itself in the conduct of the story until the end: the particularization is everywhere adequate to the demands of the narrative, the daily realities of the seaman's life are rendered with professional skill – a skill born of both the author's professions. Only at the end does the breach show, in the gap between the captain's objective situation and his subjective feeling. If this gap flaws the story, it by no means destroys its intrinsic interest; and it adds to it, perhaps, an exemplary interest in its indication of the risk involved for the traditional objectives of fiction (the presentment of an "action of human beings that will bleed to a prick and are moving in a visible world") [43] when the impulse to symbolization approaches the regions of allegory. Conrad, complained Las Vergnas, "est parfois conduit à outrer les symboles. Il en est venu à considérer le symbolisme, non comme un auxiliaire de l'art mais comme son objet même ... c'est lorsqu'il [s'efforce de] 'faire' symbolique, que, généralement, il appuie, et échoue." [44] There is little question in my mind that Conrad "faisait symbolique" in this story, more radically than in "Heart of Darkness" (the *données* of which were largely given him by experience), more so probably than in any other of his fictions. I do not think that he "went aground"; but when he let his captain take his ship up to the

[43] *Letters to William Blackwood*, p. 156.
[44] Las Vergnas, *Joseph Conrad* (1938), p. 204. Las Vergnas had specifically in mind not "The Secret Sharer", but *The Shadow-Line* and "Heart of Darkness" ("les deux ouvrages où l'excès symbolique de Conrad s'est manifesté de la façon la plus flagrante"). But his charge that the extension of "the kingdom of death" in those works was evidence of a "mauvais romantisme" was, I think, sufficiently answered (anticipated rather) in the "Author's Note" to *The Shadow-Line* (*vide infra*, p. 306). In my view it is rather in "The Secret Sharer" that one sees most clearly illustrated the risks for the fictional delineator of actions in "a visible world" implicit in the impulse to "make symbolic".

gates of hell (*videlicit* Erebus) on no motive within the cognizance of his crew, and when, after hell had rejected the craft, he undertook to express the crew's emotion in "cheery cries" and the captain's in a cozy feeling of togetherness, he illustrated a methodological difficulty. I think that we may be grateful for the illustration, as well as for the story – which, though not as Zabel called it one of Conrad's "most perfect tales",[45] remains certainly one of his most suggestive.

[45] Morton D. Zabel, "Editor's Introduction", *The Portable Conrad* (New York, Viking, 1947), p. 29.

XI

THE SHADOW-LINE

Le vent se lève, il faut tenter de vivre.

Valéry, *Cimetière marin*

As *Typhoon* centers upon its eponymous storm, so *The Shadow-Line* centers upon a calm. Externally considered the two are complementary records of crises surmounted at sea, both managed with the sober authority and telling particularization that Conrad characteristically brought to material of this sort. A model of the genre, *Typhoon* stands up with anything of comparable dimensions that Conrad produced. Without benefit of narrator and with no character remotely qualifying as the author's mouthpiece, it is, like the otherwise very different *Secret Agent*, one of his triumphs of an unwaveringly objective presentment of character and episode. As such it commands admiration as a symbolic structure, offering ample scope for our reflection upon the issues it dramatizes and the human values it celebrates – with however liberal an infusion of irony. But *Typhoon*, symbolic in the large and valid sense postulated by Philip Rahv, does not present that texture of local symbolisms and thematic metaphors characteristic of, say, "Heart of Darkness". Nor are we likely to see it – as, in a certain perspective, we may see both "Heart of Darkness" and "The Secret Sharer" – as a single expanded metaphor ("ein einziger Tropus"). If the typhoon itself is symbolic – as Conrad suggested when he declared in the "Preface to the Shorter Tales" that it "takes on almost a symbolic figure" – its symbolism is wanting in the reflexive or reciprocal quality that marks his more characteristic employment of natural and atmospheric symbols (the river and forest of "Heart of Darkness", the London fog of

The Secret Agent). The function of the typhoon as adversary to MacWhirr is uncomplicated; testing his fortitude, it reflects nothing in him, in Jukes, or in any human soul aboard the *Nan-Shan.* Nor is there, in Jukes's progress from disdain of MacWhirr to a grudging appreciation, anything approximating the "unforeseen partnership" or the shock of recognition in which Zabel and Hewitt, among others, have rightly detected one of the recurrent Conradian themes.

In *The Shadow-Line* these characteristic Conradian motifs are again in evidence. The metaphoric title, the Baudelairean epigraph, the introspections of the narrator-protagonist, all invite us to penetrate the descriptive and narrative surface of the work and to discern a more intimate "interpenetration" of sea and life and a more inward nexus of human relations than we are likely to discern in its earlier counterpart.

Albert Guerard has written of this novel:

The Shadow-Line professes to deal with a physical experience so trying that it tempts the narrator-captain to share his mate's paranoid unreason. And it professes to deal, more generally, with the passage of the shadow-line between youth and maturity. But what it actually dramatizes, if unintentionally, is the living through and throwing off of an immobilizing neurotic depression.[1]

Since my view of *The Shadow-Line* has something in common with Guerard's it is embarrassing to have to say that, as formulated above, his "diagnosis" (as we might call it) seems to me to involve a misapprehension. It suggests that the manifest drama – the drama of a young seaman driven to the extremity of his resources on the maiden voyage of his first command, overcoming with the aid of the elements the difficulties encountered, and maturing morally and professionally in the process – is somehow less than "actual", a matter of empty "profession", a sort of confidence trick played on the reader. In effect Guerard suggests implicitly that Conrad has produced allegory – since it is only of allegory that we can say that the ostensible events are a mere

---

[1] Guerard, "The Voyages of Captain Korzeniowski", *The Reporter*, XVI (March 21, 1957), p. 43.

pretext, or that the latent meaning, the "undercurrent" of the narrative, has an "actuality" denied to the surface. Such a view mistakes Conrad's method.

The fact is that Conrad's performance in no way falls short of his profession, as defined by Guerard. He may (as I think he does) give us an overplus of evoked meaning – or an undercurrent of suggestion – but he does not give it to us at the expense of the narrative surface. What Conrad "actually" dramatized is a mariner's predicament – as he did in *Typhoon*, as he did in *Lord Jim*. The predicament was, like that dramatized in *Lord Jim*, related to what we may call an existential crisis, a crisis in the moral and spiritual life of the protagonist. With this difference from *Lord Jim*, however: that whereas in the earlier work the predicament precipitates the crisis (though admittedly by drawing to a head predispositions latent in Jim's character), in *The Shadow-Line* the predicament follows upon an antecedent inner crisis, discursively defined in the opening paragraphs of the tale. Again, in *Lord Jim* the original predicament, the mishap on the *Patna* – though it is recounted in intimate detail by Jim himself and subjected to the play of many cross-lights throughout the first half of the novel – does not itself constitute the principal substance of the novel; it serves rather to propel Jim into a succession of further predicaments ending with his execution in Doramin's campong. If we take his leap from the *Patna* to be a symbolic act – the symbol of his entire existence – we do not take his day-to-day or his hour-to-hour experience on deck as symbolically defining his state of consciousness, his *état d'âme*, with the same sort of strictness with which the captain's daily experience in the Gulf of Siam may be said to define his state of consciousness.

Between *Typhoon* and *The Shadow-Line* there is approximate parity of scope, but a disparity of method and a radical difference in the author's orientation toward his protagonist. In *Lord Jim* there are certainly grounds for imputing a degree of identification of author with protagonist, but it is partial at best: Marlow, in fact, may be seen here precisely as a device for limiting that identification. Jim's psyche is mercilessly probed, but it is an operation *ab extra*. With whatever technical innovations, *Lord*

Jim is a novel in the Flaubertian tradition of objective presentment, though with distinctly non-Flaubertian elaborations and refinements of method. Moreover, it is conceived (or rather it developed, since in its original conception it was to have been a short story) on a much grander scale than *The Shadow-Line*, with complications and multiple peripeties. It is, in short (to invoke a useful French distinction), a *roman* rather than a *récit*, and as such – though one of the most "inner-directed" of novels and one that bristles with symbolic imagery – not a suitable vehicle for the sort of concentrated and unitary symbolism transmissible in such compact and linear recitals as "Heart of Darkness" and *The Shadow-Line*.

This is perhaps going a long way around to suggest that I am so far in agreement with Guerard as to believe that the author of *The Shadow-Line* – in dramatizing a seaman's first command and a young man's maturation, and not under the pretext of dramatizing these vicissitudes – succeeded in symbolically evoking the "living through and throwing off" of a mental state to which the term "neurotic depression", if wanting in evocative power, is perhaps as applicable as any other. Although he permitted himself a proportion of direct psychological analysis (in the guise of the narrator's self-analysis) probably greater than in any of his writings since his earliest novels, the symbolic dimension of the work is nevertheless largely the product of the objective presentment, the continuous imaging that remained as an inveterate habit and defined to the end his fictional method. Here, as always, he gives us in the first instance an "action of human beings that will bleed to a prick, and are moving in a visible world". But when he inscribed at the head of his novel a line from a poem of Baudelaire's he strongly suggested that the natural manifestations – the becalmed sea, and succeeding breeze – which on the one hand determine the objective events of the voyage, and thus of three-quarters of his narrative canvas, on the other hand "mirror" or objectify the narrator's subjective state.

Although Conrad, his wife told us, chose his epigraphs with care, the relations subsisting between many of them and the works to which they are appended would seem to be largely a matter of

private association, with no great suggestive value for the reader
– or perhaps I should say with no *more* than a suggestive value,
often very slight. It is otherwise in the present case: here the
epigraph stands in evident relation to the text – if we read the
text as I think it should be read – serving not, perhaps as a key to
the unlocking of a mystery (in Mallarmé's sense) but as an
appreciable aid to our reflection upon the symbolic method and
content of the work. In this novel under the seal of Baudelaire,
the system of "correspondences" between man and nature, employed locally throughout Conrad's fiction for the objectification
of inner states and for the accentuation of dramatic crises, becomes an organic principle of the entire work.

"D'autres fois, calme plat, grand miroir / De mon désespoir":
this is the epigraph, from Baudelaire. The metaphor of the sea as
man's mirror is recurrent in that poet: one finds it most explicitly
developed in *l'Homme et la mer*.[2] The lines of Conrad's epigraph,
however, are the concluding lines of *La Musique*, a treatment of
the Baudelairean theme of *correspondances*. Music, the initial
subject of the poem, becomes in metaphor a sea, with the poet as
auditor transformed into a ship vibrating to the sea's agitation. I
quote the sestet of the poem (a modified sonnet):

> Je sens vibrer en moi toutes les passions
> D'un vaisseau qui souffre;
> Le bon vent, le tempête et ses convulsions
> Sur l'immense gouffre
> Me bercent. D'autres fois, calme plat, grand miroir
> De mon désespoir! [3]

The verses antecedent to Conrad's fragment account for the
"d'autres fois", which in the epigraph has no referent; and "le bon
vent" may be taken to identify the natural agency which shatters,
in the novel, the enchanted mirror, the "calme plat" which lies at
the center of the work and which reflects, if not Baudelaire's

---

[2] No. 14 of *Spleen et Idéal*. Cf. especially the following:
   "La mer est ton miroir: tu contemples ton âme
   Dans le déroulement infini de sa lame,
   Et ton esprit n'est pas un gouffre moins amer."
[3] The poem is No. 72 of *Spleen et Idéal*.

"désespoir", then something very like it – a "sense of life-empti-ness" whose "evil influence" and "bitter plausibility" define the narrator's state at the outset of his adventure,[4] and which finds its objective correlative in the becalmed sea and the ship immobilized or capriciously tossed about without direction.

The affinities of temperament and aesthetic ideal between Conrad and Baudelaire, which have been touched upon in an earlier chapter, need not be developed here other than to remind the reader that the obsessive image of the "abyss", illustrated in chapter VII, has its counterpart in Baudelaire (cf., e.g., *l'Homme et la mer, De Profundis clamavi*) and that the sea, whether in its surface manifestations or in its primary signification as "le gouffre", was for Baudelaire as for Conrad a recurrent symbol of the human psyche.[5]

Before going on to consider the texture of image and event by which the symbolic evocations are realized I want to suggest briefly what seems to me a probable relation of *The Shadow-Line* to the work of another major poet – *viz.*, to "The Ancient Mariner". In speaking of *The Shadow-Line* as "a prose 'Ancient Mariner' ",[6] F. R. Leavis did not elaborate, and his analysis, though suggestive enough, did not give any very explicit warrant for the designation, other than the obvious sequence of events: a vessel becalmed, then set in motion by a favoring breeze. It is notable that Coleridge is one of the major English poets never mentioned or quoted by Conrad in his published writings, so that there seems to be no objective evidence that he knew "The Ancient Mariner". On the other hand there is a strong presump-tion that so inveterate a reader of the literature of voyages would not have neglected this most conspicuous of poetic voyages: and

---

[4] *The Shadow-Line*, p. 49.
[5] Cf., in addition to *La Musique* and *l'Homme et la mer, l'Obsession*, and such prose-poems as *Déjà* and *l'Invitation au voyage* (in *Le Spleen de Paris*).
[6] Leavis, *op. cit.*, p. 187. Much earlier Maud Bodkin, without establishing any terms of critical comparison between the two works, testified to a mental association between them. Cf. Maud Bodkin, *Archetypal Patterns in Poetry: Psychological Studies of Imagination* (London, Oxford Univer-sity Press, 1934), pp. 33 f.

the presumption is strengthened by several images (one in *Victory*, one in *Lord Jim*, one in the work under consideration) suggestive of one of the most familiar images in the poem: "As idle as a painted ship / Upon a painted ocean." The most unmistakable echo is the concise simile in *Victory* (page 178), "like a painted ship on a painted sea". The image in *The Shadow-Line* (closer to the Coleridgean image in its referent than the one in *Lord Jim*) is the simile of the ship standing "as motionless as a model ship set on the gleams and shadows of polished marble".[7] The image from *Lord Jim* (closer to Coleridge's in its physiognomy) is that of the *Patna's* wake "like the phantom of a track drawn upon a lifeless sea by the phantom of a steamer".[8]

The view of Coleridge's poem which, relating it to the Dejection Ode, sees it as a symbolic presentment of a state of depression and moral isolation, is well known.[9] Although this view of the poem, identified with D. W. Harding and Kenneth Burke, had not, so far as I know, been put forth in Conrad's day, I think we may assume that it was the sort of construction to which his temperament would have predisposed him. This is not the place to enter into the critical controversy over the Harding-Burke interpretation of "The Ancient Mariner": but since the matter arises from my context I shall simply say that where it is not advanced "reductively", as an exclusive account of the poem, I find it persuasive and indeed inescapable. As to the general ordonnance of the poem,

---

[7] *The Shadow-Line*, p. 76. This image, together with the narrator's morbid vision of the ship as "a floating grave" (p. 92), was cited by Frederick Karl as evidence of a relation between Conrad's novel and Coleridge's poem (Karl, *A Reader's Guide to Joseph Conrad*, p. 275n.).
[8] *Lord Jim*, p. 16.
[9] Cf. D. W. Harding, "The Theme of *The Ancient Mariner*", *The Importance of Scrutiny: Selections from SCRUTINY: A Quarterly Review, 1932-38*, ed. Eric Bentley (New York, George W. Stewart, 1948), pp. 174-181; especially the following (pp. 175 f.) which I take to summarize Harding's thesis: "The human experience around which Coleridge centres the poem is surely the depression and the sense of isolation and unworthiness which the Mariner describes in Part IV.... "This, the central experience, comes almost at the middle of the poem. It is the nadir of depression to which the earlier stanzas sink; the rest of the poem describes what is in part recovery and in part aftermath." Cf. also Burke, *The Philosophy of Literary Form*, pp. 71-73.

Conrad would probably have seconded Lamb's view that it was "fertile in unmeaning miracles".[10] In the strict descriptive meaning of the word, Conrad was a confirmed "naturalist": that is to say, he was a confirmed anti-supernaturalist; and it is precisely in the "Author's Note" to *The Shadow-Line* that he most unequivocally expressed this bias – in stinging reply to an obtuse criticism that thought it part of the author's purpose to impose upon the reader Burns's view of supernatural agency:

The world of the living contains enough marvels and mysteries as it is; marvels and mysteries acting upon our emotions and intelligence in ways so inexplicable that it would almost justify the conception of life as an enchanted state. No, I am too firm in my consciousness of the marvellous to be ever fascinated by the mere supernatural, which (take it any way you like) is but a manufactured article, the fabrication of minds insensitive to the intimate delicacies of our relation to the dead and to the living, in their countless multitudes; a desecration of our tenderest memories; an outrage on our dignity.[11]

But I think we may assume also that Conrad, pocketing the outrage on his dignity, would have responded to much in Coleridge's poem – to the subtle simplicities of the ballad metre, to the coruscating images derived from that literature of mariner's tales in which he himself was steeped, above all to the moral and psychological crisis of the Mariner; and I should like to advance the hypothesis that it was, in part, owing to the influence of the poem that he stressed certain themes in the novel. Specifically I see this putative influence of "The Ancient Mariner" in the recurrent stress on the narrator's latent guilt-feelings which, seizing on various emergent occasions, find repeated expression during the ship's ordeal; in those delusions of the mate – haunted by the evoked image of the narrator's half-mad predecessor, to whom he attributes a power of posthumous mischief – which caused Conrad to fall afoul of his critics and which, without constating any supernatural apparatus, evoke an aura of the supernatural recalling Coleridge; and in the frequency of metaphors drawn from the realm of magic and enchantment. This was, of course, by no

[10] *Letters of Charles Lamb*, ed. Alfred Ainger (London, 1897), I, p. 95.
[11] *The Shadow-Line*, pp. vii f.

means a new source of metaphor in Conrad's work. Absolutely speaking one can find more images deriving from this source in the densely metaphoric *Lord Jim* or "Heart of Darkness"; relatively speaking they are nowhere more conspicuous than in *The Shadow-Line*, in which metaphoric expression is much less pervasive a feature of style.[12] Finally, there is the title-image itself, first introduced into the text on the opening page of the novel. Within the novel the metaphoric sense of shadow-line – as the doubtful region dividing youth from maturity – is involved, by way of Burns's delusions, with the imagery of enchantment. It coalesces with the area of immobilizing calm whose imaginary boundary lies at the mouth of the Gulf (in "latitude 8° 20′″"), where Burns has given sea-burial to the late Captain, whom he imagines as "ambushed" there, an evoked shade, blocking the passage to the open sea.[13] In this ambiguity of the title-image, this adumbration of an imaginary geographic line coinciding with the metaphoric line, I think we may see a distinct suggestion of the strategy that prompted Coleridge to situate his calm – and thus the moral crisis of his becalmed mariner – in the region of the Equatorial Line.

Before I trace briefly the recurrence of the metaphoric theme of enchantment – and of one or two others related to it – a short résumé of the narrative content is in order. In dealing with it briefly I have no intention of relegating it to any critical limbo or denying its dramatic "actuality". But its dramatic structure is uncomplicated, and the sequence of events is readily summarized.

The opening pages present us with the situation of an English seaman (the unnamed narrator) on the threshold of the middle years, who, in the grip of an undefined disgust with himself and his life, resigns a mate's berth ("in that, to us, inconsequential

[12] There is in this novel a region of prose unexampled in the work of the Marlow period – ten pages from p. 15 through p. 24 – which for all practical purposes may be said to be bare of figurative locutions. The frequency of metaphors is generally greater in the pages devoted to the voyage.

[13] *Ibid.*, pp. 81-83. Cf. Conrad's admission to Sidney Colvin: "Mr. Burns's craziness being the pivot is perhaps a little accentuated", in which we may see a significant hint that it is precisely in the area of evoked "enchantment" that the novel was most independent of the lived experience upon which it was based (*Life and Letters*, II, p. 182).

manner in which a bird flies away from a comfortable branch") [14]
and resolves to give up the seaman's calling and return home. An
unaccountable impulse makes him await his homeward passage
not in a hotel, but in the Officers' Home of the eastern port
(Singapore) in which he finds himself. Here he is exposed to the
interrogations of the elderly Captain Giles as to his motives and
plans – irritating, since he has nothing to declare in the way of
either commodity. Giles's surreptitious intervention puts him in
the way of a command. In the upshot, the narrator succumbs
– partly to Giles's insinuations, partly to his own combative anger
at the discovery that the Steward of the Home, from self-regarding
motives, has set on foot a cabal against him in favor of another
candidate. He applies for the berth, is employed, and proceeds up
the Gulf of Siam to claim his command in Bangkok. The remainder
of the novel, comprising about three-fourths of the whole, is, in
substance, an elaborated log of the narrator's first command.
Circumstances conspire against his success: a baffling calm which
immobilizes the ship; an outbreak of fever which disables the
crew and kills several men. The dead hand of the narrator's
hypochondriac and more than half-mad predecessor weighs on the
ship: among his legacies to his successor are an emotionally un-
stable mate (Mr. Burns) and a rifled quinine supply. In the face
of these disheartening circumstances the narrator survives his
ordeal: a favoring wind releases the ship and revives the spirits of
captain and crew; in the end, having brought the ship safely back
to port, he prepares to take her out again the next day, with
favorable auspices.

To say, as Douglas Hewitt has said, that "the doubts which
assail the captain are reasonable and simple" [15] is, I think, to
oversimplify and overrationalize. The statement scarcely gauges
the extent to which the narrator (in his imagination, if not in his
reason) is infected by the mate's delusions; nor does it take into
account all that we are told of the arbitrary and irrational quality
of those assailing "doubts" which, though finding reasonable occa-

[14]   *The Shadow-Line*, p. 5.
[15]   Hewitt, *Conrad: A Reassessment*, p. 116.

sions in the objective situation, existed antecedently to it in the form of anxiety, of the feeling of "life-emptiness". Apart from the notations cited, we read in the early pages of "moments of bore-dom, of weariness, of dissatisfaction" (p. 4); of "a dreary, prosaic waste of days" (p. 7). There is also the metaphor of emergence from the "enchanted garden" of youth (p. 3), reminding us of the *hortus conclusus* of "A Smile of Fortune", reminding us too that, for all the enchanted atmosphere of the voyage, the novel is, in one of its aspects, another tale of disenchantment. In the present instance, however, it is a double disenchantment, occurring in sequence – the first unaccounted for as to its origins and barren as to its consequences; the second involving a stripping-away of illusion under the lash of reality and the burden of responsibility, resulting in a sense of continuity with tradition, of professional solidarity, and of community with the living.

The opening image of the enchanted garden is followed by the narrator's assertion (apropos of the berth he had just thrown up) that "I could not have been happier if I had had the life and the men made to my order by a benevolent Enchanter" (p. 5). There is no recurrence of the motif in the thirty-five following pages, devoted to the machinations of the steward and the countermoves of Giles over (so to speak) the inert psyche of the torpid and disenchanted narrator. Immediately upon the triumph of Giles's policy and the investiture of the narrator with his first command, the metaphoric theme is reintroduced, in the same tonality as in the opening pages. Captain Ellis (the "deputy-Neptune") becomes a fierce but benevolent sort of fairy, the narrator himself a marine Cinderella, who occupies his "spellbound" ship in the enchanted state of the fairy princess mounting her pumpkin coach (pp. 39f.). Except for an isolated epithet the motif is suspended through the first forty pages following the captain's embarkation. Images drawn from the familiar region of dream and nightmare (pages 72, 80) prelude its re-entry in the characteristic tonality that will mark its recurrences in the remainder of the book. On page 83 the calm is identified as an "evil spell", and this becomes the key-image of the voyage. It recurs on page 88 (where the captain imagines the quinine to be a "magic powder" to counter its "mysterious malefices"); it recurs again on page 115, and finally on page 125 with a reference to the breaking of the spell, the laying of the "malicious spectre".

The image links, on the one hand, with Burns's delusions about the "evil intention" of the captain's spectral predecessor and his recollections of the curse pronounced on ship and crew (p. 61), on the other with the captain's own premonitions of the ship as a "floating grave" with crew all dead or dying (pp. 92, 102) or Burns's evocation of a Flying Dutchman of the China Sea (p. 94). Akin to these images are the recurrent images of poison and decomposition ("poisoned air"; "something going on in the sky like a decomposition, like a corruption in the air".[16])

These, then – together with the image of the "deadly enemy" in Ransome's breast [17] – are the principal metaphoric themes, in this rather sparsely metaphoric novel, with which Conrad re-enforces the title-image itself, the image of the shadow-line between youth and maturity, explicitly evoking the *Grenzsituation* the novel explores. Later, at the height of the narrative crisis, the captain's journal entries make more explicit the psychic ingredients of the antecedent mental crisis: a diffused guilt-sense ("I feel as if all my sins had found me out" [18]); anxiety and self-doubt ("Now I understand that strange sense of insecurity in my past. I always suspected that I might be no good. And here is proof positive, I am shirking it, I am no good" [19]). No eloquence is expended on the descriptive presentment of the state: the images and the bare statements are allowed to do their work with a minimum of rhetorical encumbrance. In *The Shadow-Line*, as in "The Smile of Fortune" and "The Secret Sharer", Conrad has taken eloquence and twisted its neck. Or if there is eloquence in these perfunctory

---

[16] *The Shadow-Line*, pp. 86, 106. And cf. on pp. 70, 92.
[17] *Ibid.*, p. 68; also p. 112 ("the dreadful knowledge of the enemy"), p. 133 ("our common enemy"). And cf. on p. 73, "something very fragile or very explosive to carry about his person". The reference is to the steward Ransome's weak heart.
[18] *Ibid.*, p. 106. Cf. also the following: "No confessed criminal had ever been so oppressed by his sense of guilt" (p. 96). An exhaustive analysis of the narrator's state would have to dwell on this morbidity of conscience, and could hardly avoid reference to the Freudian superego.
[19] *Ibid.*, p. 107.

notations it is (in marked contrast to the early Conrad who devoted paragraphs on end to an adjectival elaboration of the
mental states of his characters) the Pascalian eloquence which
mocks at eloquence.[20]

From these discursive and metaphoric hints we may formulate
the captain's moral condition in one of a number of terms supplied
by the vocabulary of religious or existential thought: in terms of
the medieval acedia, of the Baudelairean despair or the Baudelairean ennui, of existential anxiety, or of the "neurotic depression"
of Guerard's formula. Or we may invoke the significant term
(though one weakened by trivial contexts) of "doldrums" – a
mariner's word in whose metaphoric application we may see
adumbrated the symbolic operation Conrad has performed in his
novel. But it is in the events of the voyage itself that the narrator's
state is most adequately defined for us, that the brief discursive
hints are objectified, made matter of art and imposed upon our
imagination. In a sense the objects and events of the narrative
compose the moral state. Within the context of the controlling
symbol of the paralyzing calm, the subordinate details – capricious
and fitful gusts of breeze (for this is the doldrums, not the dead
calm of "The Ancient Mariner"), the "decomposing" skies, the air
"stagnant and oppressive", the "sulkily" smouldering sun, the
looming presence of Koh-ring – figure as ancillary details in the
landscape of depressive anxiety which the narrative objectifies.[21]
The predicament of the crew assumes also (as in "The Ancient
Mariner", though never departing from the natural plane) a
symbolic relation to the captain's state. The fever that grips most
of the seamen objectifies his "sickness of soul" (p. 109) and
focusses his sense of guilt, since through neglect (or rather what a
morbid conscience interprets as neglect) he has failed to discover
that the quinine supply is exhausted, a fact cunningly camouflaged

[20] I find in *The Shadow-Line* only one brief relapse into the sort of diction which marked (and for some readers marred) "Heart of Darkness".
Cf. on p. 108: "There was in it [i.e., the impenetrable blackness] an effect
of inconceivable terror and of inexpressible mystery."
[21] *Ibid.*, pp. 105 f., p. 84. Cf. Baudelaire's sonnet *De profundis clamavi*
(No. 30 of *Spleen et Idéal*), in which the poet projects what may be
termed the inner landscape of despair.

by his predecessor.[22] Burns's incipient madness, his delusions concerning the malign influence of the narrator's dead predecessor, however stubbornly resisted, find their echo in the narrator's thoughts, in momentary doubts of his own sanity. "My position's bad enough", he remarks to Burns, "without being worried with your silly fancies"; but the "silly fancies" of malign and irrational agencies at work are part of the essence of the position, psychologically considered, and the narrator does not escape their infection.[23]

Finally, the apprehensions of Ransome, with his precarious heart, objectify what I think we may take to be the basic anxiety that lies at the bottom of the experience of crossing the shadow-line from youth (which denies death) to maturity (which accepts it and learns to live with it): i.e., the shrinking from death (*timor mortis*) that manifests itself as a shrinking from life. Except in occasional metaphor ("It's like being bound hand and foot preparatory to having one's throat cut"; "The quietness that came over me was like a foretaste of annihilation" [24]), death as a personal contingency is not touched upon in the narrator's thoughts: as in "The Ancient Mariner", as in certain dreams, it is projected upon "the others" – in the general illness of the crew (suggesting to the narrator the repeated vision of the ship as a "floating grave", derelict with a dead crew [25]); in the death fear of the captain's dead predecessor as reported by Burns (p. 94); and most explicitly in the person of Ransome, whose precarious hold upon life is repeatedly before us, though his own terror of his condition and the captain's sense of community with him clearly emerge only at the end of the novel.

Conrad's protagonist thus reveals the three related types of anxiety – all involving the threat of "nonbeing", the denial of

---

[22] *Ibid.*, pp. 93 f. Burns's plausible assumption is that the quinine had been sold by his former captain.
[23] *Ibid.*, p. 102. For the captain's suspicions of his own sanity, cf. pp. 100 f.; also the following (p. 82): "I felt the inexpugnable strength of common sense being insidiously menaced by this gruesome, by this insane delusion."
[24] *Ibid.*, pp. 107, 108.
[25] *Ibid.*, p. 92; and cf. p. 102.

man's "spiritual self-affirmation" – discriminated by Paul Tillich:

> The awareness of this threefold threat [of nonbeing] is anxiety appearing in three forms, that of fate and death (briefly, the anxiety of death), that of emptiness and loss of meaning (briefly, the anxiety of meaninglessness), that of guilt and condemnation (briefly, the anxiety of condemnation).[26]

Of these, the third – articulated in the journal entries – is objectified principally in the episode of the missing quinine; the second, articulated principally in the opening paragraphs of the novel, and furnishing the psychological *donnée* of the work, is objectified in the evoked image of the crazed predecessor and more immediately in the contagious delusions and apprehensions of Burns. It is the "anxiety of fate and death" (as we are not surprised to learn) that is distinguished by Tillich as the "most basic, most universal, and inescapable".[27] It is the apprehension of death that furnishes the material of the final paragraph of *The Shadow-Line*. Ransome's leavetaking of ship and captain sounds the final note of the book – one of insistence upon the common human fate:

> Left alone in the cabin, I listened to him going up the companion stairs cautiously, step by step, in mortal fear of starting into sudden anger our common enemy it was his hard fate to carry consciously within his faithful breast.[28]

What is conscious in Ransome illumines what was unconscious in the captain.

[26] Paul Tillich, *The Courage to Be* (New Haven, Yale University Press, 1952), p. 41.

[27] *Ibid.*, pp. 42 f. I cite Tillich's typology of anxiety for its concision and for what seems to me its peculiar aptness to the work under consideration. But his discrimination of the source of the "basic" anxiety can be found elsewhere in theological and psychiatric writings, and is implicit or explicit in much of the world's imaginative literature: e.g., in Conrad, in a passage in "Falk" in which the narrator, identifying as complementary aspects of the life-instinct Falk's hunger for Lena and the hunger which led him to cannibalism, declares that "we are in his case allowed to contemplate the foundation of all the emotions – that one joy which is to live, and the one sadness at the root of the innumerable torments" (*Typhoon*, p. 224). Or cf., in "Heart of Darkness", Marlow's pronouncement on lies: "There is a taint of death, a flavour of mortality in lies – which is exactly what I hate and detest in the world – what I want to forget" (*Youth*, p. 82).

[28] *The Shadow-Line*, p. 133.

Here (played down in the course of the novel, and fully revealing itself only in the closing paragraphs) is another of Conrad's
"unforeseen partnerships".[29] No more than in "Heart of Darkness" or "The Secret Sharer" can the full meaning of this obscure
relationship be exhausted in a formula. Carl Benson offered a
useful one when he remarked, in the course of an interesting
comparative study of *The Shadow-Line* and "The Secret Sharer",
that Ransome is "employed significantly to emphasize the opposition of a sick heart, or soul, in a sound body and a sound soul
in a sick body".[30] The formula satisfies our sense of symmetry,
and it probably defines in part Conrad's intention; but it does not
seem to me that it accounts for the inwardness of the relationship
or its deeper meaning for the reader. For my own formula, however, I claim no more than that it comes closer to accounting for
my own response to the novel.

Does Ransome's departure from the ship signify the final
exorcism of the "basic anxiety"? It is, in any case, the culminating
event of the story, setting its seal (for whatever we may make of
it) upon the whole; and remembering the importance Conrad set
upon his endings, we cannot avoid questioning it for any summa-

---

[29] With this "unforeseen partnership" cf. Malraux's explicit account of
the bond between Claude Vannec and Perken, in *La Voie Royale*, a novel
in which one may detect more than one suggestion of Conrad's influence:
"Il ne restait entre eux – pour les attacher – que ce que les êtres ont de
plus profond. . . .

Et tout-à-coup, Claude découvrit ce qui le liait à cet homme qui l'avait
accepté sans qu'il comprît bien pourquoi: l'obsession de la mort" (André
Malraux, *La Voie Royale; Les Puissances du désert, I*, Paris, B. Grasset,
1930, pp. 52 f.).

[30] Carl Benson, "Conrad's Two Stories of Initiation", *PMLA*, LXIX
(March, 1954), p. 53. Cf. Haugh's assertion that Ransome "is symbolically
useful as a sort of double for the captain, whose heart must undergo
seasoning of another sort in this weird cruise" (Robert F. Haugh, *Joseph
Conrad: Discovery in Design*, Norman, University of Oklahoma Press,
1957, p. 85). Moser's view – that Conrad tries, and fails, "to suggest the
presence of evil" in endowing Ransome with his physical flaw – seems to
me gratuitous (Moser, *Joseph Conrad: Achievement and Decline*, p. 139).
Is not the evoked figure of the late captain (though Moser sees in him
"a very external evil") sufficiently suggestive for the purpose? What Ransome, in his role of invalid, embodies is man's mortality – the precarious-
ness of his life tenure, in which we may trace the origin of his anxiety.

rizing word or any light it may throw upon the whole. We have already had evidence, in his immediately preceding dialogue with Giles, of the captain's newly-won maturity of outlook. In the light of this we may perhaps say something like the following: If death (together with the other spectres that haunted the captain: the spectres of guilt and meaninglessness) has not lost its sting, the sting is at any rate mitigated, deprived of its immobilizing power. Brought into the light of consciousness the captain's fears are neutralized; having confronted the human condition he is equal to his fate, and the terror of "nonbeing", concentrated in Ransome, departs from him.[31] These formulations are conjectural, an admitted groping in the dark, and it may be felt that they tend to reduce to allegory the complexity and ineradicable ambiguity of symbol. We have Conrad's own testimony that he suppressed some of the content of the episode which was the prototype of the fictional episode, and that the suppression was prompted by a deliberate instinct for concealment, for safeguarding from profane hands certain autobiographic arcana; [32] and I think we must accept that the "meaning" – the full meaning – of the fictional episode is as little amenable to a final summary as are the last paragraphs of "The Secret Sharer". Nevertheless, I would propose with some confidence that in this final identification of death as "the common enemy within", reenforcing our earlier sense of an obscure community between Ransome and the narrator, Conrad has objectified an implicit element of the narrator's crisis which, as subjective (and presumably unconscious) content of his own psyche, has been all but suppressed in the body of the narrative.

Here it is worth noting that Jessie Conrad objected to the title of this work on the grounds that it suggested the image of mortali-

---

[31] The reference could be expanded to include Burns, who also relinquishes his berth.

[32] The passage in question (from a letter of February, 1917, to Sidney Colvin) affords a hint, inexplicit but highly suggestive, at the intensity of Conrad's relationship with the prototype of the fictional Ransome: "My last scene with Ransome is only indicated. There are things, moments, that are not to be tossed to the public's incomprehension, for journalists to gloat over. No. It was not an experience to be exhibited 'in the street' " (*Life and Letters*, II, p. 182).

ty in *Psalms* xxiii, 4.[33] I suspect that Mrs. Conrad – who knew
something of her husband's relation to the idea of death – was not
being extravagant and that in his image of the shadow-line Conrad
has, in some sense, given us a sort of marine equivalent of the
Psalmist's Valley of the Shadow – a valley which has not un-
commonly been traversed by imaginative men "nel mezzo del
cammin", at the threshold of full maturity and self-possession.[34]

The Shadow-Line, originally published with the sub-title "A
Confession", is, with "Youth", the most nearly autobiographical
of all Conrad's fictions. On this point we have Conrad's repeated
assurances: in the "Author's Note", in which he speaks of it as
"personal experience seen in perspective"; [35] in a letter of 1917 to
Pinker, in which he asserts that it is "not a story really but exact
autobiography"; [36] in the letter to Sidney Colvin already cited, in
which he repeats the phrase, adding the assertion, "*J'ai vécu tout
cela*", and even expressing the conviction that the very speeches
were "verbally accurate", and that all but one of the names were
authentic.[37] The Colvin letter implies, in fact, that Conrad in his
own mind expressly differentiated *The Shadow-Line* from his
works of fiction; and three weeks later we find him writing to the

[33]   Jessie Conrad, *Joseph Conrad and His Circle*, pp. 193 f.
[34]   That Conrad in his middle years was much possessed by death is warranted by biographical, as well as by fictional, testimony. A striking instance may be found in Jessie Conrad's account of his proposal of marriage: "He had begun by announcing that he had not very long to live and
no intention of having children; but such as his life was (his shrug was
very characteristic), he thought we might spend a few happy years together" (Jessie Conrad, *Joseph Conrad as I Knew Him*, p. 105). That
there was an ambivalence in his orientation to death may be gathered from
such a passage in the correspondence as the following (in the letter to
Mme Poradowska quoted in the foregoing chapter): "Why are you afraid?
And of what? Is it of solitude or of death? O strange fear! The only two
things that make life bearable!" (*Letters to Marguerite Poradowska*, p. 72).
Cf. on this whole question Jocelyn Baines's account of the young Conrad's
attempted suicide at Monte Carlo. This was an event of Conrad's early
youth, but one that appears to have cast a long shadow.
[35]   *The Shadow-Line*, p. ix. The experience seen in perspective was his
abandonment of a mate's berth on the S.S. *Vidar*, in January, 1888, and
his subsequent assumption of command of the barque *Otago*, shipping out
of Bankok.
[36]   *Life and Letters*, II, p. 181.
[37]   *Ibid.*, II, p. 182 f.

same correspondent that "I shrink from calling it a Tale".[38] For all this, the "Author's Note" speaks of it, repeatedly if shrinkingly, as a "story" and a "tale", and its destiny has been to enter the canon of English fiction.

In returning to the autobiographic source from which seven years earlier he had drawn up, in a different pail, "The Secret Sharer", Conrad nicely illustrated the inexhaustibility of any experience to a deeply reflecting mind of the sort James postulated when he counseled the writer to be one of those on whom nothing is lost. "For when", as Conrad wrote in his "Author's Note" to the later work, "we begin to meditate on the meaning of our own past it seems to fill all the world in its profundity and its magnitude." [39] Critics have naturally compared the novel and the story to see what crosslights they might throw on each other – most assiduously among them Carl Benson in the comparative study already cited. I have only one serious issue to take with that able and suggestive study. Benson sees *The Shadow-Line* as a record of an initiation which is "the communal counterpart to that of 'The Secret Sharer' ". In it "the dark and narrow inwardness" of the earlier work "is counterpointed by the deliberate outwardness of human responsibility".[40] Insisting that the captain's initiation in "The Secret Sharer" is "humanly abortive",[41] Benson does not remind us that Conrad explicitly states the reverse, that the *declared* outcome is the achievement (or at any rate the prospect) of "silent knowledge and mute affection, the perfect communion of a seaman with his first command".[42] Thus his view of the story seems to imply, without explicitly indicating, some such disjunction as I have argued between the captain's objective situation at the end of that story and his subjective feeling about it.

We may see in the argument defensible grounds for preferring the novel to the story. What seems to me exceptionable is Benson's view of *The Shadow-Line* as "Conrad's critical judgment of the

---

[38] *Ibid.*, II, p. 184.
[39] *The Shadow-Line*, p. ix.
[40] Benson, *PMLA*, LXIX (March, 1954), pp. 46, 56.
[41] *Ibid.*, p. 46.
[42] *'Twixt Land and Sea*, p. 143.

earlier story".[43] As we have seen, Conrad was well satisfied with "The Secret Sharer", and there is no evidence of any wavering in his apparent conviction that he had realized his intention in that work. True, *The Shadow-Line* is a turning back, seven years later, to the same autobiographical material, and not perfunctorily but with a genuine *élan*, clearly under an impulsion to handle the material from a different angle and with a different stress. But this implies no more than that the earlier treatment did not exhaust for him the meaning of the experience it explores; and have we any reason to assert that *The Shadow-Line* came nearer than its more "inward" precursor to that imagined goal? It risks less, attempts less in the way of symbolic transmutation, relying more confidently (though not, as I have suggested, supinely) on the symbolic values inherent in the given, the lived-through and remembered experience. It is, perhaps in consequence, a more nearly perfect work. And certainly the "communal" aspects of first command are more fully developed in *The Shadow-Line* than in "The Secret Sharer": the rapport between captain and crew, only postulated in the earlier work, is realized in the later. But each work must be seen as the response to an independent creative impulse; neither judges, and neither diminishes, the other.

In one of the letters to Sidney Colvin already cited, Conrad declared of *The Shadow-Line* that in it "experience is transposed into spiritual terms".[44] The statement is significant since it defines a process opposite to that of allegory, in which preconceived spiritual (or moral) conceptions are cast into simulacra of life, of lived experience. There is a strong temptation for the critic – concerned primarily with the work as a finished product, an object, and only marginally with the provenience of the material – to see the process as reversed. Filled with his intuitive apprehension of ideal or spiritual values transpiring through the recorded events, he tends to see the events, even the most apparently casual, as deliberately contrived or manipulated to illustrate these values. If he is perceptive, and sensitive to fictional and poetic (as well as to moral and social) values, no great harm is done; if he is not he

[43]   Benson, *loc. cit.*, p. 56.
[44]   *Life and Letters*, II, p. 183.

may treat the text like a Euclidean theorem or a logical apparatus for proving something the critic wants proved. Paul Wiley, I think, though not an imperceptive critic, falls into this trap in his dealings with *The Shadow-Line*, which he sees as an allegory of "guilt and absolution".[45] Aside from the fact that this judgment fails to reckon with the subjective nature of the "guilt", or with the way in which the narrator's guilt feelings are involved with other symptoms of anxiety, Wiley's terminology is misleading.

I have affirmed throughout this study, and want to reaffirm here near its close, that I think the Coleridgean distinction between the allegoric and the symbolic is important and useful, and that I do not see Conrad as an allegorist but as a novelist *pur sang*, impelled by the pressure of imagination into symbolic expression but deriving his initial impulse from lived experience. This is to reaffirm, in the face of my repeated insistence upon the deliberateness of many of his artistic procedures, my conviction that unconscious impulse figures importantly in his work. It is what Coleridge predicated of genuinely symbolic art, as distinct from allegory, when he wrote that allegory "can not be other than spoken consciously; – whereas in . . . the symbol it is very possible that the general truth represented may be working unconsciously in the writer's mind during the construction of the symbol".[46] I think, then, that we do well to accept as a valid account of the genesis of this novel Conrad's declaration that experience – the experience of his first command on the *Otago* in the Gulf of Siam – has been transposed, in *The Shadow-Line*, into spiritual (or psychological) terms.

When this has been said, it has to be acknowledged that Coleridge's logical opposition between allegory and symbol,

---

45 Paul L. Wiley, *Conrad's Measure of Man* (Madison, University of Wisconsin Press, 1954), pp. 200, 209. Wiley's discussion (pp. 199-214) is otherwise useful, stressing the recurrent Conradian themes of fidelity to duty, of solidarity and continuity (in this novel broken and then restored). But Wiley is determined to make Conrad an allegorist, and I cannot avoid the feeling that – as Coleridge remarked to Mrs. Barbauld of "The Ancient Mariner" – there is "too much moral" in his *Shadow-Line*. This is not, of course, to dismiss the serious moral implications of the work; but they scarcely account for its imaginative impact.
46 Coleridge, "Lecture VIII, on Cervantes", *Complete Works*, IV, p. 265.

though important and even essential in arriving at a general view of a writer's method and in accounting for the genesis of individual works, cannot in every instance – and particularly not when we attempt an imaginative reconstruction of the compositional process – be maintained with the strict rigor with which it is formulated. Apart from certain works which seem to resist any confident assignment to one or the other category, there are those which appear to mix the two modes – i.e., works fundamentally symbolic in their conception which at one or more points interpolate deliberate allegorical elements. I think that the figure of *L'Aveugle* in *Madame Bovary* may be said to be such an interpolation, and I suspect that the same might be said of Mr. Jones in *Victory*.

More relevant to our context, however, is this: that, insisting upon the genetic primacy of the lived experience, of the imagined events and their agents, we are yet not obliged (either in Coleridgean theory or in common sense) to believe that the symbolized meanings, or the "general truths represented", or the "valeurs idéales", must be, in all cases and from beginning to end of the creative process, unconscious products, mere autonomous secretions thrown off from the actions represented. Here I recall again Goethe's "ohne es gewahr zu sein, oder erst spät". For many (if by no means for all) of the symbolized meanings we intuit in an imaginative work we may conjecturally postulate a point in the creative process at which what had originally been unconscious, or inchoate, emerges into full consciousness. At this hypothetical point we may postulate the beginning of a process of reciprocal action of the symbol, or of the "valeurs idéales", upon the narrative surface, modifying the direction of character and events. If, in the present case, we knew at what point Conrad chose his Baudelairean epigraph (or when it imposed itself upon him), or if we had evidence of a contemporaneous reading of "the Ancient Mariner", we would have interesting clues to some such conjectural process – to the motives (for example) that led him to modify the autobiographic *données* by making Burns and his delusions "the pivot", as he called him, entailing with it the discursive and metaphoric stress on the theme of enchantment. Or to the motives that lay behind his decision to close the work with the departure of Ransome and the evocation of "our common enemy".

Since Conrad's correspondence (unlike Flaubert's) gives us virtually nothing in the way of contemporaneous hints as to his imaginative processes, we are left with our conjectures. Without pursuing these further I shall close this chapter by quoting and briefly commenting on an *ex post facto* statement of intention: Conrad's remark in one of the letters to Colvin that "my object was to show all the others and the situation through the medium of my own emotions".[47] Of this I would say that Conrad achieved his object in a convincing and objectively realized narrative with a firmly textured surface; but that in achieving it he achieved also a symbolic presentment of his narrator's psychic state (*état d'âme*) which, paradoxically, might be defined by reversing the terms of his statement. That is to say that symbolically he has evoked the emotional and moral state of the narrator (whether it was also Conrad's is critically irrelevant) through the medium of the "others" – of the malarious crew with their sick bodies, of the deluded Burns with his sick fancies, of the devoted Ransome with his sick heart.[48] And to the personages of the drama one must add, to complete the account, the "mirroring" function of the elements: the becalmed sea and the capricious winds, the rain and the quickening breeze.

Otto Ludwig wrote (apropos of Shakespeare's dramatic method, which he opposed to Schiller's) that "the action, the event, occurs as a necessary consequence and at the same time as a symbolic externalization of the inner development".[49] It cannot of course be

[47] *Life and Letters*, II, p. 184.

[48] My analysis has stressed the symbolic significance of Ransome's faulty heart-beat. Here I had better make it clear that I do *not* reduce the living character to a *memento mori* or a mere projection of the captain's anxiety. He exists as much in his moral strength as in his physical weakness. I would endorse the view of Ian Watt (who, in a perceptive essay, showed himself aware of the importance of the death-motif in the novel) that Ransome, in his "contained serenity, ... represents most fully the dynastic inheritance". Neither as character nor as symbol can he be reduced to a unitary formula (Cf. Ian Watt, "Story and Idea in Conrad's 'The Shadow-Line'" *Critical Quarterly*, II, Summer, 1960, p. 145).

[49] Quoted in Eric R. Bentley, *The Playwright as Thinker, a Study of Drama in Modern Times* (New York, Reynal & Hitchcock, 1946), p. 72.

said that the action (or inaction) of wind and water in the Gulf of Siam, or the delusions of Burns, or Ransome's eccentric heart-beat are (in any natural order of events) "necessary consequences" of the narrator's inner state; but one does feel them as "symbolic externalizations" of it, and feeling this one accords to them a poetic, an imaginative, necessity.

Cf. Conrad to Edward Noble, in a letter of October, 1895: "You must treat events only as illustrative of human sensation, – as the outward sign of inward feelings, – of live feelings, – which alone are truly pathetic and interesting. You have much imagination. ... Well, that imagination (I wish I had it) should be used to create human souls: to disclose human hearts, – and not to create events that are properly speaking *accidents* only" (*Life and Letters*, I, p. 183).

BIBLIOGRAPHY

Allen, Jerry, "Conrad's River", *Columbia University Forum*, V (Winter, 1962), pp. 29-35.

Baines, Jocelyn, *Joseph Conrad* (New York, McGraw-Hill, 1960).

Baudelaire, Charles, *Œuvres complètes*, éclaircissements, notes et commentaires de Jacques Crépet, 13 vols. (Paris, Louis Conard, 1930-1952).

——, *Le Spleen de Paris: Petits poëmes en prose, suivis des Journaux intimes et de Choix de maximes consolantes sur l'amour* (Paris, Editions de Cluny, 1939).

Bayley, John, *The Characters of Love* (New York, Basic Books, 1960).

Beerbohm, Max, *A Christmas Garland* (London, Heinemann, 1938).

Benson, Carl, "Conrad's Two Stories of Initiation", *PMLA*, LXIX (March, 1954), pp. 46-56.

Bentley, Eric R., *The Playwright as Thinker: A Study of Drama in Modern Times* (New York, Reynal & Hitchcock, 1946).

Bewley, Marius, *The Eccentric Design* (New York, Columbia University Press, 1959).

Björkman, Edwin, "Joseph Conrad, A Master of Literary Color", *Review of Reviews*, XLV (May, 1912), pp. 557-560.

Bodkin, Maud, *Archetypal Patterns in Poetry: Psychological Studies of Imagination* (London, Oxford University Press, 1934).

Bradbrook, M. C., *Joseph Conrad: Poland's English Genius* (Cambridge, The University Press, 1941).

Brown, E. K., "James and Conrad", *Yale Review*, XXXV (Winter, 1946), pp. 265-285.

Burke, Kenneth, *The Philosophy of Literary Form* (Baton Rouge, Louisiana State University Press, 1941).

Burkhardt, Johanna, *Das Erlebnis der Wirklichkeit und seine künstlerische Gestaltung in Joseph Conrads Werk* (Marburg, H. Bauer, 1935).

Cassirer, Ernst, *Language and Myth* (New York, Dover Publications, n.d.).

Chase, Richard, *The American Novel and Its Tradition* (London, Bell, 1958).

Chevrillon, André (See *Nouvelle Revue française*).

Claudel, Paul, *The Correspondence, 1899-1926, between Paul Claudel and André Gide*, translated by John Russell (New York, Pantheon, 1952).

Clemen, Wolfgang, *The Development of Shakespeare's Imagery* (New York, Hill & Wang, 1962).

Clemens, Florence, "Conrad's favorite Bedside Book", *South Atlantic Quarterly*, XXXVIII (July, 1939), pp. 305-315.
——, "Joseph Conrad as a Geographer", *Scientific Monthly*, LI (November, 1940), pp. 460-465.
Coleridge, Samuel Taylor, *Complete Works*, edited by W. G. T. Shedd, 7 vols. (New York, Harper's, 1853).
Conrad, Jessie, *Joseph Conrad and His Circle* (New York, Dutton, 1935).
——, *Joseph Conrad as I Knew Him* (Garden City, Doubleday, Page, 1926).
Conrad, Joseph, [*Collected Works*; Canterbury Edition] (Garden City, Doubleday, Page, 1924) [Same pagination as Kent and Malay editions, also the Concord and the Personal editions].
——, *Conrad to a Friend: 150 Selected Letters from Joseph Conrad to Richard Curle* (Garden City, Doubleday, Doran, 1928).
——, *Letters from Joseph Conrad, 1895-1924*, edited with Introduction and Notes by Edward Garnett (Indianapolis, Bobbs-Merrill, 1928).
——, *Letters of Joseph Conrad to Marguerite Poradowska: 1890-1920*, translated from the French and edited with an Introduction, Notes, and Appendices by John A. Gee and Paul J. Sturm (New Haven, Yale University Press, 1940).
——, *Letters to William Blackwood and David S. Meldrum*, edited by William Blackburn (Durham, Duke University Press, 1958).
——, *Lettres françaises*; avec une introduction et des notes de G. Jean-Aubry, 4ième éd. (Paris, Librairie Gallimard, Editions de la Nouvelle Revue française, 1930).
Cornell, Kenneth, *The Symbolist Movement* (New Haven, Yale University Press, 1951).
Crankshaw, Edward, *Joseph Conrad: Some Aspects of the Art of the Novel* (London, John Lane, The Bodley Head, 1936).
Croce, Benedetto, *Aesthetic as Science of Expression and General Linguistic*, 2nd ed. Translated by Douglas Ainslie (London, The Macmillan Company, 1929).
——, *The Poetry of Dante*, translated by Douglas Ainslie (New York, Henry Holt and Co., 1922).
Curle, Richard, *Joseph Conrad: a Study* (New York, Doubleday, 1914).
——, *The Last Twelve Years of Joseph Conrad* (Garden City, Doubleday, Doran, 1928).
Daniel-Rops, Henry,* *Carte d'Europe* (Paris, Perrin & Cie., 1928).
Demorest, D. L., *L'Expression figurée et symbolique dans l'œuvre de Gustave Flaubert* (Paris, Louis Conard, 1931).
Dickens, Charles, *The Works of Charles Dickens*, Gadshill Edition, 34 vols. (London, Chapman & Hall, 1903).
——, *Bleak House*, introduction by G. K. Chesterton, Everyman's edition (London, J. M. Dent, 1907).
Dumesnil, René, *Gustave Flaubert: l'homme et l'œuvre*, avec des documents inédits (Paris, Desclée de Brouwer & cie., 1932).
Estaunié, Edouard (See *Nouvelle Revue française*).

* Library of Congress entry. The author himself (real name Henry Petiot) employs the pseudonym "Daniel-Rops" without addition.

Faguet, Emile, *Flaubert (Collection des grands écrivains français)* (Paris, Hachette, 1899).

Fernández, Ramón, "L'Art de Conrad" (See *Nouvelle Revue française*).

Flaubert, Gustave, *Œuvres complètes*, 21 vols. (Paris, Louis Conard, 1921-1954) (Includes 13 volumes of correspondence as follows:
—, *Correspondance*, nouvelle édition augmentée, 9 vols., *Ibid.*, 1926-1933;
—, *Correspondance: Supplément*, 4 vols., *Ibid.*, 1954).

Ford, Ford Madox, *Joseph Conrad: A Personal Remembrance* (Boston, Little, Brown, 1924).

Fowler, H. W., *A Dictionary of Modern English Usage* (New York, Oxford University Press, 1944).

Gatch, Katherine H., "Conrad's Axel", *Studies in Philology*, XLVIII (January, 1951), pp. 98-106.

Gide, André, *Dostoïevsky (Articles et causeries)* (Paris, Plon, 1923).

—, *The Journals of André Gide*, translated by Justin O'Brien, 4 vols. (New York, Knopf, 1947-1951).

—, *Pages de Journal (1929-1932)* (Paris, Gallimard, 1936).

—, (See also *Nouvelle Revue française*).

Gillet, Louis, *Lectures Etrangères: Première Série* (Paris, Plon-Nourrit, 1924).

—, "Le nouveau roman de M. Conrad, *The Arrow of Gold*", *Revue des deux mondes*, 6ième période, LIII (1 octobre 1919), pp. 676-685.

Gillon, Adam, *The Eternal Solitary: Joseph Conrad* (New York, Bookman Associates, 1960).

Goethe, Johann Wolfgang von, *Sämtliche Werke*, 40 vols., Jubiläums-Ausgabe (Stuttgart and Berlin, Cotta, 1922-40).

Gordan, John Dozier, *Joseph Conrad: the Making of a Novelist* (Cambridge, Harvard University Press, 1940).

Guerard, Albert J., *Conrad the Novelist* (Cambridge, Mass., Harvard University Press, 1958).

—, "The Heart of Conrad", *Nation*, CLXVI (3 January 1948), pp. 21-22.

—, "The Voyages of Captain Korzeniowski", *The Reporter*, XVI (21 March 1957), pp. 42-44.

Gurko, Leo, *Joseph Conrad: Giant in Exile* (New York, Macmillan, 1962).

Harding, D. W., "The Theme of *The Ancient Mariner*", *The Importance of Scrutiny: Selections from SCRUTINY: A Quarterly Review, 1932-1938*. Ed. by Eric Bentley (New York, G. W. Stewart, 1948), pp. 174-181.

Harding, M. Esther, "The Shadow", *Spring*, 1945.

Hardy, Thomas, *Tess of the D'Urbervilles* (New York, Harper, 1921).

Haugh, Robert F., *Joseph Conrad: Discovery in Design* (Norman, University of Oklahoma Press, 1957).

Hawthorne, Nathaniel, *The Complete Novels and Selected Tales*, edited, with an introduction, by Norman Holmes Pearson (New York, The Modern Library, 1937).

Hay, Eloise Knapp, *The Political Novels of Joseph Conrad: A Critical Study* (Chicago and London, University of Chicago Press, 1963).

Heller, Erich, *The Disinherited Mind; Essays in Modern German*

Literature and Thought (Philadelphia, Dufour and Saifer, 1952).

Hemingway, Ernest, *A Farewell to Arms* (New York, Scribner's, 1929).

Hewitt, Douglas John, *Conrad: A Reassessment* (Cambridge, Bowes & Bowes, 1952).

Hicks, John H., "Conrad's Almayer's Folly: Structure, Theme, and Critics", *Nineteenth-Century Fiction*, XIX (June, 1964), p. 24.

Hopkins, Gerard Manley, *A Hopkins Reader*, selected and with an introduction by John Pick (New York, Oxford, 1953).

Huneker, James Gibbons, *Ivory Apes and Peacocks* (New York, Scribner's, 1915).

——, *Steeplejack*, 2 vols. in one (New York, Scribner's, 1922).

Huret, Jules, *Enquête sur l'Evolution littéraire* (Paris, Charpentier, 1901).

James, Henry, *The Bostonians* (London and New York, Macmillan, 1886).

——, *Notes on Novelists, with some Other Notes* (New York, Scribner's, 1914).

——, *The Wings of the Dove* (Westminster, Constable, 1902).

Jean-Aubry, G., "Joseph Conrad's Confessions", *Fortnightly Review*, CXV (May, 1921), pp. 782-790.

——, *Joseph Conrad, Life and Letters*, 2 vols. (Garden City, Doubleday, Page, 1927).

——, *The Sea Dreamer: A Definitive Biography of Joseph Conrad*, translated by Helen Sebba (Garden City, Doubleday, 1957).

——, "Souvenir (Fragments)" (See *Nouvelle Revue française*),

Karl, Frederick R., *A Reader's Guide to Joseph Conrad* (New York, Noonday Press, 1960).

Kenner, Hugh, *The Poetry of Ezra Pound* (Norfolk, Conn., New Directions, 1951).

Lamb, Charles, *Letters of Charles Lamb*, edited by Alfred Ainger, 2 vols. (London, Macmillan, 1897).

Langer, Susanne K., *Philosophy in a New Key: A Study in the Symbolism of Reason, Rite, and Art* (New York, Penguin Books, 1948).

Las Vergnas, Raymond, *Joseph Conrad* (*Les grands écrivains étrangers*) (Paris, H. Didier, 1938).

——, *Joseph Conrad, romancier de l'exil* (Lyon, E. Vitte, 1959).

Leavis, Frank Raymond, *The Great Tradition: George Eliot, Henry James, Joseph Conrad* (New York, George W. Stewart, 1948).

Lehmann, John, "On Re-reading 'The Rover'", *The Open Night* (New York, Harcourt, Brace, 1952).

Lenormand, H.-R., *Les Confessions d'un auteur dramatique*, 2 vols. (Paris, Albin Michel, 1949-1953).

——, *Le Simoun*, édition définitive (Paris, Crès & cie., 1921).

Lewis, C. S., *The Allegory of Love: A Study in Medieval Tradition* (London, Oxford University Press, 1938).

Lippman, Edward Arthur, "Symbolism in Music", *The Musical Quarterly*, XXXIX (October, 1953), pp. 554-575.

Lohf, Kenneth A., and Sheehy, Eugene P., *Joseph Conrad at Mid-Century: Editions and Studies, 1895-1955* (Minneapolis, University of Minnesota Press, 1957).

MacCarthy, Desmond, "Joseph Conrad", *Portraits* (New York, Oxford University Press, 1954), pp. 68-78.

MacShane, Frank, "Conrad on Melville", *American Literature*, XXIX (January, 1958), pp. 463-464.

Mallarmé, Stéphane, *Œuvres complètes*, texte établi et annoté par Henri Mondor et G. Jean-Aubry (*Bibliothèque de la Pléiade*) (Paris, Gallimard, 1945).

Malraux, André, *La Voie Royale; Les Puissances du désert*, I (Paris, B. Grasset, 1930).

Mann, Thomas, *Die Entstehung des Doktor Faustus: Roman eines Romans* (Amsterdam, Bermann-Fischer, 1949).

——, "The Making of 'The Magic Mountain' ", *Atlantic*, CXCI (January, 1953), pp. 41-45.

Martino, Pierre, *Parnasse et symbolisme (1850-1900)*, 3ième éd. (Paris, Librairie Armand Colin, 1930).

Miller, James E., "*The Nigger of the 'Narcissus'*: A Re-examination", *PMLA*, LXVI (December, 1951), pp. 911-918.

Mondor, Henri, *Vie de Mallarmé*, édition complète en un volume (Paris, Gallimard, 1941).

Moore, Carlisle, "Conrad and the Novel of Ordeal", *Philological Quarterly*, XLII (January, 1963), pp. 55-74.

Morf, Gustav, *The Polish Heritage of Joseph Conrad* (London, Sampson Low, Marston, 1930).

Moser, Thomas, *Joseph Conrad: Achievement and Decline* (Cambridge, Mass., Harvard University Press, 1957).

Mudrick, Marvin, "The Artist's Conscience and *The Nigger of* 'The Narcissus' ", *Nineteenth-Century Fiction*, XI (March, 1957), pp. 288-297.

——, "Communication: Mr. Stallman's Remarks", *Kenyon Review*, XIX (Summer, 1957), p. 483.

——, "Conrad and the Terms of Modern Criticism", *Hudson Review*, VII (Autumn, 1954), pp. 419-426.

——, "The Originality of Conrad", *Hudson Review*, XI (Winter, 1958-59), pp. 546-550.

Muir, Edwin, *Latitudes* (New York, Huebsch, 1924).

——, *The Structure of the Novel* (London, The Hogarth Press, 1954).

Murry, John Middleton, *The Problem of Style* (London, Oxford University Press, 1922).

Nouvelle Revue française, XXIII (Décembre 1924), pp. 649-806 ("Hommage à Joseph Conrad", articles on Conrad by: André Chevrillon, Edouard Estaunié, Ramón Fernández, André Gide, Edmond Jaloux, G. Jean-Aubry, Joseph Kessel, H.-R. Lenormand, André Maurois, Paul Valéry).

O'Connor, William Van (ed.), *Forms of Modern Fiction: Essays Collected in Honor of Joseph Warren Beach* (Minneapolis, University of Minnesota Press, 1948).

Pater, Walter, *The Renaissance: Studies in Art and Poetry* (London, Macmillan, 1924).

Pierre-Quint, Léon, *André Gide: His Life and Work*, translated by Dorothy M. Richardson (New York, Knopf, 1934).

Pongs, Hermann, *Im Umbruch der Zeit: das Romanschaffen der Gegenwart*, 2. erweiterte Auflage (Göttingen, Göttinger Verlagsanstalt, 1956).

Pritchett, V. S., *The Living Novel* (New York, Reynal & Hitchcock, 1947).

Proust, Marcel, *Pastiches et mélanges* (Paris, Gallimard, 1919).

Rahv, Philip, "Fiction and the Criticism of Fiction", *Kenyon Review*, XVIII (Spring, 1956), pp. 276-299.

Raphael, Alice, "Joseph Conrad's Faust", *Goethe, the Challenger* (New York, Jonathan Cape & Robert Vallou, 1932), pp. 39-83.

Raymond, Marcel, *De Baudelaire au Surréalisme* (Paris, Corrêa, 1933).

Retinger, J. H., *Conrad and His Contemporaries: Souvenirs* (New York, Roy Publishers, 1941).

Spurgeon, Caroline F. E., *Shakespeare's Imagery, and What It Tells Us* (Cambridge, The University Press, 1935).

Stallman, Robert Wooster (ed.), *The Art of Joseph Conrad: A Critical Symposium* (East Lansing, Michigan State University Press, 1960).

——, "Life, Art, and 'The Secret Sharer'", in O'Connor, William Van, ed., *Forms of Modern Fiction . . .* [q. v.].

Stawell, F. Melian, "Conrad", *Essays and Studies by Members of the English Association*, VI (1920), pp. 88-111.

Strich, Fritz, *Der Dichter und die Zeit* (Bern, A. Francke, 1947).

Symons, Arthur, *Dramatis Personae* (Indianapolis, Bobbs-Merrill, 1923).

——, *Notes on Joseph Conrad, with some Unpublished Letters* (London, Myers & Co., 1925).

——, *The Symbolist Movement in Literature* (London, Heinemann, 1899).

Temple, Ruth Zabriskie, *The Critic's Alchemy: A Study of the Introduction of French Symbolism into England* (New York, Twayne, 1953).

Thibaudet, Albert, *Gustave Flaubert, 1821-1880: sa vie, ses romans, son style* (Paris, Plon, 1922).

——, *La Poésie de Stéphane Mallarmé: étude littéraire*, 11ième éd. (Paris, Gallimard, 1926).

Tillich, Paul, *The Courage to Be* (New Haven, Yale University Press, 1952).

The Times Literary Supplement, LVI (12 April 1957), pp. 217-219.

Tindall, William York, "Apology for Marlow", *From Jane Austen to Joseph Conrad: Essays Collected in Memory of James T. Hillhouse*, edited by Robert C. Rathburn and Martin Steinmann, Jr. (Minneapolis, University of Minnesota Press, 1958), pp. 274-285.

——, *The Literary Symbol* (New York, Columbia University Press, 1955).

Turgenev, Ivan, *Rudin: A Novel*, translated by Constance Garnett (London, Heinemann, 1894).

——, *Smoke: A Novel*, translated by Constance Garnett (New York, Macmillan, 1896).

Turnell, Martin, *The Novel in France: Mme de LaFayette, Laclos, Constant, Stendhal, Balzac, Flaubert, Proust* (Norfolk, Conn., New Directions, 1951).

Ujejski, Józef, *Joseph Conrad*, traduit par Pierre Duméril (Paris, Société française d'éditions littéraires et techniques, 1939).

Ullmann, Stephen, *The Image in the Modern French Novel: Gide, Alain-Fournier, Proust, Camus* (Cambridge, The University Press, 1960).

——, *Style in the French Novel* (Cambridge, The University Press, 1957).

Urban, Wilbur M., *Language and Reality* (London, Allen & Unwin, 1939).

Valéry, Paul, "The Existence of Symbolism", translated by Malcolm Cowley, *Kenyon Review*, XIX (Summer, 1957), pp. 425-447.

——, *Variété* (Paris, Gallimard, 1924).

——, *Variété II* (Paris, Gallimard, 1930).

——, *Variété III* (Paris, Gallimard, 1936).

Van Ghent, Dorothy, "On *Lord Jim*", *The English Novel: Form and Function* (New York, Rinehart, 1953), pp. 224-244.

Villiers de l'Isle-Adam, *Œuvres complètes*, 11 vols. (Paris, Mercure de France, 1914-1931).

Wallace, Alfred Russel, *The Malay Archipelago*, 2 vols. (London, Macmillan, 1869).

Warren, Austin, "Myth and Dialectic in the Later Novels of Henry James", *The Kenyon Critics, Studies in Modern Literature from The Kenyon Review*, edited by John Crowe Ransom (Cleveland, World Publishing Co., 1951), pp. 42-57.

Watt, Ian, "Conrad Criticism and The Nigger of 'The Narcissus'", *Nineteenth-Century Fiction*, XII (March, 1958), pp. 257-283.

——, "Story and Idea in Conrad's 'The Shadow-Line'", *Critical Quarterly*, II (Summer, 1960), pp. 133-148.

Wells, H. G., *Experiment in Autobiography* (New York, Macmillan, 1934).

——, Review of *An Outcast of the Islands*, in *Saturday Review*, LXXXI (16 May, 1896), pp. 509 f.

Wheelwright, Philip, *The Burning Fountain: A Study in the Language of Symbolism* (Bloomington, Indiana University Press, 1954).

Wiley, Paul L., *Conrad's Measure of Man* (Madison, University of Wisconsin Press, 1954).

Williams, Porter, "The Matter of Conscience in Conrad's *The Secret Sharer*", *PMLA*, LXIX (December, 1964), pp. 626-630.

Wright, Walter F., ed., *Joseph Conrad on Fiction (Regents Critics series)* (Lincoln, University of Nebraska Press, 1964).

Wüscher, Albert, *Schau und Veranschaulichung der Aussenwelt bei Joseph Conrad* (Thayngen, K. Augustin, 1934).

Wyzewa, Teodor de, "Un Conteur anglais: M. Joseph Conrad", *Revue des deux mondes*, 6ième période, XX (15 avril 1914), pp. 935-946.

Young, Vernon, "Lingard's Folly: The Lost Subject", in Stallman, R. W., ed., *The Art of Joseph Conrad . . .* [q. v.].

——, "Trial by Water: Joseph Conrad's *The Nigger of the Narcissus*", *Accent*, XII (Spring 1952), pp. 67-81. (Reprinted in Stallman, R. W., ed., *The Art of Joseph Conrad . . .* [q. v.].)

Zabel, Morton Dauwen, *Craft and Character: Texts, Method, and Vocation in Modern Fiction* (New York, The Viking Press, 1957).

——, "Editor's Introduction", *The Portable Conrad* (New York, The Viking Press, 1947).

INDEX

Conrad's titles are indexed under the entry for Conrad himself